History, Buddhism, and New Religious Movements in Cambodia

History, Buddhism, and New Religious Movements in Cambodia

Edited by
John Marston
and
Elizabeth Guthrie

University of Hawai'i Press
Honolulu

Printed in the United States of America
09 08 07 06 05 04 6 5 4 3 2 1

Library of Congress Cataloging-in-Publication Data

History, Buddhism, and new religious movements in Cambodia /
edited by John Marston and Elizabeth Guthrie.
p. cm.
Includes bibliographical references and index.
ISBN 0-8248-2666-3 (hardcover : alk. paper)—
ISBN 0-8248-2868-2 (pbk. : alk. paper)
1. Buddhism—Cambodia—History—20th century.
2. Cambodia—History—20th century. 3. Buddhism and
politics—Cambodia. I. Marston, John A. (John Amos).
II. Guthrie, Elizabeth.
BQ466.H57 2004
200'.9596—dc22
2004003500

University of Hawai'i Press books are printed on
acid-free paper and meet the guidelines for permanence
and durability of the Council on Library Resources

Designed by the University of Hawai'i Press Production Staff

Printed by The Maple-Vail Book Manufacturing Group

Contents

III. The Ethnography of Contemporary Cambodian Religion

IV. The Transnationalism of Cambodian Religion

Acknowledgments

We would like to thank David Chandler, Charles Hallisey, and Saurabh Dube for their insightful comments on an early draft of the manuscript and for their commitment to the importance of Cambodian religion as a topic. We would also like to thank our editor at the University of Hawai'i Press, Pamela Kelley, for her encouragement and common sense throughout.

Obviously, we owe a debt of gratitude to all the contributors of this book and their patience in what has been a much longer process than originally anticipated. We would especially like to thank Anne Hansen, Teri Yamada, and Ashley Thompson for their readiness to answer questions about points of Buddhism as well as the ins and outs of transliteration systems and fonts.

We thank Peter Gyallay-Pap for the photograph of the Dhammayātrā. We would also like to thank Ed and Kitty Higbee for help in digitalizing images and formatting projected covers of the book, as well as for the personal support they have given to Elizabeth Guthrie during the creation of this book.

Thanks to the Center for Asian and African Studies of El Colegio de México for providing John Marston with an institutional framework conducive to working on a project of this kind, including the technical support of secretaries and photocopying. The computer center of El Colegio de México also provided invaluable support.

Notes on the Transliteration System

Khmer words are transliterated using the system devised by Saveros Pou and published in 1969 (Lewitz 1969).

Scholars writing about Cambodia in recent years have generally relied either on Pou's system (and the variations of it worked out by François Bizot and the Library of Congress) or on what is known as the "Franco-Khmer transcription system." The latter was developed in 1983 by Franklin E. Huffman as a refinement of a system used by the French in the colonial period. The Franco-Khmer transcription system has as an advantage the fact that it results in a reasonable approximation of Khmer pronunciation. It has often been chosen by anthropologists and political scientists, especially those writing in English.

We have opted for the Pou system for various reasons. First, it is a true transliteration system; that is, there is a one-to-one correspondence between Khmer characters and the transliterated characters such that—unlike the Franco-Khmer transcription system—one can predict with a degree of accuracy the Khmer spelling based on the transliterated words. Second, the system follows established patterns of transliteration for other Indian-derived writing systems. One plus of the system is that Khmer words derived from Sanskrit and Pāli often reveal their roots in transliteration. For this reason, the Pou system is often preferred by scholars with a textual focus, especially those writing about religion, literature, and the arts.

Some of the pitfalls of the Pou system should be pointed out, however. The most striking of these is that it often results in a representation of Khmer words that seems to have little to do with pronunciation. The primary reason for this is that Khmer consonants fall into two series in such a way that the same vowel symbol will be pronounced differently according to whether it attaches to a first- or a second-series consonant. The Pou system corresponds directly to the vowel symbol and does not reflect the variation in pronunciation. Thus, for example, the vowel in the word "*tā*," with a first-series consonant, is pronounced much as it is written. However, the vowel in the word "*jā*," with a second-series consonant, would be pronounced "ea." Generally, in this book, where there is a significant difference between transliteration and pronunciation we give the pronunciation in parentheses after the first mention of the word.

Another issue that has proved thorny is the representation of inherent and final "a" in Khmer. Sometimes the "a" sound is represented by the absence of a symbol in Khmer, but this occasionally leaves ambiguous the question of whether there should be a transliterated "a." This has proved to be especially touchy in words derived from Pāli. The transliteration of Pāli itself requires invariably adding a final "a" for a sound that is not represented by a Pāli letter. However, this "a" is rarely actually pronounced in Khmer words derived from Pāli. This raises the question of whether the Khmer transliteration should include the final "a" of the Pāli root (since spelling obviously derives from the Pāli spelling) or should drop the final "a" (given that the syllable is absent in Khmer pronunciation). For example, in the case of the Khmer word for "temple," pronounced "vihear," the question is whether it should be transliterated *"vihār"* or *"vihāra."* We have found examples of scholars opting for both.

Our decision has been, when the term in question clearly represents a Khmer word, to not use the final "a." At the same time, however, when we refer to basic Buddhist concepts that are well known in their Pāli representation, we will write them using the final "a." In particular, we write "Buddha," *"dhamma," "sangha," "vihāra," "cetiya,"* and *"samaṇera"* as such, even though in Khmer pronunciation there is no final "a." Written this way, they arguably should not be considered transliterations of Khmer, but as the standard Western representation of Buddhist terms.

Where a nontransliterated spelling for proper names has been well established, we have not transliterated them. We have also made the decision, in the case of proper names for which the exact Khmer spelling was not readily available, to use whatever spelling was used in the source from which the word was taken.

Another dilemma for us has been the representation of some key religious terms that are written and pronounced differently by scholars focused on Sanskrit and Pāli traditions: *dharma/dhamma, karma/kamma,* and *cakravartin/cakkavattin.* Both Sanskrit and Pāli have been important to the Cambodian religious tradition; this is illustrated by the fact that there are alternative spellings for the Khmer word for *dharma/dhamma,* one reflecting Sanskrit roots and one Pāli roots. At the risk of seeming inconsistent, we have opted to use the Sanskrit-derived terms in the articles by Ashley Thompson and Hang Chan Sophea, which draw heavily on Sanskrit inscriptions, and elsewhere to use the Pāli-derived terms.

Introduction

Directly or indirectly, the chapters in this book all relate to the question, "What is particularly Cambodian about Cambodian religion?" In other words, they are concerned with the ways that Cambodian ideas and practices of religion relate to the ideas and institutions that have given shape to Cambodia as a social and political body—to a Cambodian "nation," if you will. We are using the term "nation" very broadly, and, as we will discuss below, the authors in this book have very different ways of approaching the idea of "nation," but all are concerned with the processes of religion giving meaning to social interaction, and that meaning in each case in some way includes "Cambodian" identity.

The origins of this book were e-mail conversations between the two editors in which we speculated about how interesting it would be to have a book about the many small, unusual religious movements that can be found in Cambodia today. We organized a "Cambodian Religion" panel for the 1998 Annual Conference of the Association for Asian Studies in Washington, D.C. As we discussed our ideas with the other panel members, we came to see the need for a volume in English that would showcase some of the current and exciting research being done by a new generation of scholars. Cambodian religion—like, in fact, all religions—is often characterized as a conservative force in society: traditional, static, and unchanging, or worse, removed from society and outside historical processes. We believe that in Khmer society, religion is deeply involved in processes of change, if not, in fact, often the matrix of social change itself. The chapters in this book clearly illustrate Cambodian religion in a perpetual process of reforming and recreating itself. The historical chapters in this book illuminate the chapters on contemporary ethnography, and vice versa, not because Cambodian religion has not changed or is conservative, but because processes of change relate to social memory, sometimes in complex ways.

Cambodian religion first became the object of Western academic study in 1879, when Orientalists Hendrik Kern and Auguste Barth began publishing their translations of Cambodian Sanskrit inscriptions. At that time, the civilizations of Indochina were widely perceived to be once-great societies in decline that needed to be rescued by European colonization. As Penny Edwards describes in chapter 3, the French set up organizations that helped to systematize the study of Cambodian religion, such as the École Française d'Extrême-Orient in 1898, a Pāli religious school in 1914, and the Institut Bouddhique in 1930. During the colonial period, members of the École Française d'Extrême-Orient dominated Khmer studies. An immense body of French scholarship, such as Coedès' seven-volume work on the *Inscriptions du Cambodge* and Giteau's research on Khmer religious art and architecture, was created that emphasized Cambodia's status as an "état hindouisé d'Indochine." The temples and inscriptions from the Angkorean period, considered by many to be the most valuable and authoritative remnants of Cambodian culture, always received the most funding and scholarly attention. Research informed by these traditions of French scholarship has continued into the present day, focusing on the information that can be gleaned from ancient temples, the numerous Khmer inscriptions, and the Khmer chronicles (Pou 1989; Mak Phoeun 1984; Mannikka 1996; and Vickery 1998, among others).

One of the first ethnographers of Cambodia was Adhémard Leclère (1853–1917), an administrator of the French protectorate who rose to the position of Résident in Kratie Province. He translated many Khmer religious texts as well as royal chronicles and recorded his observations of religious ceremonies in several books that were for many years the only source for Cambodian religious practice. The work of Leclère, an amateur who did his research in the vernacular and in the field, was at first considered less important than the work of scholars trained in the classical languages of Buddhist studies who endeavored to uncover the secrets of Angkor. Today, however, Leclère's work seems to be an important precursor to the ethnographical research of Porée-Maspero (1962), Martel (1975), Bizot (1976, 1988), Forest (1992), and the Khmer scholar Ang (1986).

There was little writing in English about Cambodian religion prior to the Civil War period, with the exception of short articles by Ebihara (1966), Kalab (1968), and a chapter in Ebihara's dissertation (1968), all more concerned with peasant social systems than religion per se. Chandler wrote several articles on the intersection between religion and politics (1974, 1976, 1983). In the 1980s, a Khmer scholar residing in the United States wrote an insightful description of the relationship between Cambodian Buddhism and politics between 1954 and 1984 (Sam 1987).

A volume in English published out of a refugee camp also explored the relationship between Buddhism and politics from the perspective of the Cambodian resistance movement of the time (Khmer Buddhist Research Center 1986). In the 1990s, work began to appear describing Cambodian religious practices in countries of resettlement, for example, Kalab (1994), Mortland (1994), Higbee (1992), Ledgerwood (1990), and, especially, Smith-Hefner (1999).

The contributors to this volume are scholars whose primary research on Cambodia began in the 1990s, when Cambodian political developments created new openings for Western researchers in the country and a new momentum for the study of Cambodian culture. The chapters compiled here show religious practice relating to Cambodian "nation" in very different ways. Contemporary theory holds "nation" to be a modern social formation, whereby an imagined community develops in relation to a clearly defined geographical entity and a bureaucratic state apparatus. This is the kind of nation Edwards is referring to as she describes under French colonialism the development of state bureaucratic apparata, an education system, and book publication in support of the state vision of Cambodian Buddhism—a Buddhism seen as separate from the secular institutions of the state. This vision of nation also meant the institutionalization of the vernacular language as a national language.

Scholars have attempted to describe how a premodern Southeast Asian polity differed from this, using terms such as "*maṇḍala*" to describe polities with no clear geographical boundaries that took form as a configuration of relationships connected to a symbolic center. Wolters (1979), in an article on Cambodia's "protohistory," suggested that a Khmer kingdom, with its own identity as such, was never established; there was only the cult of kingship—the form of the personal cult of the man who had seized the kingship. These *maṇḍala* are the kinds of formations Ashley Thompson is describing in her chapters on Cambodian kingship (chap. 4) and the cult of the Maitreya, or "Buddha-to-come" (chap. 1). She convincingly describes the metanymic role of kingship and the cult of Maitreya as unifying processes in the formation of the Khmer geobody. Whether or not we can call these processes of social unification configurations of "nation," such "premodern" social formations (which have in fact existed in quite a variety of historical periods and in states of very different scale) have continued to be a dynamic of the modern Cambodian state and as such continue to stand, in modern society, as powerful symbols. The tension between a "premodern" *maṇḍala* social formation and emerging modern institutions is explicit in Anne Hansen's chapter about religious identity in the face of French colonial reforms (chap. 2). Less explicitly, this tension underlies many of the chapters in this book.

The chapters by Hang Chan Sophea (chap. 5), Didier Bertrand (chap. 7), and John Marston (chap. 8) also concern the power of religious iconography in ways that perhaps suggest the continuing power of social formations organized around symbolic centers—especially the icons of kingship in Hang's chapter. Marston's chapter shows the iconography of Angkor assuming great weight in a millennial cult focused on the idea of the Khmer nation. Angkor Wat doubtless functioned historically as a symbol of spiritual power informing configurations of *maṇḍala;* a contemporary cult of the kind Marston describes searches for a similar symbolic center, while at the same time taking on modern sociopolitical meanings in relation to Cambodian society. As Bertrand's chapter describes them, the pantheon of *pāramī* that manifest themselves through contemporary Cambodian mediums are less clearly symbols of nation; however, they also show the power of central icons to give meaning to Cambodian society—and perhaps in their totality do suggest a set of reference points for Cambodian nation.

Almost all the chapters in this book show Cambodian religion looking backward to a mythico-historical past at the same time that practice is shaped by the memories of a more immediate, cataclysmic history and adjusts to a continuing process of social change. In this way they relate to a process of constructing narratives of the nation moving through time. Chapter 10, by Teri Shaffer Yamada, especially shows how a particular narrative of the defense of the Khmer nation is used ritually to promote unity among Cambodians—in her specific ethnographic work, among Cambodians living overseas.

While we are uncomfortable using the term "postmodern" to refer to the recent intensification of transnational processes, we recognize these processes coming into play in the religious practices of diasporic Cambodians and in the ways transnational support and organizations have intensified recent Cambodian religious movements, as we see in the chapters by Yamada, Marston, and Kathryn Poethig (chap. 9). In cases like these Cambodian identity comes to be defined and emphasized as contrasting with other national identities through the very transnational processes that bring these national identities into contact.

From a broad perspective, all religious practices are transnational, and in emphasizing *Cambodian* religion, we do not wish to ignore the continuities among the earlier religious practices of monsoon Asia, the continuities of tradition among Theravāda Buddhist countries, or the underlying unities among all religions. What we choose to emphasize, however, amid the flux of religious practice are some institutions and belief systems shaped by their connection with the history of a given place, Cambodia.

Cambodia is conventionally described as a Theravāda Buddhist country, and few Cambodians would question this characterization. As in other Theravāda countries, however, there is a complex relation of Buddhist religious practices to "non-Buddhist" practices that are nevertheless deeply ingrained in Khmer culture in what is sometimes called syncretism, or synchronism. Cambodian scholars themselves describe their religion as a mixture of animism, Brahmanism, and Buddhism (Phang 1963; Yang 1987; Ang 1986, 1988). Scholars of Buddhism have struggled to define the exact relation of complementarity and unity among these different traditions (Kirsch 1977; Tambiah 1970; Gombrich 1988, 23–31), while until recently Cambodian Buddhists have shown little need for self-consciousness about the precise boundaries between these practices. We will not try to define a precise sociological model of this "syncretism." It is worth pointing out, however, that the chapters in this book tend to be less concerned with examining the "pure" animist, Brahmanist, or Buddhist tradition than with exploring the social complexity, with its concomitant ironies, that arises in the unclear boundaries of these traditions—just as this volume is also concerned with the social complexity in the unclear boundaries between religious practice and political formation.

What is missing from this volume? The chapters in this book are concerned with the religious practices of the dominant population of Cambodia, the Khmer, and do not attempt to touch on the religious practices of ethnic Vietnamese, the largely Muslim Cham and Chvea, or the numerous small ethnic minorities of the Cambodian northeast. There is also no discussion of Chinese religious practices, even though there is evidence of a fascinating mixture between religious practices identified as "Chinese" and "Khmer" among Cambodians, regardless of their personal identification as "Chinese" or "Khmer."[1] Among the religious practices of ethnic Khmer, perhaps the chief gap in this volume is the absence of discussion of Christianity, which has been discussed historically by Ponchaud (1990). While still little studied (an article by Poethig [2001] on the dual citizenship of Cambodian-American Christians is an exception), recent conversions related to the return of refugees from border camps and evangelization by overseas Cambodians may yet prove to be an important social development.

Notes

This general introduction was written jointly by John Marston and Elizabeth Guthrie. The introductions to each of the four parts should be regarded as the work of Marston.

1. A conversation with Kobayashi Satoru helped illuminate some of these tendencies for us.

PART I

Cambodian Religion and the Historical Construction of Nation

Since Durkheim, it has been a maxim that modern society entails increasing social division of labor, including a tendency to separate religion from other fields of activity. This is not always the case even in the Cambodian society of today, where, as chapters in this book show us, the spiritual is often not rigidly categorized as a separate sphere. It is especially important to remember, when looking at the early history of Cambodia, that there was never a rigid division between the practice of religion and statecraft, art, education, medicine, or even exchange, even though French colonial policies promoted this kind of division.

Scholars believe that Indian influences began in the area of Cambodia at around the beginning of the Christian era, with Indian artifacts found in the area dating to the second and third centuries C.E. (Chandler 1996a; Bhattacharya 1997). Chinese references to the area begin in the middle of the third century C.E., and stone inscriptions in Khmer and Sanskrit begin to appear by the fifth century. Prior to the adoption of elements of Indian religious practice, there probably existed shrines to the spiritual eminence of a place, or *anak tā*, similar to what is still universally found in Cambodia. Such spiritual eminences were associated with the soil and with ancestors buried in the soil; Mus, in a classic article (1975), saw in this relationship the rudiments of dynastic law and territorial law in Southeast Asia. Then, as now, *anak tā* may have been worshiped in the form of stones. As has been argued for other parts of Southeast Asia, the later importance of phallic stones, or *śivaliṅga*, for Khmer cults devoted to Śiva may have evolved logically out of this earlier practice (Wolters 1979; Slamet-

Velsink 1995; de Casparis and Mabbett 1992). Likewise, it has been speculated that early Southeast Asian religious practice that made ritual use of elevated places and artificial mounds may have been a precedent for the temple-mountains so characteristic of the Angkor period.

Indian influence from early on included both Buddhist and Brahmanist practices centered on cults to Viṣṇu and Śiva.[1] By the ninth century there was evidence of syncretism between Buddhism and Śaivism. Early Indian-influenced religious practice was very intimately associated with statecraft: it was a means for a ruler to generate the spiritual power necessary to conquer and rule. Put in terms of Geertz's model of the classic Southeast Asian polity, *negara,* it created the framework whereby a ruler could enact the theater of being the center of a social universe. Religious practice also empowered rulers through its capacity to give meaning to oaths of loyalty and the corresponding curses on those disloyal. The fact that Indian religious practice was associated with the introduction of writing meant social bonds could more easily be concretized where there was not immediate physical contact between people; this may have facilitated the extension of rule over wider areas.

Most scholars date the Angkor period from 802 C.E. to 1431 C.E., a time when a series of kings succeeded in consolidating empires and during which there was a florescence of monumental buildings. The later date is the year traditionally ascribed to an attack on Angkor by Ayuthayan forces. The early date is identified in inscriptions with the creation of the *devarāja* cult, but religious practice had much continuity with what came before. We will not attempt to describe the art and architecture of Angkor except to say the obvious: it is a great marvel that has continued to capture the imagination of Cambodia and the world. During the Angkor period, art and architecture served both ritual and political purposes. Angkor continues to have deep meaning for Cambodians as a national symbol and as a symbol of a kind of spiritual power.

Much has been written about the cult of the *devarāja,* a word scholars once translated as "God-king" but has alternatively been translated as "god of the kings." What is clear is that the *devarāja* cult was related to the cult of Śiva, it empowered Angkor's kings, and it provided a thread of unity linking successive monarchs during this period. A full genealogy of the priests devoted to the cult, found in one inscription (Ledgerwood 1995, 248), suggests that the matrilineal succession among these priests was more regular than the patterns of succession of the kings themselves.

Many surviving inscriptions from the Angkor and pre-Angkor periods have to do with donations to religious foundations. According to Hall (1985), there was a hierarchy of religious foundations during the Angkor period, with regional religious foundations feeding into the central foundations of Angkor itself. Communities of people were bonded to religious foundations in relations that had some of the properties of slavery, although the status of temple "slaves" may not have been particularly low.

During the Angkor period, a range of Buddhist and Brahmanist practices coexisted, just as, in India, they had developed historically in relation to each other. Inscriptions composed in Sanskrit and Khmer and religious iconography carved in stone attest to a longstanding tradition of religious asceticism, a tradition particularly associated with the cult of Śiva—although the precise relation of these ascetics to temple foundations and Brahmanist and Buddhist religious practice is not completely understood. An interesting question is whether this ascetic tradition arose for the first time in conjunction with the adoption of Indian-influenced ideas about centralized, hierarchical states or was also linked to pre-Indic practices. Although Angkor kings most often associated themselves and their reigns with the cult of Śiva, the largest and most famous of the temple complexes, Angkor Wat, was dedicated to Viṣṇu. As Thompson discusses in chapter 1, tradition holds that one of the most famous kings of the Angkor period, Jayavarman VII (r. 1181–1220), the last of the great builders, was Buddhist. His temple-mountain, Bayon, has been interpreted as a Mahāyānist structure devoted to the bodhisattva Avalokiteśvara, whose face (represented by the features of Jayavarman VII) appears repeatedly on the temple's four-sided towers. While Jayavarman promoted Buddhism during his reign, shrines to Śiva and Viṣṇu were also included in his construction projects.

A key document to understanding the religion practiced at Angkor is a late thirteenth-century description by a Chinese ambassador, Zhou Daguan (Chou Ta-Kuan 1993). Zhou Daguan's account describes Angkor in the century after Jayavarman VII, during a period when there were no longer the massive building projects associated with classical Angkor. He describes the simultaneous presence of Brahmanist, Buddhist, and "Taoist" religious practices. Zhou Daguan's description of Buddhist monks with shaved heads and saffron robes is usually interpreted as proof that the Theravāda tradition was in existence at Angkor by the late thirteenth century. The Khmer would have been familiar with forms of Theravāda Buddhism long before this period through their contacts with the neighboring Mon (de Casparis and Mabbett 1992, 294). However, it was not until the late Angkor period that the Khmer kings began associating themselves and their reigns with Theravāda Buddhism. During this period there was a shift to Sinhalese forms of Theravāda Buddhism throughout the region, and inscriptions note that Buddhist monks from Burma, the Tai and Mon areas, and Cambodia went to Ceylon to study. In fact, there is a tradition that a son of Jayavarman VII was one of the monks who went to study Sinhalese Buddhism (Keyes 1977a). And Lao chronicles indicate that Theravāda Buddhism was first brought to Laos by a king who had acquired it while exiled to Angkor in the mid-fourteenth century (Reynolds and Clifford 1987).

In recent years, François Bizot, Olivier de Bernon, and others have documented a significant body of Buddhist texts that has been preserved in Cambodian monastic libraries. This work is still in progress, but these texts and associated Buddhist practices are apparently the remnants of non-Theravāda forms of Buddhism popular throughout the region before the Theravāda became dominant. The fact that the texts and practices have survived well into the twentieth century suggests that it is impossible to understand the practice of Cambodian Buddhism without recognizing "the presence of two factions: one orthodox, coming from the official Buddhism of Sri Lanka, the other heterodox, coming from ancient traditions of India, already in place at Angkor" (Bizot 1976, 27; trans. of original French).

While historical roots and the degree of connection to an Angkor tradition is not clear, forms of Brahmanism have continued to be associated with the Cambodian court, where a small number of Brahmans is still maintained to conduct royal ritual. Although these traditions were abandoned with the monarchy itself in the socialist periods, they were revived with the reintroduction of the monarchy in 1993 (de Bernon 1997). Nevertheless, some form of Theravāda Buddhism has been royally recognized and linked to the ideology of rule since the late Angkor period, and it became the dominant form of religion during Cambodia's Middle period—some five hundred years between the fall of Angkor and the establishment of the French protectorate (Thompson 1999).

One theory holds that the shift away from monumental architecture in stone associated with Angkor relates to a Buddhist emphasis on impermanence. However, it is probably more accurate to say that during the Middle period, Theravāda Buddhism flourished. Many Buddhist temples were built throughout the region of inexpensive materials (wood, tile, thatch), rather than expensive and labor-intensive stone monuments. During this period, Cambodian men were ordained into the Sangha as a rite of passage. There they achieved some literacy, and as a result, a greater percentage of the population had access to Buddhist teachings and scriptures.

The Portuguese missionary Gaspar da Cruz spent a year in Cambodia in 1556, during the reign of King Ang Chan. While his statement that one-third of the population was monks (Cruz 1569, 61) might be hard to believe, it is remarkably similar to the statement cited in Edwards (forthcoming) that in 1880, a French surveyor in the area of Kampong Luong found one monk and one novice for every six inhabitants. At the very least, these figures suggest that during the long period after the establishment of Theravāda Buddhism, up to and including the early French colonial period, one could in given places and at given times find particularly intense participation in the monkhood.

The Thai kingdom of Ayutthaya rose as a power during the late Angkor period, and a series of Siamese invasions was one reason that the Cambodian capital moved to the area around modern-day Phnom Penh. During the Middle period, Cambodia fell increasingly under the domination of Siam and, later, Vietnam, with the two powers competing to control Cambodia in the later part of the period. The threat Siam posed to Cambodia figures in two well-known myths, the Khleang Moeung story discussed by Yamada in chapter 10 and the story of a sacred bull and jewel, Braḥ Ko and Braḥ Kaev, lost to Siam, a myth that continues to have great resonance for Cambodians.

The term "Braḥ Kaev" is the same term used to refer to the Holy Emerald Jewel, carved in the image of a Buddha, that is the palladium of the Chakri dynasty of Thailand (known in English as the Emerald Buddha). Thai myth has the stone passing from India to Sri Lanka to Cambodia before continuing its historically documented path to Chiang Mai, Laos, and Bangkok (Reynolds 1978; Tambiah 1984, 214–219). It is interesting that the Khmer story, like the Thai, has Braḥ Kaev moving from Cambodia to Thailand in what clearly represents a loss of cosmic power—even though, as the story is generally told by Cambodians at the present time, Braḥ Kaev is a human figure. The story suggests the loss of a palladium, justifying and empowering kingship, to Thailand. The predicted return of Braḥ Go and Braḥ Kaev to Cambodia has powerful millennial overtones for many Cambodians.

By the time of the arrival of the French, as Hansen (chap. 2) and Edwards (chap. 3) show, Thailand's dominance as a center of Theravāda Buddhism was sufficient enough that the French felt compelled to build up an alternative Buddhism more based in Cambodia.

Chapter 1 (Thompson) is particularly unusual and revealing, since so little has been written about the Cambodian Middle period. Using the evidence of inscriptions and the art and architecture of the Middle period, Thompson argues that the reign of Ang Chan in the sixteenth century was a cultural watershed in Cambodian history. This chapter demonstrates that the national unity that Ang Chan was able to achieve was linked to the elaboration of the cult surrounding the Maitreya, or Buddha-to-come. Thompson shows how Middle-Cambodian iconography of the Maitreya draws on Angkor-period iconography in ways that link it to ongoing religious practice.

If the cult of Maitreya gave unity and direction to the Cambodian kingdom under Ang Chan, the "modernizations" of French colonialism offered new constructions of national unity, which would replace or interface with those already in existence. Chapters 2 and 3 both deal with the French colonial period. Each considers the French colonial period as a crucial point in a process of modernization that would change the relation of Buddhism to the nation state.

In chapter 2 Hansen explores changing identity in relation to the kinds of moral order proposed in Buddhist texts during the colonial period. She opens her chapter with a consideration of the social and moral chaos that Cambodia experienced in the nineteenth century and how it was experienced in relation to a particular cosmological vision, a society ordered by hierarchy with the king as its exemplary center. She offers evidence of the millennial thinking during this period and shows how it relates to Buddhist prophetic texts. Hansen then goes on to discuss processes of modernization that took place under the French, which undermined hierarchies and questioned traditional cosmologies. She explores the changes in the moral universe represented by Ukñā Suttanta Prījā Ind in a lengthy ethics manual in which we see a critique of superstition and evidence of an emerging discourse of ethical purity and the beginnings of new ideas of nation.

In chapter 3 Edwards focuses more specifically on the period following Ind and the specific institution building by Cambodian monks and French scholars that resulted in new ways of experiencing religion, deriving ultimately from philosophies of modernity and the attempts of the French to create religious institutions separate from those of the state. She discusses the reformist Dhammakāy movement within the Cambodian monkhood and, in particular, the roles of two scholar-monks, Chuon Nath and Huot Tat, and how they helped to set the parameters of a new national Buddhism under French colonialism—a "rational" Cambodian Buddhism oriented to printed text and the close analysis of Buddhist scriptures. Parallel to this, she discusses the impact of French scholars, focusing on the role of Suzanne Karpelès, in developing institutions that linked religion to a vision of nation.

Note

1. Scholars vary in the choice of a term to refer to Indian-influenced devotional practices in Southeast Asia. I have chosen to use "Brahmanist" as a general term to refer to non-Buddhist, Indian-derived practices, rather than to refer to "Hinduized" or "Indic" religious practices—terms that have their own limitations. I do not thereby mean to suggest the existence of a class of Brahmans or emphasis on a cult of Brahma per se. My usage corresponds to the way contemporary Cambodians often refer to "Brahmanism" *(brahmaññsāsnā).*

–1–

The Future of Cambodia's Past

A Messianic Middle-Period Cambodian Royal Cult

Ashley Thompson

This chapter concerns the political and religious history of Cambodia during the Middle period, the relatively undocumented centuries after the fall of Angkor and before the French protectorate. More precisely, it concerns what might be called an indigenous conception of history, a certain relation to the past that was set on the future, and that seems to have arisen during the sixteenth century in conjunction with Theravāda Buddhism. In other words, this chapter is about history in the making, when the object of historical study is also in the process of "doing" history.

The phenomenon I shall attempt to identify and interpret here concerns a particular political-religious cult involving the *stūpa,* a sculptural ensemble consisting of four Buddha statues, or a Buddha with four faces, and the future Buddha Maitreya.[1] This cult appears repeatedly at religious sites of notable political importance in the Cambodian Middle period: Wat Nokor (in present Kompong Cham Province), Tralaeng Kaeng (Lovek), Angkor Wat (Siem Reap), and Wat Phnom (Phnom Penh). Though the origins and meanings of this cult can be understood only in the context of a particular span of Cambodian history, the phenomenon under study defies the very notion of linear chronology insofar as it conflates a repetition of the past and a rehearsal of the future in a performative show of sovereignty. So as is often the case in addressing history and religion, the history of religion, and religious history (if not the religion of history), we are faced with seemingly incompatible ways of living with the past, where fiction may rework fact only to become itself an element in factual history, where belief can bring about or reanimate events even as events inspire belief, and where past, pre-

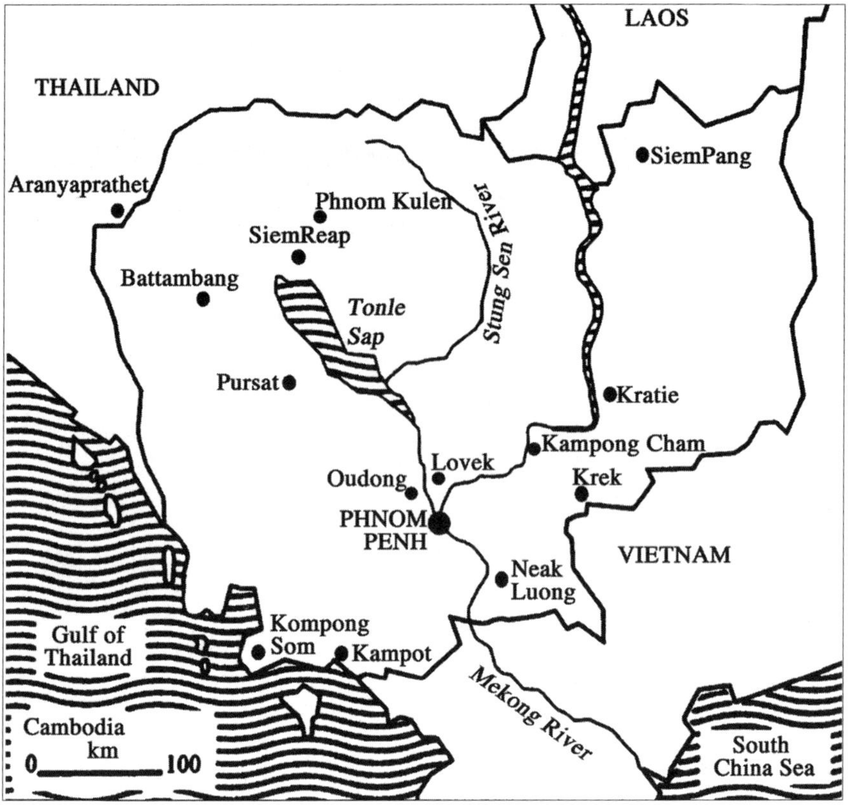

Map of Cambodia

sent, and future are inextricably implicated in each other. Accordingly, I will conclude this chapter with reference to a series of contemporary cults that reenact in a particular way the Middle-period phenomenon in question.

The *Stūpa* and the Savior in Cambodian History

While studying the transition from the Angkor period to the Middle period, and in particular the apparition of the *stūpa,* or *cetiya* (pronounced "chedei"),[2] I became increasingly aware of the future Buddha Maitreya's unique importance to Cambodian culture (Thompson 1998). The *cetiya,* a Buddhist monument to the dead that is also considered a place of gestation before rebirth,[3] gained prominence in Cambodia just as the religions of the Angkorean Empire lost their sway. I shall attempt to demonstrate here that the substitution of the *cetiya* for the sanctuary tower of the ancient Khmer *prāsād* presages the emergence of a cult dedicated to, or at least closely linked with, Maitreya.[4]

The association between the appearance of the *stūpa* and that of a Maitreya cult should not surprise us. Indeed, according to Indian iconographic codes, the future Buddha is identifiable by the *stūpa* he wears in his headdress. But the few remaining statues and the scarce epigraphic evidence that have survived from the Angkor period indicate that this divinity (not unlike the *stūpa* itself) was relatively rare and not the object of widespread worship at that time.[5] The inscription of Wat Nokor, dated July 15, 1566, the year of the tiger, bears what is to my knowledge the first textual mention of Maitreya in Theravāda Cambodia. From that moment on, Maitreya reappears frequently—in inscriptions, manuscripts, invocations—and continues to play a significant role in Cambodia today.

A careful reading of the sixteenth-century inscription of Wat Nokor in conjunction with the study of the temple itself is, I believe, essential to identifying and interpreting the rise of Maitreya in the Cambodian cultural complex. While invoking Maitreya, the inscription recounts the transformation of the temple's central sanctuary, dating from the thirteenth century, into a *cetiya.* Elsewhere I have demonstrated that this type of architectural transformation—from the *prāsād* to the *cetiya*—was a hallmark of Middle-period cultural expression (Thompson 1996). In this chapter I will explore the association between these architectural transformations and the rise of the cult of Maitreya at a particular moment in Cambodian history.

Before examining the archaeological and textual evidence pointing to this Middle-period phenomenon, I would like to briefly discuss the general philosophical, legendary, and historical contexts from which Maitreya emerges. Maitreya is the only bodhisattva, or "being (destined to reach) enlightenment," to consistently figure in Theravāda Buddhism, which distinguishes itself from Mahāyāna in rejecting the doctrine of exterior salvation incarnated by the multiple bodhisattvas. Of these beings "as numerous as grains of sand"[6] that find expression during the Middle period, only Maitreya emerges with a specific identity. These are the main elements of his story as they are generally known in Cambodia today.

> A past disciple of the "historical" Buddha, the *bodhisattva* Maitreya currently lives in the paradise of the "Satisfied," Tuṣita. At a given yet unknown moment of the present era in which our earthly world is gradually sinking into chaos, as the Buddhist religion approaches the point of disappearing, a *cakravartin* king will rise to power, and Maitreya will descend—in time to save the world. Reborn into an eminent family at the time of this *cakravartin* named Saṇkha, and having reached adulthood, he will abandon mundane life to follow the path to enlightenment. Under his aura, the Buddhist order will reign anew. Maitreya will teach

> the *Dharma,* with the *cakravartin* himself as his most eminent disciple. By accumulation of merit, mortal men and women aspire to be reborn during the time when Maitreya will live on earth. Faithful followers of his teachings, at his side, they will also, finally, attain *nirvāna,* or the saintly state of *arahant*—or else receive the prediction of such future peace.[7]

In studying certain iconographic, epigraphic, and ethnographic sources it is possible to isolate other elements of the beliefs that have developed around the figure of Maitreya in Khmer culture. One such legend predicts that upon reaching Buddhahood, Maitreya will open the *stūpa* (or the mountain) where Kaśyapa, another disciple of the historical Buddha, is awaiting his arrival. Awakened from his cosmic meditation, Kaśyapa will offer to his new master the robe of his past master. This legend is often invoked to explain Maitreya's iconographic emblem, the *stūpa* in his headdress.[8] Whether the iconographic association between Maitreya and the *stūpa* precedes or is derived from this legend, it suggests that the themes of renewal, renaissance, and "revolution," as well as the promise of salvation—themes incarnated by the *stūpa*—lay at the origin of conceptions of the future Buddha.

Indeed, if Maitreya is the only bodhisattva shared by the two Buddhist vehicles, it is no doubt due in part to the importance of these messianic themes to Buddhist historiography—because the history of Buddhism past and future has a familiar form in which Maitreya plays a crucial role: that of the rice mortar *(tpāl').* One of the most commonplace household objects in Cambodia, the mortar is wide at its top and progressively diminishes in girth, just as Buddhism, once widespread, is now diminishing. But like the mortar, which narrows at the middle only to expand again toward the base, so will Buddhism flourish once more at the arrival of Maitreya. It is widely believed in Cambodia today that only a handful of Khmer people, as many as will fit under the shade of a *bodhi* tree, will remain after the ultimate dissolution. In making an offering at any temple, it is common to be blessed in return with some version of the following phrase: "*sūm puoṅ suoṅ oy dān' braḥ sī āry metrīy,*" roughly, "May you be reborn at the time of Maitreya." Maitreya will arrive—and his future presence has preceded him, irrevocably transforming the expectant world of Theravāda Cambodia for centuries now.

The fifth and last Buddha of the present era, Maitreya, is inscribed in a precise future and is experienced in the present time as a historical event—if not *the* historical event—still to come. However, his illustrious future role has an important antecedent: a reincarnation of the historical Buddha, Maitreya is a key figure in the life of the historical Buddha upon which Theravāda, in particular, bases its doctrine and claim to legitimacy. And thus the promise of Maitreya's return is not that of a new world order, but rather the restoration of the old. He is therefore revolutionary in the etymological sense of the word: Maitreya will be returning when he arrives to consecrate the political renaissance of the *cakravartin* king. But he figures in external salvation only insofar as the state and its individual members are determined, or predetermined, to receive him. Only those who have accumulated enough merit to be reborn at his side will be saved. As Nattier remarks in "The Meanings of the Maitreya Myth,"

> Unlike Amitābha Buddha or any of the distinctively Mahāyānic celestial *bodhisattvas,* Maitreya appears simply as a traditional Buddha, whose preaching reaches only those whose *karma* has prepared them to hear his message. His actions are "intransitive," as it were, in contrast to the "transitive" efforts of those Buddhas and *bodhisattvas* who intervene directly in the cosmic process in order to save their followers.[9]

In light of these considerations, Maitreya can be seen to embody a relation to the future that gained special relevance, I believe, in Cambodia's Middle period, a relation in which individual action and preordained destiny commingle in an unstable balance.

Though all the relevant details cannot be discussed here in full, I hope to demonstrate that the specific conjunction of political events and religious evolution in Cambodia over the course of the sixteenth century opened the way for Maitreya's rise to a position of unique importance in Khmer culture, as reflected notably in certain influential cult practices. By the time the capital at Angkor fell in the fifteenth century, Theravāda Buddhism had overcome Cambodia's Brahmanist and Mahāyānist traditions. Yet it is essential to recall that the past never ceased to haunt the Theravāda descendants of the Angkor period.

The symbolic implications of the religious and political circumstances of the transition from Angkor-period to Middle-period Cambodia would seem to have foreshadowed the country's future. Angkor's last prominent king, Jayavarman VII, reputed to have saved the country from the devastation of civil war and invasion by the neighboring Cham Empire, was associated through iconographic, epigraphic, and probably ritual production with the Buddha—and particularly with the Buddha Protector-Savior (Jayabuddhamahānātha). This type of royal representation can be seen as an indication of the king's future reincarnation as the Buddha Savior. Moreover, Jayavarman VII, like his father, was expressly associated with Lokeśvara (Avalokiteśvara), the bodhisattva savior of Mahāyāna tradition who works everywhere at all times for the salvation of beings.[10] He is, notably, the bodhisattva who protects the Buddha's teachings in our time, pending the advent of the Buddha Maitreya. Taking up Buddhism where Jayavarman VII left off, the Theravāda tradition brought to Cambodia its own (version of the) past. The memory of Jayavarman VII and, as we will see, his iconographic signature, were not abandoned after the fall of Angkor. The story of the bodhisattva savior associated with the *cakravartin* king, which had long informed the development of other Theravāda Buddhist states, resonated with particular meaning in Middle-period Cambodia.

The definitive removal of the capital south from Angkor was and continues to be a powerful symbol of royal and political dissolution. As the Khmer capital was repeatedly displaced over the following centuries, another coherent symbolism, indissociable from the Middle period and born at once of continuity and rupture with the past, came to preside over the foundation of each new capital. Political upheaval and the loss of the traditional seat of power provoked—as in the past—the powerful need for a savior. And indeed the sixteenth century saw the rise of a Buddhist king who succeeded in restoring order to the land, seemingly against all odds. This was Ang Chan, whose reign spanned a good part of the century, and a good part of the country.

Khmer historical legend recounts that after having returned from exile in Siam to restore domestic unity by overthrowing a usurper of the throne, Ang Chan, the legitimate successor, established independence from neighboring Siam and reconquered territory it had taken. Founding his new capital at Lovek, Ang Chan then marked the political consolidation by making religious foundations across the country, notably in the Angkor region. The restoration of the monarchy thus found concrete expression in the restoration of the ancestral heritage. The Khmer royal chronicles, which were the vehicle for a powerful historical imagination, emphasize Ang Chan's strict moral rectitude. Like a *cakravartin* king, his political success is attributed to sincere religious devotion. Ang Chan's works were pursued by his son Paramarājā I and grandson Braḥ Sattha up until the final fall of Lovek at the end of the sixteenth century.

The figure of the savior, formulated in the image of the *cakravartin* king or the future Buddha Maitreya, or more precisely through an association or fusion of the two, appears consistently over this period. In a typical case of the syncretic incorporation of Cambodia's ancient heritage into the new Theravāda framework, the Brahmanic god Viṣṇu, particularly in his avatar of Rāma reformulated as a Buddhist monarch and savior, returns to play a similar role. The miraculous appearance of an *anak mān puṇy* (a type of pseudomythical messiah figure), whose accumulated merit, corroborating his historical legitimacy, brings him to (predetermined) political power, is repeatedly recounted in the royal chronicles and other "historical fictions" concerning the Middle period.

These figures can each be seen as variations on a single theme, a theme that may not have been invented ex nihilo in the Middle period, but was certainly distilled then and is particularly potent today. Khmers still await the imminent arrival of Cambodia's savior—the king, Rāma, Maitreya, or *anak mān puṇy*—and the restoration of Cambodia's political and moral order.

A Present Absence: Spatial Representations of the Buddha Wat Nokor

Situated on the outskirts of the provincial seat of Kompong Cham, the Wat Nokor complex was originally built as a Mahāyāna temple under the reign of Jayavarman VII around the turn of the thirteenth century. It was then transformed for the Theravāda faith through both architectural and iconographic modifications during the Middle period. The central compound of Wat Nokor consists of five towers, four at each corner of the temple's innermost enclosure surrounding a central sanctuary tower. In the sixteenth century the square lower portion of this sandstone sanctuary was topped with a circular sandstone *stūpa* (fig. 1.1*a*). Three of the Buddhist reliefs sculpted onto the pediments of the four antechambers giving onto Wat Nokor's central sanctuary have also been dated to the sixteenth century (fig 1.1*b*). A modern *vihāra* lying immediately to the east of this central structure and actually engulfing the facade of its eastern antechamber shelters the sixteenth-century inscription mentioned above. The inscription is composed of two texts, one in Pāli and the other in Khmer, both recording the physical transformation of the ancient sanctuary into a *stūpa*.[11]

The Pāli text first introduces its protagonist, a man named Siri Sogandhapada, or Mahāparamanibbānapada. The first of these names is presented as a royal title, the second is religious; both are posthumous and indicate that their bearer has entered the Buddhist afterlife.[12] After having described, in third-person narration, the fervent and pious nature of this man and his royal wife, as well as the reliquary that has been built for them atop the *prāsād,* the text shifts into the first person as the deceased man speaks.

> Indeed, in the pleasurable ancient kingdom called Jayavīraśaktinagara, [I held] power, with appointed ministers, with innumerable men of valor. Then I vanished from where I was born. In Tuṣita heaven I enjoy agreeable happiness, the pleasure of desire, surrounded by relatives, borne by infinite strength; this is the attainment of infinite pleasure. Having qualities and keeping the observances, advancing with intelligence, of great merit, I will be *cakravartin,* King, until Maitreya has vanished from Tuṣita. When, amongst human beings, he has reached full omniscience on the throne of Enlightenment, then I [will] abandon all pleasure with my wife and, having heard the eminent *Dharma,* having obtained in his presence the lower and higher ordinations, I will have attained the state of *arahant* with distinction.

This projection of Buddhist legend is well grounded in Khmer history. It has been amply demonstrated that the various modern names of Wat Nokor, Phnom Bachey, and Phnom Bachey Ba-ar find explication in this narration from the past. Jayavīraśaktinagara, which is thought to correspond to the name of the site dur-

Fig. 1.1 *(a) Stūpa-prāsād,* Wat Nokor; *(b)* Pediments with Buddha figure underneath, Wat Nokor; *(c) Stūpa* with four Buddhas, Vihār Yay Peou; *(d) Stūp,* Wat Nokor; *(e)* Buddha, Tralaeng Kaeng, Lovek; *(f)* Four-faced finial, *vihāra* roof, Tralaeng Kaeng, Lovek. Drawings by Say Sopheap

ing the reign of Jayavarman VII, survives in both the "Nokor" *(nagara)* of Wat Nokor and the "Chey" of Bachey, a condensation of Braḥ Jaya (noble victorious one). Ba-ar is none other than Braḥ Āry (noble lord), a shortened version of the common Khmer appellation of Maitreya, Braḥ Sī Āry Metrīy.[13]

On close examination, a number of otherwise anomalous structures found on the grounds of Wat Nokor today can be given special meaning in connection to this vow. Vihār Yāy Bau is a small cement pavilion situated between the temple's second and third enclosures, to the northeast of the transformed central sanctuary that is both *stūpa* and *prāsād, "prāsād-stūpa."*[14] The pavilion harbors a curious object of worship: at its center is a stone *stūpa* surrounded by four stone Buddhas, each seated at one of the four cardinal points with its back to the *stūpa* (fig. 1.1*c*). What is worshiped at Vihār Yāy Bau is not any one of the individual Buddhas or the *stūpa,* but the ensemble of five elements. It is true that within Khmer Buddhist sanctuaries the main icon is often accompanied by a number of smaller ones, along with offerings, various ritual objects, and so on. But here the ensemble is treated as a fixed unit and in practice functions in a similar way to the central icon found in most *vihāra.* A nearly identical configuration can be seen in Vihār Cās', another open pavilion to the southeast of the central *prāsād-stūpa* and between the temple's third and fourth enclosures.[15] Here, the Buddhas are recent cement replicas, but the *stūpa,* sculpted in stone, can be dated to an earlier era.[16]

While this configuration of a *stūpa* surrounded by four Buddhas as a single object of worship inside a sanctuary or *vihāra* first strikes the eye as an anomaly in Cambodia, it is more easily recognizable elsewhere in Buddhist Asia. Such ensembles are known to represent various groups of five elements in Buddhist theology, the five points in space (including the zenith) in conjunction with the five transcendental Buddhas, five aspects of Buddhahood, the five parts of the Buddha, five episodes in the Buddha's life, the five senses, and the five Buddhas of our era.[17] Nonetheless, if we look closely, we recognize this configuration, albeit in less distinct forms, at a significant number of other sites in Cambodia. Indeed, upon reexamining Wat Nokor, it becomes clear that the two secondary structures I have described can be seen as reduced models of the central *prāsād-stūpa* structure as a seated Buddha image is placed in each of the antechambers of the central sanctuary (see fig. 1.1*b*). In other words, the transformed central element at Wat Nokor as it appears today can itself be seen as a *stūpa* surrounded by four Buddhas facing in the four cardinal directions.

Further consideration has led me to see in this ensemble a powerful and telling iconographic representation fundamental to Middle-period Khmer religious practice, and which elucidates the complex relations between this practice and the sociopolitical evolutions of the time. In a classical Indian context, the ensemble of four Buddhas and a *stūpa*—or rather, of one *stūpa* that "is" five Buddhas—can represent Buddhahood and, insofar as Buddhahood is beyond time, timelessness.[18]

Yet in the case at hand it is significant that this appeal to timelessness is made repeatedly at a particular time and place, at certain important sites in Cambodia during the Middle period. It is tempting to see in this ensemble an additional signification as the five Buddhas of the present era. But the appearance of Maitreya in the epigraphy and the marked political renaissance intimately associated with Theravāda Buddhism, two historically overdetermined and very real facts, must not, in my opinion, be written out of this Buddhist history. Although in theoretical or metaphysical terms the *stūpa* can be identified with the five Buddhas, four of which are represented anthropomorphically on or around the *stūpa*'s body, we cannot occlude or ignore the essential iconographic heterogeneity between the anthropomorphic Buddha statues and the "aniconic" or abstract form of the *stūpa*.[19] The *stūpa* and the Buddha are the same, yet different. Timelessness is embodied here not through a straightforward repetition of a single image, but instead through an ensemble in which repetition is expressed with explicit reference to time in the form of the funerary monument.

From its first appearance in Buddhist art, the *stūpa* has evoked the presence of the Buddha in his very absence. Of course one could argue that the anthropomorphic representation—as all representation—functions in a similar manner, standing in for what is not there. Yet the image of the *stūpa* carries this structural spectrality of art to its logical limit, as if the iconographic incommensurability of the Buddhas and the *stūpa* at the core of this configuration corresponded to the chasm between a "figurative" past and a future that has yet to take form, a future materialized as such by the nonfigure of the *stūpa*. As the funerary monument is simultaneously a site of gestation, so the presence of the four Buddhas evokes the absence of the fifth to come. To this degree, at least, the *stūpa* cannot help but figure Maitreya, or rather prefigure him nonfiguratively. The *stūpa* "is" the presence of an irredeemable absence, like any funerary monument, but as a Buddha itself identified with the four others emanating from it, the *stūpa* here represents a presence to come. This is perhaps an unconventional reading of the symbolism of the *stūpa*, and yet it in no way contradicts more traditional views. The point is not to reduce the *stūpa* to a representation of Maitreya, or to suggest that sixteenth-century Khmers did so in any direct or rigid fashion; I aim instead to highlight the messianic or Maitreyan dimensions of the *stūpa* with reference to this remarkable cultic configuration of singular importance for Middle-period Cambodia.

A stone sculpture, kept inside the Wat Nokor *vihāra* adjoining the central complex and placed on a pedestal flanking the central altar to the south, reiterates this sixteenth-century message (fig. 1.1*d*). It is a votive object, called in modern Khmer a *stūp* (Giteau 1975, 133–135). Almost two meters in height, this *stūp* is a rectangular mass crowned with a circular lotus motif finishing in a dome. On each face of the rectangle a niche is framed by *nāga* figures, strikingly similar to those framing the sixteenth-century pediments of the antechambers giving onto

Wat Nokor's central sanctuary. With an image of the Buddha sculpted into each niche, this small *stūp* is yet another reduced representation of Wat Nokor's central structure.

Though these observations concern contemporary conditions at the temple, what they reveal of a systematic pattern of condensation/multiplication across the temple grounds of an evocation of the vow contained in the temple's sixteenth-century inscription—the vow to return in the time of Maitreya—is not simply a recent phenomenon. The various cult objects I have described, as well as explicit worship of Maitreya, can be traced in descriptions of Wat Nokor written by French visitors as early as the late nineteenth century.[20] While the temple caretakers and local worshipers can no longer decipher the Pāli inscription in full, those people who maintain the cults of Wat Nokor have inherited, and indeed perpetuate, its memory.

Historians have traditionally attributed the transformation of Wat Nokor to Ang Chan. Indeed, the date of the inscription, 1566, is also the date of this king's death as it is given in many of the chronicles. One is tempted to see in Mahāparamanibbānapada the posthumous name of Ang Chan, and so in the *cetiya*, the tomb of this king. However, although the renaissance that Ang Chan represented undoubtedly played a major role in the renovation of Wat Nokor, the terms of the inscription do not allow us to affirm that he was the founder or the beneficiary of the *stūpa* itself (Thompson 1999, 342–343).

Tralaeng Kaeng

A remarkably similar construction, Tralaeng Kaeng, at Lovek, is more clearly associated with Ang Chan. One chronicle describes the foundation of this religious site, which was central to the new capital: "The King ordered an artisan to make a statue of the Buddha appearing back to back and facing out to the four cardinal points" (Khin Sok 1988, 149–150).[21] Like the *stūpa*-Buddha configurations at Wat Nokor, the central statue worshiped at Tralaeng Kaeng today, an early twentieth-century replica of the legendary original, is a single iconographic ensemble, effectively one statue made of four Buddhas joined at their backs by a tall column ending with a lotus motif resembling the top of a *stūpa* (fig. 1.1*e*). The *vihāra* accompanying this construction, the royal chronicle continues, was consecrated in 1530, the year of the tiger.[22] Inside this sanctuary today there is a *stūp*, a small stone monument with a Buddha image sculpted on each of its four sides, and crowned with a pyramidal form. Like the *stūp* and the pavilions at Wat Nokor, this constitutes yet another reduced representation of the ensemble, which I am arguing can be identified as a Middle-period cult. In this context it is not insignificant that four faces can be seen at the summit of Tralaeng Kaeng's modern roof, literally dominating the remains of this Middle-period capital (fig. 1.1*f*).

Angkor Wat

While the kingdom's capital was maintained at Lovek after its foundation by Ang Chan until its fall at the end of the sixteenth century under the reign of his grandson Braḥ Sattha, the Angkor region was reinvested by the monarchy at the same time. In particular, the twelfth-century Vishnuite temple of Angkor Wat had become a major center of Theravāda Buddhist worship by the second half of the sixteenth century. The monarchy and the elite reappropriated this most powerful symbol of the Angkor period for their personal salvation and the salvation of the kingdom (Thompson 1999, chap. 2). A number of votive texts in Khmer inscribed on columns of Pākān (the uppermost level of Angkor Wat) and of the adjoining gallery known as Braḥ Bān' are especially revealing in the context of the present study. One Pākān inscription brings us the words of the Queen Mother in 1578. After praising her son's devotion manifest in his restoration of the ancient temple, she expresses her own wish to be reborn a "great man" *(mahāpurus)* in the time of Maitreya. At Maitreya's side she (or he) will follow the path to *nibbāna.*[23] A subsequent inscription engraved on a column at Braḥ Bān' and dated 1579 records the good works and vows of King Braḥ Sattha himself.

> When His Majesty the great devotee rose to the throne as protector of the royal line, he sought to elevate the religion of the Buddha in truth by restoring *[sāṅ']* the great temple of Braḥ Bisṇulok [Angkor Wat],[24] stone by stone, he restored its summit with its nine-pronged spire, embellishing and covering it in gold. Then he deposited the sacred relics[25] transferring the fruit of his royal works to the four august ancestors,[26] in homage above all to his noble father the deceased King, as well as to his august ancestors of the past seven generations. . . . After this, His Majesty, the great and pure devotee, recalled a vow he had once made to propagate *[sāṅ']* the teachings of the Buddha in truth in the country of Kambujā, to elevate the glory of the royal family to its past brilliance, to stave off its ruin: may we be granted peace, success and stability.[27]

Another inscription at Angkor Wat, written in or after the year 1586, records pious foundations made by a dignitary at the temple. This inscription, engraved on another column of Pākān, begins by recounting the foundation of a *vihāra* by the dignitary and his wife in the year 1566, year of the tiger (the same year as the foundation at Wat Nokor described above). The text continues to describe the good works accomplished by the same dignitary some twenty years later.

> The dignitary Abhayarāj, brimming with faith, restored the cruciform stone tower with its four stone Buddha images conserved in this five-towered *prāsād.*[28] . . . [After listing the various offerings made, the inscription continues to note that the dignitary Abhayarāj] deposited sacred relics. . . . [Transferring the merit gained

through these acts to relatives and others, he then expressed the wish to] become a perfect devotee of the *bodhisattva* Braḥ Sī Āry Metrīy.[29]

Thirteen years would pass before the dignitary Abhayarāj accomplished and archived other religious acts at Angkor Wat. In the meantime, the capital at Lovek had fallen to the Siamese, and King Sattha had taken refuge abroad. Recalling—or perhaps repairing some of the same religious foundations made in the past—another inscription, dated 1599, provides more clues to the role the Buddhist cult at Angkor Wat had in the establishment (or reestablishment) of national order.

> [O]ur hearts brimming with faith, we built[30] a four-faced tower with stone and metal Buddhas symbolizing Braḥ Bisṇulok.[31]

Here again, it is the repetition of a single form, the reiteration of the same, that counts in this religious-political cult. Through the gift, the donors are united with their ancestors, placing themselves in a direct line of descent. In their act, they "construct," "restore," or "realize" the four-faced temple, which, I believe, represented an appeal to timelessness as the four manifestations of the Buddha (past), forming and emanating from the *prāsād,* invoke the Buddha (to come).

The information contained in these inscriptions is underscored by archaeological and ethnological evidence at the temple itself. The uppermost terrace of Angkor Wat supports five towers, one at each of the four corners of the first enclosure and a fifth in the center; each of these sanctuaries originally opened to each of the four cardinal directions. However, the central sanctuary would undergo significant modification during the Middle period. Each of its four entranceways was blocked up with sandstone, into which was sculpted a standing Buddha image (fig. 1.2*a*). Modern scholars have paid little attention to this late modification of Angkor Wat. However, we see once again four Buddhas surrounding a crowning pyramid and facing each of the four directions. The fact that several *stūp* were kept in the gallery of Braḥ Bān' well into the twentieth century can hardly be a coincidence.

This modification of the central sanctuary at Angkor Wat apparently took place at the end of the sixteenth century, during the particular political and religious context I have been describing here. The reliefs sculpted onto the stone entrances of the central sanctuary can be dated to the same time. Together, the iconography and texts tell us that during the sixteenth century particular attention was paid to the restoration of the sanctuary summit, relics were deposited, and Maitreya was invoked. Again I would argue that the renovations of the uppermost level of Angkor Wat sometime around 1580 were part of a religious-political movement.

The inscription concerning the offerings and vows made by the king himself is particularly enlightening. This text is dated 1579, just after Braḥ Sattha had risen to power. As the royal chronicles illustrate repeatedly, the initial duty of a new king is to render homage to his ancestors, in particular the last king: the son inaugurates his reign in laying his father's remains to rest. Braḥ Sattha's text reveals the importance of this gesture as both a perpetuation of the royal line and of the Buddhist religion, both seen as essential to the preservation of the kingdom's stability. Closed off to the mundane world, the central sanctuary of Angkor Wat served, I believe, as a *cetiya* for this king father, Paramarājā I.[32]

a

b

c

Fig. 1.2 *(a)* Buddha, the Pākān, Angkor Wat; *(b)* Buddha at Wat Phnom, Phnom Penh; *(c)* Viṣṇu, National Museum, Phnom Penh. Drawings by Say Sopheap.

The four past Buddhas are in fact associated with the royal ancestors in Braḥ Sattha's text. It tells us that in depositing relics (or building a reliquary), this monarch transferred merits to *saṃtec braḥ jī tā pūn braḥ aṅg nu saṃtec braḥ vara-pitādhirāj snoṅ guṇ braḥ kanloṅ pabitr jī adi.* While we can read this expression as literally designating four ancestors, first and foremost being Braḥ Sattha's deceased father, the phrase "*saṃtec braḥ jī tā pūn braḥ aṅg*" can also designate four Buddhas. This second interpretation is supported by the fact that no particular group of four ancestors is recognized and revered as such in Khmer culture. The principal Buddha of a *vihāra* is, moreover, traditionally called *braḥ jī* (august ancestor). This linguistic ambivalence is corroborated by modern ritual practice at the temple itself in which the four Buddha images sculpted into the entranceways of Angkor Wat's central sanctuary are associated with sacred ancestors. Each of the four images is also worshiped as one of the four past Buddhas. Any of the numerous local caretakers of this central sanctuary will readily identify these religious ancestors by name: Kuk Sandho, Nāg Gamaṇo, Kassapo, Samaṇa Gotam.[33] The western image[34] is also known as *braḥ buddh braḥ pītā,* "august Buddha, august Father" (perhaps the *braḥ varapitādhirāj* of the inscription); the southern image is *braḥ buddh braḥ mātā,* "august Buddha, august Mother." According to my informants the caretakers, this is because those Buddhas contain the *dhātu* (the relics or the essence) of the father and the mother.

And of course, no one has forgotten Braḥ Sī Āry Metrīy. Two elaborately adorned Buddha statues placed before the standing Buddha of the eastern entrance are worshiped as Braḥ Sī Ār. Moreover, in enumerating the four Buddhas of Pākān, local worshipers invoke the future Buddha to the north, at Wat Braḥ Sī Ār Metrīy, a short distance away in Angkor Thom. According to a number of caretakers at Angkor Wat, Maitreya is the last of the five brothers, the eldest and wiser still than his younger siblings who have come and gone. The future Buddha is also finally evoked in the figure of the central sanctuary itself. In this last interpretation, the four corner sanctuaries representing the four past Buddhas surround Maitreya still to come.

Angkor Wat has become an omnipresent icon in recent years for Cambodia's reconstruction or rebirth. Yet this symbolism has deeper roots than commercial iconographic trends might suggest. For many people across the country, it is here at Angkor Wat, the most imposing expression of Khmer cosmological order, where Maitreya will arrive. It would seem that this colossal monument to the dead has long been a place of gestation for Cambodia's future.

Phnom Penh

The royal chronicles tell us that the site of Wat Phnom in Phnom Penh was founded in response to, or in reverence of, the unexpected arrival of a bronze statue of the Buddha with four faces (or, according to some versions, four images of the Buddha), along with a stone statue of Viṣṇu. To commemorate the marvelous discovery of these statues floating downstream, the *bhnaṃ* (hill, pronounced "phnom"), was built. According to the royal chronicles, the Viṣṇu image was placed at the foot of the hill to the northeast; the four-faced Buddha image (or the four Buddhas) was placed in a *vihāra* built at its summit. Upon arrival at the site, Baña Yat, the founder of the capital there, erected a *stūpa (braḥ cetiya)* directly west of this *vihāra.* Another smaller *stūp* was erected atop a small sanctuary *(guha)* within the great *stūpa.* Transferring the bronze Buddha image(s) to the pedestal of the inner *stūp* itself, Baña Yat is said to have erected a model of the original statue in the *vihāra.* Other Buddhas were brought from Angkor and placed in the lower sanctuary supporting the *stūp* within the great *stūpa* (Khin Sok 1988, 70–71; *Vāṃṅ Juon* 1929, 90–92). While the concrete historical validity of this legend is suspect, if only for its attribution of the *stūpa,* which is stylistically dated to the sixteenth or seventeenth century (Marchal 1954), to Baña Yat in the late fourteenth or early fifteenth centuries, the iconographic preoccupations it expresses are consistent with those reflected in the Middle-period cult outlined above at other sites across the country.[35]

The modern cult disposition of Wat Phnom sheds light on the site's legendary history. Though the great *stūpa* is entirely closed, inside the *vihāra* we see a large *stūp* with a Buddha image sculpted in each of its four niches, rising immediately behind the central Buddha image. Unlike the vast majority of central *vihāra* statues in Cambodia today, Wat Phnom's central statue represents not the historical Buddha, but rather Braḥ Sī Āry Metrīy (fig. 1.2*b*).

Each of the *stūpa*-Buddha ensembles I have described here—Wat Nokor, Tralaeng Kaeng, Angkor Wat, and Wat Phnom—is associated with the actual foundation of a city, or the symbolic appropriation or occupation of territory. During the politically troubled Middle period, this type of gesture no doubt responded to particularly urgent needs and hopes. The innovation was to draw not only on the past, but also, in a concrete manner as indisputable as a sandstone *stūpa,* on the future. In these uncertain times for the Cambodian ruling classes, the symbolism of the iconographic ensemble was no doubt a powerful and particularly economical means of marking—and thereby performing—the reestablishment of political-cosmological order, capitalizing in effect on the perpetual presence to come of the "revolutionary" savior.

The Bayon as Paradigm

The quadruple Buddha image that appears faithfully at major royal foundations and *stūpa*s during the Middle period was, I believe, prefigured at the Bayon, a Mahāyāna temple built by Jayavarman VII, the last of Angkor's savior-kings and the first of Cambodia's Buddhist monarchs. The filiation between Jayavarman's Buddhist kingdom and the Theravāda kings of the Middle period, manifested in the repeated appearance of four-faced *prāsād* and *stūpa*s, reflects profound conceptual and pragmatic links. First, as I have suggested above, each of these traditions was intimately tied to precise political aims responding to specific though not incomparable historical situations. Jayavarman VII was, as he proclaimed, the monarch who saved Cambodia from annihilation by the Chams and who reconstructed a largely decimated or at least desecrated country. He was explicitly associated with the Buddha and with the bodhisattva savior Avalokiteśvara. Responding to similar refoundational imperatives, Middle-period rulers looked, I believe, to reincarnate within the Theravāda context the model of salvation represented by Jayavarman VII: the four-faced tower.

Scholars and Khmer people alike have long speculated about the origins and meanings of the four-faced tower. Of course it is entirely appropriate that the four faces should have inspired such a multiplicity of interpretations. Replicated in space, the tower with four identical faces shows the repetition of the unique to be a defining characteristic of divinity. The *Saddharmapuṇḍarīka-sūtra,* a Mahāyāna text evoked as a possible source for the complex iconography of the Bayon, incessantly repeats that the Buddha appears differently to different people, always choosing to appear in a form the beholder can perceive. I do not mean to suggest that we should abandon other, more traditional, approaches to the Bayon or Khmer religious iconography in general. Yet neither should we neglect the interpretive drive that the Bayon has long provoked. If indeed there ever was a single intended meaning in the four-faced towers, the very fact that that meaning has been infinitely refigured over centuries is not without meaning, in and of itself. One of the principal functions of a monument or a statue, aside from evoking or conveying a certain story or history, lies in the interpretation of the history the monument or statue itself has undergone. In this sense, the multiplicity of interpretations of the Bayon is a reflection of the temple's innate monumental and iconographic power.

In what follows, I shall recall only two of the many hypotheses concerning the Bayon's four faces—two hypotheses that are particularly intriguing in light of the Middle-period evidence presented above. The first, advanced initially by Filliozat, evokes the Buddhist center of Nalandā, of which another example can be found in the Nepalese *stūpa* painted with four stylized faces (Filliozat 1969b, 45–48). This possible relation is notable because the architectural body incorporating the four faces is in this case explicitly a *stūpa.* One tradition identifies the Nepalese *stūpa*-faces as *kṣetrapāla,* territorial manifestations of a single god.[36] It is even possible that this lead could give us new clues to that most elusive of Angkorean mysteries: the "original" identity of the four-faced Bayon-period figure. An obvious first step in this direction would involve the five mysterious gods known as *mahākṣetra* or *pañcakṣetra*, a set of guardian divinities that would seem to have played a key role in Khmer royal cult since at least the Middle period. Two inscriptions at Angkor Wat indicate the role of these gods in rituals performed at this temple in the sixteenth century and in association with the four-faced *stūpa-prāsād.*[37] Today, these divinities are placed around the ritual space delimited for a variety of royal ceremonies, one at each of the four cardinal points, and the fifth to the northeast.

The second hypothesis I want to recall, from a series of readings by Boisselier and Woodward, echoes not only the evidence outlined above but also traditional Khmer interpretations of the four-faced towers of the Bayon era as the manifestation of Brahma. Boisselier notes that the epigraphy of Jayavarman VII's reign explicitly states that the Khmer kingdom or capital was the earthly replica of the Paradise of the Thirty-three Gods (Traitriṃsa), with Indra at its head; in this metaphor or parallel, the Bayon temple complex, with its numerous towers, represents the Traitriṃsa Assembly. Drawing from Pāli and Siamese sources, Boisselier further suggests that the Bayon was a representation of a visit Brahma once made to this Assembly. In the form of the Gandharva Pañcaśikha, Brahma replicated himself thirty-three times to appear singularly before each of the thirty-three gods. Integrated into Siamese cosmological traditions, this scene evokes a new consecration of the king *(indrābhiṣeka)*. The Bayon is thus the realization on earth of the Traitriṃsa, implying that Brahma Pañcasikha appeared on the occasion of the consecration of Jayavarman VII and his capital (Snellgrove 1978, 410; Jessup and Zephir 1997, 117–120). Pursuing Boisselier's textually based hypothesis, Woodward notes that one of the architectural modifications to the Bayon could have corresponded to the *indrābhiṣeka* of Jayavarman VII, and to an ideological change in the court. At that moment, he argues, the four faces of the towers would also have changed in signification, to be thereafter identified with Brahma Pañcasikha appearing everywhere at once before the Divine Assembly. The change in signification of the four faces would have followed (or presided over) a change in the political history of the kingdom (Woodward 1981). It is tempting to link this second hypothesis to the Middle-period evidence discussed above that associates the four-faced Buddha-*stūpa* configuration, along with the image of the crowned Buddha (or king set under the four faces), with certain rituals serving to affirm political and territorial sovereignty in foundation ceremonies for capital cities or important religious centers.[38]

The iconographic signification proposed by Boisselier is presumably not what was originally intended at the Bayon. It may rather reflect a later reinterpretation, perhaps even dating from the period when Theravāda Buddhism had conquered Cambodia. It is significant in this respect that Boisselier's reading is largely based on Theravāda texts written in Pāli and Siamese. However, I do not want to jump to hasty conclusions as to the significance of such semantic and iconographic "ruptures"—in this case either during the reign of a single king or between two so-called historical periods. Indeed, the break between the Angkor and Middle period is too often taken as a self-evident and unproblematic given.[39] On the strength of such Cambodian examples, I would argue more broadly that in cultural terms rupture and continuity are not mutually exclusive. For the purposes of this chapter, I shall limit myself to two comments. On the one hand, the Middle-period kings established their cities and their legitimacy by integrating themselves into a historical lineage of descent from the Angkorean kings. In this way, they revived an ancient Angkorean tradition of performatively establishing continuity across inter-reign ruptures and at the same time bridging the gap caused (or at least symbolized) by the fall of Angkor. More specifically, the cult of the *stūpa* with four Buddhas must have served to link the Middle-period kings to Jayavarman VII through a cultural "citation" of what had become his iconographic emblem. Furthermore, and in a sense more important, the power of this cult must have consisted in its repetition ad infinitum of the miracle of repetition that the quadruple image may be seen to represent, above and beyond the question of its singular iconographic identity or meaning. In homage to the work of Paul Mus on this subject (notably Mus 1936), I would say that any precise identity of the divinity represented—or even of the monarch representing—is inseparable from the multiplicity that composes the representation, that is, from the repeated manifestation of one entity over time and across space. The Middle-period ruler reproduced the miracle that consists of reproducing the miracle. Installing oneself on the throne meant having oneself consecrated by the four-faced image. The image that the king installs as central deity in turn installs the king as sovereign monarch, and this double performative recalls the quasi-messianic conversion accomplished by Jayavarman VII.

Other Media of Expression

Iconographic representations of Maitreya have of course varied in space and time. Positive identification of statues or images can be problematic when Maitreya's most distinctive characteristic, the *stūpa* in his headdress, is absent. He can be represented as a scantily clad ascetic or as a royal figure draped in luxurious robes and jewelry. With two or four arms, and sometimes a vase and/or a wheel in hand, Maitreya shares certain traits with Viṣṇu. He is often accompanied by a tiger.

To my knowledge, no Middle-period Khmer statues of Maitreya have been positively identified to date. Indeed, the case of Maitreya in the Middle period begs the much more general question of identity, of "positive" iconographic identification, and of the attribution of the attribute. What I am attempting to formulate here about repetition, about multiplication of or as the same—something on the order of an applied theory of the supplement—bears directly on this question. I would argue that in the context of the Brahmano-Buddhist traditions of iconographic identification, which are intimately implicated in religious practice and the question of aesthetic codes, there must be a space left open for a certain indeterminacy. This is often a simple consequence of a multiplicity of identifications, but it can also, and particularly with regard to Maitreya, be understood as a certain structural openness to future readings or interpretations.

From this perspective it is instructive to look again at the various iconographic clues that can be traced more or less directly to Maitreya. While the *stūpa* appears as an architectural element in space throughout the Middle period, it disappears as an iconographic attribute of this divinity. Middle-period statuary, however, was marked by a relative proliferation of images of the "adorned" or "royal" Buddha. In these images, the Buddha appears richly adorned, typically with jewels and a crown as symbols of his sovereignty or (future) spiritual transcendence. Today in modern representations, Maitreya is systematically depicted as an "adorned" Buddha. Furthermore, a number of Middle-period adorned Buddhas are systematically worshiped today as Braḥ Sī Āry Metrīy. Once again, this cannot be taken as proof, but it does suggest the possibility that at least some of these statues were meant to represent Maitreya.[40] In any case, the iconographic evolution in which the traditional representations of Maitreya—his four arms, his attributes, including the *stūpa,* his asceticism—gave way to representation as an adorned Buddha can be attributed at least in part to an intensification of the association between the future Buddha and the *cakravartin* king in the Theravāda complex.[41] The two seemingly contradictory representations of Maitreya, as an ascetic or as a prince, together find meaning in the figure of the *cakravartin,* a transcendent man bound to rigorous observance of moral precepts.

In light of this connection, the appearance of Viṣṇu in the various examples of the Maitreya cult I have described need not be seen as fortuitous. In the myth of the origin of Phnom Penh, Viṣṇu descends with the four-faced Buddha from the north (from the former royal capital at Angkor?) to found the new southern capital. And the fact that Ang Chan completed the work of his ancestors in sculpting Vishnuite bas-reliefs in the galleries of Angkor Wat indicates much more than simple tolerance for or respect of the ancient religious tradition. This divinity reemerged throughout Middle-period Khmer expression as an important symbol of the monarchy's power to protect social order.[42] Viṣṇu's appearance represents the reincarnation of the past as future salvation. In this sense, the ancient Brahmanic god accompanies Maitreya in the reincarnation of Cambodia as a Theravāda kingdom.

One of the finest pieces of Middle-period Khmer art, a bronze statue traditionally identified by art historians as Viṣṇu, may in fact be seen as an association of the two gods (fig. 1.2*c*).[43] Discovered in the northern Khleang of Angkor Thom and now in the collection of the National Museum in Phnom Penh, this statue is thought to date from between the fourteenth and the sixteenth centuries. The four-armed figure is represented in elaborate dress, carrying an orb, a wheel, a conch, and a mace. He wears only a topknot on an otherwise cleanly shaved skull. The strands of hair are passed upward through a hollow cylinder at the center of a pearl-studded band and are allowed to fall back again on the outside, forming a bell-shaped headdress. This headdress may have been meant as a representation of a *stūpa*, something suggested not only by its form,[44] but also by its content: like tiny relics, pieces of gold leaf and rock crystal were found within the center cylinder. In light of iconographic clues combined with the evidence outlined above, I think it is possible that this image, carrying the attributes of Viṣṇu, yet with a *stūpa* as a diadem, represents a fusion of Viṣṇu and Maitreya, a fusion of the Brahmanic and Buddhist saviors depicted in their association with royalty.[45]

Waiting on the King

In the guise of a conclusion, I would like to give just a few more indications of how this vision of the future from the past may inform certain modern religious and political phenomena. A contemporary form of the Maitreya-Viṣṇu fusion is found, for example, at Wat Kien Svay Knong in Kandal Province, where Hanuman, Rāma's monkey general, is worshiped as an *anak tā* (territorial spirit). In the cement pavilion erected in the early 1990s in honor of Anak Tā Kaṃhaeṅ, as this Hanuman is called, a wooden sculpture of the "royal" Buddha is placed next to a newly fabricated cement image of the monkey general. The wooden statue is identified by local worshipers as both Rāma (Viṣṇu's reincarnation) and Braḥ Sī Āry Metrīy, in direct association with His Majesty King Norodom Sihanouk. One brief example suffices to illustrate the political implications of this religious cult. Prior to the 1993 elections, the principal caretaker of Anak Tā Kaṃhaeṅ at Kien Svay Knong, an *ācāry,* was arrested by local officials because of his support of the royalist FUNCINPEC Party, and in particular his anticipation of the king's imminent return to Cambodia after a long exile. One night, after the *ācāry* had been imprisoned for several weeks at the district headquarters (the bastion of the Cambodian People's Party, FUNCINPEC's political rival) Hanuman made an unexpected visit, ripping up papers and overturning tables and chairs. The local officials were terrorized, and the *ācāry* was released.

Norodom Sihanouk may not be the only person to embody the promise of Maitreya's coming in Cambodia today. Nonetheless, the image of the king remains transcendent. Though he returned to the country in 1991, His Majesty's frequent departures maintain a continually renewed anticipation of his arrival—his physical absence enhancing his spiritual presence. Indeed, from the perspective of the present chapter, this is a continuation of a long history of Khmer royal mobility: Cambodia's kings have always been on the move. But while it had always been a feature of Cambodian kingship, it was the very hallmark of the Middle period, as the seat of hereditary Khmer power became an ever-moving target for would-be usurpers. In conjunction with attempts to establish the chronology of reigns, these innumerable displacements of the court have been studied at length, and the unique historical context of each one must be emphasized. Yet I think we can nonetheless speak of a certain ongoing or stationary aspect to this notorious shiftiness. There is of course no Khmer monopoly on the phenomenon. However, during at least the Middle period—and in a distilled or sublimated fashion with the current king, during this post-protectorate era that bears some resemblance, however superficial, to the Middle period—this movement, which always articulates departures and returns, takes on particular significance. This continuous pattern of presence-absence has conferred a spectral power on royal leaders that is related to the extraordinary and uncanny power of the memorial in general, and of the *stūpa* in particular. For a memorial, as I have said, is the presence of an absence. Its presence marks the absence of someone who has departed, and who thereby acquires a spectral status, neither simply absent nor simply present. It is not alive, of course, but it is animated by a sort of eternal intentionality, a permanent reference to the dead as token of the impermanence of the living.

The *stūpa,* and in particular the hybrid nature and role of the *stūpa* that developed in Middle-period Cambodia as I have attempted to outline them here, performs this function in exemplary fashion. And yet in certain circumstances, in a certain configuration or set of configurations, a *stūpa* can stand in for a very special savior who is not here now but who will be or should be later, tomorrow, or in some future life; it can stand in for the (future) Buddha, one might even say for the

Fig. 1.3 Mural of Sihanouk, Wat Nokor (A. Thompson)

future itself, insofar as one may hope that there will be one. The structure of the memorial (and of culture in general, which can always be seen as a memorial system) is disturbingly unstable. The seemingly staid and at least partially performative symbol of closure, of the successful accomplishment of mourning's work, can come about or veer wildly; it can reverse the poles without warning and begin by beckoning to the future. It is the remains of the future, so to speak, all there is of it here and now—which does not mean that it guarantees it in any way, but rather that it calls it forth and stands as testimony or promise of its realization.

So Maitreya is not simply the future Buddha crowned with a *stūpa;* he "is" the *stūpa,* according to this beguiling, spectral, conditional yet performative species of being he exemplifies and authorizes. And the extraordinary and apparently irresistible if somewhat covert pull exercised by Maitreya and by the *stūpa* in Cambodia from the Middle period onward can thus be seen as driven by this bewildering temporal cantilever: the *stūpa* is or represents Maitreya insofar as he is promised to us, it is the presence among us of the promise of what is yet to come, it is the present absence but also the absent presence—already here—of a promising and uncompromised future.

A mural painted in 1995 in a newly renovated *vihāra* on the Wat Nokor temple grounds demonstrates King Sihanouk's unique symbolic power in contemporary Cambodia (fig. 1.3). The sponsors of this painting have depicted themselves, husband and wife, flanking the king before the temple of Angkor Wat. The king is in the position of the central sanctuary that corresponds to the *stūpa,* surrounded by the four Buddhas or ancestors *(saṃtec braḥ jī tā pūn braḥ aṅg),* and thus also to the Buddha to come so often conflated, as I have suggested, with a *cakravartin* king. The merit-gaining act of sponsoring the reconstruction of the *vihāra* brings the couple one step closer to salvation. Reenacting ancestral tradition even as they render it nearly unrecognizable, it is in attending this protean king—fixing him and framing him in a visual representation before the very emblem of past glory, but facing forward, facing the observer and thus the future, perhaps already in the future with their backs to the *stūpa*s of their former lives—that they seek to influence their destiny beside this remarkable returning regent.

Notes

This chapter began as a paper given at the conference Cambodia: Myth and Memory, held at Monash University, Australia, December 1996. In chapter 2 of my dissertation (1999) I explored in greater detail many of the issues raised and rethought the initial conclusions presented at Monash. The hazards of publication have meant that a sequel to this piece, in which the basic arguments are summarized in order to expand my readings of the foundation of Phnom Penh, appeared in 2000. The present version aims to shed some of the detail of the dissertation work while further refining my interpretations. I wish to extend my thanks to P. S. Jaini, A. von Rospatt, and D. Chandler, who have given me invaluable commentaries on this chapter. Once again, I am thoroughly indebted to Ang Choulean for his insight into many of the issues discussed here. Unless otherwise noted, translations are my own.

1. Khmer draws freely on Sanskrit as well as Pāli for Buddhist terms. I use the Sanskrit form "Maitreya," as opposed to the Pali "Metteya," throughout this paper, as this is the form in which the future Buddha is generally referred to in Khmer. Similarly, for other words of Indian origin in this chapter (*cakravartin, nibbāna,* etc.), I have chosen to use the form most frequently used in Khmer.

2. The Pāli term *"cetiya"* (in Khmer pronounced "chedei") is used today in Cambodia to designate Buddhist funerary monuments. Variations in regional pronunciation suggest that the Sanskrit form of the word, *caitya,* may once have been widespread. On the use of the terms *"stūpa"* and *"caitya"* in other Buddhist contexts, see Bareau 1960, 240–241; 1974, 18–24; Trainor 1997, chap. 2; and Schopen 1989, 1991.

3. In contemporary Khmer religious belief and ritual practice, the entire *stūpa* is associated with the womb, echoing the technical term for the *stūpa* dome: *garbha,* or "womb."

4. A note is in order on the various terms used in this chapter to describe Cambodian sacred buildings or places of worship. *"Prāsād"* designates an ancient Khmer temple complex (Brahmanist or Mahāyānist) or one of its distinctive tower sanctuaries. "Temple" refers to any religious complex, ancient or modern. "Wat" refers specifically to Theravāda Buddhist temples (Middle period or modern Cambodia). The presence of the term "wat" in the names of ancient temples such as Angkor Wat or Wat Nokor signals that a Theravāda Buddhist temple is located somewhere within the complex. A *"vihāra"* (pronounced "vihear," from the Sanskrit-Pāli) is a pavilion or hall located in a wat that houses a central Buddha image and is used for Buddhist rituals. "Sanctuary" can refer to a *prāsād* tower (especially in the phrase "central sanctuary"), to the space inside such a tower, or to a *vihāra.*

5. Maitreya seems to have been an important divinity during pre-Angkorean times in what is now northeastern Thailand. See Mowry 1985 and Chutiwongs and Leidy 1994. Maitreya is only rarely encountered in the Khmer epigraphic record. See K. 163 (Coedès 1954, 6, 100–101), K. 225 (Coedès 1951, 66–67), and K. 198 (Coedès 1954, 147–149). References to the advent of the future Buddha also appear in the epigraphy of Jayavarman VII, though the name Maitreya does not. See K. 227 (Coedès 1930, 309–315). An inscription at the Bayon recording the renewal of Śaivaism after the reign of Jayavarman VII provides a final intriguing reference to the future Buddha in a non-Theravāda context: K. 470 (Coedès 1942, 187).

6. This expression, common in Middle Khmer epigraphy, and related practices (such as votive tablets covered in tiny images of the Buddha) all bear witness to the continuing importance of Mahāyāna concepts during the Middle period.

7. For a presentation of the variations in Maitreya's story in South and Southeast Asian written sources, see Jaini (2001, 451–500). The only textual source that relates the history of Maitreya and is known to have influenced the Khmer Maitreya tradition is the *Pañcabuddhabyakaraṇa.* Composed in Chiang Mai / Laos around the fifteenth century, this paracanonical legend narrates Maitreya's birth as a lion. See Martini 1969, 125–144. The Siamese *Paṭhamasambodhi* elaborates at length on the character and history of Maitreya:

Metteyyabuddhābyakaraṇa-parivatta (chap. 21). For a historical presentation of the *Maitreyavyākaraṇa* (as well as a translation of the Tibetan text), see Lévi 1932. My thanks to Anne Hansen for having shared her knowledge of the Maitreya tradition in Thailand with me and for her bibliographical assistance. For a general history of textual and iconographic references, see Bhattacharya 1980.

8. Bhattacharya (1980, 108) challenges this interpretation: "in the post-Gandharan period Maitreya lost his predominance. The *stūpa* in his crown or *jaṭā* is now a parallel to the figures of the *kuleśas,* either representing the eternal *dharmakāya* or *parinirvāna* of the previous Buddhas." In the context of Middle Cambodia, one might take this hypothesis one step further and suggest that the *stūpa* functions in paradigmatic fashion as the *kuleśas,* representing a lineage, thus a past inheritance, only insofar as it stands for or promises rebirth in the future, and thereby a certain conception of timelessness.

9. A. van Rospatt, personal communication, suggests that we mitigate any sharp distinctions between the two traditions on this point, as one is born in Sukhāvati also by virtue of one's karma while Schopen (1978, 147–153) suggests that we consider the world of Maitreya to be "*functionally* identical with Sukhāvati."

10. Lokeśvara is himself associated with the Amitābha Buddha who is in charge of the paradise of Sukhāvati. In twelfth- and thirteenth-century Khmer representations, Lokeśvara is portrayed with a miniature image of Amitābha in his headdress.

11. This easily accessible monument was visited if not studied by most early explorers and researchers. A thorough study of the temple's architecture and decor can be found in Parmentier 1917. For a study of the temple's Middle-period reliefs, see Giteau 1967. My translation of the sixteenth-century Pāli inscription relies largely on Filliozat 1969b.

12. For a résumé and analysis of arguments put forth by Vickery to support another interpretation of the text's opening lines, see Thompson 1999, 105, 342–343.

13. For a more thorough explanation, see Filliozat 1969b.

14. Counting from the innermost out.

15. Also known as Vihār Bichey Bi-ar, a variant of Bachey Ba-ar.

16. These two *stūpas* may in fact be the upper portions of larger structures that were dismantled long ago.

17. See for example Gutschow 1997, 174–185, and Frédéric 1992, 134. Frédéric associates this particular representation with Mahāyāna Buddhism, in which the *stūpa* represents the "supreme Buddha" corresponding to Mahāvairocana and Krakucchanda, the first of the five Buddhas of the present age. The ensemble is also known, however, in Theravāda Buddhism; a number of relic caskets from Śrīkṣetra are adorned on their four sides with four images of the Buddha, which accompanying inscriptions identify as the four Buddhas of the past (Chutiwongs and Leidy 1994, 26).

18. I am indebted to A. von Rospatt for helping me think through these issues.

19. Though the direct worship of a *stūpa* as an image of the Buddha is exceedingly rare in Cambodia, certain practices do suggest the personification of the monument. One of these is the use of the classifier "*aṅg*" for *stūpa,* which is otherwise reserved for the Buddha, royalty, or divinities.

20. See, e.g., de Villemereuil 1883, 264–275, Aymonier 1900, 1:333–337, Parmentier 1917, 28–29, and Giteau 1975, 133–135.

21. This is the colossal quadruple figure (of which only the stone feet remain) located under the pyramidal roof of the *vihāra* of Tralaeng Kaeng.

22. The historical validity of this account contained in the royal chronicles, written several hundred years after the events they describe, is of course open to debate.

23. IMA 2. See Krassem 1985, 2–4; and Lewitz 1970, 99–126.

24. Here I understand *braḥ bisnulokaprākar* as a compound noun, "temple of Braḥ Bisnulok," reiterating the preceding term, "*mahāprāsāddh*" (great temple).

25. Or "consecrated the sacred reliquary." See Thompson 1998.

26. Or "Buddha images" *(saṃtec braḥ ji tā pūn braḥ aṅg)*. See explanation of this alternative translation below.

27. IMA 3. For a critical edition of the full text, see Lewitz 1970; my English translation differs slightly from her French.

28. I have slightly modified Lewitz' French translation (1971, 114–115) while remaining as close as possible to the original text, in order to highlight the conjunction of epigraphic and archaeological evidence. That *pañcaprāsād* designates the five towers of the uppermost level of Angkor Wat, rather than referring to a "tower with a five-story roof," is confirmed by modern usage of a variation of this term: *prāsād prāṃ*. The ambiguity of the term "*sāṅ*," frequently employed in the IMA to mean either "build" or "restore," must be taken into consideration in each of the inscriptions from Angkor Wat cited here. Though it is clear that the *prāsād* was only restored, we cannot be certain whether the Buddha images mentioned were newly sculpted or restored. It is possible, for example, that this dignitary restored the "four ancestors" of Braḥ Sattha's inscription represented by four Buddhas sculpted during or before his reign.

29. IMA 4.

30. Or "repaired" *(sāṅ)*.

31. IMA 6. Again, I have modified Lewitz' translation.

32. Further archaeological evidence contributes to this interpretation. Explorations inside the central sanctuary in the 1930s revealed, among a collection of statuary fragments, a stone recipient thought to have been used as a sarcophagus. (See Marchal and Trouvé 1935, 1936; and Coedès 1941.) Vestiges of a fire suggest that a cremation could have been held there; however, archaeologists at the time of initial exploration were uncertain as to whether these vestiges resulted from their own fumigations during research or dated to an earlier historical period. Though we cannot confirm that this sarcophagus held the remains of Braḥ Sattha, it seems to have been enclosed in the *cella* as a sort of sacred relic.

33. These are the popular Khmer versions of the Pāli names Kakusandha, Konagamaṇa, Kassapa, and Gotama, in which the first two names include the animals associated with the first two Buddhas: the *kuka* (cock) and the *nāga* (serpent or dragon). Although the order varies some depending on the informant, in general we find Kuk Sandho to the north, Nāg Gamaṇo to the west, Kassapo to the south, and Samaṇa Gotam to the east.

34. Or, according to some, the eastern image.

35. For a more thorough discussion of the Phnom Penh cult outlined below, see Thompson 2000.

36. Or *caturmahārāja,* the guardians of the four cardinal points. Cf. Gutschow 1997, 40 ff.

37. IMA 3 and 6, Lewitz 1970, 1971.

38. Today, the four-faced towers are popularly identified with Brahma, perhaps a "cultural memory"?

39. The one Middle-period inscription at the Bayon (K. 479), often cited for its testimony to a royal return to Śaivism, not only records the performance of Śaivaite ceremonies under a fourteenth century king, but also refers to the Buddha of the future.

40. Giteau 1975 speculates on this possibility for stylistic reasons but reaches no conclusion due to the absence of any single mark allowing for positive identification. For a thorough discussion of the identity of the adorned Buddha, see Mus 1928.

41. The adorned Buddhas of the Angkor period have never been identified with Maitreya. In fact, there has been little research into the origins of new iconographic constructs—imported from Pagan, nascent Siam, or Sri Lanka?—during the late Angkor period and early Middle period.

42. It has largely been through the *Rāmakerti,* the Middle-period Khmer version of the *Rāmāyaṇa,* that Viṣṇu, as Rāma, has been integrated into Theravāda Cambodia. See Pou 1977a and b; 1979, 1982.

43. Inventory no. Ga 5457, National Museum of Phnom Penh.

44. As in India, Cambodia's earliest *stūpa*s were bell-shaped (Marchal 1954).

45. For information about the *stūpa*-diadem and the intermingling of Brahmanic and Buddhist elements it implies, see Lobo in Jessup and Zephir 1997, 341. Woodward, personal communication, sees no reason to identify the divinity as Maitreya.

–2–
Khmer Identity and Theravāda Buddhism

Anne Hansen

It has become commonplace in scholarly and popular works on Cambodia to place Buddhist definitions of self and community squarely at the center of the articulation of what it means to be Khmer. "How can I be a tree without my roots?" a Khmer-American woman commented in an interview, referring to Theravāda Buddhism.[1] Religion has deep roots in the Khmer traditional society, not only in artistic and cultural life, but also in shaping the personality and the mentality of the Khmer people entirely, a contemporary manual on Khmer culture suggests (Welaratna 1993, 30). Similar linkages between being "Khmer" and being "Buddhist" are frequently recorded in the literature on Khmer diasporic communities and individuals, as well as in studies of contemporary Cambodia (Smith-Hefner 1999, 16, 21–63; Mortland 1994, 72–73; Mahoney and Edmonds 1992, 13; Welaratna 1993, 56; Ebihara 1990, 21, 42–44; Keyes 1994, 43).

This chapter examines the equation of "Khmerness" with Theravāda Buddhism during a period of sociopolitical reforms and Buddhist renovation in Cambodia, extending from the mid-nineteenth century until 1930, when the Buddhist Institute—one of the primary vehicles for the development of later Khmer Buddhism and nationalism—was established in Phnom Penh (fig. 2.1). The Theravāda had existed in Cambodia at least since the thirteenth century and had been the dominant religious school ever since, as evidenced in chronicles, inscriptions, art, literature, and architecture. Newer scholarship on Buddhist history, however, has made it increasingly problematic to assert that the Buddhist traditions existing in Cambodia prior to the latter half of the nineteenth century were the same as those we have presently come to understand as the "Theravāda" (Bizot 1976,

1992; Strong 1992). Further, the self-conscious imagining of a "Khmer" identity associated with a distinctive language, ethos, culture, and nation, and particularly with a distinctive way of being Buddhist, was a product of the cultural politics of the nineteenth century.

The notion of Theravāda orthodoxy is explored in this chapter, one that came to be increasingly interwoven with Khmer identity in the 1930s. It was put into place over the course of a century of reforms connected with the rubric of modernization throughout Southeast Asia. These far-reaching reforms, aimed at restructuring political administration along with institutions such as slavery, education, and the *sangha* (described by Edwards in chap. 3 and Hansen 1999, 20–108) challenged assumptions about the validity of a moral hierarchical arrangement of space and power and corresponding notions of the place of the human being in that cosmology. In this context, it is unsurprising that the Buddhist visions of cosmic order that dominated nineteenth-century notions of social and individual identity were subjected to an increasingly self-conscious reappraisal.

I begin this chapter by examining several universalized cosmological conceptions of identity that appear in key religious texts of the nineteenth century and that are also expressive of sociopolitical organization during this period. In the rest of the chapter, I contrast this older rendering of person and community with an emerging discourse of religious purification at the beginning of the twentieth century that sought to accommodate new, localized notions of identity such as Khmer ethnicity and culture. The change was not a total rupture or disjuncture with past understandings of order and identity, but rather the development of new currents of intellectual scrutiny that both reflected and reflected on modern notions of temporality. This development may represent the culmination of the historical process Sheldon Pollock has termed the "vernacularization" of southern Asia, a process that he understands to have occurred largely between 1000 and 1500 C.E., as the use of local languages began to supercede the cosmopolitan influence of Sanskrit as the language of literary-cultural practices (Pollock 1998, 6–37). Simultaneously, it is possible to see in the period of colonial creation of nation-

Fig. 2.1 Seal of the Buddhist Institute

states the processes that in Cambodia have led to the creation of new cosmopolitan or translocal identities through the discourses and experience of communism, the Vietnam War, diaspora, and contemporary global Theravāda Buddhism. Most recently, the latter has become the ideological vehicle for international conceptions of rural development and human rights education in Cambodia.

Identity and Order in the Nineteenth Century

Postcolonial cultural theory has pointed to the inadequacies of insisting that one can identify only one or even several wholly consistent conceptions of identity or of order at play during a particular historical moment, let alone represent them historiographically as universal or monolithic ideas (Chakrabarty 2000, 3–23). The sources for understanding topics as amorphous as order and identity are obviously many. Scholars of Southeast Asia have examined representations of order apparent in architecture, law texts, chronicles, prophecies, village rituals, maps and geographical knowledge, and Buddhist biographies, for example, and how they express and construct political and social organization and identity (Wyatt and Woodside 1982; Tambiah 1970, 1976; Thongchai 1994; Jory 2002). This multiplicity of conceptions of order and identity cannot be fully treated here, but it should be assumed that the "semio-political operations" I examine (Thongchai 1994, x) also function in a world that contains alternative, complementary, and sometimes competing value systems. In fact, the Buddhist reformist ideology I will discuss represents one such emerging alternative. But in order to understand the discursive impact of the reformist movement on early twentieth-century Cambodia, it is helpful to consider the more hegemonous identity discourse to which it reacts. I will discuss several key textual renderings of the social community and individual self that were influential in the nineteenth-century Khmer intellectual milieu and then turn to an examination of how these discourses were represented in Khmer political culture.

The turn-of-the-century monks and scholars who became engaged in reformist activities were themselves schooled at least partially in a different educational climate from the one they sought to introduce. Literati, trained and educated for the most part in Buddhist monastic schools during the nineteenth century, learned texts that articulated a Buddhist vision of a morally constructed universe existing in a cosmic time frame. The cosmos, with its multiple worlds, moved through continuous cycles of decline and regeneration that mirrored the contiguous decline and regeneration of the *dhamma,* or Truth, among beings. The identity of individuals was morally derived as well, determined by their *kammic* status as they moved through a hierarchically ordered cosmos of levels of rebirth *(gati)* depending on their accumulated stores of "merit"—derived from good or beneficial actions in past lives.

Well-known religious texts of the period, some of which were best known outside monastic circles in their oral and visual forms, include versions of the *Trai Bhūm,* a cosmological text, and the *Jātakas,* along with other related Buddhological biographies (Jacob 1996, 49; Coedès 1957, 349–352; F. Reynolds 1976b, 53–57; 1976a, 203–220; McGill 1997, 200–202).

The moral and hierarchically ordered nature of social and individual identities was also implicit in poetic texts used in the period to inculcate students in political and family norms and values. Pāli Buddhist *nīti* texts, studied by monks, and *cpāp',* a genre of didactic poetry widely learned in a sung oral form in Cambodia (Moura 1883, 1:303), provided rules of conduct for rulers and the governed, men and women, and children and parents. These texts emphasized one's role in relation to others and the actions or behavior appropriate to that role, patterning an idealized replication in social relations of the ordered hierarchical arrangement of beings in the larger cosmos.

The representation of the being/community moving through a hierarchically structured moral cosmic time frame was reinforced in ritual contexts as well. Performative actions emphasized the place of the person in the moral cosmological scheme as well the transfer of merit in order to facilitate a more advantageous birth in the next life. State funerals observed by Leclère at the turn of the century, for instance, conveyed this cosmological structure writ large, reproducing in ritual form the cosmological map of the world. In the case of the cremation of the Queen Mother in 1899, the corpse was made to represent Mount Meru, and ritual ceremonies enacting the rotation of the sun and moon were performed as part of the transfer of merit to the deceased queen (Leclère 1900, 368–376). In 1906, Leclère witnessed the ordination ceremony of King Sisowath, which explicitly recreated the cosmology of the *Trai Bhūm* through the enactment of a meticulously orchestrated procession depicting the king as the *cakkavattin* of the text (Leclère 1916, 46–47).

Other cases of ritual performances of texts described by Leclère (but found in other Southeast Asian contexts as well) illustrate the discursive power of these texts in everyday religious life (Leclère 1899, 188–189, 193; McGill 1997, 203–205; Tambiah 1970, 160–168; 1985, 87–122; Kingshill 1976, 152, 274–279). The *Vessantarajātaka,* the narrative of the bodhisattva's penultimate life, was traditionally recited at funerals and used in sermons in order to reinforce the perfection of generosity or gift giving. Recitations of the *Nimi-jātaka* and *Braḥ Mālăy Sutta* focused on the fruition of beneficial and wicked acts in various levels of the heavens and hells (Leclère 1899, 213–214).

These powerful and definitive religious conceptions of the arrangement and identity of social communities and individual selves were moored in a nineteenth-century political world characterized most prominently by unrest and upheaval in which the same kind of moral and hierarchical arrangements of space and power inscribed by the texts were coming unhinged. Writing on Cambodia during this period, historian David Chandler has commented that "[i]t would be difficult to overstress the atmosphere of threat, physical danger, and random violence that pervades [Khmer] primary sources and indeed so much of everyday life in nineteenth-century Cambodia" (Chandler 1983, 122). In the late eighteenth century, the Siamese, after repeated military incursions, had incorporated the northwestern Khmer provinces of Battambang and Siem Reap into their administrative control (Tauch 1994, 1–12). By the early 1800s, the Vietnamese had also begun to exert a quasi-colonial control in the southern and eastern regions of Cambodia, attempting to introduce Vietnamese administrative models, agricultural methods, and cultural forms to the Khmer (Chandler 1983, 126–127; Khin Sok 1991, 78–98; Leclère 1914, 406–429). With the decline of Vietnamese influence in the 1840s, a treaty was finally made with the Siamese, who installed a Siamese-educated Khmer prince, Ang Duong, on the Cambodian throne in 1848.

The upheavals of the nineteenth century, moving from the decades of war with Siam and Vietnam into a series of rebellions later, were chaotic not only because of the uncertainty and violence that warfare entailed, but also because of the toll inflicted on the hierarchical sociopolitical order. Although scholars of Southeast Asia have perhaps overstated the extent to which the *Trai Bhūm* conception of cosmography alone has dominated the spatial imagination of Southeast Asians (Thongchai 1994, 20), Khmer social and political relationships during this period appear to have been largely hierarchical and expressive of a map of the moral cosmos with a righteous king at its center.

This vision as a deeply ingrained schema for social organization in precolonial Southeast Asian societies has been the subject of a great deal of scholarly consideration (Wolters 1999, 27–40; Heine-Geldern 1956; Tambiah 1976, 102–131; 1985, 252–286; Thongchai 1994, 16–18; Schober 1995, 307–325). Prior to the creation of the modern Southeast Asian states, a process that crystallized around the turn of the twentieth century, it has been suggested, kingdoms were not conceived as bounded spaces but as a kind of vacillating geopolitical process. Termed *maṇḍalas* (galactic polities) by scholars, these kingdoms were patterned on the reduplication of ordered cosmic hierarchies drawn from religious visions of the universe. The most powerful kingdoms (in terms of military, economic, and cultural dominance) served as the "centers." Power radiated out and away from the centers to weaker surrounding principalities that signaled their vassal status by paying annual tributes in the form of gifts such as trees crafted from gold and silver, local products, and corvée labor.

These geopolitical notions were linked to the larger hierarchical and cosmological conceptions of space and power that I have discussed. So, too, was individual identity. The sum of one's moral virtue and religious practice determined not only the realm of one's rebirth, but also one's social standing and circumstances in that life. Social rank, then, was tied not just to one life, but also to countless lifetimes within the cosmic frame.

Nineteenth-century Cambodia was a highly stratified society in which a few people wielded power over most of the rest of the population. The office of the monarch occupied the central position, albeit one that was closely predicated on upholding the *dhamma.* To become a king, one's moral standing from previous lives was obviously high. Yet to be king also involved the promulgation of benefit—of merit—for the whole kingdom, largely through acts that promoted religion such as building temples and collecting Buddhist texts—acts that were moral imperatives besides being politically wise. Kingship in Theravāda Southeast Asia, defined in large part by the Buddhist ideal of the *cakkavattin* and the legendary reign of King Aśoka, necessitated that the king act as the moral fulcrum of the kingdom as well as its political center.

With the king occupying the position of greatest authority, the Khmer court was divided into departments, or houses, in which the highest-ranking members of the court—the king, the *mahā obhayarāj* (second king),[2] the *mahā uparāj* (heir apparent), and the queen—each had control over a certain number of high officials and the provinces that fell under their respective jurisdictions. The provinces were divided into sub-units known as *sruk,* consisting of several *bhūmi* (villages). A royally appointed governor administered each province with lesser officials under him at the *sruk* and *bhūmi* levels. These officials were joined by other ministers with higher and lower grades of rank such as *ukñā* who owed allegiance to various members of the royal family and had duties ranging from collecting taxes to writing poetry. Each of the titles that might be conferred on nobility carried with it a *hūbān'* (a level of rank) that in combination with the royal house from which the title was issued rendered one official clearly "above" or "below" another (Khin Sok 1991, 163–236). There were lower-ranking officials as well, such as judges, who were appointed locally by the governor or one of his underlings. Although, technically, anyone could be appointed to offices, officials were selected largely according to the functioning of what has been termed a "patron-client system": as a reward for services rendered or favors done, or in response to gifts presented to a higher-ranking patron or the king (Khin Sok 1991, 216–217; Moura 1883, 248–250).

The system held together, observed one contemporary French official, as tenuously as all governments on earth, based on a ritual known as *bhịk-dịk-saṃpath* (drinking the water of the oath) (Leclère 1904, 735–741; 1916, 220; Moura 1883, 248–256; Khin Sok 1991, 202–206; Porée and Porée-Maspero 1938, 152). Twice each year, members of the court and regional officials gathered in the capital to swear allegiance to the king by reciting an oath in which they promised loyalty in thought, deed, and military support and by drinking water that had been sacralized by the king's Brahmanic priests who soaked weapons in the water to be administered. Just as the behavior of the king was linked to the well-being of both the state and the *dhamma,* the nobles' duties went beyond supplying armies and corvée, labor. They were expected to behave as moral exemplars, upholders of the *dhamma* and *sangha* as well as the king.[3]

The conception of rulers as moral exemplars whose *kammic* inheritance led them to be reborn in positions of authority and rank is at once an ideal and a source of ambivalence and tension in the history of the period. Although the *cau-hvāy sruk* (provincial leaders) held enormous power over the people in their jurisdictions, including the ability to levy taxes and labor and to commute or inflict capital punishment, their hold on power was fragile in the sense that they could be stripped of their rank and privileges at the will of their own higher-ranking patrons (Khin Sok 1991, 215, 239; Chandler 1983, 105). When an official fell from power, it followed that his many retainers would also lose their positions relative to him, thus potentially triggering the realignment of social networks within an entire locality.

Since social order was dependent on the smooth flow of the reciprocal benefits conferred by patron and clients on each other, it suffered when either or both sides could not fulfill their obligations. Warfare and unrest placed demands upon local leaders to levy armies and laborers. The constant wars also caused massive destruction in many regions of Cambodia. Entire populations fled into the forest or were captured as prisoners of war and forcibly relocated with the conquering armies, the survivors destined for slavery (Pavie 1898, xx; 1995, 68; Khin Sok 1991, 239, 269; Bowie 1996, 114–126).[4]

Under these conditions, raising revenues from agricultural and other sectors became more difficult. This situation caused tension in the relations between elites and peasants, evidenced in the mood of spiritual and material dissatisfaction that led to tax revolts and millenarian movements in the second half of the century. The strain that these forms of turbulence placed on the different strata of society added to the weakening of a hierarchically ordered social structure that was simultaneously undergoing challenges from the reform-minded administrations coming to power in both Siam and French-controlled Cambodia.

The close of two centuries of regional warfare gave rise to a period of reconstruction in Cambodia. While social reconstruction was begun under Ang Duong and continued into the reign of his son Norodom (1860–1904), the circumstances of life for many Cambodians remained harsh. Unrest throughout the remainder of the century both contributed to the slowness of the recovery process and signaled continuing unease on the part of the population. This dissatisfaction was in turn exacerbated by the transformations in the social arrangement of power in the kingdom necessitated by French political control.

From 1863, when Norodom (r. 1864–1904) agreed to a protectorate treaty with the French, the monarch's real power had begun to diminish as he was increasingly forced to rely on the French military to protect his interests against civil unrest. In spite of this arrangement, as far as most Khmer were concerned, French interference in their daily lives was minimal, since for the most part the Khmer monarchy maintained its administration of the kingdom through the 1880s. This perception began to crumble in the mid-1880s with the introduction of French-initiated governmental reforms that sought to diminish the power of Khmer elites to administer and raise revenue from villages under their jurisdiction in the countryside.

The French presence did bring a greater degree of peace to the countryside in the regions they controlled, but besides the piracy and banditry that was a constant problem at the time, revolts and rebellions continued to erupt in both Thai- and French-controlled Khmer areas throughout the rest of the century. Motivated in part by political considerations such as taxation, the rebellions also reflected a millenarian religious thought that was common among the peasantry in other parts of Southeast Asia as well throughout this period.[5] This current of "semio-political operations," to use Thongchai Winichakul's phrase (Thongchai 1994, x), represents one more alternative discourse on order and identity during this period. At the same time that millenarianism critiqued and checked the authority of the king as the moral center of the cosmos, however, it also flowed out of and reinforced the very same map of power and social formation that placed the king at its center.

Generally, the millenarian rebellions were led by charismatic religious leaders termed *anak mān puṇy* (those possessing merit) whose religious authority was linked to prophecies and Buddhist texts predicting the birth of the epoch of the Buddha to come, Maitreya, and to the ideal of the *cakkavattin,* or wheel-turning *dhamma*-king associated with Maitreya's epoch. The Maitreya prophecy has emerged from obscure origins in a number of Mahāyāna and Theravāda Buddhist historical contexts (see chap. 1; also Sponberg and Hardacre 1988). In various versions, it predicts cycles of decline of the *dhamma,* connected with an unrighteous ruler whose errors of judgment engender the proliferation of poverty, violence, and immoral behavior and diminish the average span of a human life to a few years. Following the decline, which only a few people survive, the *dhamma* is renewed and gradually regenerates. The human population increases and develops under the guidance of a righteous ruler until the epoch of the next Buddha, Maitreya, when the people are ready to benefit from the preaching of another Buddha. In the late nineteenth-century Khmer versions of these movements, their "millenarian" nature (Collins 1998, 346–347, 378–383, 395–413) involved the belief that in the midst of social turmoil, the arising of a righteous leader termed a *dhammik* was imminent; the *dhammik* would usher in a new golden age of justice and *dhamma,* preparing the way (at some unknown point in the future) for the coming of the next Buddha.[6]

In Cambodia, the rise of millenarian thinking during the latter half of the nineteenth century is evidenced by political revolts and by the popularity and circulation of prophetic texts. Millenarian leaders, presenting themselves as figures (or incarnations) of the past and connecting themselves with the *dhammik* and the eventual arrival of Maitreya in the future, personified a moral solution to dissatisfaction with the present. In Cambodia, as in northern Thailand and Burma, bloody confrontations resulted when millenarian followers armed primarily with protective tattoos, amulets, and mantras were slaughtered by conventionally armed government troops.

Turn of the century French administrative records give clear evidence of the extent to which the French feared these religiously potent millenarian figures. A nineteenth-century official's account of the political necessity of beheading and then displaying the severed head of Borkampor, leader of an 1866–1867 revolt, focuses on the necessity of demonstrating Borkampor's demise to a populace largely convinced of his religious powers of invulnerability (Leclère 1914, 457; Collard 1925, 81–82; Maspéro and Porée-Maspéro 1938, 49–52; Reddi 1970, 33–39; Moura 1883, 159–171).[7] Following this rebellion, colonial officials were so alarmed by the connection between millenarianism and rebellion that they put monks and others demonstrating even minor displays of religious power under surveillance. This fear is evidenced throughout turn of the century administrative records and reports. For instance, an administrative report on the tax rebellion of 1885–1887 in Kampot highlights the claims of invulnerability made by one of the revolt's leaders.[8] In another case in 1916, two monks were arrested and disciplined for proffering tattoos that conferred invulnerability, thereby "pushing the inhabitants to revolt," according to administrative correspondence on these monks' activities.[9] In a 1917 case, an elderly provincial monk was put under surveillance after he earned the respect of nearby villagers for taking up residence in an abandoned temple. Fearful that the solitary monk would develop a reputation for prowess in meditation, colonial officials quickly alleged he was "stricken with madness" and sought to have him removed to a monastery in Phnom Penh where he could be closely watched.[10]

The millenarian mood of the populace in the late nineteenth century is also evident in the composition and circulation of Buddhist prophetic texts that interpreted contemporary political events in the kingdom through the lens of Buddhist cosmic history (Maspéro 1929, 299; de Bernon 1994, 83–85; 1998, 43–66). This group of texts, sometimes referred to as *damnāy* (prophecies) and apparently composed during this period, enumerated predictions made by Gautama Buddha concerning the future fortunes of the *dhamma* in the epoch preceding the birth of the next Buddha, Maitreya. Although Khmer intellectuals evidently knew the texts, they appear to have circulated much more widely as part of the literary-oral culture that existed well into the twentieth century.[11] Literate persons, most likely men who were or had been monks, copied or memorized important texts and recited them to others. The act of interpreting the texts, as they appear to have been used, was an effort to ameliorate present anxiety and dissatisfaction through establishing moral causation and effect in the past and future. The circulation of these texts in the written form—a form understood to be as powerful and authoritative as the ideas it contained (Swearer 1995, 18–22)—may have contributed to the acceptance of millenarian discourse during this period.

Along with the immediate political concerns that fueled millenarianism, it seems likely that the preponderance of millenarian movements during this period expressed a moral crisis, a way of responding to social unrest that conveyed a longing for the restoration of remembered, idealized conceptions of meaning and order. These idealized conceptions were based on the *kammic* ordering of existence and identity and the cosmic history of the degeneration and regeneration of the *dhamma.* As Thompson suggests in chapter 4, Buddhistic assumptions about history went beyond the conception that the past was the model of a better, more righteous world; the past was in fact a template for what the future would become as sentient beings cycled from Buddha era to Buddha era. This historically charged interpretation of the present, then, meant that factors such as natural phenomena (e.g., drought) or social conditions such as the oppression caused by overtaxation could be interpreted in terms of the degeneration of the *dhamma,* which in turn could be linked to past or present moral causes, such as the unrighteous behavior of a king or the yielding of power by illegitimate or morally suspect individuals.

The second half of the nineteenth century saw increasing fragility and corruption in the Khmer administrative system, which in turn gave French colonial officials greater opportunities and justification for accelerating their intervention in the kingdom.[12] The disruption of sociopolitical hierarchies in Cambodia that developed and intensified under French political control had wider ramifications for the society than simply the wresting of political and economic control from certain elite families. As I have suggested, hierarchies were deeply ingrained cultural metaphors employed in religious and cosmological schemas that expressed ideas about identity, harmony, and moral order.

At the same time that the privileging of a hierarchically organized, spatially and temporally cosmic religious construction of identity was eroding in French-controlled Cambodia, an emerging current of thought recognized by some Thai Buddhists sought to separate cosmology from notions of religion and morality. The forces that ushered in these new currents of thought, it has been argued, were not primarily the result of knowledge of Western technology and science brought to Siam during this period, but rather the concurrence of the introduction of Western science into the reform-minded, rationalistic climate of Bangkok intellectualism under Mongkut (Tambiah 1976, 200–229; F. Reynolds 1976a, 203–220; Thongchai 1994, 37–47). Mongkut's religious reforms, known as the Dhammayut movement, emphasized an orthodoxy based on scripturalism, a demythologizing rationalism, an effort to intellectualize monastic education and to spread this purified religion to laypeople—to the exclusion of magical ritual practices and the centrality of narrative texts, such as the *Jātakas*, for teaching and interpreting the tradition (Tambiah 1976, 208–219; C. Reynolds 1972, 81–112; Griswold 1961, 23). Mongkut and members of his court who formed much of the reform-minded class of intellectuals were interested in Western science even as they worked to introduce religious and administrative reforms in the kingdom. In 1867, one of Mongkut's officials published a book (the first Siamese-printed book) called *Kitchanukit,* which argued for the reinterpretation of Buddhism away from the erroneous cosmological views of the world promulgated by the *Trai Bhūm* and toward an understanding of Buddhism that emphasized moral conduct in the context of an individual's present life (Reynolds 1976a, 214–216; Thongchai 1994, 41; Ivarsson 1995, 56–86).

In Cambodia, the convergence of reformist influences from the French, Siamese, and Khmer elites themselves began to have an impact on the cultural politics of the late nineteenth and early twentieth centuries. Social, administrative, and fiscal reforms imposed by the French colonial government had a growing influence on social structures beginning around the turn of the century. Although the initial religious changes in nineteenth-century Cambodia were neither as dramatic nor as self-conscious as to warrant being called reforms, the renovation of Khmer Buddhism begun during the reign of Ang Duong continued into the early twentieth century and was invigorated by French patronage. By the 1910s and early 1920s, the influence of Siamese religious reformism on young monks in Cambodia combined with French efforts to strengthen Khmer Buddhist education had triggered the formation of a reformist wing in the Khmer *sangha.* While these young monks were Mahānikāy rather than Dhammayut, their reformist ideas reflected the Dhammayut passion for purification and scripturalism.

These shifts in intellectual and religious discourse were inseparable from the political dimensions of reformism in Cambodia during this period. Beginning in the late nineteenth century, the French and Siamese governments—the two political powers controlling Khmer-inhabited areas—were both reforming social structures in the region in ways that further contributed to the corrosion of the traditional hierarchies that defined and ordered social identities. In both Siam and Cambodia, new administrative policies were enacted that sought to reshift the "galactic" arrangement of power in the kingdoms to one in which the central government had tighter control over all parts of its increasingly definable territory and over all levels of government. In Cambodia, the administrative reforms introduced by the French beginning in 1876 (but put more aggressively into force after 1884) included the elimination of numerous royal ranks and ministry positions, reform of the judicial and taxation systems in the kingdom, and the abolition of all forms of slavery.[13]

These reforms, intended as part of a larger French effort not only to consolidate and ensure their own political control but also to reform what they perceived as the indigenous structures of inequality and corruption among non-European members of society, caused considerable social upheaval for turn-of-the-century Khmer. Efforts by French colonials to abolish traditional social practices such as slavery challenged basic assumptions on which society had rested, including the idea that social life was structured by a karmic ordering of beings based on their moral histories in the cosmos.

Religious Purification and Cultural Identity in the Early Twentieth Century

By the early twentieth century, the confluence of social and religious reforms within colonized Cambodia led to the development of a heightened sense of Khmer cultural identity that was connected, among educated Khmer, with an emerging discourse on religious purification. This move among reformists toward the "domain of the spiritual" clearly evokes Chatterjee's widely acknowledged analysis of intellectual and emerging nationalist responses to colonial ideology in India and elsewhere. The colonial subject, he suggests, divides reality into material and spiritual domains. The material domain is perceived to be subordinate to colonial control and Western technological superiority; the spiritual, on the other hand, is understood to be too interior to be controlled and simultaneously a domain in which the East can claim superiority. It is in this latter domain, Chatterjee has argued, that "nationalism launches its most powerful, creative, and historically significant project: to fashion a 'modern' national culture that is nevertheless not Western" (Chatterjee 1993, 6).

It would be an exaggeration, I think, to suggest that in turn-of-the-twentieth-century Cambodia, the religious domain served as a self-conscious wellspring of nationalist aspirations. But there are strong parallels to the situation that Chatterjee observes in India. Khmer intellectuals needed a way to respond to French frustration with Khmer technological and scientific backwardness (Moura 1883, 303, 315–316; Leclère 1899, xi–xiii), often expressed in the form of incredulity that the contemporary Khmer were the descendants of the great Angkorean civilization. Typical of this assessment of the Khmer were the comments of an official who arrived in Cambodia in 1884.

> Heredity has developed the sentiment of his [the Khmer] powerlessness and weakness to such a degree that in the presence of the work of his ancestors he sincerely doubted the latter. What a lot of times we have heard Cambodians imputing the construction of the Angkorean monuments to genies! (Collard 1921, 138)

Given their contact with these sorts of sentiments, it is unsurprising that Khmer intellectuals came increasingly to examine their local identities in terms of the universal and translocal language of Buddhism. Buddhism commanded respect even from colonials. French officials were politically astute enough to recognize the prominence of the *sangha* in Khmer society and the legitimating power the *sangha* lent to the monarch who supported it. Some colonial officials were also genuinely attracted to Buddhism as a rationalist, ethical alternative to Christianity —qualified with the assertion that the original message of Buddhism had become corrupted by the "intellectual weakness of the masses it has morally governed" (Leclère 1899, xiv; Hallisey 1995, 45–46). Finally, as I have already suggested, in a political sense the French were also clearly fearful of Buddhist forms of indigenous power.

But Khmer intellectual absorption in religious reform was not simply or merely a self-conscious effort to articulate a response to the colonial experience. The rebuilding of religious institutions in Cambodia had begun prior to colonial influence and was further expanded because of French patronage. Rather, given the historical context of colonialism and modernist reforms being introduced in French Indochina and Siam, concern with religious purification became a medium for self-scrutiny and grappling with modernist ideas for the obvious reason that religion was already one of the primary sources for Khmer imaginings of reality. Dominant intellectual conceptions of self and community, as I have suggested, had been constructed in Buddhist terms throughout the nineteenth century. Most of the kingdom's literati were either monks or former monks; Khmer literature, arts, and architecture were religious; history, in its chronicular form, was the history of the relationships between kings, the *sangha,* and the *sāsanā* (religion). Further, Siamese thought continued to exert a strong influence on the Khmer throughout the nineteenth century, so Siamese intellectual concern with scripturalism and monks educated in Bangkok carried other tenets of religious purification back to Cambodia.

These ideas were bolstered by support from the French colonial administration who, motivated by political expediency, favored a demythologization of Khmer Buddhism as a more rational and acceptable alternative to what they viewed as the unscientific and degenerate tendencies reflected in traditional Khmer cosmological thought. As a discourse of religious purification developed in Cambodia, it encompassed new modes of textual production, Pāli education, and heightened attention to Khmer language and folklore.

While the French colonial administration tightened its hold on political power in Cambodia through reforms initiated in the late nineteenth century, French attention to Khmer religion did not begin in earnest until the early twentieth century. French officials who had dealt with millenarian revolts throughout the late nineteenth century and witnessed the rebuilding of Buddhist architecture, textual collections, and education during Norodom's reign were keenly appreciative of the key role of Buddhist monks in Khmer society as the largest group of literati in the kingdom and as educators and figures endowed with morally charged power in the eyes of the populace.

In late nineteenth-century Cambodia, the two most prominent Khmer monks of the nineteenth century, Saṃtec Saṅgharāj Dien (1823–1913), who became the *sangha* head in 1857, and Saṃtec Sugandhādhipatī Pān (1824–1894), the monk who is credited with establishing the Dhammayut sect in Cambodia either in 1854 or 1864,[14] were both educated and ordained in Bangkok (Khin Sok 1991, 269–271; Leclère 1899, 523–524; Flauguerges 1914, 175–182). From the mid-nineteenth century until the 1920s, Bangkok was the center of Buddhist education in the region. Khmer monks who aspired to higher Pāli studies or who wanted to collect or copy manuscripts were obliged to travel there, often spending months or years in Siamese monasteries. As a result of this exposure, the general intellectual atmosphere of reformist scripturalism, and the tenets of religious purification and rationalism coming from Siam, were transmitted to Khmer monks of both sects.

While no Khmer version of the Siamese *Kitchanukit* was produced in Cambodia, Siamese-inspired rationalism and demythologization was current in Khmer monasteries during the nineteenth century. While too few details are known about Khmer monastic education prior to the early twentieth century, some of the monks who were educated in this milieu went on to influence the next generation of students with ideas about renovation and reform. Leclère's late nineteenth-century accounts show that even before the intellectual influence of European colonialism had become deep-seated in Cambodia, some Khmer monks were debating traditional Buddhist cosmological ideas (Leclère 1899, 130–133). While the demythologizing discourse seems to have developed at a more cautious pace in Cambodia than in Siam, after the turn of the century it was fortified by French colonial views of Khmer Buddhist cosmology as scientifically backward. A subsequent movement toward a more rationalized Buddhism, understood to be more "pure" or in tune with original Indian Buddhism, emerged among a new generation of monks and Pāli scholars. With the death of Saṃtec Saṅgharāj Dien in 1913, the influence of religious reformism became even more pronounced in Cambodia as a result of the rise to prominence of younger Mahānikāy leaders promoted by the French, notably Chuon Nath (1883–1969) and Huot Tat (1891–1975?), discussed by Edwards in chapter 3.

French interest in patronizing the reinvigoration of Buddhist education in Cambodia developed largely after the turn of the century. Although it would appear that, ideologically, French and Siamese approaches to Buddhist education had much in common, the French position toward the Dhammayut sect was highly antagonistic, and fear of Siamese cultural and political influences taking hold in Cambodia through the organ of Dhammayutism became the official motivation for the colonial administration's policies toward the Khmer *sangha* in the twentieth century. By the turn of the century, it is clear that Siamese influence and, in particular, the travel of monks to Siam for study had become a cause for alarm among the French colonial administration and was one of the primary factors leading to the initiation by the French of a major program for revitalizing Buddhist education, including the establishment of new Pāli schools at Angkor in 1909 (which ultimately failed) and Phnom Penh in 1914 (see chap. 3; Hansen 1999, 94–101).[15]

In spite of the motivations for stemming the influence of Siamese reformism in the protectorate, on an ideological level many French ideas for religious renovation were drawn from or identical to those of Siamese reformists, emphasizing rationalism and scripturalism in the study, interpretation, and practice of Buddhism. The reasons for the strong similarities between Siamese and French views on Buddhist education are perhaps best understood in relation to the small nucleus of French scholars charged by the colonial government with revitalizing Khmer Buddhism, whose introduction to the workings of Buddhist community life and education originated in Bangkok. The two most influential French scholars installed by the École Française in Phnom Penh, George Coedès and Suzanne Karpelès, both came to Phnom Penh by way of Bangkok, where each was affiliated at different points in their careers with the Vajirañāṇa Library, an institution established in 1882 in Mongkut's honor by his children (Coedès 1924; Filliozat 1969a, 1–3).

Significantly, Siamese reformist notions initiated by Mongkut, although stemming largely from indigenous notions of orthodoxy and purification, were to a certain extent influenced by and compatible with European scholarly understandings of Buddhism. Both Siamese and European views favored a rational, demythologized, historical, and philological approach to the study of canonical texts as its central tenet and tended to devalue the traditional centrality of the performance and transmission of "apocryphal" narrative texts such as the *Jātaka*s, the cosmological understanding of ethics, and the performance of certain domestic and agricultural rituals viewed as animist or Brahmanic corruptions of original Buddhism. As the French moved the Khmer *sangha* toward the introduction of printed canonical texts and other Buddhist works in Cambodia, their importation of Siamese reformism became further entrenched. Educating Khmer monks in the task of editing and translating the *Tipiṭaka* and commentaries, they insisted that the texts used as a basis for this work should be those of Siamese origin, since the production of critical editions (which they considered reliable) had already been initiated decades earlier in Siam under Mongkut.[16] Thus, the oddly jarring result of French efforts to combat the influence of the Siamese Dhammayut in Cambodia was in fact the promotion of a renovated Khmer Buddhism that closely resembled the rationalized Buddhism introduced by Mongkut in Bangkok a half century earlier. As in Siam, while key issues such as the style of wearing robes, the carrying of the alms bowl, and the manner of pronouncing Pāli were not adopted by the Mahānikāy, many of the intellectual, pedagogical, and scriptural interpretation methods and ideas initiated by Mongkut influenced the subsequent development of religious practice and doctrine in both sects.

The trend toward the intertwining of new definitions of Buddhist orthodoxy with a more particularistic, localized conception of identity that had begun to take shape in Cambodia in the 1910s and 1920s is reflected in the career and writing of one of the most important Khmer intellectuals of this period, Ukñā Suttantaprījā Ind (1859–1924). A Mahānikāy-affiliated monk, Ind trained in Phnom Penh and Battambang and spent nearly a decade in Bangkok. Ind disrobed in 1897 to become a provincial official in Battambang under the Siamese governor. While living in Battambang, he wrote poetry and a treatise on versification, completed numerous vernacular translations of Pāli works, and painted temple murals (Tauch 1994, 98–99). After Battambang was retroceded to the French protectorate in 1907, Ind was awarded the rank of Ukñā Suttantaprījā and called to Phnom Penh to serve as a member of the controversial first Commission du Dictionnaire Officiel Cambodgien and the commission designated to oversee the curriculum of the École de Pāli.[17] Serving on both of these commissions, Ind was immersed in the discussion of the Sanskrit and Pāli origins of Khmer language and literature and pedagogical and curricular reform in Buddhist education. His interest in collecting Khmer folklore, which would become the focus of later Khmer constructions of "national literature," apparently developed in response to these involvements[18] and is expressive of a heightened interest in Khmer language, literature, and culture that developed during this period. In 1921, Ind finished composing a lengthy text entitled the *Gatilok* (Ways of the world). An ethics manual directed at the problem of living as a moral Buddhist in the modern world, the *Gatilok* was one of the first Buddhist books purposely written for print.

Ind's text uses Khmer folklore (as well as Indian and French fables) as a basis for Buddhist ethical reflection. While narrative has long been used as a medium for Buddhist ethical reflection (Hallisey and Hansen 1996, 305–313), one distinctive dimension of Ind's folktales in the *Gatilok* is the prominence given to local identities. In one case, the humorous Khmer story of a Khmer son-in-law forced to contend with the stupidity of his three elder brothers-in-law and father-in-law about local natural phenomena is used by Ind to demonstrate the characters of those who lack *satisampajañña* (the ethical quality of mindfulness and discrimination) (*GL*, 3:44–47). Another local narrative tells the story of a hill-tribe boy who migrates to the Khmer lowland after the brutal murder of his entire family; this story is used to explore ethical problems connected with responses to human injustice (*GL*, 2:50–58).

Along with the incorporation of local geography and cultural practices, Ind also employed a localized temporal frame for his examination of Buddhist moral identity. Most of the narratives focus on the causal relationship between one action and its immediate consequences—often unintended or unforeseen—representing what Ind refers to as *gatiloka* (ways of the world). While *gatiloka* is most commonly used in Pāli literature to refer to the five (sometimes six) realms of existence into which humans can be reborn in the three worlds of gods, humans and animals, and hell-beings as a consequence of their *kammic* identities (i.e., Feer 1884, 152–161), in Ind's definition, "*gati*" is reinterpreted as the "ways" of acting or behaving in the immediate present. *Gatiloka,* "ways of the world," is then contrasted with *gatidhamma,* "ways of *dhamma.*"

The "self" in Ind's work is understood in a simile that directly reflects both his preoccupation with purification and with the notion that human identities are partially rooted in the "world" *(lok),* which represents whatever is constructed from the thought, speech, and actions of sentient beings. All beings with minds are formed from a combination of "*dhamma*" and "world," he asserts in the simile, as if they were gold alloys made from gold and copper.

> All the different beings are different from each other because *dhamma* and *lok* are put together in the same way that the textures of gold alloys are different because the element copper is put together with the element gold in varying large or small amounts. . . . A bright yellow color shining forth from the texture of a gold alloy belongs to the category *(jāti)* of gold. The various colors of red in the texture of the gold alloy indicate the category *(jāti)* of copper. (*GL,* 1:7–8)

The parts of a human being that are subject to the processes of birth, death, and change, such as the body and feelings or reactions, are of the world, *lok.* These aspects of the world shape human identity just as the amount and grade of copper in a gold alloy determines its overall color and appearance. Whatever knowledge or truth the being possesses is not subject to death or change because it is "of the *jāti* of *dhamma.*" Like gold in an alloy, its brilliant, pure color shines forth from any being that possesses it. A person's unique identity is thus determined by the combination of *dhamma* and *loka* that he or she creates through thought, speech, and actions. Identity is keyed to the clarity of one's moral vision, dependent on *satisampajañña,* mindfulness, and discrimination, and likewise, the identity of the larger group is shaped by the moral qualities and *satisampajañña* of its individuals. This understanding of identity, while not wholly divorced from traditional cosmic constructions of identity discussed earlier, appears to be nonetheless reflective of a transformed temporal and spatial orientation. The larger cosmic time frame of personal development is deemphasized in this vision of the individual, and the conception of the moral well-being of the world or community is less dependent on the figures at its fulcrum, such as the king, than on the moral reverberations of individuals interacting with each other.

While Ind does not employ modern words such as "national" *(jāti),* "nation" *(prajājāti),* or "society" *(saṅgam)* in the *Gatilok,* his writing represents a move toward these concepts. In his commentary, he sometimes seems to be grappling with a notion of "culture," although he lacks terminology for the concept. Instead, he often employs the word *"jāti,"* which he uses not in its modern connotation but in its Pāli-derived sense of "kind, category, birth, or genealogy," to inscribe a notion of the simultaneous internal connectedness through language, ethos, and worldview (in the Geertzian sense; Geertz 1973, 89–90) of *jāti manuss yoeṇ* (people of our kind), as well as the external separation from others of different groups such as *jāti pārāṅsaes* (the French) (*GL,* 3:40–42). This same semantic transition was already occurring in Siam by the time Ind spent some years in a Bangkok monastery (Thongchai 1994, 134–135). The Guesdon Khmer-French dictionary published in 1930 (but researched and compiled in the several preceding decades) defines *jāti* as "existence, being, or birth" (Guesdon 1930:I, 517). By the time the Khmer-Khmer dictionary was published in 1938, however, as Edwards (chap. 3) points out, the word *"jāti"* had become the basis for modern Khmer words connected with its present notion of "nation" *(prajājāti)* (Institut Bouddhique [1938] 1967, 1989, 1:667).[19] While Ind's distinctive use of the concept of *"jāti"* in combination with his incorporation of Khmer folklore was probably not overtly intended to convey or celebrate nationalist ideas, it shows the development of this discourse in process. Considering the prominence of Ind's work, it may well have contributed to this process. The publication of Ind's compilation of *Gatilok* stories in *Kambujasuriyā* was followed by a nationwide effort to collect and publish Khmer folklore for the next several decades. In 1938, a group of readers wrote a letter to the recently established Khmer newspaper *Nagararavatta,* commenting that the newspaper should continue to help aid the development of Khmer nationalism by printing *gatilok-gatidharm* stories "because Khmers increasingly liked to read stories, more than before."[20]

Various passages in the *Gatilok* exemplify the concern during this period to articulate notions of a new Khmer Buddhist identity along reformist lines. Ind draws on several examples of local religious practices to examine ignorance that originates, he argues, with people's inability to recognize that whatever is good and advantageous in the world is always paired with misfortune and dissatisfaction. "Even though people do not want [negative experiences] they will surely have them because the nature of reality is such" (*GL,* 3:29). Again, the cultivation of *satisampajañña* underlies Ind's analysis. Those people who do not possess this quality of moral discernment chase "quick fix remedies" offered by various types of *grū,* healers, teachers, and others who claim to possess special powers.

> [A]ll of these *grū* are charlatans. They always fake people out with tricks, making boastful claims that this is effective, accurate and quick; it cures all diseases.
>
> Hearing this, subjects of the kingdom generally scatter in a clattering panic,

> gathering up candles, incense and money to go rent boats and consult these effective *grū*. At times like these, Chinese boat captains can command a high price for their boats. (*GL*, 3:30–31)

Ind points to local cults surrounding village or territorial spirits and deities as inappropriate from the standpoint of Buddhist orthodoxy. Not only does participation in the cults demonstrate a lack of "rationalistic" discernment among their followers—which he articulates as an absence of *satisampajañña*—but it also leads them to disappointment and further suffering. In one passage, for example, Ind gives lengthy consideration to a well-known Khmer cult involving a sacred, magical bull, Braḥ Go, who was supposed to have been captured by Siamese soldiers during the eighteenth century (Ly and Muan 2001). Ind is highly critical of the claims and legends surrounding the bull. He makes his point with a humorous anecdote about the inevitable result when villagers surround a stray bull that they believe to be Braḥ Go, escaped from Siam. Charging at the crowd of adoring worshipers gathered around him, the bull leaves a tangle of broken limbs and trampled flowers and candles behind him. The story becomes a vehicle both for lampooning the Braḥ Go cult and for reflecting on the proper and authentic heritage of Khmer Buddhists. "Please consider whether or not the villagers [described in this narrative] possessed the *satisampajañña* to analyze the circumstances surrounding this cow" (*GL*, 3:35). Upon reviewing the flawed logic of those who maintained, among other claims, that the bull could have lived for two hundred years, he concludes,

> You should not believe a word of this old legend. . . . Among all of us Khmer, who uphold and venerate the *Sāsana* of the Fully Enlightened Buddha Gotama, the Highest Teacher . . . why should we venerate a cow, holding its name sacred, grieving deeply for Braḥ Go, whom the Siamese kingdom has captured? If we Khmer were to grieve for a "Braḥ Go" or uphold the sound "go," it should be for the name "Braḥ Gotama," because our Lord Braḥ Buddha is descended from the "Gotama" lineage, containing the sound "go." In *Sruk Khmer*, cows are domestic animals, used to pull carts and to plow rice fields, and we kill them for their meat as well. . . . This is why we should not venerate cows. Today, one cow is like another. (*GL*, 3:37–39)

Ind's response to another cult surrounding Yāy (Ancestress) Deb (an image considered by Hang in chap. 5) demonstrates similar concerns about the purity of Khmer Buddhist practices.

> [T]here are some groups who believe in and venerate statues of Yay Daeb [*sic*], and pray to Yay Daeb with their desires. People who worship Yay Daeb know nothing about her history. When she was alive, was she a goddess or a human

> being? Whose wife was she? What was her husband's name? When she was alive, did she possess some manner of merit and virtue enabling her to help free Khmer from suffering, or to defeat the enemies of the Khmer, or to protect against disease? Did she perform good deeds associated with our land in some manner? Is Yay Daeb's history found in chronicles or in any Pāli religious scriptures that tell us why we should believe in and worship her and make the claim that she has special powers? For example, we can take the figure of Joan of Arc in French history, whom the French respect and venerate because when she was alive, she helped save her king. She became a general who raised an army and went to war against the enemy, capturing back territory belonging to her people. Later, when she had exhausted her merit, she fell into the hands of her enemies, who burned her alive. All of the people in her kingdom remember the good deeds of this girl who helped save their land. They erected a statue of her as an extraordinary woman so those of her same *jāti* could honor and venerate her as one of their own, right up to the present time.
>
> Returning to Yay Daeb, when she was alive, in what manner did she free our Khmer *jāti* from suffering, causing ancient people to want to build a statue for all Khmer to worship and venerate her down to the present day? . . .
>
> Did you know that the word *daeb* is a translation of the Sanskrit *"daitya,"* meaning "demon," and that the history of this demon is as an enemy to humankind? How did people come to believe that they should worship her or that the word *"daeb"* isn't really the word *"daeb"* at all, but is a transformation of the sound "deb," referring to Nāṅ Debdhīta, which alludes to Nāṅ Umābhagavati, the consort of Lord Śiva? Because people of an earlier time were followers of the religion of Lord Issarādhipatī [Śiva]. Out of respect for Nāṅ Umābhagavatī as the wife of Lord Śiva, they erected a statue of her . . . and called her "Yay Deb" . . . which over a long period of time, came to be pronounced as "Yay Daub." Did you know this? But even if we regard the statue as Nāṅ Umābhagavatī, it is not right that we who are *upāsaka-upāsikā* [lay followers] of the Buddhist *sāsanā* worship and venerate a statue of Yay Daeb. Doing so causes us to become troubled, to lose the Going to the Three Refuges that is our heritage, to be bankrupt and naked. (*GL*, 3:39–43)

This passage documents the effort to shape a new Khmer religious practice, purified of the same kinds of nonscripturalist practices found undesirable by the Dhammayut sect in Siamese Buddhism, but at the same time, one that is self-conscious of a distinctively Khmer history and identity. The religious, social, and political changes enacted over the course of a century in Cambodia had contributed to the introduction of new visions of self and community. As Buddhists, Ind's vision asserts, Khmer recognized and shared in the Refuge of the Triple Gem, the culmination of a unique and proud Khmer history and identity.

Here, we can see Ind's reshifting of the older cosmological framework for ethics to encompass newly emerging notions of identity that were more modern in their recognition of cultural, ethnic, and religious differences. The passage also focuses on the need for Khmer religious identity to be authentic and purified of corrupt influences, both animist and Brahmanic, thus making it at once more "Khmer" and more "Buddhist." He shifts the emphasis from understanding moral development through a universalized cosmic time frame to examining the development of the moral quality of *satisampajañña* in everyday life, including, in his consideration, the lives of ordinary Khmer monks, villagers, wicked officials, and well-known Khmer narrative folk heroes such as Judge Rabbit and Thanonchai the trickster. In the *Gatilok*, the stories of Khmer Buddhists acting in the world, juxtaposed with the stories of Theravāda moral exemplars such as the Bodhisattva, emphasize the particular cultural heritage of the Khmer as Buddhists, followers of a universal *dhamma*. Whereas the nineteenth-century Buddhist constructions of identity discussed previously were less concerned with the particular and local dimensions of one's *jāti* than with the larger cosmic dimensions of one's course through the realms of rebirth, in Ind's work we see the working out of a Buddhist identity more rooted in the particular, local conditions of place, time, ethnicity, and social conditions, as well as in the context of the universal human propensities toward ignorance, carelessness, and malice.

Ind was probably not holding up these notions as a nascent nationalist refutation of the French colonial perception of the Khmer as corrupt and backward, but rather as a means of rethinking and repositioning the Buddhist moral path in the emerging modern world as a way for good Khmer Buddhists, and good human beings living in the world, to behave. This same local-translocal tension would be voiced more strongly in the rhetoric of Khmer nationalism, closely intertwined with Buddhism, which developed in the following decades.

Khmer intellectual understandings of self and community, I have suggested, had found expression in cosmicized Buddhist moral terms throughout the nineteenth century. By the early twentieth century, social and religious reforms within colonized Cambodia led to the development of a sense of Khmer cultural identity that was expressed in large part through efforts at effecting religious purification, Pāli education, and heightened attention to Khmer language and folklore. While the notions of self and community connected to this movement in a work such as Ind's *Gatilok* were still Buddhist, they contain a concern with the local and with difference—why human beings are "different from each other"—that shifts attention to the worldly as well as *dhammic* aspects of identity: one's situatedness in geographies of ethnicity, language, religion, and culture. Throughout the rest of the century, the development of different and competing discourses of authentic "Khmerness" in anticolonial and postcolonial nationalist ideologies, *dhammic* socialism, and ultimately in the emergence of the strongly anti-Buddhist communism of the Khmer Rouge contained the assumption that Theravāda Buddhism was an "essential" component of Khmerness, a force either to be embraced or eradicated. At the present time a new renovation of Theravāda Buddhism is underway in Cambodia, this time seemingly influenced by the introduction of a new cosmopolitan vernacular, the global discourse of human rights.

Notes

I am grateful for helpful comments from the three anonymous readers who reviewed this volume, and to John Marston, Elizabeth Guthrie, and Mark Bradley for comments on earlier drafts of this chapter. I have also benefited from colleagues' responses to versions of this chapter presented at the Association for Asian Studies Conference and the Centers for Southeast Asian Studies at the University of Wisconsin, Madison, and Northern Illinois University. Thanks also to Yoeum Ngin and Tauch Chhuong.

1. Research notes, East Boston, Massachusetts, 1987–1989.

2. This title was given to kings who abdicated in favor of their heirs, or in some cases was used to designate highly ranked princes (Khin Sok 1991, 174–175).

3. It is difficult to tell from Moura's text whether this is a translation or a paraphrase of the oath. Coedès, however, compares Moura's translation to a version of the oath sworn to Suryavarman I, noting many similarities in content and wording (Coedès 1913, 16–17).

4. While it is problematic to wholly accept French colonial accounts of the extent of the brutality of Southeast Asian practices of warfare during this period, numerous French sources indicate the high toll in human suffering that these relocations engendered.

5. Collins 1998, 346–413; Keyes 1977b, 283–302; Ishii 1986, 171–187; Tambiah 1984, 293–320; Tai 1983; Adas 1979, 34–40, 88–89, 99–102; Sarkisyanz 1965; Herbert 1982.

6. Ed. note: modern references to Braḥ Pād Dhammik are cited in chapters 7 and 10 of this volume. One of the *grū pāramī* written about by Bertrand (chap. 7) is claimed to be Braḥ Pād Dhammik (see editor's note in endnote 11 of his chapter).

7. Borkampor, sometimes transliterated as "Poukambo" or "Pokamābo," is the name of a son of King Ang Chan (r. 1806–1834) who apparently died a few hours after birth. Leclère reports that this Borkampor was the third "imposter" who took this name (Leclère 1914, 457*f*).

8. This report was written by Leclère, apparently around 1900. NAC box 542, file 5181.

9. NAC box 903, file 10126.

10. NAC box 900, file 10093.

11. E.g., one of Ukñā Suttantaprījā Ind's narratives in the *Gatilok* is meant to parody such a text. See Ind, "Story of the Crow and the Civet-cat," in *GL,* 3:81–83.

12. Beginning after 1876, the rhetoric of corruption and the condemnation of slavery became the ubiquitous official justifications used by the French colonial administration to defend their efforts to enfeeble Norodom. For example, see Collard 1925, 151.

13. Moura 1883, 1:329; 2:178–180; Janneau 1914, 617–632; Aymonier 1900, 98–102; Collard 1925, 116; Forest 1980, 337–357; Wyatt 1969, 50–52; Thanet 1998, 161–186.

14. The sect was established in either 1854 or 1864. Khin Sok, excerpting a biography from the 1912 Phnom Penh publication of the periodical *Preah Vinaya Vannana,* gives the

date of the founding of the Dhammayut in Cambodia as 1854 (Khin Sok 1991, 271). The Khmer Dhammayut tradition may well prefer to attribute the founding of the sect to the reign of Ang Duong, considered a period of Buddhist piety and purification, rather than to the more troubled reign of Norodom. Osborne cites a "continuing oral tradition" of the founding of the sect in Ang Duong's reign (Osborne 1969, 11). Most other sources follow Leclère's 1864 date (Leclère 1899, 403).

15. "M. Sylvain Lévi à le Résident Supérieure, 21 décembre 1922," AEFEO box 23, folder K3, "École de Pāli, 1922–29," doc. 1407; "George Coedès à le Résident Supérieure, 16 décembre 1912, Hanoi," [addendum to "Director EFEO à Gouveneur Général, Hanoi, 28 décembre 1912," AEFEO box 23, folder K3, "École de Pāli, 1909–1918]; "Ordonnance royale de 13 aout 1909," AEFEO box 23, folder K3, École de Pāli, 1909–1918"; NAC box 908, file 10172; NAC box 908, file 10173.

16. J. Filliozat, personal communication. The effort to obtain credible texts from Bangkok is also evident throughout the correspondence preserved in AEFEO, as scholars wrote to colleagues in Siam requesting copies of texts.

17. "Roume, Gouveneur Général d'Indochine à Coedès, professeur EFEO, 28 aout 1915," AEFEO box 34, file 2; Coedès, "Note relative à la Confection d'un Dictionnaire Cambodgien, 1915," AEFEO box 24, no folder no., file 1; Lomberger, "Circulaire no. 35, 30 avril 1926," AEFEO box 34, folder 2, file 67; "Administrative chef du 2eme Bureau à Directeur Imprimerie du Protectorat, Phnom Penh, 6 mai 1926," AEFEO box 34, folder 2, file 67.

18. This becomes evident in *Kambujā Suriyā* and in a later collection of Khmer folklore published between 1959–1974 by the Commission des Moeurs et Coutumes titled *Prajum Rioeṅ Bren Khmaer.* Even as late as 1950, Pang Khat attributes his interest in producing a Khmer version of the *Hitopadeśa* to the influence of Ind (Pang Khat 2493 [1950], i).

19. P. Edwards, personal communication: the word "nationalism" *(jātiniyam)* developed still later.

20. P. Edwards, personal communication, interprets this quote from *Nagarvatta* December 17, 1938, 1–3, as a reference to Ind's work.

–3–

Making a Religion of the Nation and Its Language

The French Protectorate (1863–1954) and the Dhammakāy

PENNY EDWARDS

In 1863, as legend has it, the establishment of the French protectorate of Cambodia ushered in a ninety-year period of peace, prosperity, and stability that has been characterized as a "colonialism without clashes" (Forest 1980) and contrasted with previous centuries of war, chaos, and cultural attrition. Among the instances rupturing this mythology, two stand out: the Sivutha Rebellion of 1884–1885 and the Umbrella War of 1942.

The Sivutha Rebellion was the first protracted, armed show of opposition to French rule. Close to four thousand colonial troops were rushed in from Annam to crush the rebellion, inciting widespread fear and hatred. This episode marked a critical shift from the piecemeal character of the protectorate's first twenty-one years to a period of more sustained and direct European intervention and intrusion into indigenous theaters of power. From 1885 onward, the secular space staked out by the enforced reforms was gradually strengthened and expanded. These processes paved the way, from the early 1900s onward, for a secondary assault by the colonial government and its institutions into an area of society long deemed sacred and outside the orbit of worldly political power, namely the Cambodian Buddhist *sangha*.

In 1942, the twilight of French rule was marked by a much shorter but no less symbolic conflict, this time between the *sangha* and the colonial state. Staged in Phnom Penh, the confrontation involved a peaceful protest by more than one thousand monks, whose signature parasols earned it the name "Umbrella War" in Khmer lore, and its swift and brutal dispersal by truckloads of *sûreté* (colonial police). The monks were protesting the arrest, defrocking, and jailing of Achar

Hem Chieu, a highly revered teacher from the École Supérieure de Pāli whose crime was the alleged delivery of anti-French sermons. An estimated five hundred of the protesters came from a reform movement led by two extraordinarily talented monks, Chuon Nath (1883–1969) and Huot Tat (1891–1975?).

These two "wars," nearly sixty years apart, were both protests against the violation of accepted parameters of conduct by the French administration in its engagement with the Khmer polity (1884) and the Khmer *sangha* (1942). The Sivutha Rebellion was an armed response to the fiscal denuding of the Khmer monarchy, the Umbrella War a collective cry of anger at the defrocking of a Khmer monk. This brute assertion of colonial and secular power echoed the persecution of those people whose religious faith, racial origin, political beliefs, or sexuality offended the narrow norms prescribed by Marshal Pétain's Vichy regime (1940–1944). Among those affected were officials of Jewish background working in the colonial administration, most notably the energetic and erudite Suzanne Karpelès (1890–1969) (fig. 3.1). In the two decades between joining the École Française d'Extrême Orient (EFEO) in 1922 and being expelled from government office because of her Jewish lineage in 1941, Karpelès carved out a critical intellectual and institutional space for the growth of Cambodia's indigenous Buddhist reform movement, which the protectorate referred to as the "renovation" of Khmer Buddhism.

Two colonial developments were critical. One was the progressive institutionalization of the *sangha* and its separation from the realm of state politics as a strictly "religious" entity. Another was the emergence of a reform wing of the *sangha*, known at first as the Mahānikāy *thmī* (new Mahānikāy)[1] and later as the Dhammakāy.[2] To avoid confusion, I refer to this group as the Dhammakāy throughout this chapter, except where I am directly quoting from sources using the term "Mahānikāy *thmī*."

The Dhammakāy's quest to authenticate and validate Buddhist doctrine aligned modernist prescriptions for a return to scriptural purity and a revalorization of the past with the spatial and temporal framework of the nation, making room for the emergence of a new category in Cambodia, that of *sāsanā jāti* (national religion). The intellectual roots of the Dhammakāy lay in Siam, not France. But the geopolitics of colonialism created the climate for the emergence of the Dhammakāy as a local movement, centered in Phnom Penh.

From their arrival in 1912 at Wat Unnalom, the headquarters of the Mahānikāy order, to the Umbrella War of 1942, Nath and Tat steered the growth of the Dhammakāy in ways that borrowed from the doctrinal legacy of the Dhammayut, built upon the recent refashioning of the language of Buddhism by the prominent intellectual Ukñā Suttantaprījā Ind, and mobilized new methods for disseminating their message, notably through Khmer vernacular print media.

Although framed by two hallmark episodes of colonial violence, this story is presented here neither as a sustained violent encounter nor one dominated by a unilateral exercise of epistemological violence wrought on Khmer domains by European dictators, but in the spirit of a conversation between Khmer *sangha* and European scholars. This conversation was fraught with tension and was bilingual in more than one sense. It involved reconciliation and negotiation between contesting visions of time. It required the acquisition of French by Tat and Nath and of Sanskrit and Khmer by European scholars. It was inflected by a categorical consciousness, which I believe to have been lacking from Cambodia prior to the colonial encounter. In its emphasis on the promotion of vernacular Khmer as a

Fig. 3.1 Suzanne Karpelès (S. Karpelès)

medium for the transmission of Buddhist precepts and learning, this conversation produced a twin category to that of "national religion": that of a "national language" *(bhāsā jāti)*. Like any conversation, it was far from all-revealing. It was, at times, a strategic conversation, one involving bluff and counterbluff, points of convergence, concealment, divergence, and dissimulation by both sides.

My focus here is on the place of nationalism as a site of convergence between the colonial and monastic voices engaged in this conversation. The modern concept of the nation, I suggest, provided an intellectual and conceptual framework through which certain members of the *sangha* were able to synergize the disenchanting projects of modernity with their visions for the moral rectification of Khmer Buddhism. My argument owes much to existing works on nationalism and modernity and studies of the production of colonial knowledge categories elsewhere (Anderson 1991; Bhabha 1994; Chakrabarty 2000; Cohn 1996; Duara 1995).

In its focus on the reform movement, this chapter marginalizes the voices and visions of those within the Mahānikāy who were opposed to the Dhammakāy agenda for reform. Here I would like to briefly suggest that the so-called Mahānikāy-*cās'* were driven not by an intellectual death wish, but by a desire "to keep alive a life-form in ways where the questions of modernity, while not irrelevant, [were] not central to the ways in which [they] made sense of their lives" (Ganguly 2001, 5–6). Viewed this way, the Mahānikāy-*cās'* are as much "presentists" as "traditionalists."

Disenchanted Times: Authenticating Buddhism, 1860–1900

Colonial regimes of discipline and subjugation were not restricted to military occupation, colonial prisons, and other violent institutions, but also included the subordination of indigenous interpretations of the world to European perceptions. A principle means of bringing the colonized into line involved the promulgation of knowledge forms, such as linear history, which simultaneously enabled and naturalized "major institutions" of colonialism while themselves becoming "seriously embedded" in a broad array of state institutions (Chakrabarty 2000, 32). Key vehicles for the transmission of these historicist narratives were new, secular public arenas, notably schools and museums, and a new form of public messaging, namely print media (Anderson 1991).

The historicist narratives introduced under the French protectorate of Cambodia comprised visions of descent from a glorious Angkorean past and prospects of ascent to a thoroughly modern future, which deviated from indigenous readings of time as at once cyclical and, in its accommodation of spirits and living beings in the same temporal space, multilayered. It was in the inscription of this disenchanted vision into the world of religion that colonialism provoked the keenest displays of anxiety and controversy.

The school of Buddhist studies that emerged in Europe during the early nineteenth century was dominated by Indologists who considered Buddhism "an historical projection, derived exclusively from manuscripts and blockprints" (Lopez 1995, 7). The resultant reification of Buddhism in European imaginations focused Buddhist studies on the pursuit of master texts. Deposited in European libraries, isolated from the popular practices in which they were embedded in local cultures, such texts allowed the European construction of Buddhism as a "transhistorical and self-identical essence" (Lopez 1995, 12). Such scientific study allowed Buddhism to enter what Chakrabarty has described as the "godless, continuous . . . empty and homogeneous" time of history, a time that offers no scope for the agency of "Gods, spirits, and other 'supernatural forces'" (Chakrabarty 2000, 32). In this vein, colonialism's knowledge project in Cambodia, like its counterparts in India, sought to shear Buddhism of its supernatural accretions and, simultaneously, to document and authenticate a material, scriptural body of Khmer religion.

The initial stages of this process, from the 1860s to circa 1900 consisted of sporadic efforts by colonial administrators to accumulate a material body of Cambodian religious culture for French institutions. Self-taught in Khmer, with no academic grounding in Orientalist disciplines, these early collectors differed from the more formally trained scholar-officials of the early twentieth century and may more aptly be described as "scholar-entrepreneurs."

The pioneer of this work was the French naval lieutenant Doudart de Lagrée. Despite basic proficiency in Khmer and the support of the king, de Lagrée's nationwide search for Khmer literature and religion in 1863 yielded only a few sūtras.[3] In 1875 the French engineer Félix-Gaspard Faraut (1846–1911) collected some one hundred manuscripts, mostly poems of Indian origin and Buddhist "myths." Four years later, France's Bibliothèque Nationale commissioned Faraut to build a collection of Khmer literature. Faraut found that while the titles of works were well known in some wats, the texts were either missing or "poorly transcribed copies of originals."[4] In the late nineteenth century, the colonial administrator Adhémard Leclère (1853–1917) produced the first European study of Buddhism in Cambodia, *Le Bouddhisme au Cambodge* (1899).

These early French attempts to procure and catalogue Cambodia's Buddhist manuscripts and relics were paralleled by indigenous movements to purify and reform Southeast Asian Theravāda Buddhism.[5] The beginnings of these reform movements are usually associated with the establishment of the royally sponsored Dhammayut sect in Siam in the 1830s. The Siamese Dhammayut promoted the rigorous study of the Pāli canon, which aimed to "cleanse" Buddhist practice of "false" accretions and superstition and emphasized reflection rather than rote learning.

Established in Cambodia in the 1850s and granted royal recognition as an official sect, the Khmer Dhammayut also encouraged monks to question the authenticity of traditional Buddhist practice (chap. 2; Keyes 1994). The Dhammayut met with strong antagonism from some quarters of the Mahānikāy, but there were also Mahānikāy monks who found their teachings compelling. King Norodom (r. 1860–1904), monks, and secular literati made regular visits to Bangkok's "many institutes of learning" to peruse its "numerous Pāli manuscripts."[6]

The first Khmer typographic characters were cast in Paris in 1877 (Népote and Khing, 1981, 61). In 1885, hoping to bring around Cambodians alienated by France's brutal suppression of the Sivutha Rebellion, the governor of Cochinchina, Charles Thomson, ordered the establishment of a Khmer printing press for the production of Khmer-language tracts promoting the benefits of French rule.[7] The targeted audiences were the pupils of wat schools.[8] By 1902, a second printing press had been established in Phnom Penh (Gervais-Courtellemont, Vandelet et al., n.d., 67). This was followed in 1904 by the royal Khmer printing press for the publication of sūtras, laws, and regulations (Jacobs 1996, 10).[9] Thomson's proposed mode of inscription (print), media (flat sheets of paper for posting on walls), and content (vernacular language designed to be understood by the common public) differed sharply from traditional monastic ways of producing, circulating, and phrasing the written word. However, print media cohered with the textual bias and emphasis on scriptural "authenticity" exhibited by the Dhammayut movement and by European scholars.

The European valorization of Buddhist scriptures as historical documents, like the scriptural emphasis of the reform movements, differed from long-standing ways of seeing religious texts in Theravāda Southeast Asia. In Cambodia, as elsewhere in precolonial Southeast Asia, written texts were part of a performative tradition of Buddhist practice in which the word and art of listening were both modes of literacy and means of accumulating merit (Marston 1997, 14; Florida 1995, 11–12; Taylor 1993, 64–45, 74; Keyes 1977a, 118; Hansen 1999, 71–75).

The role of colonial scholarship in the transition from this aural tradition to a textual bias is nicely captured in a somewhat contradictory appraisal by Leclère, who enthuses about the performative life of the story of the Buddha's enlightenment, the *Braḥ Paṭhamasambodhi-kathā,* and at the same time effectively silences that text in its translation, scrutiny, and print production in his *Livres Sacrés* (Leclère 1906b). Leclère's enthusiastic account of a recital at a Cambodian wat stresses the "live" function of this text as a vehicle for generating merit: the monk raised his voice "high, clear, almost singsong—One felt that he knew that the Khmer letters have another value when they reproduce a word of the holy language." The audience savored each word with utter reverence and in absolute silence as if, Leclère wrote, "it really was the life of the Master, the Teacher—that they were hearing." But despite applauding such life in the delivery of texts, Leclère does not see texts themselves as something that should have a life beyond the "authentic," as reflected in his criticism of scribes, particularly those from Siam and Burma, whose transcriptions of Buddhist texts were more "adaptations" than "translations" (Leclère 1906b, 9; Hallisey 1995, 52).

In France, the study of Asian religion gained particular momentum with the establishment and expansion of the Musée Guimet in Paris in 1889. That year also saw the establishment of the École Coloniale in Paris, signifying the emergence of a career colonial civil service. Twelve years later, in 1901, the EFEO was constituted in Saigon under the directorship of the eminent Indologist Louis Finot. The combined effect of both schools was to institutionalize specializations in Orientalist studies and colonial governance. As Said has noted elsewhere, Orientalism and its disciplines were in many respects the handmaiden of colonial practice (Said 1978). The 1900s saw a shift in the "ownership" of colonialism's knowledge projects away from figures like Leclère, increasingly discredited for his "lack" of formal Orientalist training, to three key figures: George Coedès, Louis Finot, and Suzanne Karpelès.

Reforming Buddhism from Phnom Penh, 1900–1922

The protectorate's attitude toward Buddhism during the first decades of the twentieth century differed from the laissez-faire character of the earlier years. The impetus behind this change was in part the fallout from the Dreyfus Affair (Neher-Bernheim 2002), which stimulated reflection on the need to protect religious freedom, but also triggered an anticlerical backlash, resulting in the passage in parliament of the 1905 act decreeing the separation of church and state.

The percolation of this 1905 act through to colonial Cambodia had two paradoxical effects. One was a literal application of the act through educational reforms that resulted by the 1920s in the excision of all religious subjects from the curricula of what the French called "renovated temple schools." A second effect was to allow for the creation of secular institutions of higher learning, where monks could study religion as an academic subject.

In 1904, following the death of King Norodom, the reform-minded King Sisowath acceded to the Cambodian throne, and the governor-general of Indochina (GGI), Paul Beau, launched an Indochina-wide reform of indigenous education. The Commission to Study the Reorganization of Education in Cambodia was promptly established, made up of a prince, a palace official, a Mahānikāy designate, and seven French members. The Dhammayut's lack of official representation on the committee presaged prolonged resistance by the Dhammayut order against colonial intrusion in monastic education.[10] The commission recommended French-language use and practical education, Khmer manuals in "morals and sciences," and teacher training courses for monks.

Although this program did not gain substantial momentum until the mid-1920s, from its inception it represented a critical projection of the protectorate's view of the place of Buddhism within society and its parallel vision for the place of the state, and its institutions, within Buddhism.

The retrocession of Battambang, Sisophon, and Siem Reap from Siam to Cambodia in 1907 heightened the protectorate's concern to control and monitor the traffic of monks between the two countries and to erect a clear, cultural boundary around Cambodia. The protectorate, hoping to attract the best and brightest novices and monks from the capital and provinces, inaugurated with great fanfare the School of Pāli at Angkor in 1909.[11] The Royal Ordinance of 1909, which established the school, also claimed that the royal printing press would reproduce Pāli scriptures "more meticulous than any Bangkok production," placed a near total ban on Khmer monks traveling to Siam for study, and appealed to royalty, ministers, mandarins, and all subjects to donate funds to the school.[12] The school failed to attract local support, funding, or pupils and closed in 1910.[13] Khmer monks—in particular those from the Dhammayut order—their paths eased by new roads serviced by an expanding network of buses, continued to make their way to Bangkok to study (Lester 1973, 115).

It is at this juncture that a more meaningful challenge to Siamese influence on Buddhism within the protectorate's new boundaries began to assert itself from within the Mahānikāy. In 1912, the recently ordained twenty-eight-year-old Chuon Nath and the twenty-year-old Huot Tat were appointed to Wat Unnalom. They were not the only Mahānikāy monks who favored reform of Buddhism. However, it was Nath and Tat who emerged as leaders of the movement in the 1910s and who would anchor the rethinking of Buddhism in a self-consciously Khmer context.

Born and educated in central Cambodia, Nath and Tat had reached boyhood after the crisis of 1884–1885, during what might be called an enduring crisis of deepening colonial intervention in indigenous institutions.

A sense of energetic curiosity in what was new glimmers throughout Tat's narrative of their Phnom Penh experience. On their own initiative, Tat relates, they surreptitiously learned Sanskrit and Pāli from an Indian peddler and studied French at night behind closed doors. Their covert encounters with French were a rendezvous not only with a new language, but also a new medium, in the form of the modern book. In the absence of vernacular Khmer novels or of a vernacular Khmer press, these literary encounters and their subsequent training in colonial centers of learning where French was the medium of instruction may have encouraged their promotion of vernacular Khmer as a language for the transmission and explication of the Buddhist scriptures, in both print and sermons.

In 1914, the protectorate founded another School of Pāli in Phnom Penh[14] and proclaimed new restrictions on travel by monks to Siam for language studies.[15] Located in the palace, the school—sponsored by the EFEO, supervised by the Ministry of Public Education, and ultimately controlled by the Résident Supérieure du

Cambodge (RSC)—had sixty students.[16] Its director was the esteemed and erudite Thong, a master of the Pāli language (Finot 1927, 523), and Finot, still director of the EFEO, was on the school's board of councillors (Goloubew 1935, 528).

During the same year (1914) a new *mahāsaṅgharāj*, Kae Ouk, was appointed by Sisowath to lead the Mahānikāy following the death of Dien (see chap 2, p. 53). Ouk's installation as *mahāsaṅgharāj* made him the supreme authority at Wat Unnalom. The next few years saw a battle of words and wits between Ouk—described by his detractors as stubborn, traditionalist, and not especially erudite—and Nath, Tat, and other reformist monks in residence at Wat Unnalom. The crux of this conflict was Nath's and Tat's push to replace Cambodia's ancient monastic traditions with new and unfamiliar practices drawn from new translations of the Pāli *Vinaya* that originated in Thailand and were deemed more textually authentic.

Nath and Tat enjoyed the support of some members of the royal family, one of whom offered to sponsor a daily sermon on the *Vinaya* throughout the *vassā* period. In an early show of support for the young monks, Ouk selected Nath, Tat, and a reformist monk named Um Sou to deliver the sermons. In a radical deviation from the traditional rote recital of scriptures, Nath, Tat, and Sou delivered sermons they had composed themselves, explaining the *Vinaya* to their fellow monks. The high levels of attendance and the lively debates so antagonized some senior monks that they complained to Ouk, who from this point on positioned himself against the reformists and cancelled the sermons. But the seeds of reform had been sown.

This was at first an underground movement. With the exception of Nath, Tat, and Sou, monks did not dare reveal their interests in the *Vinaya* precepts for fear of upsetting their superiors. By night, Nath, Tat, and Sou pored over manuscripts and distilled what they considered to be their true essence, making extracts and annotations in their own books. By day, they continued to debate and preach in their daily discussions with other monks. Nath's and Tat's criticism of such mainstays of Mahānikāy practice as the recitation of the *Jātaka*s, their advocacy of preaching in both Pāli and Khmer, and their argument that sermons should provoke reflection and enhance understanding of the *Vinaya* gradually percolated through Mahānikāy temples in the capital and beyond. These innovations antagonized members of the Mahānikāy far beyond Wat Unnalom, notably in the central and southeastern provinces of Kompong Cham, Svay Rieng, and Prey Veng.

In 1911, the protectorate formalized a program of wat school reform under a royal ordinance that made secular subjects, and Khmer language lessons, compulsory at all wat schools (Morizon 1930, 180–181).[17] These policies were revived in the aftermath of widespread peasant protests in 1916 (Porée and Porée-Maspéro 1938, 183), and in the late 1910s, newly trained secular inspectors of temple schools began monitoring development of the reforms in the central and southeastern provinces.

Alarmed by such developments, and by Nath's and Tat's agenda, a group of Mahānikāy monks petitioned King Sisowath, who summoned Nath and Tat to the palace. During this royal audience, Nath presented an eloquent defense of the reformist interpretations of the *Vinaya,* demonstrated his bilingual Pāli-Khmer mastery of scriptures, treatises, and commentaries, and stressed the value of study (Tat 1993, 17–18). Sisowath was allegedly so impressed by Nath's erudition that he dismissed the petitions. But the dispute was far from settled in the minds of Nath's detractors. In 1917 or 1918, perhaps partly in response to expanding secular intrusion into wat education, a group from within the Mahānikāy persuaded the king to combat reformist elements within the *sangha.* Issued on October 2, 1918, Royal Ordinance 71 recognized the Mahānikāy and Dhammayut as the only two lawful Cambodian sects; prohibited monks from spreading new, unauthorized religious theories; and prohibited Mahānikāy and Dhammayut monks from any breaches of the traditions established in the time of the now deceased supreme patriarchs Dien and Pān (Tat 1993; Keyes 1994, 47–48).[18] Shortly after the ordinance was proclaimed, Nath and Tat completed two books on the *Vinaya,* which they then took to the Khmer Ministry of War and Education, requesting permission to publish. Within a week, the ministry had ruled that

> [t]he Council of Ministers will not allow *bhikkhu* or *sāmaṇera* to study *vinaya* . . . in paper books . . . [It] will only allow the study of the *vinaya* [inscribed] on palmleaf manuscripts. Any *vinaya* in a paper book like this is considered New Vinaya *(vinaya thmī),* which is different from the tradition in the time of Saṃtec Braḥ Mahā Saṅgrāj Dien. (Tat 1993, 22)

This perception of the intrinsic sacrality of palm-leaf texts clashed severely with the prescriptions of Nath, Tat, and their supporters, who believed that "palm-leaf or paper books were only materials. . . . There was no difference between them" (Tat 1993, 22). The ruling triggered a flurry of clandestine copying and circulation of Nath's book by monks and novices (Tat 1993, 24–25). In late 1918, RSC François-Marius Baudoin intervened to allow the publication of *Sāmaṇera Vinaya* (*Vinaya* for novices) against the wishes of Ouk and other senior religious authorities. Sponsored by Ukñā Keth, five thousand copies were printed. Subsequent attempts by a number of monks to ban the book and to expel Nath, Tat, and Sou from Wat Unnalom for their violation of Royal Ordinance 71 failed, partly because both Sisowath and his son Prince Monivong supported the book. Despite the best efforts of those he dubbed "traditionalists" or "old Mahānikāy" to obstruct the youthful push for knowledge, wrote Tat, "they couldn't stop progress. Books for study and practice were being churned out" (Tat 1993, 17, 30–32).

Despite its checkered beginnings, the School of Pāli established by the protectorate emerged as a key site in which monks from Tat's and Nath's generation, and the next, could embrace European, rationalist subjects such as science and geography, further their attempts to distill the essence of Buddhist teachings and articulate the correct *Vinaya,* and consolidate textual knowledge and linguistic skills to rival and, in some cases, surpass, their seniors. In 1922, in a move approved by the protectorate and the EFEO, and possibly initiated by its director, Thong, the École de Pāli was restructured as the École Supérieure de Pāli and installed in new premises with a new curriculum featuring Buddhism, Sanskrit, Pāli, French, Cambodian history, Khmer language, Khmer literature, geography, and an optional course in modern science (Finot 1927, 523).[19] The new school included a custom-built library designed to hold and conserve printed works on Buddhism and Buddhist manuscripts in Pāli, Sanskrit, and Khmer and to realize the school's new function as a conservatory of "all works, documents and texts bearing on Buddhist history, literature and theology."[20] The year 1922 also saw the construction in Phnom Penh of Cambodia's first public library, the Central Library, which held about five thousand books, mostly in French (Lévi 1931, 197–198). These libraries consolidated the place of modern print media as tools for practice and learning and consigned palm-leaf texts and other traditional forms of manuscripts to the archives. The designation of the palm-leaf text as fragile and obsolete symbolized the dilution and fragmentation of the Khmer *sangha*'s authority over the interpretation, conservation, and circulation of scriptural materials.

In 1922, Finot met with RSC Baudoin and impressed upon him the importance of including Pāli and Sanskrit on secondary and elementary school curricula in Cambodia. Later that year, Nath and Tat set sail for Hanoi to study Sanskrit with Finot at the EFEO. Tat's later account of this journey, and of their time in Hanoi, indicates clearly that the two young monks were guided not just by religious conviction and scholarly ambition, but by a firm sense of purpose as the potential guardians of Khmer culture. A sense of solitude and alienation from the majority within the Mahānikāy is also evident. Few came to see them off, and following their departure from Phnom Penh,

> some monks and lay people . . . spoke out against us and said: "Those two monks have disappeared to Hanoi, perhaps they'll never come back, the administration has got rid of them." (Tat 1993, 42–43)

Shortly after arriving in Hanoi, Nath and Tat complained to Finot about the restrictions on publishing Buddhist texts in Cambodia. Finot lobbied on their behalf and persuaded RSC Baudoin to authorize the École Supérieure de Pāli to print and disseminate books (Tat 1993, 51–53). In late 1923 Finot's protégés returned to Phnom Penh competent in Sanskrit, able to decipher ancient Khmer inscriptions, and well versed in the geography and history of Buddhism in India and China. During their sojourn in Hanoi, Nath and Tat had also experienced the beginnings of a national and political consciousness, something later described by Tat as an "awakening" (Tat 1993, 47–48).

During the next two decades, Nath and Tat channeled their new skills and political awareness into developing the concept of Buddhism as the Khmer national religion *(sāsanā jāti)* and promoting vernacular Khmer as the national language *(bhāsā jāti)*. Their popularization of these notions was paralleled by the ascendance of their reform movement within the Mahānikāy and their own journey from the margins of the Buddhist establishment to the center of the Cambodian nationalist movement. The institutional climate in which they mapped the scholarly and cultural boundaries of a *sāsanā jāti* was massively strengthened and expanded by Suzanne Karpelès.

Reforming Buddhism from the Outside In, 1922–1930

The daughter of wealthy parents who owned trading stations in Pondichèry, Karpelès developed an interest in Oriental civilizations at an early age (Ha 1999, 110). After graduating from the École Pratique des Hautes Études in Paris, she was posted to Hanoi with the EFEO in January 1923.[21] In Hanoi, Karpelès collated a Pāli text from Ceylon with a Khmer manuscript. She then moved to Phnom Penh in 1925 and lived in Cambodia until 1941 (Filliozat 1969a, 1–3).

Karpelès was unusual among Orientalists of the time in that she saw Cambodians not as purely the "object" of her research, but as its main audience. Karpelès' personal religious orientation is unclear, but we do know that she, like her mentor George Coedès, came from a Jewish background (Ha 1999, 110). In 1923, Karpelès visited the National Library in Bangkok for final training in librarianship and to conduct research on collating Khmer and Pāli manuscripts. After meeting with its chief curators George Coedès and Prince Damrong, Karpelès began to lobby for the establishment of a national library in Cambodia (Filliozat 1969a, 1). With backing from RSC Baudoin and King Sisowath, Cambodia's Royal Library was established in 1925 to research, collect, conserve, and reproduce the "ancient manuscripts scattered in temples and individual homes [and] often kept in material conditions detrimental to their conservation."[22] Impressed by Karpelès "erudite zeal and energy," Finot appointed her as director (Goloubew 1935, 528). Sponsored by the Cambodian government, the Royal Library housed Khmer, Siamese, and Burmese works in print and on palm leaf, alongside modern Asian and French works (Lévi 1931, 197–198; de Pourtalés 1931, 113). As one *sûreté* report later declared, the protectorate hoped that the Royal Library would "eliminate the need for monks to visit Bangkok" and that, together with the École Supérieure de Pāli, it would "curb emigration and check Siamese influence."[23]

This new investment in elite education triggered fresh interest in colonial reform of temple schools at the primary level. In the early 1920s, a new gloss was put on "educational reform" with a nationwide program for "renovated wat schools" (Porée and Porée-Maspéro 1938, 183). This renovation involved the bifurcation of religious and secular arenas *within* temple grounds through the insistence that wat schools keep religion out of the classroom and adhere to an official curriculum.

Karpelès' portfolio as director of the Royal Library included a series of Khmer tales and historic texts[24] and encompassed the publications of the École Supérieure de Pāli.[25] In 1926, the library sold over nine thousand volumes "suited to national tastes, at modest prices" (Teston and Percheron 1931, 338, 526). In 1927, Karpelès launched Cambodia's first Khmer-language journal, *Kambujā suriyā* (Cambodia sun), a monthly journal of Khmer Buddhism, culture, and history (Jacobs 1996, 214–217). Also in 1927 the Societé Anonyme d'édition et de publicité indochinoises launched *Sruk Khmaer,* the Khmer edition of the Indochinese monthly *Extrême-Asie,* featuring articles on Buddhist literature and poetry as well as agricultural advice and local news.[26] Compiled by French and Khmer staff, *Sruk Khmaer* reached a circulation of two thousand in its first year.[27] Between 1927 and 1930, close to sixty thousand of the Khmer texts produced by the Royal Library were sold through the Buddhist Institute's bookstores, which numbered fifty-seven by 1930, and via a "book-bus" purchased in 1930 (Teston and Percheron 1931, 338, 526).

These journals and works on Cambodian history, culture, and religion consolidated the transition from a scribal to a print culture in Cambodia. They also provided vital arenas for the formulation of new ideas about Buddhism and nation, allowing Tat, Nath, and other reformists to translate their prescriptions for Khmer Buddhism into a body of thought and literature that, popularized through libraries, preaching, and outreach activities, enabled the Dhammakāy to project their vision of Buddhism as the authentic model. These claims to authenticity and purity resonated with emerging proto-nationalist preoccupations, which had crystallized by the late 1930s into a nationalist discourse celebrating the pure *(suddh),* authentic *(bit),* and original *(ṭoem)* Khmer.

Importantly, except where they were reproducing historic texts or Buddhist verses, these publications adopted a prosaic style of journalism and reporting in vernacular Khmer. They thus represented a significant step toward establishing a reading public among Khmers in Cambodia and were equally critical in consolidating the emergence of vernacular Khmer as a field of national meaning.

As the vernacular literature on Khmer Buddhism expanded, so did its target audience. Locked out of Cambodia's geographic borders but conversant in many facets of Khmer culture, the Khmer Krom—ethnic Khmers living in Cochinchina—became a target of both the Royal Library's activities and educational reform from the late 1920s onward, when Tat carried out a number of tours of wats in Khmer Krom communities[28] and GGI Pierre Pasquier made a much-publicized visit to Khmer wats in Cochinchina.[29] In 1927, Henri Gourdon, the honorary inspector of public education in Indochina, recommended expanding Cambodia's program of "renovated education" to serve Cochinchina's three hundred thousand-strong Khmer population.[30] The protectorate of Cochinchina duly launched a campaign of wat school reform, promoting professional teacher training and "rational teaching tools" in Khmer-speaking areas (Gastaldy 1931, 99). In May 1928, the Ministry of War and Education launched a new series of Khmer language school texts.[31] In 1929, following her own fieldwork among Buddhist communities in Southwest Cochinchina and Laos, Karpelès proposed the creation of a Buddhist Institute (Filliozat 1969a, 2).

The Buddhist Institute and the Dhammakāy, 1930–1942

On May 12, 1930, the Institut Indigène d'Études Bouddhiques de Petit Véhicule was inaugurated at a ceremony held at the Royal Library by King Monivong of Cambodia, King Sisavong Vong of Laos, Pasquier, and Coedès, who had succeeded Finot as director of the EFEO (Teston and Percheron 1931, 338). Addressing some two thousand monks from Cambodia, Cochinchina, and Laos, Monivong described the institute as "a house of Franco-Buddhist friendship" for French, Lao, and Cambodian intellectuals.[32] The founding mandate of the institute was to rescue Cambodian Buddhism from "degeneration." A corollary aim was to foster cooperation between Cambodian and Lao monks and the French administration, apparently so as to replace the Khmer and Lao *sangha*'s long-standing orientation toward Siam with loyalties toward Indochina (Teston and Percheron 1931, 338; Chandler 1992, 18). Studying "minor differences" between Cambodian practices and those in Siam was one means of severing the *sangha*'s links with Siam (Ghosh 1968, 198–199). A more immediate means involved redirecting the attention of Khmer *sangha* to Khmer communities in Cochinchina. Speaking as the secretary of the institute, Karpelès defined its zone of action as Cambodia, Laos, and "a large part of the provinces of Southwest Cochinchina, where more than 200,000 souls who have remained deeply Cambodian and profoundly attached to the land of their birth, continue their fervent practice of Buddhist precepts despite a number of obstacles."[33]

The Khmer population of Cochinchina was estimated at 320,000 in 1931, including 3,900 Khmer pupils enrolled at an estimated 229 wat schools (Gastaldy 1931, 98, 101). By this stage, the staff of the Royal Library and the Buddhist Institute enjoyed a mobility, autonomy, and freedom of association unmatched by other official organizations in the protectorate. That year, thirty monks who had been trained at the École Supérieure de Pāli were dispatched to wat schools in Cochinchina (Marquet 1931, 157). The Royal Library's book-bus also ensured the dissemination of Buddhist Institute publications to Cochinchina.[34] In 1931 Cambodian troops in Saigon and Cambodia were included on Buddhist Institute preaching tours, and the Buddhist Institute founded several special libraries at military cantonments in Cambodia and Saigon. Nath applauded the success of these efforts in making troops and militia "fervent adepts of Buddhism" and improving the morality of the Cambodian military.[35] The ascendancy of the Dhammakāy in Cambodia was accelerated by the institutional and logistical support provided by French colonial authorities as well as the proselytizing activities of Nath, Tat, and their colleagues.

In 1930, the Buddhist Institute established the Committee for the Translation of the *Tipiṭaka* and began production of a complete Khmer-Pāli edition (Khing 1993; Jacobs 1996, 76–77). In August 1931, *Sruk Khmaer* heralded the printing of the *Tipiṭaka* in Khmer and Pāli as "a matter of interest for all 'true' *(bit)* Khmers, that is, those who love their country *(sruk)* and race *(jāti)* and have a strong belief in Buddha" and argued that printing the *Tipiṭaka* would ensure Cambodia's status in the region as a world-renowned center of Buddhism on par with Burma, Siam, and Sri Lanka.[36] In November 1931, two thousand monks gathered in the royal palace to witness the presentation of the final manuscript of the first volume of the *Tipiṭaka* to France's visiting minister of colonies.[37]

In a speech on this achievement, Nath praised the École Supérieure de Pāli and the Royal Library and applauded Karpelès' dedication.[38] Several years later, the Franco-Khmer poet Makhali Phal (aka Pierrette Guesde) dedicated her poem celebrating the first Khmer volume of the *Tipiṭaka* to "S. K. [Suzanne Karpelès], who loves my country" (Phal n.d., frontispiece). However, not all Cambodians shared these sentiments. Karpelès' projects were held in disdain by several French-educated members of the Cambodian elite and by the Dhammayut. Where the Francophone elite resented Karpelès' crusade as an obstacle to Cambodia's modernization, the Dhammayut apparently begrudged the access to higher religious learning that her institute offered the Mahānikāy. Both groups were united by a prejudice against the Khmer language, which they saw respectively as outmoded by French and Siamese.

In 1931, the French-educated Prince Areno Iukanthor lampooned Karpelès as a "blue-stocking" (*bas bleu,* a pejorative term for a lady of learning, with connotations of feminism) of common origins and aristocratic aspirations whose exoticist attempts to structure a traditional culture represented a "public danger." In a convoluted comparison between the Maid of Zion and the Maid of Orleans (Joan of Arc), Iukanthor also appeared to link Karpelès' Jewishness to lack of patriotism. Iukanthor's mother Princess Malika and the scholar-administrator Guillaume Monod allegedly shared Iukanthor's views of the Buddhist Institute (Iukanthor 1931, 278, 419, 428).

In 1932, internal colonial reports began to register strong antipathy to the Buddhist Institute among the Dhammayut sect, especially in the western provinces.[39] A 1933 *sûreté* report noted a virtual Dhammayut blockade against Royal Library publications, particularly in Battambang, Siem Reap, and Sisophon, and attributed this to Dhammayut fears that the Royal Library and the École Supérieure de Pāli were giving the "primitive" Mahānikāy access to knowledge considered Dhammayut terrain and to the Dhammayut's disdain of the Khmer-Pāli version of the *Tipiṭaka* as inferior to the Siamese edition.[40]

The expansion of Khmer print production was paralleled by several campaigns aimed at creating a vernacular, Khmer-speaking universe. In 1931, Louis Manipaud was appointed to the Department of Education to "create a monastic teaching corps," a task that he energetically pursued, with particular emphasis on the use of vernacular Khmer as the medium of instruction.[41] Manipaud created a team of Khmer-speaking French inspectors to monitor adherence to the official syllabus. In 1934, he championed the "systematic diffusion of Khmer" through renovated wat schools in areas where ethnic Khmers formed a minority, including the Gulf of Siam, Battambang, and Pursat, and the following year he sent two monks to establish a Khmer school for the Thai-speaking Cambodian population in Koh Kong (le Grauclaude 1935, 19).[42]

In the 1930s, Karpelès drafted a number of Khmers from Cochinchina into her project to reanimate Cambodian Buddhism and culture (Becker 1985, 50–51). The most prominent recruit was Son Ngoc Thanh (1908–c. 1975). Born in Cochinchina and educated at a wat school, a colonial secondary school, and a French high school and university, Thanh joined the Royal Library as a clerk in 1933. In 1935, he moved to the Buddhist Institute, where he worked on the Committee of Cambodian Mores and Customs (Chandler 1992, 18).[43] He also used his position to ensure that monks dispatched on preaching tours by the institute were "strongly nationalist, good talkers and skilled in persuading the soldiers, using the Buddhist style of enlightenment, to love their country" (Mul 1982 [1971], 117–119). Vernacular Khmer was the medium of these sermons.

A June 1937 article in the journal *Nagaravatta* described the Royal Library as "the heart of the Khmer country," a fecund site of Khmer customs and social mores and a "meeting place for Khmer scholars who disseminate these precepts to the Khmer nation."[44] The seminar series begun in 1927 continued into the late 1930s, bringing together institute and library staff, *sangha,* and secular intellectuals such as *Nagaravatta*'s editor, Pach Choeun (like Son Ngoc Thanh a Khmer Krom), people from Phnom Penh and the provinces, and French Orientalists. Buddhist Institute publications were circulated among the audience.[45] In 1937, Karpelès launched a Buddhist Institute radio program, which was given provincial airplay by the mobile book-bus.[46]

This extended field of religious institute activities expanded the influence of reformist monks and intensified regional discord between the Dhammayut and Dhammakāy. Touring the western provinces in July 1933, King Monivong impressed upon the *sangha* the "sacrifices" made by the French administration to "renovate Buddhism" and urged the *sangha* to drop their divisive differences.[47] In July 1937, a front-page column in *Nagaravatta* implicitly blamed the feuding between the Dhammayut and the Dhammakāy for fracturing Cambodia's Buddhist unity. Warning that such factionalism could lead to the decline of Buddhism, the paper urged its readers not to worry about who was a Dhammayut, a Dhammakāy, or an "old-school Mahānikāy," but as the "Khmer race *(jāti khmaer)*, united in one Buddhism, and making merit with Buddhist monks in [the name of] Buddhism."[48] In early 1938, a *Nagaravatta* editorial implicitly endorsed the reformist movement in the *sangha*, urging its readers to discard the ignorance and prejudices of olden times.[49] In 1938, the ascendance of the reformists within the Mahānikāy was reflected in the election of a Dhammakāy as Mahā Sangharāja of the Mahānikāy order (Coedès 1938; Kiernan 1985, 4). The following year saw the formation of a Buddhist Association modeled on a new wave of secular associations and dedicated to transcending factionalism within the *sangha* by spreading knowledge of Buddhism among the "disciples of Buddha" in Cambodia.[50]

On July 3, 1940, the GGI, Jean Decoux, issued a decree confirming the Cambodian Buddhist Institute's responsibility for directing and coordinating studies of Theravāda Buddhism in Indochina, and especially in Cambodia and Laos.[51] Issued weeks after the fall of France to Germany and Decoux's declaration of pro-Vichy loyalties, the decree may have been an early attempt to reinforce Indochina's geocultural boundaries and thereby strengthen the *sangha*'s immunity to political overtures from Siam. In September, Decoux's government, unable to reinforce its military position, allowed Japan to station troops in Indochina (Brötel 1986, 176). But ideologically, Indochina's colonial administration remained Vichy territory, as reflected in its enforcement of the Vichy Statute on the Jews of October 3, 1940. The statute prohibited all Jews—defined as those possessing two or more grandparents of the Jewish "race"—from public office (Neher-Berhnheim 2002, 1097–1100). Application of the statute was selective.

Undermined militarily by the presence of Japanese troops, Vichy Indochina focused its energies on a cultural struggle to gain and retain indigenous allegiance. Specifically, Decoux's administration sought to prevent Japan from stimulating anticolonial nationalism through cooptation of the *sangha* through such organizations as the Buddhist Association. Citing Coedès' expertise and ability to combat Japanese influence in this sphere, the Résident Supérieur of Tonkin granted him an exemption from the statute (Raffin 2002, 369). Retained in office, Coedès spearheaded a "highly erudite cultural team" tasked with galvanizing local cultural nationalisms, Vichy style, in the service of greater France (Goscha 1995, 80).

Coedès' special treatment made the dismissal of Karpelès an ideological necessity for Decoux's government to prove its pro-Vichy credentials. She was an easy target. As an educator involved in publishing and the highest female officeholder in the French protectorate, Karpelès not only violated the Vichy statute, but also subverted Vichy gender ideologies, which held that a woman's place was as a reproducer of a pure French race and confined the place of female educators to home economics (Edwards 2001).[52] Karpelès was among fifteen Europeans forced from office in Indochina for being Jewish (Raffin 2002, 369). Stripped of her post and fearing for her security, she left Cambodia in 1941 and retired to the country of her childhood, Pondichèry.[53]

The following year, Decoux's government announced plans to romanize the Khmer language through the enforced adoption of a system of romanization devised by Coedès. Both secular intellectuals and members of the *sangha* saw the proposed romanization as an attack on their elite status (Keyes 1994, 49; Chandler 1991, 170). But the strength of opposition and the depth of feeling on the issue indicates that more than social privilege was at stake. To many, romanization threatened the erasure of the very essence of Khmer culture in its violation of one domain—the Khmer language—which, largely due to the activities of Nath, Tat, Karpelès, and others, they now conflated with the Khmer nation. Where the so-called "traditionalists" had vetoed modern print media, all factions rallied against this campaign, which threatened to strip the Khmer language of all vestiges of indigeneity and religiosity.

The most outspoken opponents of the campaign were Achar Hem Chieu, a teacher at the École Supérieure de Pāli, and Achar Nuon Dong, a graduate of the school. On July 18, 1942, the *sûreté* arrested Achar Hem Chieu and Achar Nuon Duong for preaching anti-French sermons to Khmer troops, and the "Umbrella War" ensued. The subsequent internment and exile of key agitators broke the backbone of the nationalist movement. *Nagaravatta* was shut down.

The defrocking of Achar Hem Chieu and the discharge of Karpelès from government office both bore the imprints of a new absolutism, which used modernity's categories of religion, gender, and nation to extraordinarily destructive ends.

The Umbrella War and Vichy ideology triggered a reassessment of protectorate policies vis-à-vis the Buddhist Institute and the École Supérieure de Pāli. The institute's greatest crime, in the eyes of both RSC Gaultier and the head of the information department, J. Desjardins, was crossing the line between religion and politics. In December 1942 Gaultier openly accused the institute of breaching its mandate and espousing political sympathies in its texts, thus catalyzing the July demonstrations.[54] Ordered to stay outside of politics, the institute was also warned not to become a school of theology.[55] Once favored as a buffer against Siamese influence, the Dhammakāy were now condemned as an "anti-French minority" and the Buddhist Institute was accused of spreading Dhammakāy influence in Cambodia via its publications.[56] Monks attached to either the Buddhist Institute or the École Supérieure de Pāli were henceforth banned from preaching. But so as not to alienate the *sangha* completely, and in line with the Vichy regime's emphasis on such official emblems of nation as flags and anthems, in 1942 the protectorate commissioned Nath to write the words and music of Cambodia's first national anthem (Harris 2000, 12, 16ff).

Conclusion

The path from Nath's ordination in 1912 to his role as an official architect of nation in 1942 was also a journey from the margins of the Mahānikāy to a position as moral custodian of a national culture. This linkage between moral authority and national identity was itself a sign of transition in Cambodian religious life, which had witnessed the gradual conflation, under colonial rule, of a belief system—Buddhism—and the idea of a racially pure group—"the Khmers"—into a new category: "national religion" *(sāsanā jāti).* As the founding director of the Royal Library (1925–1941) and the Buddhist Institute (1930–1941), and as chief publications officer for the École Supérieure de Pāli (1925–1941), Karpelès had engineered an institutional framework for the documentation and codification of this category. The language in which these new categories were framed and articulated—that of vernacular Khmer—acted as the thread linking new discourses of Buddhism to new imaginings of a Khmer nation. As we have seen, language itself—its manner of inscription, its content, and its dissemination—was a major domain through which the Dhammakāy managed the tension between the *appeal* of scientific, rationalist explanations of the world and the latent *threat* of erosion of indigenous cultural sovereignty. From the 1910s onward Dhammakāy projects promoted and effected the transformation of the language of religious education by broadening the scriptural reproduction and delivery of Buddhist sermons from Pāli to include Khmer. In their insistence that meaning, and not the style or medium of reproduction, was everything, Nath and Tat ostensibly divested the scriptures of the magico-religious aura of the sacred writing at the same time that they sought to purify Mahānikāy sermons and texts such as the *Jātaka* tales from what they considered an excess of superstition and hyperbole. They also favored the replacement of the scribe with the reliability and clarity of the printer's block. These engagements with the technology and vocabulary of modernity imprinted history's "Godless, empty" time into the domain of Buddhist scriptures. That transformation was, apparently, completed through their insistence on the use of Khmer, which furnished their "rational" school of Buddhism with a national "Khmer" flavor. However, as we have seen, this process did not empty the Khmer written script of its meaning. Instead, the Khmer vernacular, produced in print media, emerged as a modern form in which the words of Buddha were fused with the magico-religious aura of a new divinity: the nation.

The crystallization of the notion of the nation as both a spiritual domain and ethnocultural site occurred through a gradual process from the 1900s to the 1930s.

Through their print projects and their spells of study and teaching at the protectorate's schools and institutions, Nath and Tat helped to forge the common vocabulary for a conversation centering on notions of the nation and the national, which dominated Franco-Khmer exchanges between European scholars and reformist monks in the late 1920s and 1930s, and which also framed a series of exchanges between Khmer monks across factions and Khmer intellectuals. The performance and dissemination in research institutes, schools, textbooks, and newspapers of this vocabulary of the national helped to cement notions of a nationally framed Khmer cultural and religious collectivity.

The passage from Ind's notion of *jāti* to that of *jāti* (as used by the 1930s in such compounds as *jātisāsanā*) was a journey not only from the local to the national, but from more stylized renderings of Khmer to a vernacular Khmer. In this, Nath and Tat were not complete pioneers, but were heirs of Ind's refashioning of the language of Buddhism. Where Ind had developed a universal and translocal discourse of *jāti* with local implications (see chap. 2), Nath and Tat developed a specifically national language of Buddhism with particular geographic and historic dimensions. These developments, while increasing intimacy between reformists and European scholars, were matched by a rising antagonism between figures such as Nath and those within the Mahānikāy who sought to make sense of their world differently, through their continued engagement with present practice, and those in the Dhammayut who considered Nath's and Tat's Khmer vernacularization of Buddhism demeaning. In their sustained conversation with secular Khmer intellectuals and colonial scholar-officials, Nath and Tat proved extraordinarily versatile cross-cultural negotiators who staked out a central space for their interpretation of Buddhism within the dominant discourse of Khmer nationalism as it emerged in the 1930s.

Superficially, the Buddhist reform movement and colonial attempts to replace Buddhist cosmologies with a scientific cognitive grid cohered in their renunciation of those things held to be beyond the pale of reason: notably magic and superstition. However, as we have seen, modernity's apparent erasure of the "magico-religious aura" (Népote and Khing 1981) of the written word through the processes of print production championed by the reformists was a trompe l'oeil, as was the reformists claim to be against superstition. By the Umbrella War in 1942, the reformists had consecrated a new superstition in the form of the Khmer nation, whose divine status was now located in the Khmer language. The lure of that superstition lay in its constant reiteration—not as an "irrational" leap of faith, but as a modern, rational ideology that enjoyed a solid basis in documented "tradition." Religion was seen to offer a respectable base for that tradition and was also seen, by European administrators, as a domain in which the cultivation of good relations would procure mass support for colonial projects.

But where this reform movement broke faith with secularism was in its refusal to dispense with the magico-religious elements enshrined not only in the Khmer script, leading prominent reformists to oppose romanization, but also in the very fabric and clothing of Khmer monkhood, as epitomized in the reaction to the defrocking of Achar Hem Chieu. High colonialism and the machinery of modernity—print media, secular research institutes, libraries, museums, and "renovated" temple schools—never quite managed to disrobe indigenous religion.

Notes

I would like to thank several anonymous readers for their valuable comments on an earlier version of this paper, and John Marston and Elizabeth Guthrie for generously sharing their wisdom and information. I gratefully acknowledge funding from the Centre for Cross-Cultural Research in the form of a Postdoctoral Fellowship, which allowed me to develop this chapter for publication.

1. The term "Mahānikāy *cās'*" was used in reformist and colonial texts to refer to Mahānikāy monks who were opposed to the Buddhist reforms promoted by the Mahānikāy *thmī*. By using these terms, my intention is *not* to validate hegemonic paradigms of the Mahānikāy *cās'* as a "backwards-looking" sect. Rather, I suggest that the very notion of such bipolar categories was largely a colonial legacy.

2. The Cambodian Dhammakāy movement should not be confused with the Thai Thammakāi sect based at the Wat Phra Thammakāi near Bangkok. See Jackson 1989, 199–221.

3. Archives d'Outre-Mer (AOM) GGI 24210 RSC Huyn de Vernéville to GGI March 30, 1895, 1–6; Migot 1960, 303.

4. AOM GGI 24210 RSC Huyn de Vernéville to GGI March 30, 1895, 1, 3, 6.

5. The rationalist framework of Southeast Asia's Buddhist reform movements parallels similar reform movements in Enlightenment Europe and was, in part, inspired by them (Hallisey 1995, 48).

6. *Braḥ rājjātipay nae saṃtec braḥ mahāsaṅgarāj sanniyuk* [Speech by the Venerable Supreme Patriarch and chief of monks]. *Kampujā suriyā* 1.7 (1927):7–13.

7. AOM INDO GGI 11804 Badens to Messieurs Guilland and Martinon, January 16, 1886.

8. AOM INDO GGI 11804 Governor, Saigon to Representative of Cambodia, September 5, 1885.

9. AOM FP APC 46 1 (file 5) Son Diep to Auguste Pavie, May 13, 1904.

10. AOM INDO GGI 1579, November 15, 1904.

11. "École de pāli d'Angkor," *BEFEO* 9 (1909):824. This was not purely a colonial creation; Mahā Sangharāj Dien, head of Wat Unnalom, was also credited with the initiative (Flauguerges 1914, 175–182).

12. "École de pāli d'Angkor," *BEFEO* 9 (1909):825.

13. "La section de Phnom Penh de la Société d'Angkor," *BEFEO* 11 (1911):252–253; *BEFEO* 14 (1914):95.

14. "École supérieure de pāli," *BEFEO* 35 (1935):463.

15. AOM FM INDO NF 570 RSC Baudoin to GGI Au sujet de la surveillance des bonzes au Cambodge Phnom Penh, April 2, 1916, 1–9.

16. *BEFEO* 14 (1914):95.

17. AOM INDO GGI 2702 RSC to GGI, March 24, 1916, 2.

18. AOM INDO GGI 65502 RSC to GGI, June 3, 1927.

19. "Cambodge," *BEFEO* 22 (1922):428; "École supérieure de pāli," *BEFEO* 35 (1935):463.

20. *BEFEO* 22 (1922):428.

21. Ibid., 444. Karpelès is likely to have met with scholars-in-residence Tat and Nath during this time.

22. AOM INDO GGI 65502 RSC Report First Trimester 1925, April 17, 1925, 5.

23. AOM INDO GGI 65539 *Sûreté* Phnom Penh, "Sectes Réligieuses au Cambodge," July 20, 1933, 2.

24. "Bibliothèque royale du Cambodge," *BEFEO* 30 (1930):212.

25. "École supérieure de pāli," *BEFEO* 35 (1935):464.

26. *Société Anonyme d'édition et de publicité indochinoises: Les éditions d'extrême Asie: Extrait des statuts 1928.* Phnom Penh: Imprimerie S.E.K., 1928, 1.

27. "Why you should read *Sruk Khmaer,*" *Sruk Khmaer* 1 (1927):1.

28. Tat, "Tournée d'inspection dans les pagodes cambodgiennes du Sud-oeust de la Cochinchine," *Kambujā suriyā* 3 (1929):39–62; Tat, "Suite et fin," *Kambujā suriyā* 3 (1929).

29. *Sruk Khmaer* 3.27 (1929):2.

30. AOM INDO NF 259 Dossier 2226, 39–40.

31. "Sictīy jūn ṭaṃṇiṅ aṃbī sīevbhau vijjā Khemarābhāsā" [Information about Khmer-language educational books], *Sruk Khmaer* 11 (1928):3

32. "Bibliothèque royale du Cambodia," *BEFEO* 30 (1930):212; *BEFEO* 30 (1930):185.

33. "Rapport du Secrétaire de l'Institut," *BEFEO* 31 (1931):337–338.

34. Ibid.

35. "Discours du vénérable Nath, représentant du clergé cambodgien," *BEFEO* 31 (1931):339.

36. "Aṃbī poḥ bumb *Tipiṭaka*" [About printing the *Tipiṭaka*], *Sruk Khmaer* 21 (1931):1

37. "Le voyage ministeriel en Extrême-Orient," *L'Illustration* 21 (1931):364.

38. "Discours du vénérable Nath, representant du clergé cambodgien," *BEFEO* 31 (1931):339–340.

39. AOM INDO RSC 321 "Annual Report of Resident of Siem Reap," June 1, 1931–May 31, 1932, 3, 13.

40. AOM INDO GGI 65539 *Sûreté* Phnom Penh, "Sectes Religieuses du Cambodge," July 20, 1933, 2.

41. AOM INDO RSC 269 RSC Lavit to Chef Local du Service de l'Enseignement à Phnom Penh, November 12, 1931, 1–2.

42. AOM INDO RSC 269 "Louis Manipaud, le Délégué de SM à l'Enseignment Traditionnel, Rapport annuel," 1933–1934, 9, 20.

43. "Pravattikār nae rājkār Khmaer" (History of the Khmer administration), *Nagaravatta,* June 26, 1937, 1–3.

44. "About the Radio at the Royal Library in Phnom Penh," *Nagaravatta,* June 12, 1937, 1.

45. "Sictīy gāp prasoer rapas' anak srī kramuṃ karpīlaes jā sakaniyuk nīy braḥ rāj baṇṇalāy" [The goodness of Miss Karpelès, head of the Royal Library], *Nagaravatta,* April 9, 1938, 1–2.

46. "About the Radio at the Royal Library in Phnom Penh," *Nagaravatta,* June 12, 1937, 1.

47. AOM FM INDO NF 577 RSC Sylvestre Confidential Report to GGI no. 499-SPK, titled *Voyage de SM Monivong dans les Provinces de son Royaume,* July 18, 1933, 2.

48. *Nagaravatta,* July 10, 1937, 1.

49. "Pariya thṅai sau Dhammayut niṅ Mahānikāy" [Saturday report: Dhammayut and Mahānikāy], *Nagaravatta,* January 29, 1938, 1.

50. "Sictīy jūn ṭaṃṇiṅ aṃbī buddhikasamāgam" [News about the Buddhist Association], *Nagaravatta,* January 21, 1939, 1; "Sictīy camroen nae buddhikasamāgam" [The progress of the Buddhist Association], *Nagaravatta,* July 29, 1939, 1.

51. AOM INDO RSC 464 GGI Arrèt, July 3, 1940, article 1.

52. The disappearance and deaths of numerous Karpelès are recorded at Yad Vashem, The Holocaust Martyrs' and Heroes' Remembrance Authority, Yad Vashem, Israel.

53. J. Filliozat, personal communication, June 10, 2002.

54. AOM INDO RSC 464 Letter from RSC to Secretary General of Buddhist Institute, December 18, 1942.

55. AOM INDO RSC 464 RSC to Secretary General of the Buddhist Institute, June 22, 1943, 2, 5, 8.

56. AOM INDO RSC 464 M. Desjardins Chef de la Service Local d'Information de la Propagande et de la Presse to RSC, April 22, 1943.

PART II

The Icon of the Leper King

The two chapters in Part II deal with the complex, multilayered meaning of the leper king image in historical and contemporary usage. Thompson and Hang originally planned to write a chapter on the leper king together. In the end, the two projects developed independently to the degree that they decided to make separate chapters. We group them together in one section to emphasize that the historical and theoretical issues considered by Thompson in chapter 4 and the ethnographic and art-historical descriptions of Hang in chapter 5 explore one topic. While Part II focuses on a single salient icon rather than a theme, the chapters invoke themes found throughout this volume and do so in a way that links the themes of Part I with those of Part III. Thompson's and Hang's chapters show the relation of the Khmer religious past to contemporary practice. Like all the chapters in the book, they are concerned with the degree Khmer religious practice reflects and shapes ways of conceiving a Khmer geobody. Like several other chapters, they also explore how iconography acquires social meaning in the actual practice of Khmer religion. The saliency of the icons Hang describes is underlined by the fact that they are among the *pāramī* who enter one of the *grū pāramī* in chapter 7 (Bertrand); the cult of Yāy Deb also figures in chapter 2 (Hansen), which mentions its critique by a colonial-era reformer.

Perhaps one way of introducing these two chapters is to refer to a journal entry by William Harben, a U.S. diplomat based in Phnom Penh during the politically chaotic 1970–1975 Lon Nol period.[1] Harben wrote about the statue of Braḥ Aṅg Saṅkh Cakr that Hang describes in chapter 5.

> People are saying that the beheading of the concrete statue of King Kralang [*sic*]—The Leper King—by a deranged man is an omen that the country will soon be headless, that Lon Nol will soon be overthrown.

Harben and a colleague went to check it out and found it restored.

> We were surprised to see that not only had the head been put back on, but the statue repainted in an even more garish hue than formerly in order to hide the scar around the concrete neck. A lump running completely around the neck showed, however, that the head had been cemented back on.
>
> "There must be an anti-omen squad at work," I observed. . . . I wondered how much of this hocus-pocus is self-generating. Are some of the omens actually hexes against the regime? If one wanted to get rid of Lon Nol, and consulted a wizard on the best way to go about it, the wizard might very well suggest knocking the head off a royal statue—on the same principle of sticking pins in a wax doll resembling the target.

The incident dramatically illustrates the importance of the statue as a cult site in the 1970s; its importance perhaps increased in chaotic times. It also illustrates the degree to which in the popular mind, consistent with Thompson's argument in chapter 4, the body of the statue was associated with the body of the "kingdom."

Chapter 4 is concerned with religion in the broadest sense of the term, as a worldview that can embrace conceptions of kingship and of healing, a usage that is further illuminated by the concrete ritual practice described in chapter 5. The theme of the leper king is only part of a broader discussion of healing and pardon in relation to kingship. Thompson develops the idea of the king as a body standing metonymically for his kingdom, whose corporal well-being corresponds to its well-being, paralleling the ways that the body of the Buddha is conceived as integrating and ordering the physical world. Thompson discusses the concept of healing as associated with inscriptions describing medical care at the time of Jayavarman VII and analyzes legends of the leper king as they intersect with those surrounding Jayavarman VII. The connection between the body of the king and that of the state figures as well, she shows, in the legend of the fall of the sixteenth-century Khmer capital and in the role of King Norodom Sihanouk in modern times (and even, as Harben's journal entry shows, in the role of Lon Nol, as president of the consciously nonmonarchical Khmer Republic).

As she did in chapter 1, Thompson suggests in chapter 4 alternative, seemingly premodern, ways of defining Cambodian nation—ways that, as she points out, may contradict the democratic ideals of the nation-state and yet figure in the actual practice of Cambodian modernity.

Chapter 4 also provides a far-reaching interpretation of Khmer conceptions of healing as they relate to the metonymic extension of the body. Thompson's discussion is sure to shed light on future research on traditional healers *(grū khmaer)* and suggests ways of looking at the kinds of religious practitioners described in this book's later chapters, most involved to some degree in healing: the *grū pāramī* described by Bertrand and Yamada (chaps. 7 and 10), the cult figure of a hermit monk described by Marston in chapter 8, the Phnom Penh abbot treating AIDS patients described by Guthrie in chapter 6.

Chapter 5 is about the statue of the leper king in the Cambodian National Museum and four nearly identical statues in Phnom Penh and Siem Reap. Hang describes the characteristic features of each, what is known of its history, and the different ways it functions as a shrine. Among the many fascinating implications of this chapter is how it brings out the dualities created between the different statues, starting with that of the leper king in the National Museum and its contemporary, the Yāy Deb statue in Siem Reap, which, while virtually the same, is ascribed a female identity by the public. Similarly, a modern replica of the leper king statue on the grounds of the National Museum is called Yāy Deb and given a female identity. Its recent creator describes it as serving to protect the original in the museum as a second, diversionary image, much like the role of second kings described in chapter 4. Finally, we have a leper king statue in front of Wat Unnalom in Phnom Penh (the one referred to in the Harben journal) now associated with the political party FUNCINPEC, which is complemented by a similar statue associated with the Cambodian People's Party.

From the perspective of the large picture of Cambodian religious practice, chapter 5 serves as one particularly salient example of the veneration of shrines in Cambodia, both in personal homes and in public places. While many shrines are devoted to the Buddha or iconography associated with Buddhism, many are not. Obvious examples are the spirit *(devatā)* shrines found in individual homes or bordering temples and *anak tā* shrines associated with each village and each wat. Other non-Buddhist iconography is venerated: statuary of the Hindu pantheon; the icons, in statuary, drawings, and photos, of Braḥ Kaev and Braḥ Go; statues of forest ascetics and ancient warriors—perhaps the same range of iconic figures that inhabit the *grū pāramī* mediums Bertrand describes in chapter 7.

Of these shrines, as Thompson and Hang bring out, the leper king statues have special resonance by how they recall Khmer *national* identity and by the degree they represent, in all its complexity, the institution of Cambodian kingship.

Note

1. Our thanks to David Chandler for making this passage from Harben's journal available to us.

-4-

The Suffering of Kings

Substitute Bodies, Healing, and Justice in Cambodia

Ashley Thompson

I have gathered here a rather eclectic collection of material—parts of a twelfth-century inscription and a twentieth-century royal chronicle, as well as different sorts of archaeological, ethnographic, and linguistic data, along with snippets of Freud, Kantorowicz, and Foucault—to piece together a certain image of the king, and of kingship, in Cambodia. I call it "the king as substitute body," or "the substitute body of the king," and examine the various implications this image has for Khmer healing practices in the largest sense—inseparable as they are, even in the modern context I will argue, from religion. But already in the quilting together of these disparate fragments, something of the subject should transpire: it is a question of wholes and parts. The debate is an old one, but it has taken on new urgency in postcolonial contexts: enlightenment universality versus inassimilable otherness; metadiscourse versus untranslatable idiom; colonial essentialism versus nihilistic relativism. These issues are inextricably implicated here in what can be taken for an indigenous Khmer example. Indeed an example is always, precisely, a replaceable singularity. And so beyond these sterile oppositions, I shall attempt to show that in a certain history of Khmer royalty, the substitute body of the king is both transcendent or universal *and* uniquely particular. In my very methodology, navigating between different time periods and different cultural or intellectual traditions, I aim to test boundaries between the one and the other.

The king as substitute body, which has, I believe, played a central role in the Khmer Buddhist tradition, is in no way limited to Buddhism or to Cambodia. A particularly striking example can be seen in a related cultural practice by which a "scapegoat king" is both maintained as a revered protector of the community and charged with the collective ill, to be expelled as a vile threat.[1] Like the prohibition of incest, the institution of the scapegoat king has long been seen as a "cultural universal." Freud, an avid armchair anthropologist, devotes a long section of *Totem and Taboo* to "The Taboo of Rulers" in the chapter on the "Ambivalence of Emotions." He puts it as follows: "The behavior of primitive races towards their chiefs, kings, and priests, is controlled by two principles which seem rather to supplement than to contradict each other. They must both be guarded and be guarded against" (Freud 1918, 56).[2] As Freud says, "the person in line for the succession often used every means to escape it," and "it is often necessary to use force to compel the successor to accept the honor" (Freud 1918, 63). Freud actually mentions a Cambodian example, taken from Frazer's *The Golden Bough:* that of the dual kings of the Jaraï, an Austronesian minority living in the mountainous regions to the northeast of the country. Well into the nineteenth century, the Khmer court regularly sent tribute to these famous Kings of Water and Fire. In 1883, Moura described the Kings of Water and Fire as being "nominal, spiritual or mysterious rather than effective" monarchs with no "political or administrative authority." His knowledge of them was based solely on hearsay: "In the Cambodian provinces neighboring the savage tribes, we were unable to find a single person having visited the forests of the Jaraï" (Moura 1883, 432–433). We will cross paths with these mysterious double kings a bit farther on, but keeping in mind precisely their duplicity, I would like to evoke another preliminary example.

From the Middle Ages through the Renaissance, English jurists and theologians speculated and legislated at length on the king's two bodies. They distinguished the king's body natural from his body politic or mystical body. The first was material and mortal, while the second was immaterial and immortal. Whence the famous cries heard at royal funerary ceremonies from the beginning of the sixteenth century: "The king is dead! Long live the king!" These seemingly illogical calls "powerfully demonstrated the perpetuity of kingship" (Kantorowicz 1997 [1957], 410–413). But each of the bodies is dependent on the other. The king's physical body stands in for a metaphysical body that outdoes it but cannot do without it. Or to quote Kantorowicz again, the king's Two Bodies "form one unit indivisible, each being fully contained in the other" (Kantorowicz 1997 [1957], 9).

We can see in this duality a structure that is essential to the scapegoat king, with the mortality of the natural body of the king serving as a gage or a guarantee of the immortality of the body politic. A similar structure can be found in Khmer Buddhist culture where the time-bound living king *embodies* the essentially atemporal *dharma.* Here the royal body is one in a series of substitute bodies, including the Buddha and the *stūpa,* each being an image of Mount Meru, which substitute one for the other in substituting for the kingdom or the universe governed by the *dharma.*[3]

What, then, might this have to do with healing? Though his interpretation is quite different, it is not insignificant that Freud's first example in "The Taboo of

Rulers" is that of "the remarkable case of the king's touch becoming the healing and protective measure against the very dangers that arise from contact with the king" (Freud 1918, 57). For the purposes of my argument here, a first clue is provided by the English term "to heal" (see Derrida 1996). A close linguistic cousin of "holy" and descendant of "whole," "healing" harks back to a religious sense of re-membering what has been dismembered. Perceiving the individual body as integral to a communal or political whole embodied by the king implies an analogy between, on the one hand, the relationships between the part and the whole and, on the other, those between the physical and the meta- or supra-physical. The part can aspire to wholeness only insofar as the physical can communicate with the mystical. And this is where the king's bodies come in, because the king is at once a part for the whole and the whole in a part, or, to borrow once again from medieval English legal terminology, he is a "Corporation sole" in which the species and the individual coincide like the mythical "self-begott'n bird," the phoenix (Kantorowicz 1997 [1957], 388–395). It is my belief that in Cambodia, attempts to heal the king, the community, or the individual subjects of the king inevitably have recourse to complex strategies of integration, embodiment, and substitution between these various co-implicated bodies. Of course this supposes that no body is a simple, self-same monad, but at once a part of the whole of the communal body (or bodies), and simultaneously a whole in and of itself, or rather a potential whole. Indeed, it is, I think, this teleological promise of wholeness that drives the overlay of metonymical relations through which the king as substitute body, and as embodiment of substitution, plays a crucial role in healing.

I have organized this chapter in roughly chronological order so as to situate modern phenomena in their historical context. However, it is the historical process itself that is in question here. Healing, as I will discuss it, involves the reintegration of the past into the present, through the body of the king, or substitutes thereof. Yet this process of re-membering, and its inextricable co-implication of physical health and social justice figured in the substitutional body of the king, obeys a teleological or even messianic orientation. Reworking past and present, healing is all about the future.

Policies of Public Health

My historical pilgrimage begins in the late twelfth century with Jayavarman VII, a Mahāyāna Buddhist and the last prominent king of the Angkor period. His reign set the stage for many of the transformations that followed the fall of Angkor and the emergence of modern, Theravāda Buddhist Cambodia. During Jayavarman VII's reign, a certain conjunction of the physical health of the people and the social health of the kingdom through the figure of the king was formulated in an unprecedented manner. This first Cambodian "public health policy," though not perhaps a full-coverage social security system, included the foundation of 102 "hospitals" *(arogyasālā)*. A royal edict was inscribed on a stele at each hospital.[4] These Sanskrit inscriptions seem to have been identical copies of a long poem composed for the occasion. As we will see, the Hospital Edicts can be read on one level at least as a kind of treatise on the multiplicity—and substitutability—of the body of the king.

The poem opens with a homage to the Buddha and a reference to the Mahāyāna Trikāya doctrine.

> I. Homage to the Buddha, who has the forms of *nirmāṇa* (apparition), of *dharma* and of *saṃbhoga* (enjoyment), who surpasses the duality of being and non-being, who, impersonal, personifies non-duality.[5]

The reference to the Trikāya in the poem's first stanza gives some insight into the intellectual-religious context during the reign of Jayavarman VII. It also offers a primary clue to the substitute body structure I am proposing. Harrison (1992, 44) has recapitulated the canonical interpretations of the Trikāya doctrine as follows:

> Taking these in ascending order of abstraction, the *nirmāṇa-kāya* usually translated "apparitional phantom body," "phantom body," "transformation body," etc., is the physical manifestation of Buddhahood, the ordinary perishable human form, as exemplified by the "historical Buddha," Siddhārtha Gautama. The *saṃbhogha-kāya* ("body of bliss," "reward body," "enjoyment body," etc.) is a more exalted and splendid manifestation of the enlightened personality, still in the realm of form, but visible only to *bodhisattvas,* those of advanced spiritual capabilities. By contrast, the *dharma-kāya* ("*Dharma*-body," "Body of Truth," "Cosmic Body," "Absolute Body," etc.) is both formless and imperishable, representing the identification of the Buddha with the truth which he revealed, or with reality itself. As such the *dharma-kāya* is often linked with various terms for reality... and has even been regarded as a kind of Buddhist absolute, or at least at one with it.... The *dharma-kāya* is understood as the primal "source" or "ground" from which the other two types of bodies emanate.

One of the principal substitute bodies of the king is the image of the Buddha: the king gives body to the Buddha on earth and in our time.[6] As speculation on "the nature of Buddhahood, the nature of reality, and on the relationship between them" (Harrison 1992, 45), the doctrine of the Three Bodies constitutes a theoretical reflection on the nature of representation itself, at once bridging and creating the gap between the manifest and the ineffable, between the human and the divine.

While the superposition of these two spheres is one of the very premises of Khmer (royal) culture, the poem simultaneously enacts a sort of inaugural descent from this most abstract theological domain beyond the mundane binary (to be or not to be, *bhavābhava*) to the suffering world of Jayavarman's subjects. Thus the second and third stanzas give homage to one particular form of the Buddha: the Bhaiṣajyaguru, or the Buddha as healer.[7]

> II. Homage to Jina Bhaiṣajyaguruvaiḍūryaprabhārāja (Buddha the Victorious, master of the science of healing, king brilliant as *vaiḍūrya* (cat's eye) who gives peace and health to those who simply hear his name).

The reference to the Bhaiṣajyaguru in stanza II is another clue to the religious milieu in Cambodia at the time. The image of Bhaiṣajyaguru was certainly worshiped in Jayavarman's hospitals, and some form of the *Bhaiṣajyaguru sūtra* may have been known as stanza II reiterates one of the its main points: simply hearing the name of Bhaiṣajyaguru "gives peace and health" to the hearer.[8] Here I am arguing that the "hospitals" dedicated by Jayavarman VII to Bhaiṣajyaguru can also be understood to comprise a strong metaphorical dimension, aimed at curing social or spiritual ills as well as physical sickness.

> III. May Śrī Sūryavairocana (Sun-god), burning with splendor, and Śrī Candravairocana (Moon-god), spouse of Rohiṇī, who both disperse the darkness of sickness from the people, be victorious at the sides of this Mount Meru, king of saints.

This last expression, the "Mount Meru, king of saints," constitutes a powerful metaphor in the present context. The Bhaiṣajyaguru is to the rest of the Buddhist saints as Mount Meru is to the rest of the universe. We will encounter a similar case of substitution as a literary trope a few stanzas farther on in the image of Prajāpati. But the immediate successor to this Meru of saints, in the sequence of the poem, is the king, Jayavarman VII.

> IV. There was a king, Śrī Jayavarmadeva, son of Śrī Dharaṇīndravarmadeva, born of a princess of Jayādityapura: he obtained royalty [in the year marked] by the Vedas, the sky, one and the moon [1104 C.S. or 1182 C.E.] [Or: he obtained royalty by the single unction of the Veda sky].

We pass from the Buddha to the Buddha-healer to the king, a king born both of his human parents and of the heavens. In other words, Jayavarman VII is situated in both the divine line of gods and the natural line of royalty; he is twice born, a common conception of the king in Angkorean epigraphy. I have discussed this double birth elsewhere in connection with issues of genealogy and the myth of hyperlegitimate masculine (royal) lineage (Thompson 2000); here, however, the motif of the double birth can be seen as a consequence of the duality of the king's body. The king must be understood, like the Buddha, as both unique and multiple, comprising incongruous parts, each of which is a whole, such that he "exists" at several different spatial, temporal, and symbolic levels. In this sense, the double or multiple birth is simply a consequence of the king's multiple modes of existence.

The next four stanzas of the poem elaborate on the exploits of the king in combating his enemies to bring salvation to the land. In stanza IX we begin to see that the mystical superiority of this monarch is manifest, in particular, as he rids the people of sickness. Having liberated the land, the king's actions mirror those of the Buddha-healer worshiped in the hospital chapels, as a succession of figures are evoked in the poem to represent these royal healing powers. First, the king is Prajāpati, the creator of the world who is eternally dismembered and re-membered in perpetual recreation. Next, he is the Bull who is the universe in the image of Prajāpati: with four legs in the first cosmic age *(kṛta),* the Bull is dismembered over time, losing a leg in each of the three subsequent cosmic ages, until Jayavarman VII arrives in extremis to turn the tables, renaissance king and miracle doctor who makes the Bull whole once again.

> IX. When, due to the exhaustion of their merit-based life force, the people neared destruction, like the destruction of the last cosmic age, then like Prajāpati at the beginning of time, he [i.e., Jayavarman VII] created a prosperous renaissance where the Bull was complete.
>
> X. Seeing that the earth, whose sky had been made by his power, was oppressed by death, he determined the ambrosia of remedies for the immortality of mortals.

Like Prajāpati who both creates the universe and is the universe recreated, the king repairs the Bull, which is at once the universe and the king.

> XI. Transforming the last age *(kāla)* into the first age *(kṛta),* [the king] restored the limbs to the Bull, whose feet, mutilated by the three cosmic ages, the royal doctors had been unable to heal.
>
> XII. Vanquishing the Bull of other kings, going as he pleases in the park of the universe [three worlds], the Bull, which he had made strong, prospers and bellows.

The Bull is *in* the universe here rather than *being* the universe, and yet it is the king of bulls, vanquishing and thus effectively uniting the multiple bulls or bulldoms in a teleological reunification of a membered and thereby dismembered universe.

This parallel between, on the one hand, the universe as a whole composed of multiple kingdoms and, on the other, the whole kingdom composed of a multitude of subjects is crucial. The king is both a part and a whole, and his ability to circulate from one plane to another through a process of continual substitution is, I believe, the key to his healing powers. Only in giving body to his subjects does the king embody the kingdom. Consubstantial with the dismembered body of the people, it is effectively his own body that the king pieces back together as he heals a suffering Cambodia. The text continues.

> XIII. The illness of the body of the people was for him the illness of the soul—and that much more painful: for it is the suffering of the kingdom, which makes the suffering of kings, and not their own suffering.

After this conflation of suffering bodies, through that of individual with collective ills, superimposed on that of physical and metaphysical ills, the inscription employs an elaborate metaphor associating war and healing.

> XIV. With warriors—doctors—versed in the science of arms—medicine—he destroyed the enemies which infested his kingdom—illnesses—by means of these arms: remedies.

This equation of healing and military conquest—doctors using the remedies of medicine to cure sickness are warriors using the arms of warfare to destroy enemies—is remarkably daring. While this might seem to be a rhetorical device, insofar as medicine is understood as ridding the body of internal ills, Jayavarman VII began his liberation of Cambodia by overcoming domestic dissension, reunifying the dismembered kingdom before going on to expel the Cham invaders.[9] Cambodia is presented in this locution not as one kingdom among others within the universe, but as the universe itself: if the Cham are *internal* enemies, then Jayavarman VII's Cambodia is the kingdom of kingdoms. Of course such an interpretation, making use of a rather strict binary opposition between inside and outside, may seem suspect, especially insofar as this implies a concept and relation to borders in some ways foreign, indeed, to ancient Southeast Asia. I would argue, however, that on the one hand the text in question itself makes abundant use of binary logic (friend/enemy; health/sickness; arms/remedies; life/death, etc.), and on the other, the very equation of sickness with war, and the problematics of internal dissension and counterinsurgency, complicates and in some sense deconstructs in advance the simple oppositional logic it nonetheless instrumentalizes. So, not only does the king promote public health programs to heal the bodies of his subjects, but he is himself a powerful antibody repulsing or neutralizing the enemies that have slipped through the body's permeable, perhaps discontinuous, borders. Taking on the enemy in the body of the people, he is simultaneously the superbody encompassing all bodies and the antibody within.

The next stanza takes a less bellicose approach, addressing the ever-topical question of healing—and pardon—in the aftermath of war.

> XV. He entirely washed away everyone's faults, cleansing the faults which were illness [brought about by] the faults of the cosmic age.

The stanzas are a prelude to the announcement in stanzas XVI–XVIII of the foundation of the hospital, in conjunction with the consecration of a statue of Bhaiṣajyaguru, along with statues of his acolytes, "for the perpetual relief of the illnesses of his [the king's] subjects." The rest of the inscription details the assignment of medical personnel, supplies, and general order to the hospital complex. While the presence of the cult of Bhaiṣajyaguru at Angkor is intriguing, what interests me more here is that the king grants or effects a form of pardon associated with cleansing and healing. It is this conception of the Cambodian king, mediated as it were in the Hospital Edicts through the figure of Bhaiṣajyaguru, that I would like to consider in more detail here.

One of the few prerogatives of the modern constitutional king, the royal pardon is a very real political tool, which can be seen to derive its power from a conception of the king as substitute body linking the divine and the lay spheres. As Derrida (with reference to religious/juridical contexts other than Khmer) has discussed at length, the royal pardon is the legal exception to the law. By giving the sovereign the right to pardon, the law paradoxically legislates with regard to that which escapes the legal system. In this sense, the king stands within the law, but is above the law. This paradoxical position of the king is essential to the functioning of the royal pardon. In its common usage, the concept of pardon seems to depend on an identification of the victim with the pardoner: one can only pardon an aggression that has been committed against oneself. A complete stranger to the victim cannot pardon the aggression or the aggressor. However, the victim's family members, insofar as they were aggressed in the communal body they form with the victim, may have some claim to exercise a right to pardon. This offers insight into the significance of the king's body, as a body of substitution, for pardon. If the king alone can grant pardons in the juridically effective sense, it is because his body proper is simultaneously a public body: in or through the king's body, the proper is somehow coextensive with the improper. In this sense the king suffers in "his" body whenever his subjects suffer. The power to heal and the power to pardon are thus intimately associated in the Hospital Edicts as they are attributed to Jayavarman VII, this unparalleled king of suffering. I shall return to this important connection shortly, articulating the question of health with that of justice.

To what extent can the general model I have just described, with its reference to Western juridical and monarchical traditions, be said to correspond to the situation prevailing in Cambodia's Buddhist kingdom at any one point in its long history?[10] I have often stressed the idea that Southeast Asia is an "object" of study that radically resists *definition* as an object, precisely. So much so that I see "Southeast Asian studies" as involving interdisciplinary work in an essential way, and to be in a privileged, if paradoxical position for engaging in a crucial self-reflexive critique, investigating not only its ostensible object, but simultaneously and inseparably also the investigation itself. One cannot study "Southeast Asia," according to my working hypothesis, without questioning the study of Southeast Asia in the process. And this goes particularly, paradigmatically, for the study of the Cambodian Middle period. At the very least, such an approach helps to avoid the twin perils of what Pollock has called "defensive indigenism" on the one hand (1996, 234), with its relativist, often nationalistic overtones, and essentialist, (neo-) colonialist universalism on the other. In the present case, it is important to consider the possibility that our particular example here, the significance and dynamics of the substitute body of the king in Buddhist Cambodia, will help us to rethink what I call a "general model" and to reconsider the presuppositions involved in such a discourse predicated on establishing well-defined borders between cultural traditions and constructs.

This is a question of the utmost importance for the study of "culture" at the present moment. Because while the self-assured universalism of a project such as Frazer's *The Golden Bough* can no longer be taken at face value, neither can it be simply falsified or written off. In this regard, I consider a general deconstruction of the (concept of the) border, and of the relations between the general and the particular, to be the inevitable horizon of an investigation such as this one. But it is important, having said this, not to fall back into a comfortable binary opposing theory, be it deconstructive, and the particulars of a singular, historically overdetermined example. We must hold out the hope that any insight we can gain into the substitute body of the king, for example—but the point here is precisely that the "example" can no longer be taken for what it once seemed to be—will illuminate not only our theories, but our understanding, and use, of theory "itself."

A modern example can be taken from the Cambodian Constitution. Promulgated in 1993, this constitution reflects the Paris Accords of 1991 and inherits a great deal from Western legal doctrines. Yet it *also* reflects Khmer Buddhist traditions. As a constitution, standing at the (re)foundation of the law, it has a liminal relation to the law. Indeed, Article 27 of the constitution grants the king the right to pardon. It has been said that there is no place for the pardon in Buddhism, especially Theravāda Buddhism, as it attributes to each person full responsibility for him or herself by means of *karma,* the principle of the retribution of actions. It is my belief nonetheless that the fundamental messianic aspect of the Buddha-king complex, with the corresponding share of salvation attributed to outside forces, changes the situation with regard to individual responsibilities, in some sense preempting the exclusion of the pardon that the concept of *karma* might seem to imply.[11] A systematic study has never been done of the various forms of pardon and amnesty in Cambodian history. Yet it is clear that Cambodian kings have long been vested with the power to pardon. Whether it is inscribed in a poem from the thirteenth century or the current constitution, the king's prerogative with respect to the pardon is founded on a singular conception of the king that is *universal* in more ways than one. In fact, it could be said to be the very concept of the universal. The royal pardon is only possible to the extent that the king can occupy a universal position, above the specificity of which he nonetheless is a part.

The term used in Khmer to translate the constitutional prerogative of the king is ambiguous. *Loek laeṅ dos,* literally "to lift and liberate the *punishment*" or "to lift and liberate the *wrongdoing,*" does not lend itself to a precise, invariant interpretation. The important consequences this ambiguity could have for the beneficiaries of such a gesture are no mystery to the present king. The 1996 pardon of Khmer Rouge leader Ieng Sary serves as a case in point. Ieng Sary was convicted of genocide by the People's Republic of Kampuchea courts in 1979. The pressing need to pardon him arose in the changed context of the 1990s, which saw an increasingly divided central government seeking to win over remaining Khmer Rouge factions in the face of an increasingly fervent demand on the part of some members of the international community for the establishment of an international Khmer Rouge tribunal. Given the past conviction, negotiations seeking to bring Ieng Sary and his followers into the government fold necessitated a royal pardon. Yet, with another trial looming, the pardon could serve to shield Ieng Sary from any future conviction. In "pardoning" this Khmer Rouge leader, King Sihanouk did not exclude the possibility that Ieng Sary would be forced in the future to appear before an international tribunal. Sihanouk thus suggested that the pardoned criminal had not been cleared of his crime: though he had been given remission, at least on the national level, the wrongdoing had not been erased. One could certainly interpret this maneuver as the only path open to a cunning constitutional king with no real political-military power, reduced to half measures by an unfavorable conjunction of circumstances. But let us return to the case of Jayavarman VII, who presents the pardon, it seems to me, as an attribute of the savior-king or the Buddha-healer.

A first interpretation of stanza XV (above), "He entirely washed away everyone's faults, cleansing the faults which were illness [brought about by] the faults of the cosmic age," sees it as a eulogy to the king, placing him above the gods who command the universe, according to a rhetorical hyperbole common to ancient Khmer inscriptions. The king is presented here as repairing the evils of the universe, including those that are part of its organic and preordained progression, that is, those that result from the fact that we are living in the fourth cosmic age, the age of greatest degeneration. But there is another possible reading, drawing from Barth's (1903, 462) revision of Finot's original reading, which puts Jayavarman VII in a position remarkably similar to that of Sihanouk with respect to Ieng Sary: "He entirely washed away everyone's faults; he did not excuse the faults of illness as the faults of the time." The two actions of the king here are complementary: the king purifies, but he does not excuse the evils (of illness) as the evils of the age. To refuse in this way to attribute the wrongdoings in question to cosmic bad times as universal extenuating circumstances can signify a refusal to clear the criminals of their crimes. In this interpretation at least, the savior-king's pardon does not necessarily annul the responsibility of the guilty parties. Such a conception of a two-tiered system is not explicit in the first reading given above, yet neither is it absent. With the king "washing away everyone's faults, cleansing the faults which were illness [brought about by] the faults of the cosmic age," stanza XV acknowledges individual responsibility in the very act of erasing it. The king's pardon operates only as it supercedes individual fault, or in other words, as it heals *karmic* obstructions.

Leper Kings

The most immediate heritage left by Jayavarman VII in this domain is arguably the legend of the leper king. The legend of the leper king is not exclusively Khmer and very probably not native to Cambodia. Various Indian literary traditions contain a tale of a leper king, which can in fact be read as a version of the Rāma story. Banished from his kingdom, the Indian leper king retreats into the forest, where he is healed. He meets a leprous princess also banished for her illness, whom he cures and marries. The two build a new kingdom in the forest.[12] The story in Cambodia has multiple incarnations. The earliest written evidence comes from Zhou Daguan, the Chinese emissary to Angkor at the end of the thirteenth century. Zhou Daguan's record is noteworthy as testimony not only to the antiquity of the legend, but also to an intriguing relationship between the king and the people by way of this particular disease. According to the Chinese emissary, Khmers suffering from leprosy were given special treatment *because* they were associated with a certain leper king. In his *Memoirs on the Customs of Cambodia,* Zhou Daguan writes the following:

> The people of this country heal many of their ordinary diseases by plunging into the water and repeatedly washing the head. Yet there are many lepers along the roads. Even when the lepers come to sleep with them, to eat with them, the local people do not resist. Some say it is a disease due to the climactic conditions of the country. There was a king who contracted this disease; that is why the people do not consider it with disdain. (Pelliot 1997 [1951], 23–24)

In numerous versions the leper king reigns over a neighboring kingdom and has committed some sort of moral offense, such as adultery. A pair of fake healers gains the king's confidence. Pretending to administer him a remedy, they instead bring about his death.[13] In one story told by certain inhabitants of the Angkor region today, the leper king is Braḥ Thoṅ, who founded Cambodia out of Kok Thlok Island. This young prince, himself originally banished from his father's kingdom, marries a *nāga* princess. Having blessed their union, and before returning to his underground watery kingdom, the *nāga*-king-father forbids his son-in-law to have four faces sculpted on the towers of his new royal city. The young king disobeys, and when the princess' father emerges to visit the new city, his powers are vanquished by those of the four faces. The *nāga*-king-father attempts to retreat but is forcefully drawn into the city, where he then continues to live in the central well of the Bayon Temple, at the city center, emerging from time to time to visit his daughter and attempt to kill his son-in-law. The latter kills him instead. But in the process, the *nāga* king's venom and blood stain the prince's skin. Before dying, the *nāga* king warns Braḥ Thoṅ not to attempt to clean the stains from his body. However, trying to hide the murder from his wife, Braḥ Thoṅ again disobeys his father-in-law. Soon thereafter Braḥ Thoṅ contracts leprosy. Some renowned healers urge him to commit suicide, so as to be resuscitated with a healthy body, but the king is wary of such an operation, and he tests out the remedy, unsuccessfully, on a monk. Upon discovering the effective murder of the monk, the healers banish the king to the forest and condemn Angkor Thom to be thereafter governed by monkeys. The king finds respite in the Kulen Mountains, where he is cured (Lam and So 1997, 67–71).

This story is thought to be represented in bas-reliefs at the Bayon, a temple built by Jayavarman VII in the center of his capital city (fig. 4.1, *a–f*).[14] In the northeastern corner of the temple's inner gallery, the reliefs, thought to have been carved soon after Jayavarman VII's reign, are generally interpreted as follows: a king and queen are in their palace. Onlookers comment as the king battles a *nāga*. After defeating the serpent, the king sends his servants in search of wise healers in the forest. Seated in his palace, the king is surrounded by women who examine his hands. Next, a wise man stands by the monarch, who is prostrate. The story is thought by some to conclude with an adjoining scene, which depicts the liberation of a woman (or a female statue) imprisoned within a cave, a rock, or a temple. She has been seen to represent the curative source discovered by the king in the forest.[15]

If Jayavarman VII was, as he says, a suffering king, there is also reason to believe that he was simultaneously responsible for suffering among his subjects. This was the opinion of Coedès, who went so far as to attribute the final fall of Angkor to the "megalomania" of Jayavarman VII (Coedès 1943, 205; 1963, 106). In Foucauldian terms, we are confronted in the Hospital Edicts, and through the event they constitute, with a somewhat ambiguous situation. On the one hand we have aspects of a classical sovereign power regime, based on a right to kill or cause death, while on the other we simultaneously have aspects of a "bio-power," based on the management of life (Foucault 1976, 184). Thus the king could simultaneously levy armies, thereby exercising his power of death over his subjects, and build hospitals as a result of his power to control his subjects' lives. Foucault of course recognizes the associations, interactions, and historical overlappings of these two power regimes in the West and the ambiguous compromises this can produce. Yet his argumentation is predicated on a strong periodization (bio-power historically supplanting sovereign power) and relies heavily on a binary logic of noncontradiction (controlling life is the opposite of controlling death, etc.). It seems to me necessary to attempt a deconstruction of this Foucauldian opposition, which would

Fig. 4.1 *(a–f)* Leper king reliefs, the Bayon. Drawings by Meas Saran

allow us to see the structures and strategies of "bio-power" as inseparable from the sovereign power regime itself. One key to understanding the mechanisms that make possible this apparent contradiction in terms is the system of substitution I have been discussing here. Foucault's (1976 ,180) historicized shift, "wars are no longer waged in the name of the sovereign who must be defended; they are waged in the name of the existence of all," may be reconsidered in light of the medieval European king as "Corporation sole," and then sovereignty as expressed in Buddhist constructs examined here. Understandings of the paradoxical dual practice of power that has long been noted in the tradition of the *Buddhist-king* (itself a powerful contradiction in terms) can, I believe, be furthered through examination of the system of substitution that allows for the sovereign to stand in for the all, and thereby for sovereign power to function hand in hand with bio-power.

Such an approach is hard to resist with regard to our Cambodian example if only because Jayavarman VII seems to have simultaneously manipulated sovereign power and bio-power with great address, and there is no reason to think there was any incompatibility between them in his hands. In other words, the classical opposition between life and death, and the periodizing historical shift upon which Foucault's analysis is based, seems to isolate what might be described as complementary and interdependent dimensions of Buddhist kingship as construed by Jayavarman VII.

It is my contention that the legend of the leper king, and more generally the discourse on the "suffering king" I have underlined in the Hospital Edicts and to which I shall return shortly in a contemporary example, participates in the constitution of what we might call a *spectral structure of power*—a very real power, but that does not necessarily intervene in people's lives or deaths in a fully present manner. Rather, part of its insufferable strength comes from a certain staging of absence, or departure.

Before pursuing this question, let us pause briefly at the Bayon and its "leper king" bas-reliefs. These constitute only a small part of a monumental panorama of mythical/historical representations associated with the reign of Jayavarman VII covering two concentric galleries of the Bayon. Various other pieces of evidence—including the well-known "leper king" statue, which I will come back to in a moment—support the hypothesis that the legend of the leper king was associated with Jayavarman VII, if not during his reign at least shortly thereafter.[16] Though I believe this hypothesis to be true, I do not mean to suggest that Jayavarman VII actually had leprosy, or that, as has been suggested in the past, his manifest concern for public health necessarily derived from his own personal health problems; nor do I mean to suggest that the leper-king legend in Cambodia originated or should be seen exclusively in conjunction with Jayavarman VII. I propose rather to examine a number of elements of the legend in view of illuminating certain of its conceptual underpinnings, which may at least partially account for the association of Jayavarman VII with the leper king.

First, I want to consider how the legend of the leper king can be read as a metaphorical representation of kingship in general. That is, how the leper king may be seen to represent all kings, and perhaps in particular Buddhist kings. In the first version of the legend mentioned above, the leprous king, without having committed any moral offense, is banished from his city. In the second version, he is an immoral man reigning over a foreign city. In the third, he is first not leprous and carries no moral stigma, but is banished all the same; later, having contracted leprosy after committing patricide, and then being responsible for the death of a monk, he is again banished from his own kingdom.

In each version of the legend, whether or not he has a visible illness, the king's body is considered tainted. The royal body, like a foreign body, threatens to infect the body of the kingdom and must be expelled. In the last version of the legend summarized above, the otherwise good king literally has blood on his hands. The moral offense is, however, ambiguous; although he is guilty of patricide, the crime was committed in self-defense, that is, in defense of the ruling king's body and thus in defense of the kingdom. In this sense, kings are all patriregicides: in ascending the throne, they have all put the previous king, literally or symbolically their father, to rest. A king must do away with a king in order to become one. The king is dead; long live the king. This is the very principle of the king's two bodies. Insofar as the king necessarily takes on this curse of kingship, he represents at once the body proper of the kingdom and its greatest threat. So it comes as no surprise that even as the king is venerated and protected, a propensity to banish him or to imprison him, within the walls of a palace, for example, should be festering just below the surface. Indeed, rather than being incompatible opposites, banishment and imprisonment, thrusting out and cloistering within, are in fact equivalent responses to the same malefic potentiality intrinsic to kingship.

Leprosy figures the royal blessing-that-is-a-curse in a particularly graphic manner. In medieval England and France, the king was thought to possess miraculous powers to heal the people of leprosy, or a disease that can resemble leprosy, scrofula, and the "King's Evil" (Bloch 1983, xvi, 28). The fact that leprosy can take spontaneously remitting forms undoubtedly contributed to the royal reputation for miracles, and this must have played a part in its selection as the object of the king's attention. Yet I believe the widespread transcultural association of this particular disease with the king, and particularly with the king as healer of the people, has more profound roots and ramifications. The name "King's Evil" is particularly telling: a disease that in statistical terms belongs to the people is called "the king's disease," symbolizing precisely the mirror relationship between the people and the king.

Leprosy is a physical mutilation of the body. Like Prajāpati, the creator of the universe who is perpetually dismembered in order to be re-membered, or the Bull, whose legs are progressively mutilated to be refigured intact by the restoration king, the king must embody the dismemberment of the kingdom so that it may again be renewed. Here, too, spontaneous remittal undoubtedly plays a role in the association of leprosy with the king. Indeed, beginning with the foundation of Kambujā by Braḥ Thoṅ on the island of Kok Thlok, and ending with the banishment of Braḥ Thoṅ the leper king and the abandonment of Angkor Thom, the story mentioned above recounts the cycle of the kingdom's creation and disintegration.

The statue of the leper king offers another key to understanding the legend and its historical implications (fig. 4.2). This statue, stylistically dated to the Bayon or post-Bayon period, was noted by foreign researchers in the late nineteenth century. At that time, it was venerated as the leper king, founder of Angkor Thom, and situated atop a stone terrace in the royal plaza of Angkor Thom to the northeast of the royal palace site. For a number of different reasons, it is thought that during the Angkor period, a tribunal may have been situated here, perhaps adjoining the royal cremation ground.[17] A brief inscription, dated by its writing style to the fourteenth or fifteenth century, identifies the statue in Sanskrit as "Dharmādhipati Adhirāja" (King of kings, Lord of the *dharma*)—a royal title, of course, but also a common name for Yama, the God of Justice, and of Death (Coedès 1929, 83–84). This identification of the statue with Yama has been shown to be at the origin of the modern Khmer appellation "*stec gaṃlaṅ*'" (Au 1968). The modern term "*gaṃlaṅ*'"

Fig. 4.2 Leper king statue, Angkor Thom (M. Coe)

(leprous), seems to be a phonetic distortion of the ancient Khmer "*kanloṅ*," meaning both "the way" or "the Law" (that is, the *dharma*) and "past, deceased." So the "Leper King," "*stec gaṃlaṅ*'," is very likely to have once been *stec kanloṅ*, which can be translated as "the god of law who is the god of death." This seemingly superficial, phonetic association reflects, I believe, an underlying conceptual association linking death and justice with the body of a leprous king. As the upholder of *dharma*, or more precisely as the incarnation of *dharma*, the Buddhist king, or Dharmarāja, is conflated with the god of justice and death. It is thus perfectly logical that a statue of Yama was worshiped as an image of the founder of Angkor Thom, a renowned Buddhist king. In this sense the legends noted by visitors in the nineteenth century are a form of historical memory that reaches back to the end of the Angkor period.

Yet one might still ask why the god of death and justice should be seen as a *leprous* king. Though this somewhat uncharacteristic statue was relatively degraded and spotted with lichen by the nineteenth century, I do not believe we can attribute the appellation solely to its physical appearance. But if, as I am suggesting, the association of this statue with the leper king is a cultural memory or vestige of Jayavarman VII's reign, the incorporation of the modern appearance of the statue into the "memory" attests to the vitality of the creative, or rather re-creative, cultural processes involved. The physical appearance of the statue, like the subsequent phonetic associations of the statue's name, was integrated into the cultural manifold.

But there is a deeper logic at work here that hinges on the substitute body of the king. In the legend of the leper king, the king's natural body becomes a substitute for his political or mystical body: the king takes the ills of the kingdom upon himself by means of his political body, being that of the institution of the kingship, but through the mythological displacement or substitution, the ills manifest themselves in his natural body. Now, according to the doctrine of the king's two bodies, the body politic is by definition immortal—"*le roi ne meurt jamais*"[18]—and is not "subject to Infirmities and Accidents."[19] So the interpretation I am suggesting of the leper king, in which the leprosy of the king affects only his natural body insofar as it concerns his political body and thereby constitutes the representation of a critical threat to the kingship and the kingdom, reflects in an interesting way on the two bodies model. The doctrine of the immortality of the political or mystical king serves to favor the longevity of the regime, but this doctrine can hold "true" only so long as the succession succeeds, so long as the cry "The king is dead! Long live the king" continues to performatively cement the unity of the kingship across the discontinuities between kings. The leper king, in contrast, is a sign of a regime in peril.

So it is no surprise that Cambodia's leper king is also the king who rebuilt the kingdom better than ever before. Jayavarman VII's epigraphic exegesis of the conjunction of physical health and social justice embodied by the king is given full form in the legend and its artistic representations at the Bayon. Suffering with the people's suffering, the king in these scenes finds the curative source for his own body, thereby implicitly curing the body politic. And in the process, in one way or another, he liberates a prisoner. This liberation, recalling the royal power of pardon, can in itself be seen as the cure, the event, and the result of the healing.

Recollections of Lovek

The legend of the fall of the Khmer capital at Lovek at the end of the sixteenth century tells of the immanence of the Dharmarāja and the kingdom in the substitute body of a statue. This story, as recorded in Cambodia's royal chronicles, taught in schools and told at the site of Lovek today, is based upon a conception of the interdependent integrity of the king's body natural, body politic, and body of the *dharma,* so to speak. Unable to conquer the Khmer capital at Lovek by sheer military means, the Siamese king devised a ruse by which two men versed in magic were disguised as monks and sent into Cambodia, which was at that time suffering from epidemics and famine. Traveling the Khmer countryside, the false monks worked as a team, one of them causing illness that the other would then heal. The reputation of the miraculous healers reached the Khmer king, who summoned them to his court. After their arrival, the king repeatedly fell ill only to be healed at their hands. They announced that the true source of the king's illness was to be found in the powerful and malevolent Buddha images of the royal city, in particular the colossal four-faced Buddha erected at the center of the city by the monarch's grandfather when he founded the capital. Much like the Bayon of Jayavarman VII, this four-faced Buddha represented the seat of royal power at the center of the kingdom and was intimately associated with the image of the king himself. Indeed, to cure the king's illness, the false healers proclaimed that it was necessary to dismantle the powerful statues. Following their advice, the sick king had the four-faced Buddha thrown into the river (Vāṃṅ Juon 1929, 1934, 248–249; Khin Sok 1988, 192–193).[20] However, rather than curing the king's physical ills, this action brought a series of calamities to the kingdom, which fell to the Siamese forces soon thereafter. Again, the illness that ravaged the kingdom is projected onto the king's very body and vice-versa. The destruction of his substitute body, here the body of the Buddha at the center of the capital, signifies the destruction of the kingdom and hence the sovereignty of the king.

Modern Times

As Freud noted, the king must both be guarded and guarded against. The father of psychoanalysis was of course interested in the "ambivalence of emotions." But in view of this double valence of kingship, it is not surprising that in various cultures the king is periodically expelled, physically or symbolically, during ritual ceremonies that serve to renew the precarious integrity of the kingdom. The bad is expelled and the good is retained, but, since kingship is essentially ambivalent, this purifying gesture must be periodically repeated.

A number of ceremonies performed in Cambodia around the New Year can be understood in terms of such an ambivalent response to the inevitable royal duplicity. The ritual of Stec Māgh, during which the "true" king abdicated to be replaced by a temporary king for a period of days, was practiced at court into the nineteenth century. This temporary king was seen to take on the "calamities" *(groḥ)* of the kingdom, thereby symbolically relieving the true king of this undesirable charge. In the Siamese version of the ritual (which was, unlike its Khmer counterpart, relatively well documented by foreign observers), the temporary king levied taxes at will. He and his temporary court were held in contempt, even attacked by the angry populace (see Leclère 1917, 292–318; Porée-Maspero 1969, 3, 579–649; Commission des Moeurs et Coutumes 1985, 79–82). Another ritual performed at the New Year, the royal Trot ceremony, aims to exorcise evil spirits from the body of the king in order to purify the kingdom. The evil spirits are called into the king, seated on his throne, after which they are dramatically expelled. The popular ceremonial dance, also called Trot, as well as other popular events around the New Year, retain the vestiges of a ritual regicide. In this ambulant dance drama that is traditionally performed to ensure the spiritual renewal of the village, town, city, or kingdom, a group of hunters symbolically kills what I interpret to be a metaphorical or metonymical substitute for the king: a deer, or sometimes the Buddha.[21]

Certain recurring aspects of Norodom Sihanouk's political "activities," in particular what I would call his "strategy of abdication," while generally responding in a unique and original manner to unprecedented sociopolitical situations, can be seen as rooted in these traditional ritual practices. The modern monarch's first abdication was effectively predicated on the concept of the king's multiple bodies. The king as a "Corporation sole" is elected by grace, perhaps, but not by democratic vote. In fact democracy ought to be entirely incompatible with the structures of kingship that I have been describing here. The king's body may be prone to infinite substitution, but he is nonetheless irreplaceable. Or rather, a king is irreplaceably replaceable. The substitution of bodies cannot simply obey the changing course of public opinion as reflected in polls or elections. A king must be king in spite of the people and in spite of himself. This is the heart of the issue, and it accounts for the potential shortcomings as well as the hopeful possibilities embodied in the superimposed multiplicity of kingship, and particularly with regard to the kingdom of Cambodia. This principle of substitution by which a part at one level stands in for a whole at another level (e.g., the body of the king as member of society standing in for the body of the whole society) can function only if at each stage the body in question enters into an exchange with a second body greater than itself, or at least one that is not subsumed or commanded by the first body as such. This is the source, I would argue, of the healing power of the king: the belief that the part on another level is a whole, such that the sick body (a dismembered part), if metonymically associated with or substituted for by the unique part that is the body of the king, can be healed (made whole) through such a relation to the transcendent wholeness of this regal part.

However, this principle is also what seems most incompatible with democracy, because according to the concept of democratic representation, the whole is simply the sum of the parts, and its representatives are chosen by arithmetic tally. A body is a body. A vote is a vote. There is, or should be, no particular part (a "king") that simultaneously gives body to the whole. Yet in playing on the distinction between the king's natural and mystic bodies, Sihanouk has used the resources of a certain deconstruction of this apparently implacable opposition between kingship and democracy.

Sihanouk's first abdication in 1955, when he placed his father on the throne as temporary substitute, was, from this perspective, a kind of ritual regi-sui-cide committed to protect the king, the kingship, and the kingdom in the encounter with democracy. Since returning to the throne in the 1990s, the king has repeatedly threatened abdication; furthermore, his repeated departures from the country, or his repeated announcements of withdrawal from public life, can be seen as virtual—or ritual—abdication aimed at purifying the kingship itself. Even his most vehement detractors, who see the king as the incarnation of the ills of the nation, are in fact firmly under the royal spell. By suggesting today, in an echo of some of General Lon Nol's cohorts, that the king's expulsion would restore Cambodia's integrity, they inscribe their purportedly republican discourse in this same conception of the king's substitute body.

The constant media and highly political fascination with the present king's health is further indication of the continued relevance of this royal tradition. The *Monthly Documentation Bulletin* produced by the royal cabinet provides extensive information on current events, including newspaper clippings with the king's personal commentary, photocopies of official and personal communications, accounts of royal audiences, and so on. The very first entry, at the head of each *Bulletin,* is a list of the monarch's "activities," including each of the monarch's numerous medical visits. Detailed royal medical reports are also periodically issued to the local press. The health of the king becomes crucial at times of political tension: when the body of the nation threatens to disintegrate, the king's body is especially at risk.

The perceived conflation of royal and national health motivates political strategies of all colors. In 1998, after a problematic national election, Prime Minister Hun Sen called on opposition leaders denouncing electoral fraud to resolve their conflict immediately in order to allow King Sihanouk to leave the country for urgent medical treatment. The implication was that dissension within the government threatens to harm the king's body, and the king's recovery will in turn mean the recovery of national stability. On another level, of course, this plea could be read as the poorly veiled expression of a desire to banish the king. Whether the "Strongman" prime minister was concerned with expelling the king so as to effectively substitute his own body for the king's or with healing the king's body in order to heal that of the nation, the conceptual basis of his plea remains the same: the potential for substitution among these multiple bodies of the kingdom.

Indeed, each of Sihanouk's ceremonial and periodic departures is a new banishment of this emissary charged with the calamities of the kingdom. The power of a king who makes use of his own absence is certainly a weak power. Yet it is an unrepealable, irreplaceable, and thus insuperable power, because an absent king is destined to return.

Notes

This is a revised version of portions of chapter 4 of my Ph.D. dissertation, "Mémoires du Cambodge." Many thanks, again, to D. Chandler, P. Jaini, and A. von Rospatt for their comments.

1. Frazer (1911) does not use this phrase, but in a sense his whole project concerns the *scapegoat king.*

2. The economical double use of the verb "to guard" comes from Frazer 1911; see also Derrida 1995, 125.

3. For a discussion of this phenomenon in the larger Indian context, see Snodgrass 1985, esp. chaps. 8 and 22.

4. Seventeen of these inscriptions, known as the Hospital Edicts, are identified in vol. 7 of the *Inscriptions du Cambodge* (Coedès 1937–1966). The reconstitution and translation of the text was first undertaken by Finot (1903, 18–33). Next, Barth consulted other rubbings of the inscription in order to complete and improve upon Finot's work (Barth 1903, 460–466). My renditions of the text draw on both Finot and Barth. Due to space limitations, the Sanskrit stanzas of the Hospital Edicts could not be included in this volume.

5. It is tempting to read this as a Buddhist deconstruction of "metaphysical" or "onto-theological" binary oppositions, though such a project, and the all-important questions of translation it cannot help but raise, lies beyond the scope of the present chapter.

6. Although there is not enough space here to discuss the details of the exchange, it should be noted that the opening passage of the Hospital Edicts, in giving homage to the Buddha as manifest in multiple bodies rendering the single *dharma*-body, also constitutes a portrait of the king. For reflections on this phenomenon in its Khmer context, see Coedès 1960, 179–198; and 1963.

7. Schopen, drawing on textual evidence from Gilgit, argues that modern scholars have overemphasized the strict identification of Bhaiṣajyaguru with healing. Rather, the Bhaiṣajyaguru is "potentially active in any situation which is connected with the fear of death or

the implementation of the effect of one's past actions" (Schopen 1978, 133). Birnbaum (1979) argues that the Bhaiṣajyaguru was associated with the healing of both physical sickness and *karmic* obstructions.

8. Little is known about the Khmer appropriation of the Bhaiṣajyaguru, and no complete versions of the *sūtra* have yet been identified in Cambodia, but the cult seems to have emerged at Angkor during a time when it was popular in Central and East Asian Buddhism; see Birnbaum 1979, 55–56.

9. See Coedès' reading of K. 485 (1930, 319–325).

10. Like Benveniste (1969, 8), I see no reason to exclude the possibility of "relations of correspondence" between languages of the Indo-European family and others like Khmer that are outside of it. What is at issue here is precisely this type of link between an inside and an outside, particularly as evinced by the scapegoat king and the royal pardon, "institutions," to use Benevistes' term, "in a broad sense" (1969, 9).

11. See chap. 1 in this volume for a discussion of these issues in the Khmer context during the Middle period.

12. For a résumé of the story, see Malalasekera 1974 [1938], 689–690.

13. Porée-Maspéro 1962–1969, 1, 116; 1962–1969, 3, 669–670, 677, 728, published various versions of the story, from Cambodia and elsewhere.

14. See Coral Rémusat 1940, 93–94.

15. Pursuing suggestions made by other scholars, Goloubew (1936, 566–567) was the first researcher to decipher the legendary sequence in these reliefs. The reading of the final scene was first proposed by Bosch (1932, 496–497, pl. CIX).

16. See in particular Goloubew 1936; Finot and Goloubew 1931; Goloubew 1925; Coedès 1929a; and Groslier 1969. For a thorough discussion of most of the primary and secondary sources concerning the Cambodian leper king known to date, see Chandler 1996b, 3–14. Chandler hypothesizes that the legend does not refer to Jayavarman VII but to his successor, Indravarman II.

17. See Barth and Bergaigne 1893, 97–117; Pelliot 1997 [1951], 12, 23, 35; Groslier 1969, 18–33; 1973, 128–129, 254–255.

18. The maxim "The king never dies" has been known in France since at least the sixteenth century (Kantorowicz 1997 [1957], 409).

19. Plowden, cited in Kantorowicz 1997 [1957], 14.

20. For other versions, see Villemereuil 1883, 289–291; and Moura 1883, 2:51.

21. In his far-reaching study of Trot, Lévy (1981–1984) clearly demonstrates that Trot is (or incorporates) the ritual staging of regicide.

-5-

Stec Gaṃlaṅ' and Yāy Deb

Worshiping Kings and Queens in Cambodia Today

Hang Chan Sophea

Cambodia shares a general system of beliefs with other neighboring countries: worship of mountains or other *tumuli* such as termite hills in which territorial spirits or other supernatural powers are thought to reside. These beliefs are typically labeled animism. Worship of such entities strives for the most part to ward off accident, danger, drought, and illness and to ensure well-being and prosperity. As these animist beliefs merged with more formalized religions first developed in what is now called India and were transported into ancient Cambodia, the physical and cultural characteristics of ancient Cambodia so well known today—its *prāsād* and statues—came into being. So, too, did Khmer systems of kingship develop through this fusion of religious systems, such that the greatest territorial spirit of the land, the king himself, was embodied by a great mountain temple sheltering statues representing the greatest gods.

Though these ancient sites and objects of worship may no longer carry the precise religious meaning they once did, many continue to be venerated today. In the following pages, I will study the contemporary worship of two virtually identical ancient statues and their numerous modern copies, all of which are considered to be of particular importance on a national level. These statues, located in the modern capital of Phnom Penh and the ancient capital of Angkor, are associated with Cambodia's monarchy in a variety of ways: some are venerated by today's king and queen and other members of the royal family; some are worshiped as both representations of an ancient king and incarnations and are, in one way or another, associated with today's king. While the king himself may not be worshiped as a god, through the intermediary of these images, the king is nonetheless endowed with divine stature. I aim to demonstrate a certain continuity in Khmer tradition from ancient to modern times despite, and perhaps even because of, major changes in religious and political structures.

Stec Gaṃlaṅ', or the "Leper King" of the National Museum

A statue traditionally known as Stec Gaṃlaṅ', or the "leper king" (pronounced "sdach kamlong"), is currently exhibited, as it was prior to recent wars, at the center of the inner courtyard of Phnom Penh's National Museum, situated to the north of the royal palace (fig. 5.1).[1] The statue is facing east in an open-air pavilion

Fig. 5.1 Leper King statue, National Museum, Phnom Penh (Hang Chan Sophea)

with a pyramidal roof erected at the crossroads of four paths leading out from each of the museum's four galleries, forming an enclosure around this courtyard. Surrounded by a miniature moat built into the raised platform of the pavilion, the statue stands alone, as if on an island. An incense receptacle is placed directly in front of the statue.

The leper king is sculpted in sandstone. He is seated with the left leg folded in toward the body and the right leg bent up. The last three toes of the right foot have been broken off. The left hand rests on the left knee; the right hand, of which only the base of the palm remains, is placed on the right knee. It is thought that this hand once held an attribute, probably a baton. A moustache is sculpted in low relief above the figure's fleshy lips, from which two fanglike teeth emerge. The hair is sculpted in long rows of curls draping over the statue's nape. Some hair is gathered in a bun at the summit of the head. These details, along with the modeling of the somewhat elongated torso with imposing, wide shoulders, distinguish this statue from typical Angkorean art.

Thought to date to the reign of Jayavarman VII (late twelfth to early thirteenth century) or soon thereafter, the leper king was first documented by researchers in the late nineteenth century, at which time it was worshiped atop a raised cruciform terrace to the northeast of the ancient royal palace site in Angkor Thom. This terrace, built during or shortly after the reign of Jayavarman VII, was in the nineteenth century—and is still today—called the "terrace of the leper king." The legend of this king, founder of Angkor who was inflicted with leprosy, was recorded by researchers at that time; the story is told today at Angkor often in specific association with the Bayon temple. Multiple versions of the leper king story, associated with the Bayon or the Kulen Mountains north of the Angkor plain, are told today throughout the country. Iconographic, epigraphic, and other linguistic evidence suggests, however, that at its origin the statue was meant to represent Yama, the god of death.[2] The statue was eventually transferred to the National Museum in Phnom Penh for safekeeping.[3]

Contemporary Worship

The central location of the leper king statue in the National Museum is the first indicator of its importance, not in artistic terms (for this statue is artistically less notable than many other Angkorean period pieces), but rather for its sacred value. While other statues in the museum are also worshiped,[4] museum employees consider the leper king statue to be the "assembly point" *(dī ruom* or *dī prajuṃ)* of the museum's supernatural powers *(pāramī).* (See also the discussion of *pāramī* in chap. 7). Particularly on holy days *(thṅai sīl),* flowers, incense, and candles are offered to this statue by museum or other Ministry of Culture staff as well as pilgrims from the outside. The museum waives entry fees for individuals or small groups wishing to worship this or other statues. Worshipers ask the statue, or rather its *pāramī*, to ensure health and prosperity for themselves, their families, or communities, particularly after or during times of trouble (disputes, accidents) or before projected danger (investment, elections, etc.). In the latter case, after the danger has passed and success has been ensured, special offerings are made to the statue. Students from the nearby University of Fine Arts (southern campus) worship the statue most fervently during examination periods. Special ceremonies are held by the museum staff two times per year: during the Celebration of the Dead (Bhjuṃ Piṇḍ) and at the traditional New Year. Monks are invited to recite chants in the museum offices on the second floor, after which trays of offerings, including rice, sweets, water, betel nut and areca leaves, are brought to the leper king. A classic percussion and wind ensemble *(biṇbādy)* performs a musical offering to the statue. Other statues may be venerated during these ceremonial times, yet the leper king is clearly the central and most prominent object of worship.[5]

Yāy Deb, Siem Reap Town

The statue known as Yāy Deb, or "divine female ancestor" (pronounced "yeay tep"), faces east under a *bodhi* tree *(Ficus religiosa)* on a traffic island (site in the middle of a roadway where no traffic is allowed) northwest of the king's residence in Siem Reap Town. Like the emplacement of the leper king in Phnom Penh, Yāy Deb's location is central to the town of Siem Reap. In September 1998, just days before an intergovernmental summit presided over by King Sihanouk to resolve conflict between warring factions following the July 1998 elections, the king and queen sponsored the construction and consecration of a pavilion with a pyramidal roof to shelter the statue there (fig. 5.2).

The Yāy Deb statue is virtually identical to the leper king exhibited at the National Museum, with one notable exception: Yāy Deb has no fangs. Thought to be contemporaneous with the leper king, Yāy Deb was found by early researchers at Wat Khnat Rangsei, a Buddhist pagoda built on a pre-Angkorean temple site south of the Western Baray. During the Khmer Rouge period the statue was broken into pieces and thrown into a pond in nearby Wat Damnak. Like many other statues at the time, Yāy Deb's *pāramī* are said to have prevented the iconoclasts from totally destroying her or from dragging her far from her seat of power. Having recovered the different pieces in 1985, Siem Reap residents, including the staff of the Angkor Conservation Office, transferred the reconstituted statue from Wat Damnak to its original spot under the *bodhi* tree. Since the head had entirely disappeared, in 1988 the conservation office molded a replica in cement and attached it to the ancient stone body. Mistaken for an ancient original, this head was stolen soon thereafter. The conservation office attached a new cement head, which remains today.[6]

The fact that this statue sculpted with masculine physical traits is worshiped today as a woman does not shock the traditional Khmer sensibility. Nor is it considered odd that two virtually identical statues are worshiped at once as male and female. When asked about this phenomenon, one National Museum employee explained that "the double title does not mean that these are two different statues because the statues are of a single divinity worshiped since ancient times. The masculine and the feminine cannot be divided one from the other; each is rather one manifestation of the divinity, which can appear as masculine or feminine according to different conjunctions of time and space."[7] Nonetheless, while Phnom Penh residents may recognize the feminine counterpart of the leper king in Yāy Deb, interviews with worshipers of Yāy Deb in Siem Reap suggest that few people in the provincial town know that the masculine counterpart is today the National Museum's central idol.

Fig. 5.2 Yāy Deb shrine, Siem Reap Town (Hang Chan Sophea)

Contemporary Worship

Siem Reap residents believe fervently in the *pāramī* of Yāy Deb. Multiple offerings are made to the statue on a daily basis. She is also worshiped by people from beyond the town and province.[8] Draped permanently in red and saffron robes, Yāy Deb is also regularly made up with face powders, creams, and lipstick. One of the shrine's caretakers recounts that it is primarily prostitutes who make up Yāy Deb; it is believed that if she is beautiful, those who worship her in this way will be equally so. Red fingernail polish is also periodically used to draw fangs sticking out of the statue's mouth. The divinity is reputed to most appreciate "crucified chicken" *(mān' chkaṅ)* or other types of raw, bloody flesh, and "savage liquor" *(aka sāhāv).*[9] Worshipers typically remove the meat from a chicken before spreading its wings and attaching it to a wooden cross; the crucified chicken is propped up at the statue's base. Rice alcohol is poured over a small bowl of rice, directly onto the chicken, or into a miniature cup. Offerings also include bananas and traditional cult accessories made of coconuts and areca leaves *(slā dharm tuṅ).* Live chickens are also released in front of the statue in an act seen to symbolize, if not magically realize, the divinity eating the chicken. On holy days *(thṅai sīl),* the devotees make offerings from dawn to dusk. An annual ceremony is performed in Yāy Deb's honor, during the lunar months of Phalgun or Chet, before the traditional New Year. People from all walks of life, from the town and the countryside of Siem Reap, come together for this event.

When in residence in Siem Reap, and notably on holy days, Cambodia's reigning king and queen regularly present the statue with offerings of cigarettes, betel nut and areca leaves, sweets and other food, as well as flowers. Siem Reap's military leaders are also known to solicit Yāy Deb's assistance before undertaking military campaigns, and of course to give thanks for services rendered with the savored chicken and alcohol offerings.

Local vendors and caretakers who have set up around the neighboring Nāṅ Cek-Nāṅ Cam pavilion sell photographs of Yāy Deb, along with cult accessories such as incense, candles, and lotus flowers. The faithful and the superstitious can also buy plastic pendants with miniature pictures of Yāy Deb, Nāṅ Cek-Nāṅ Cam, and Braḥ Aṅg Taṅkoe, a divinity embodied in a statue of Avalokiteśvara housed and worshiped before the royal palace in Phnom Penh. Since the reopening of public access to the Kulen Mountains, reproductions of Braḥ Aṅg Dhaṃ, the colossal reclining Buddha atop the Kulen, have recently been added to the repertoire of sacred images for sale here.

Yāy Deb of the National Museum

Another statue, identical to the leper king yet known as Yāy Deb, faces east under a *koki* tree[10] inside Phnom Penh's National Museum grounds, to the north of the museum building.[11] This is a precise cement copy of the museum's leper king, made, according to the statue's artisan Saen Chrik, in 1970 with the view of protecting the original inside the museum.[12] With rising insecurity across the country and in the capital, museum officials hoped to trick potential thieves into believing this exposed copy to be the original. Interestingly, this is, to my knowledge, the only such "security" copy displayed on the museum grounds. That the original leper king escaped recent wars unscathed is attributed by some to this stratagem, associated of course with the image's remarkable powers. Indeed, that the museum's entire statue collection remained intact is seen to directly result from the

Fig. 5.3 Yāy Deb shrine, National Museum, Phnom Penh (Hang Chan Sophea)

fact that the leper king, as the assembly point of the museum's *pāramī*, remained intact.

Contemporary Worship

Like the others described above, this statue of Yāy Deb is draped in a saffron robe. Worshipers consist primarily of museum staff and area residents, as well as students of the nearby University of Fine Arts (primarily during exams); relatively few people from beyond the immediate vicinity seem to know of this statue. Offerings like those mentioned above are made on a daily basis; more elaborate offerings, including *pāy sī* and other traditional cult accessories fashioned from banana trunk, are made on holy days. This statue is generally known by worshipers to be a cement copy of the original stone leper king, kept only meters away inside the museum, and a counterpart to Siem Reap's Yāy Deb. Some, like Saen Chrik, see the museum's Yāy Deb as a feminine manifestation of the leper king. This museum employee considers, moreover, that Phnom Penh's Yāy Deb is a substitution for Siem Reap's, allowing the divinity to be worshiped in both the ancient and modern capitals. Others consider Phnom Penh's Yāy Deb to be a divinity independent from these other images, her *pāramī* strong in their own right (fig. 5.3).

Braḥ Aṅg Săṅkh Cakr, Also known as Stec Gaṃlaṅ', Phnom Penh Riverfront

Braḥ Aṅg Săṅkh Cakr, or "august god (bearing) a conch and a disc," also known as Stec Gaṃlaṅ', faces east in a pyramidal-roofed pavilion along the Tonle Sap riverfront, directly in front of Wat Unnalom, the central wat and administrative headquarters of Cambodia's Mahānikāy sect. The pavilion is elaborately decorated with all sorts of colorful and gilt objects: curtains drawn to dramatically reveal the statue, miniature parasols flanking him, small statues, paper *pāy sī,* incense receptacles, photographs of other illustrious Buddha statues, and so on.

Braḥ Aṅg Săṅkh Cakr is reputed to have first been erected near this site in front of Wat Unnalom by King Norodom when the palace was moved from Oudong to Phnom Penh in the late nineteenth century in order to protect the new capital. During WW II-period bombings of this area, local residents sought shelter among the *stūpa* of Wat Unnalom and at this statue of Stec Gaṃlaṅ'; those who chose the *stūpa* are said to have died in the bombings, while those who sought the protection of Stec Gaṃlaṅ' are said to have survived. The statue was beheaded and repaired during the Lon Nol period, in the early 1970s.[13] Attempts to destroy the statue during the Khmer Rouge period were nearly successful. A Cham fisherman is reputed to have brought up the statue's head in his net cast near the site in the Tonle Sap River in the early 1980s. The body, however, has never been recovered. A Phnom Penh merchant purchased the head and, in 1993, offered it to King

Sihanouk after his return to the country and the throne. Members of the FUNC-INPEC party, led by two of Sihanouk's children, Norodom Ranariddh and Norodom Bopha Devi, and another, more distant royal relative, Chap Nhalyvuth,[14] sponsored the fabrication of a cement replica of the body. The new statue was consecrated before national elections in the same year.[15] It is a replica of the museum's leper king, with two notable exceptions: no fanglike teeth are showing, and this statue is complete, including toes, hands, and attribute (a bouquet of lotus buds).[16] The legend told in association with this statue is a variation on those told at Angkor, past and present.[17]

Contemporary Worship

Phnom Penh's City Hall employs a long-time local resident to care for the statue on a daily basis.[18] The majority of worshipers reside, or used to reside, in the immediate area. Many are ethnic Chinese and Vietnamese whose ancestors are said to have lived nearby on the riverbanks or in houseboats on the Tonle Sap until they were forcibly removed by the government as the city developed over the twentieth century. Many survivors of the bombings, as well as their descendants, regularly worship Braḥ Aṅg Săṅkh Cakr. The current caretaker recounts that a number of survivors' children now living abroad pay their respects to the statue when visiting Phnom Penh. According to this caretaker, in addition to the usual candles, incense, and flowers, specific offerings are made for specific purposes: mirrors are offered by those seeking to resolve marital problems; human images sculpted in clay, or dolls, are offered to cure long-term illness; a child's rattle *(kantae rae)* is offered by those searching for lost relatives; chicken, duck, or pork and fruit are offered by merchants seeking business success. Permanent accessories include Chinese divination sticks *(caṅkeḥ)*, which the caretaker will use, upon request, to tell a person's fortune. Braḥ Aṅg Săṅkh Cakr is venerated with particular fervor during the Auṃ Dịk festivities, ceremonial boat races held every November when the course of the Tonle Sap reverses, flowing south. Situated on the banks of the river, the statue has become a sort of tutelary god for contestants. Most often it is the dancer stationed at the boat's prow and thought to be endowed with the boat's supernatural energy who makes offerings to Braḥ Aṅg Săṅkh Cakr to request or thank this god for victory in the races. There is also an increase in the number of worshipers at Braḥ Aṅg Săṅkh Cakr when danger threatens the city—when, for example, grenades are set off, political factions are in confrontation, or elections are coming up.

Though the present king and queen themselves do not actually go to Braḥ Aṅg Săṅkh Cakr for worship, the royal palace regularly sends offerings to the statue on holy days, along with requests from the king to the caretaker to spread the statue's renown. When visiting Wat Unnalom, the king and queen are also said to pause at the temple entrance gate to pay their repects, through the car windows, to Braḥ

Aṅg Săṅkh Cakr. Members of the royal family who pay frequent visits to the statue include those FUNCINPEC party members cited above (fig. 5.4).

Stec Gaṃlaṅ', Wat Unnalom, Phnom Penh

Another cement replica of Stec Gaṃlaṅ' is currently displayed on a traffic island between Wat Unnalom and the river, just to the southwest of Braḥ Aṅg Săṅkh Cakr. According to the caretaker of the latter statue, this second Stec Gaṃlaṅ' was erected by members of the Cambodian People's Party (CPP) from City Hall before the national elections in 1993. The consecration of this statue was celebrated shortly after that of the previously described statue Braḥ Aṅg Săṅkh Cakr. The decision to found a second statue here was reputedly made after a group of City Hall CPP officials consulted a *grū* (healer/soothsayer) regarding upcoming elec-

Fig. 5.4 Braḥ Aṅg Săṅkh Cakr, Phnom Penh
(Hang Chan Sophea)

tions; the *grū,* a medium bearing the spirit of Stec Gaṃlaṅ', informed the officials that he could assist them only on the condition that they erect his statue in this highly visible city spot, exactly where, in fact, the "original" Stec Gaṃlaṅ' was worshiped before recent wars. Set facing north, this statue is another altered cement copy of the museum's leper king, without that statue's characteristic fangs and broken fingers and toes. It is displayed on a block pedestal and exposed to the open air (fig. 5.5).

Contemporary Worship

The lack of pomp in the statue's presentation corresponds to its relatively discreet cult. No caretaker is permanently assigned here, no annual ceremony seems to be held. Flowers and incense are offered by local residents on holy days, and occasionally by the statue's CPP City Hall founders.

Fig. 5.5 Stec Gaṃlaṅ', Wat Unnalom, Phnom Penh (Hang Chan Sophea)

Other Modern Replicas

Various other replicas of the Stec Gaṃlaṅ' statue have been erected in recent years in Siem Reap Province. Of particular note is the one currently displayed on Angkor Thom's terrace of the leper king. A copy of the original statue (made by the Angkor Conservation Office before transfer of the original to Phnom Penh in the 1960s) was placed on the terrace by restoration team members after completion of restoration work in 1999. Along with Yāy Deb of Siem Reap Town, the statue was fitted with a cement head in 1988. And like Yāy Deb's, this head was stolen; a replacement head was cast but never placed on Stec Gaṃlaṅ' for fear of a second theft. In 1999 a traditional healer from Phnom Penh was told by his spiritual master—the spirit of Stec Gaṃlaṅ'—that to maintain his healing powers he must place a new head on Stec Gaṃlaṅ' in Angkor Thom. This man and his family thus financed replacement of the head by the conservation office.[19] Now "complete," the statue sits at the center of the cruciform terrace facing east. The stone guardian statues, two of which were documented next to the leper king since the nineteenth century and the other two of which were found over the course of restoration work are now placed at the terrace's four extremities facing the cardinal points. An offering box belonging to Angkor Conservation Office authorities is placed before the statue, along with an incense receptacle.

In 1996 conservation office authorities themselves erected a cement replica of the leper king at the center of an inner open-air courtyard surrounded by newly renovated buildings inside the conservation office compound on the outskirts of Siem Reap Town. This statue is sheltered under a pavilion and faces east; incense is regularly offered in a receptacle placed at its base. Original plans to set this statue in its pavilion at the center of an artificial pond to be built in the courtyard were abandoned for financial reasons.

Another Stec Gaṃlaṅ' copy can be seen in the village of Kok Thnot on the northern dyke of the Western Baray. This cement copy was built here, along with a few other statues, as part of a tourism initiative by a local tour agency. Having encountered various authorization obstacles, the initiative was definitively abandoned after the 1997 coup d'êtat, when tourist numbers in the region plummeted. The statue would seem to be more or less neglected by local villagers, who continue, however, to worship other traditional tutelary spirits even in the absence of their physical representations—ancient statues stolen in recent years.

Conclusion

I would like to point to a few issues brought to light by this survey of contemporary worship of Stec Gaṃlaṅ' and Yāy Deb. The cult to these statues demonstrates how spiritual associations between the ancient and modern capitals of Cambodia are still maintained today. First, we should note that the same statues or replicas thereof are worshiped in both cities and that each of the statues is seen to play a role in maintaining national political integrity. More remarkably still, we should note the similar spatial configurations of these statues in each locality. Both of the ancient statues discussed here, Stec Gaṃlaṅ' of the National Museum (like all of its replicas in Phnom Penh) and Yāy Deb of Siem Reap Town, are situated to the north of the royal residence. Both are situated on an artificial island—as are the large majority of their replicas in both towns. The raised cruciform of the original leper king terrace has been reconstituted in the island accessed by four passageways of the Phnom Penh museum courtyard; likewise, the Angkor Conservation Office has replicated the museum configuration in its own leper king display. The cosmic significance of this configuration, seen repeatedly in Angkorean architectural design (e.g., a *prāsād* raised on a foundation and opening out to the four cardinal points) and reiterated in Khmer origin legends (kingdom born of an island), is well known. Here, I would like to call attention to the reconfiguration of this configuration in space and time. The many copies of Stec Gaṃlaṅ' discussed here represent more than an attempt to have the original image—or the power of the original—as one's own. Instead, they represent (or realize?) the reestablishment of cosmic order *(dharma/dhamma)* in the microsmic figure of a statue, a temple, or a capital city (all called *dharma* in ancient Khmer inscriptions). The association of each of these statues with the Khmer royalty, and with national political integrity, participates in and results from the statue's cosmic ordering role.

Notes

Translated and revised in collaboration with Ashley Thompson.

1. Inventoried as K. 1860.

2. For more details, see chap. 4.

3. According to Saen Chrik, who has been a National Museum, Plastic Arts Section employee since 1943, the statue was brought to the National Museum in 1960.

4. It is notable that the leper king is the only non-Buddhist image at the National Museum today to receive a religious cult. Unlike the many images of the Buddha that receive offerings of flowers, incense, and money from staff and museum visitors, the leper king statue is worshiped almost exclusively by Khmer devotees.

5. I have personally had the opportunity to observe this ceremony only during the New Year of 1998. An employee of the museum, Long Thul, kindly described the same ceremony as it is held at the Celebration of the Dead.

6. According to Nim Sun, vice-director of administration, Angkor Conservation Office.

7. Saen Chrik. We will see another interpretation of this phenomenon below.

8. Though this second class of worshiper would seem to be constituted largely of

people drawn primarily to the statues of Nāṅ Cek-Nāṅ Cam, displayed in a pavilion to the northeast of Yāy Deb. Having paid their homage to Nāṅ Cek-Nāṅ Cam, worshipers make additional offerings to Yāy Deb. Nāṅ Cek-Nāṅ Cam are, like the statues studied here, of national and regional importance.

9. Could we hypothesize that Yāy Deb's tastes derive from her origins as the god of death?

10. *Gagir (Hopea odorata).*

11. The statue has been in its current location for only a few years. Museum staff moved it from its previous location to the northwest of the museum building in the 1990s as the area became increasingly populated by squatters.

12. Saen Chrik, personal communication.

13. As described in the quotation by Harben in the introduction to Part 2.

14. Respectively holding the following positions in the 1998-elected government: president of the National Assembly, minister of culture, first governor of Siem Reap Province.

15. Information collected from worshipers and local residents, as well as Aum Khaem of Phnom Penh's Buddhist Institute and the statue's current caretaker, San Lon.

16. We should note the discrepancy between the statue's appellation and his physical reality. The name indicates an association with the god Viṣṇu, whose traditional attributes include a conch and a disc; yet there are no material associations with Viṣṇu discernable on the statue, neither in its ancient nor its modern forms. This anomaly should be further investigated, notably in light of the fact that Cambodia's kings, Buddhist or otherwise, have long been associated with Viṣṇu.

17. See chap. 4.

18. San Lon, personal communication.

19. According to Nim Sun of the Angkor Conservation Office and Vān Sary of the École Française d'Extrême-Orient.

PART III

The Ethnography of Contemporary Cambodian Religion

The ethnographies of Cambodian religion written before the Pol Pot period by Porée-Maspéro, Ebihara, Martel, and others emphasized—like most contemporaneous accounts of religion in agricultural societies—the seemingly timeless nature of religious life in small, autonomous communities. A new generation of anthropologists has questioned the implicit timelessness and autonomy of traditional models and sought new ways of framing ethnographic descriptions. Anthropologists of Cambodian religion are, in particular, confronted with the social changes that have come in the wake of the Pol Pot period, the fragility of village autonomy, the wholesale destruction and reinvention of religious practice. The three chapters in this section focus on this kind of flux. And in each case, the chapters consider religious ideas and spiritual leaders whose sphere of influence is not confined to the village but resonates throughout the region, sometimes even across national boundaries.

Nevertheless, it seems worthwhile to introduce this section with a simple account of traditional religious practice at the village level. It is important to invoke this image, one of great beauty and simplicity, if only because Cambodians themselves have aspired to this ideal as they reconstructed village life in the years since Pol Pot. Part of the drama of the recent developments in Cambodian religious practice has to do with the ways, for Cambodians as well as for outside observers, that what is experienced contrasts with the more tranquil and organic vision of religious practice that figures in memory.[1]

The traditional image of Cambodian religious practice puts the Buddhist temple complex, or wat, at the ritual center of village life. The central building of the wat, or *braḥ vihāra* (pronounced "preah vihea"), houses the main Buddha image of the wat and is the location of the most central rituals, some involving only monks. It is usually a tall, elaborate building, facing east, with terraced roofs arching at the corners, and often a tower. In a rural setting it is the most conspicuous building of a community and a landmark among the rice fields. Wat have one or more *sālā chān'* (eating hall), which may also contain a Buddha image, consisting of a large, sheltered space appropriate for community gatherings, especially at key festivals in the yearly cycle such as New Years' or the Day of the Dead (Bhjuṃ Piṇḍ). Housing for monks, which can vary from structures for one or two monks to large, houselike dormitories for a large number, are called *kuṭi* (pronounced "kot"). If present at a wat, the female ascetics called *ṭūn jī* will have separate housing. Around the grounds of a wat, one will also find small *cetiya,* structures that hold the ashes of the dead, usually in the shape of a small tower.

The monks inhabiting the wat are called *lok sangh.* (The Khmer term derives from Pāli *"sangha,"* which we will use when referring to the body of the monkhood.) *Lok sangh* refers to full-fledged *bhikkhu* as well as novices (*sāmaṇera;* pronounced "samane"). (*Lok* is a Khmer honorific, but in some contexts the word is also used alone to refer to a monk.) A *bhikkhu* must be at least twenty years old, while *sāmaṇera* may be ordained as young as eight years of age. This all-male community follows an ascetic lifestyle prescribed by the Buddhist *Vinaya.* The *sāmaṇera* vows to follow the ten precepts *(sīla),* whereas a *bhikkhu* has a more extensive disciplinary regimen consisting of 227 rules. In addition to adhering to their disciplinary rules and ritual obligations, many monks use their time in the wat to acquire literacy skills in Khmer and the Pāli language, to memorize liturgical chants, and to meditate. They also participate in the religious rituals of the lay community, primarily by performing a repertoire of religious chanting and by providing the Buddhist laity with the opportunity to make merit by receiving religious donations or alms.

While monks sanctify ritual by their presence and their chanting, villagers depend on lay specialists, the *ācāry* (pronounced "achar," from Sanskrit *ācārya,* or "teacher, master"), to remember the formats of rituals and to actually lead them. As in Thailand (Swearer 1976), these *ācāry,* who are often former monks, are important intermediaries between the monastic community and the lay community.

As Guthrie points out in chapter 6, some wats (although not all) may have female ascetics known variously as *ṭūn jī, yāy jī,* or *lok yāy* living on or near wat grounds. Like the *sāmaṇera,* these *ṭūn jī* and other committed lay followers vow to follow the ten, eight, or five precepts.

The calendar of Buddhist festivals has a direct connection to the agricultural cycle. Most significant for the chapters in this book is the three-month rainy season retreat called *vassā.* While monks are not totally restricted to the wat at this time, they must sleep in their home wat while conforming to a more intense disciplinary and ritual schedule. Festivals mark the beginning and end of *vassā.* In addition, two key religious festivals, Bhjuṃ Piṇḍ and Kaṭhin, are directly coordinated with the end of the retreat. Bhjuṃ Piṇḍ, in honor of the dead, takes place over a fifteen-day period beginning one month before the end of *vassā.* Laypeople come and camp out in the wat, sometimes in organized shifts, in such a way that the intensified field of merit generated by the monks in retreat extends to other villagers, intensifying their sense of community. Kathin, which can take place any time during the month after the end of *vassā,* generates merit and intensifies community in another way, when the communities associated with one wat organize processions to present robes and other monastic necessities to other wats. Bhjuṃ Piṇḍ corresponds roughly with the end of the period of intensive labor associated with transplanting rice; while it does not in a simple way celebrate the end of the transplanting process, it provides a seasonal reference point by which to compare the year's rains and success in transplanting. Kathin occurs in the period of time after transplanting and before harvest. Khmer New Year, less clearly Buddhist in orientation, occurs in April during the heat of the dry season, as though anticipating the coming of the rains and a new agricultural cycle.

If the Buddhist wat is often described as the ritual center of village life, another tradition gives greater emphasis to the *anak tā* (pronounced "neak ta") shrine to the spiritual essence of the place—a "non-Buddhist" practice that is nevertheless very much integrated into the ritual life of Cambodian Buddhists. (While each *bhūmi* will have its own *anak tā,* there will also typically be a separate *anak tā* shrine on the grounds of a wat.) If Buddhism provides a rationale for morality and serves to consecrate the ritual cycle of the year and lifecycle rituals, then the *anak tā* cult is more concerned with appealing to and appeasing natural forces as they affect agriculture and the health and well-being of humans and animals.

In addition to monks and *ṭūn jī* residing in a wat and the nonresident *ācāry* who officiate at the wat, rural communities have traditional healers called *grū khmaer* and mediums called *cūl rūp* (Khm: "enter the body"). As described in pre-1975 literature, the former were typically men and the latter typically women. A *grū khmaer* is a specialist in herbal medicine and in ritual formulas that protect the body. A medium might also be involved in healing but accomplishes this through access to the special information available from the spirit world. As Bertrand points out in chapter 7, there were two traditional categories of mediums: those who were possessed by *anak tā* and those who were possessed by a type of spirit called *ārakkh* (Skt: *ā-rakṣa,* "guardian, protector"), the latter said to run along family lines where there was a natural predisposition. The *grū pāramī* described by Bertrand do not appear in the literature for pre-1975 Cambodia.

Described in such broad terms, postsocialist religious practice seems similar to presocialist religious practice; the difference, as the chapters in this section illustrate, perhaps lies in the ways villagers' perspectives on religion increasingly relate to movements and institutions at the regional and national levels. In general, fewer young men enter the monkhood (for economic as much as ideological reasons), and there is more ignorance of basic ritual. There has been so much need for building that this has tended to become a focus of religious activity—to the extent, according to some observers, that other practices are neglected. As the chapters here illustrate, political chaos may have changed the way religion fulfills psychic needs and the pursuit of identity; the chapters perhaps also suggest that there has been a particularly dramatic resurgence in practices focusing on the supernatural in the years since socialism.

If the image of village life just presented does not seem too different from that of neighboring Thailand or Laos, this is again a function of how broadly our introductory picture is painted. While there has never been a systematic comparison, Cambodian monks who have lived in or visited Thailand say differences lie in the details of ritual procedures, the interpretation of monastic disciplinary rules, in slight differences in how robes are rolled and folded and chants are pronounced, and such issues as the hour of going to receive food from the community.[2] The role of the *ācāry* is not as universal in Thailand as it is in Cambodia.[3] Again, the very fact that Buddhism was outlawed during the Pol Pot regime and then revived means that Buddhism will be seen in a different light in Cambodia than in neighboring countries, changed by the distortions of memory as well as the new awareness that what was once taken for granted is not inevitable.

As in neighboring Thailand and Laos, the Cambodian monkhood consists of two orders, Mahānikāy and Dhammayut. As Edwards and Hansen describe in this volume (chaps. 2 and 3), Cambodia's Dhammayut sect was created on the model of the Thai Dhammayut. During the 1980s, the revived Buddhism of the People's Republic of Kampuchea was organized in a single order—in effect, if not in name, the Mahānikāy. In 1990, with the return of the monarchy, the Dhammayut was revived, but it is still extremely weak. Cambodian Buddhism also functions under the supervision of the Ministry of Religion. The precise relation of figures like *grū pāramī* or the cult leader Tāpas' to the Ministry of Religion is less clear, and while to the degree they are local phenomena, there is a tendency for the ministry to ignore them, the ministry begins to feel a need for supervision once they acquire prominence.

At the core of Guthrie's chapter on *ṭūn jī* is an ethnographic description of a Phnom Penh wat, Wat Mangalavan, and the role of female ascetics there. She describes the wat's history, its rebirth in 1990, and its growing role as a meditation center for women. She uses this description as the foundation for a wider discussion of the role of *ṭūn jī* in Cambodia. First, she discusses their contemporary and pre-1975 roles. Then, linking to the book's earlier chapters, she discusses pre-Buddhist concepts of female ordination and how traditional terminology is contested in the current debate about female ascetics' roles.

Bertrand's startling chapter describes contemporary interactions between Cambodian spirit mediums and Buddhism. His research focuses on the *grū pāramī,* a category of medium that has become prominent in postsocialist Cambodia. *Grū pāramī* draw on an elaborate pantheon of spirits, many directly associated with Buddhism. Bertrand describes the *grū pāramī*'s discipline, the roles they play in divination and healing, and the specific needs they fulfill in the confusion of contemporary post-Pol Pot Cambodia. In particular, he documents their interaction with traditional Buddhism, shows how they have achieved legitimacy in terms of traditional Buddhist practice, and explores the evolving logic of their position in relation to Buddhism.

In chapter 8, Marston describes the cult surrounding a man in rural Kandal Province, near Phnom Penh, who presents himself as a forest ascetic and claims to have the power to turn clay into stone. He was for several years able to generate a large following of people who believed that a neo-Angkorean temple he was building would usher in an age of peace and prosperity. Marston explores the way the movement is rooted in traditional iconography while also emerging from a particular political and economic climate. This chapter connects to the book's fourth section on transnationalism in Cambodian religion in that the movement has drawn significant support from overseas Cambodians.

Notes

1. I draw here on the ethnographic accounts mentioned in the introduction, especially Ebihara 1968. I also draw on my own field experience at a wat in rural Kampong Cham Province.

2. Field notes based on conversations with monks at Wat Mahā Montrey, Phnom Penh, 1993–1994 and 2002. Since public consensus often suggests that the new generation of Khmer monks lacks discipline, it is interesting that one monk emphasized his belief that while Thai monks superficially seem more rigorous, when observed closely inside the sangha, Khmer monks abided more closely the letter of the law.

3. Personal communication with Charles Keyes.

–6–

Khmer Buddhism, Female Asceticism, and Salvation

ELIZABETH GUTHRIE

While there have been many studies of Cambodian Buddhism and some recent work on Khmer Buddhism and gender (Ledgerwood 1990; Thompson 1999), the religious practice and beliefs of Cambodian Buddhist women have, by and large, remained hidden from view. This is due in part to the fact that ordained nuns *(bhikkhunī)*, the female equivalent of the male Buddhist monk *(bhikkhu)*, disappeared from Theravāda Buddhism many centuries ago.[1] Today there are no *bhikkhunī* for scholars to focus on; there are only Buddhist laywomen *(upāsikā)* and an indeterminate category of female ascetics called *yāy jī* or *ṭūn jī*.

The stars of Cambodian Buddhism are the Buddhist monks. Highly visible in their bright orange robes, these monks are objects of pious veneration by Cambodians who shower them with food and clothing and build them lavish temples. Women are confined to the periphery of this religious system due to their gender; not only are they barred from ordination as *bhikkhunī*, but orthodox Theravāda Buddhism also teaches that in order to reach *nibbāna*, women must first be reborn as men. However, casual observation of religious ceremonies at Buddhist temples reveals that Cambodian women are generous and enthusiastic supporters of Theravāda Buddhism, freely giving their time and money for the construction, decoration, and maintenance of Buddhist temples, and freely giving their husbands and sons to the Buddhist *sangha*. Why do these women persist in devotion to a religion that denies them access to the highest spiritual goals of Buddhism?

Some scholars, writing about the similar situation in Thailand, have explained this paradox by saying that Buddhist laywomen must work harder than men in order to compensate for their gender-related religious deficiencies (Khin Thitsa

1983; Kirsch 1985) while others note that women have their own special roles to play in Theravāda Buddhism (Keyes 1984). Recently, Andaya (2002) has argued that teachings about female spiritual inferiority found in the textual tradition have always been countered by the realities of Theravāda Buddhist practice. Narrative traditions such as the *Jātakas*, which abound with stories glorifying motherhood, and ceremonies such as ordination, which allow women the opportunity for public displays of piety and acquisition of merit, provide positive images of the feminine for devotees. In addition, the form of temporary ordination practiced in mainland Southeast Asia has permitted the relatively free movement of men between family and *sangha*, and the maintenance of close ties between monks and their female relatives.

While such theories may help explain why laywomen have enthusiastically supported and promoted Theravāda Buddhism over the centuries, they do not provide insight into the female ascetics who "act like nuns": the white-robed *ṭūn jī* and their counterparts who can be found living on the margins of Theravāda Buddhism throughout Southeast Asia. This chapter is about the *ṭūn jī* of Cambodia. I argue that the *ṭūn jī* are not "just" laywomen, but are the heirs of an ancient form of ordained female asceticism that was once accorded high status in Cambodia. The marginalization of the *ṭūn jī* and their ordination tradition, *puos*, seems to be recent, the result of attempts to standardize Cambodian Buddhist ordination traditions by Buddhist intellectuals during the twentieth century as well as the influx of Western ideas about women and religious asceticism.

What Is a *Ṭūn Jī*?

Ṭūn jī, yāy jī, mae jī, and *nāṅ jī* are terms used in Cambodia (and in neighboring Thailand and Laos) to designate the women who shave their heads, wear white robes, live in a monastery or hermitage, and follow the eight or ten Buddhist precepts. *Ṭūn jī* is an inverted form of the term for grandmother, "*jī ṭūn.*" *Yāy* is a term of respect that can also mean grandmother; *mae* means mother and *nāṅ* means "lady" or "woman." The word "*jī*" is derived from the Mon-Khmer kinship term "*ji*" or "*aji*" and is a prefix of deference that in pre-Angkor Khmer meant "ancestor, ancient one" (de Bernon 1996, 88; Jenner 1982, 180; Pou 1992, 188). The Buddhist precepts *(sīla)* that the *ṭūn jī* vow when they ordain *(puos)* are 1) do not kill; 2) do not steal; 3) remain celibate; 4) do not lie; 5) do not drink intoxicating beverages; 6) do not eat after noon; 7) do not listen to music or go dancing or attend performances; 8) do not decorate the body with garlands, perfumes, unguents, or jewels; 9) do not sleep on beds or sit in high chairs; 10) do not touch money (Meas-Yang 1978, 22).[2]

Ṭūn jī order themselves according to how many of the ten precepts they vow to keep, and seniority: how many *vassā* (three-month rainy season retreats) they have spent as a religious ascetic.[3] Ten-precept *ṭūn jī* dress entirely in white robes, while *ṭūn jī* observing the five or eight precepts may wear white robes or a black *saṃpat'* (a wraparound skirt made from one piece of fabric) and a white shirt. Some *ṭūn jī* are attached to a particular Buddhist temple, while others remain at home. However, during Buddhist holy days or the *vassā* period, *ṭūn jī* may go on religious pilgrimages to special religious sites or take up residence in a wat or meditation hermitage.

Ṭūn jī and their Thai counterparts, the *mae jī*, are often characterized by their fellow Buddhists and scholars as "failures, outcasts or eccentrics"; spinsters with emotional problems, or poor widows who exist on the periphery of the ordained *sangha*, begging for food and performing menial tasks at the wat such as cleaning or cooking.[4] Their low status is often linked to the fact that they follow "only" the eight or ten precepts, a form of religious devotion available to all laypeople, while a "real" *bhikkhunī* must follow the 311 precepts prescribed for them in the *Vinaya*. Poverty, rural backgrounds, and a lack of education, both secular and spiritual, are also cited as hindrances faced by *ṭūn jī* (Kabilsingh 1988, 230–231).

Some feminist scholars, equating the high status of the male *bhikkhu* with their access to the *bhikkhu* ordination called *upasaṃpadā*, are actively promoting the revival of the ancient order of *bhikkhunī* in Theravāda Buddhism. One proponent, Kabilsingh, has argued that "only when women are equally established in Buddhist study and practice can we be certain that Buddhism is well established. . . . Supporting ordained women will lead to a balanced society" (Kabilsingh 1994, 168). Another writer equates the movement for the reinstitution of the *bhikkhunī* ordination into Theravāda Buddhism to the struggle by Catholic women for ordination into the Roman Catholic priesthood (Karma Lekshe Tsomo 1988, 238). The projection of Protestant (or in this last case, feminist and Catholic) suppositions onto Buddhism is nothing new, and the reintroduction of the *bhikkhunī* order into Theravāda Buddhism may be a meritorious goal in itself. However, an obsession with the *bhikkhunī* ordination will lead us to overlook important aspects of Southeast Asian Buddhist history as well as a misunderstanding and devaluing of female religiosity in Cambodia today. As Andaya noted, the ambiguous position of female ascetics is a constant theme in Theravāda Buddhist history that needs to be researched.

> As yet dimly understood, the complex and indirect means by which illiterates accessed text-based learning and began to perceive themselves as part of a larger religious community have the capacity to reveal much about the acceptance and localization of transcultural ideas. (Andaya 2002, 30)

The inspiration for this chapter comes from visits to Wat Mangalavan in Phnom Penh, a Buddhist temple that has a large number of *ṭūn jī* in residence (fig.

6.1). The first time I visited Wat Mangalavan was during the Khmer New Year in April 1994. I was staying at an apartment across the street from the wat, and I could see from the balcony that many women dressed in white, with shaved heads, were arriving at the wat by pedicab and on foot. I heard the tinkling sound of Khmer religious music being played and found the forty *ṭūn jī* sitting in meditation in front of a reclining Buddha in the *sālā*. A few days later I saw the abbot in the *vihāra* performing a ritual to bless the laywomen's cosmetics and jewelry; no *ṭūn jī* participated in this ritual.

During a visit in 1996, I was introduced to the abbot, the Venerable Pāl' Hān, and to the *ācāry* Duan Jhun, and welcomed to do research there. The *ṭūn jī* invited me to sit with them and patiently answered questions. They gave me religious books, a fan, and a small bronze Buddha image. They tried to teach me their cycle of chanting, encouraging me to make cassette tapes so I could practice at home. My acquaintance with these women and their religious practice suggested that rather

Fig. 6.1 Wat Mangalavan, Phnom Penh (E. Guthrie)

than feeling handicapped by their gender or inability to be ordained as *bhikkhunī*, they believed that they were engaged in a spiritual quest that would lead them to *nibbāna* during their present life. These beliefs are not unique to the *ṭūn jī* at Wat Mangalavan and have a long history in Cambodia (and in mainland Southeast Asia), where

> religious vocation is not always identical to that of a *bhikkhu* for whom the 227 precepts are sometimes perceived as an accumulation of obstacles to the goal. The *bhikkhu* is not considered to be the only one able to aim for nirvāna and the *upāsaka* does not necessarily remain a householder. (Bizot 1988, 20)

A Brief History of Wat Mangalavan

Wat Mangalavan was built more than one hundred years ago in the northeastern part of Phnom Penh near Lake Boeng Kak.[5] It is close to the central market and near the Ministry of Health and the medical school. The wat takes up a city block and is surrounded by a high concrete wall. It is located in the heart of a busy, crowded commercial neighborhood. Huge trucks roar down the streets carrying loads of gravel, bananas, and tanks of water. There are always half a dozen pedicab drivers and moto-taxis waiting for passengers by the front entrance of the wat. Across the street from the wat are a number of curbside automotive repair and panel beating businesses as well as a Chinese-owned hotel, restaurant, and car wash. In this chapter I use the name Mangalavan (having good fortune/auspiciousness) for the wat because this name is painted on the front gate; Cambodia's prime minister, Hun Sen, gave the name to the wat when the building was reconsecrated in 1990. However, the wat is also known by two older names: Wat Svāy Daṅguṃ ("mango grove," a reference to the beautiful mango trees that once grew in the temple grounds) and Wat Thvāy Paṅgaṃ ("offer homage," a name associated with the Sihanouk period). Wat Thvāy Paṅgaṃ is the name most readily recognized today by people living in Phnom Penh.

The *vihāra* of the wat was built during 1970–1975 by a leading member of the wat's congregation, Iuṅ Hoṅsāt, a member of Sihanouk's government during the 1960s. After Sihanouk was deposed in 1970, Iuṅ Hoṅsāt retired from political life and devoted himself to the construction of his new *vihāra*, which was modeled after an important teaching wat in Phnom Penh, Wat Mahā Mantrī. I was told that during this time there were no *ṭūn jī* in residence as the wat had a reputation for orthodoxy. In 1975 the Khmer Rouge came to power, and Phnom Penh was emptied of its inhabitants. Iuṅ Hoṅsāt died in a labor camp in 1977. Like the other wats throughout Cambodia, Wat Thvāy Paṅgaṃ was emptied of monks and looted of its valuables, and its library was destroyed. In addition, its *vihāra* was desecrated by being turned into a car-repair factory.

After the Khmer Rouge regime fell in 1979, people began to return to Phnom Penh. In September of that year, Khmer Buddhism was officially restored in Cambodia by the new government, the People's Republic of Kampuchea. At first there were many restrictions on the practice of Buddhism, the reopening of wats, and the ordination of monks. During most of the 1980s, Wat Thvāy Paṅgaṃ was derelict. The grounds were littered with trash and rusting car parts, and squatters lived there. There were no monks or nuns in residence, although an old man lived in the wat buildings as a caretaker, and the surviving members of Iuṅ Hoṅsāt's family (who had returned to their old home across the street) joined with other neighbors to make urgent repairs to the leaking roof of the *vihāra.* After 1989, restrictions on the ordination of monks were relaxed, and wats throughout the country were allowed to reopen. On July 17, 1989, Oum Sum, the administrative head of the *sangha* in Phnom Penh, installed Pāl' Hān as *cau athikār* (chief of the monastery), and Wat Mangalavan was built anew *(sān' thmī).*

Today, the wat grounds are well maintained with trees, shrubs, a meditation garden, and many new *cetiya.* The *vihāra* has a new *nāga* staircase and is decorated with freshly painted colorful murals. Behind the *vihāra* there is a recently constructed *sālā* used for meditation, teaching, preaching, and meals. In March 1997 there were fifteen monks living in a building on the west side of the wat. Twelve were ordained *bhikkhu,* and there were three *sāmaṇera* (novices). Some medical students were living there as well.

In 1997 there were seventy-three *ṭūn jī* resident at the wat. They lived near the *vihāra* in rows of small brick and plaster buildings that resemble the monks' *kuṭi* and a group of less substantial huts constructed from scrap timber, mats, and tarpaulins clustered together under a large roof opposite the *sālā.* Their housing takes up a considerable area of the wat grounds, and they are a significant presence as they move about the wat on their daily routines. Most of these *ṭūn jī* are middle-aged or elderly women. They do their own housekeeping in their huts, and they assist in the maintenance and daily running of the wat, but they should not be dismissed as domestic servants for the monks. Nor do they beg for alms. Some are poor, but others have access to money and to family resources. Their family members (daughters, sons, and grandchildren) come to visit often and help with the building projects around the grounds and by cleaning and cooking. The *ṭūn jī* take their main meal at long tables in the *sālā,* eating food that is provided and prepared by laypeople. They are seated lower down the table than the *bhikkhu* and *sāmaṇera* (who begin to eat first), but the *ṭūn jī* occupy the same space and share the same food, which they must consume before noon.

The daily activity at the wat revolves around Ven. Pāl' Hān (fig. 6.2). His devotees come to the *vihāra* bringing items such as lipsticks, jewelry, watches, and bottles of purified water, medicinal ointments, cologne, incense, and candles. These are set out on trays provided by the *ācāry* along with donations of money for the wat. Ven. Pāl' Hān blesses the items on the trays one by one, blowing prayers over every bottle of water and cologne and tracing Pāli letters with the tip of a stick of incense on the ointments and lipsticks. Devotees also request *yantra,* squares of white or red cotton cloth silk-screened with protective words, and metal amulets that are worn around the neck or wrist for protection and good luck. Ven. Pāl' Hān offers a ritual purifying bath called *sroc dịk* (sprinkled water), which is believed to wash away evil and bring good fortune. At one point, so many people wanted to receive *sroc dịk* from Ven. Pāl' Hān that groups of men and women would queue

Fig. 6.2 Venerable Pāl' Han (E. Guthrie)

up on the hour to change into bathing robes, sit in rows on wooden benches, and get drenched by the hose-wielding monk.

Some people have private consultations with Ven. Pāl' Hān in a small room behind the main altar. They ask him for advice on a range of matters that often include serious illnesses. After the Pasteur Institute (a medical laboratory in Phnom Penh located near the wat) diagnoses people as infected with HIV, they often come to Ven. Pāl' Hān for counseling and a medicinal cure made from herbs and wine. During one month in 1996, 170 people came from all over Cambodia to Wat Mangalavan in search of his HIV cure.[6] The vitality and prosperity of the wat is believed to be a manifestation of Ven. Pāl' Hān's spiritual power. And in turn, it is Pāl' Hān's reputation for spiritual power that attracts the *ṭūn jī* to the wat.[7]

The *Ṭūn Jī* and Their Stories

The *ṭūn jī* spend a lot of time sitting and talking with the devotees who come to see Ven. Pāl' Hān. They allow women to use their huts to change into bathing robes for the *sroc dịk* ritual, and they share their food with the destitute and ill people who live on the wat grounds. Although they spend time with troubled people and with HIV sufferers (a group of people usually shunned by Khmer society), the *ṭūn jī* I spoke with emphasized that their priority is their personal spiritual development through *dhamma* study and meditation. Their involvement with troubled or ill people is a meditation on suffering and impermanence, like the walking meditation they do in the wat's garden with its brightly painted sequence of statues showing suffering people and decomposing corpses.

Meditation practice makes up a significant part of the daily routine of the *ṭūn jī*. They practice walking meditation in the afternoon, attend meditation classes in the evening, and meditate alone at night in their huts in front of a candle. The meditation teacher at the wat is a woman named Mau Phan (fig. 6.3). She told me she was born in Kampot and, although she is literate, has had no formal education. In 1979 she came to Phnom Penh to live. She was very poor and had no family to help her. She learned meditation techniques from a teacher in Phnom Penh during the 1980s. She was favorably impressed by Ven. Pāl' Hān's teachings and came to live at Wat Mangalavan in 1990. She was asked to teach meditation to the other *ṭūn jī* at the wat and now has many students. Mau Phon's story is not unusual. Her biography resembles that of other *ṭūn jī* from around Cambodia.

Another *ṭūn jī* who resides at Wat Autraiḥ in the south of Cambodia related the following about her own life.

> My name is Sū' Muay and I was born in 1959. I was born in the country in a village named Braek Ṭūn Haem in the sub district of Braek Aṃbil, Ksac Kandal district, in Kandal province. At the present time I live in Wat Autraiḥ, which is situ-

ated about fifteen kilometers by road from Sihanoukville. Before this time I lived through the Civil War. Because of my experiences of great suffering and hardship during this time, I grew very tired of my life as a layperson. In 1985, I committed myself to the *dhamma* and have since held the eight precepts.

In 1993 I met Saṃdec Mahā Ghosānanda who was organizing the Dhammayātrā Peace Walk. I was very happy because I wanted very much to have a state of peace in myself and because I also wanted peace to come to the nation. I went on the Dhammayātrā Walk for the first time during the national elections in 1993. After that I studied *dhamma* meditation, which is the fragrant path that leads to the attainment of a peaceful mind. I decided to go into Wat Champak' Mās in Takeo province during one *vassā,* and there I studied various *vidyā* (sciences).

Fig. 6.3 Lok Yāy Mau Phan (E. Guthrie)

> Also I was steadily progressing in my studies with regard to the *braḥ dhamma* that is the prerequisite action for all understanding and thought. (Löschmann 1995, 17–18)

A *ṭūn jī* presently living in Phnom Penh reported,

> I am *lok yāy* Dim Van and I am 58 years old. I practice the *dhamma* in Wat Saṃpūar Mās.[8] I have practiced the eight precepts for eleven *vassā*. Before I came to study at Wat Saṃbau Mās, I studied with the renowned *dhamma* teacher Thlāk Jay in the district of Kumārarājā in Takeo province for three *vassā*. After this, I began to look for a quiet and tranquil place. I lived in a hut and practiced *dhamma* at Wat Saṃnāk' Aṃbae Bhnaṃ for two *vassā* but I was not happy there and I traveled a long distance to take shelter at Wat Saṃbau Mās in the year 1990, and I have lived there ever since. (Löschmann 1995, 64–65)

The biographies of Mau Phon, Sū' Muay, and Dim Van have in common certain themes. First and foremost is the importance of personal spiritual practice. The second theme, which is intertwined with the first, is their independence: they have abandoned the life of a householder to have the freedom to advance their spiritual practice. This independence takes the form of mendicancy. While they attach themselves to a particular temple during the *vassā* period, they go on pilgrimages and travel freely around the country between *vassā* to learn new meditation techniques and study with renowned *dhamma* teachers.

Some scholars have linked the popularity of "lay" meditation movements among Theravāda Buddhist women to the ever-increasing influence of Western ideas (e.g., about gender equality) on the rising middle classes of Asia (Gombrich and Obeyesekere 1988, 292). While Western ideas have had an effect on Cambodian Buddhism, this effect has been tempered by decades of Civil War, the Pol Pot period, and years of isolation under socialism and is even today limited to Cambodia's urbanized elites. The *ṭūn jī* described here, poor women from rural backgrounds, do not resemble the Westernized lay meditators described by Gombrich and Obeyesekere. Instead, their desire for release from the sorrows of household life and their thirst for spiritual attainment and independence recall descriptions of female asceticism dating before the Civil War period.

Bizot, in his book *Le Chemin de Langka,* described the experiences of an old *yāy jī* who made a pilgrimage to Angkor in the 1960s to meditate in a hut. She reported that during meditation, her spirit left her body and flew away to one of the paradises.

> The encounters made in heaven fill one with joy. Grandparents and deceased friends offer us presents, gold. On their throne made of the clouds, the gods beckon us. Celestial music tinkles out into space. The perfume of the flowers pervades everywhere. An intense desire arises to stay in these divine surroundings,

> but the spirit must be strong and continue on the journey that leads to the other shore. (Bizot 1992, 36; translated from French)

During fieldwork at Wat Tep Pranam in Oudong in 1967, the students of the Royal University of Fine Arts in Phnom Penh interviewed *yāy jī* living at that wat. During the *vassā* these women observed the ten precepts, dressed entirely in white, and studied Buddhist texts. The *yāy jī* told the interviewers that they had come to study at that particular wat because of its reputation. The researchers concluded that

> [a]lthough these women are not true nuns *(bhikkhunī)* since that order disappeared a long time ago, one can give them such a title because they live in the same way as the nuns in the past. (Les Étudiants 1969, 52; translated from French)

In the 1960s Bareau (1969) recorded the existence of many female ascetics living in isolated hermitages and centers of meditation throughout Cambodia. And in the 1950s, travel writer Christopher Pym came across a group of *ṭūn jī* practicing meditation at the northwest corner of Braḥ Khan, an ancient temple near Angkor Thom in Siem Reap. These women practiced a form of meditation that they believed would let them glimpse *nibbāna.* They started meditating after dusk and continued until just before dawn. At dawn they ate a meal together and then continued meditation until late afternoon. The *ṭūn jī* meditated while concentrating on large sticks of incense that burned for three or four hours. Or they would gaze at circles cut in the wall of a hut, at colored disks, or at a statue of Buddha. One *ṭūn jī* was also taking care of a monk who lived there. She complained to Pym that looking after even one monk meant a lot of work. When there were more people to help her, she was able to spend much time in meditation and used to catch a glimpse of what she called *nibbāna* at least once a month: "Light shining at me very bright, very dazzling" (Pym 1959, 157–159).

Leclère described two sorts of female ascetics who inhabited Buddhist temples during the later years of the French protectorate, differentiating between what he called "five precept observers" and the *ṭūn jī.* The "five precept observers" lived with the *upāsaka* and *upāsikā* in the wat. Seen as veritable nuns by the populace, they followed the five *sīla* and in addition elected to observe most of the rules followed by the monks. The *ṭūn jī* lived in little huts on posts around the wat enclosure where they meditated, repaired the robes of the monks, and ornamented the altar of the Buddha with artificial flowers (Leclère 1899, 425).

The earliest Buddhist records (third century B.C.E.) show that

> the monastic ordination lineage, established by the Buddha himself, was dual in nature: men become *bhikkhu*-s, and women become *bhikkhunī*-s. Lay disciples were also classed by gender: laymen *(upāsaka)* and laywomen *(upāsikā).* (Skilling 2001, 242)

Female ascetics like the *ṭūn jī* do not appear in the Pāli canonical tradition.[9] This lacuna has prompted some scholars to view this Southeast Asian form of female asceticism as problematic. Penny Van Esterik, who did extensive fieldwork in Central Thailand in the 1970s, represents Thai Buddhist social organization by a triangular diagram that shows gender-paired laypeople *(upāsaka, upāsikā)* at the bottom and ordained monks by themselves at the top. According to her interpretation, the striving of the Thai *mae jī* after a monastic role and religious status that does not exist today forces them into an anomalous position, on the outer limits of her diagram and the outer limits of society. This, Van Esterik concludes, is why *mae jī* are sometimes viewed as "failures, outcasts or eccentrics" (P. Van Esterik 1982b, 72).

Seen from this standpoint, Buddhist female asceticism seems marginal or anachronistic, a social problem that needs to be tidied up, for example, by increased education for women or the reintroduction of the *bhikkhunī* ordination. But by doing so, we run the risk of ignoring or misunderstanding Buddhism as it has developed in mainland Southeast Asia where male and female ascetics have been an important part of Buddhist practice for centuries. In addition to the *ṭūn jī* there are the (male) *baku,* or court Brahmins (de Bernon 1997, 39); the (male) *tāpas'* of Cambodia and Thailand dressed in white robes (Bizot 1988, 21) or, as described by Marston in chapter 8, in "tiger skin"; and the (male and female) brown-robed *yathe (ṛṣi)* of Burma (Bizot 1988, 21). Cambodia's earliest written inscriptions contain references to women who were able to be ordained and apparently held high status in temples (Vickery 1998, 253). While it is not known if these ancient temple attendants had any religious beliefs or practices in common with the modern *ṭūn jī,* they used the same term for their religious ordination: *"puos."*

The Inscriptions and Ordination Terms

The word *"puos"* first appears in pre-Angkor stone inscriptions. One text, K. 557/600, found in Angkor Borei and dated 611 C.E., lists in Khmer the names of people, fields, and domestic animals being offered to divinities. On the north face of the stone there is a reference to *kantai ta pos oy [ya]jamāna kpoñ,* "women who enter into religion for the sacrificer of Kpoñ" (Coedès 1942, 2:21). An eleventh-century inscription from Angkor Thom, K. 420, also in Khmer, lists a series of fields donated to a god called Śri Vardhaman: *caṃnat svāy vradeṅ ti jauv ta teṅ tvan ta pvas,* "the establishment of Svāy Vradeṅ, which was bought by the woman Teṅ Tvan who has entered into religion" (Coedès 1952, 4:163). The significant word (for this chapter at least) in these two passages is *"pos/pvas."* The pre-Angkor-period form of the word is *"pos"*; during the Angkor period the word was spelled *"pvas."* In modern Khmer the word is written *"puos";* the Thai and Lao variants are *"buat," "buaj."* All these words mean "enter into religion" (Coedès

1942, 2:13). Pou defines *pos/pvas* as "to turn sacred. To become a religious" (Pou 1992, 320). Jenner gives the verbal forms of the words: *pnos/paṃnos,* "one who has been invested or ordained; cenobite" (Jenner 1982, 352). Vickery glosses *pos/pvas* as "become a monk, take on a religious vocation"; and *paṃnvas/paṃnos* as "one who has become a monk" (Vickery 1998, 129).

During the pre-Angkor period, there is no clear evidence of any connection between the term *"pos/pvas"* and Buddhist ordination; in fact, the term first appears in a Śaivite context (Coedès 1942, 2:67). As Buddhism increased in importance during the late Angkor period, the inscriptions begin to mention Buddhist ordination. One example is a late twelfth-century inscription, K. 485, from the Phimanakas Temple, Angkor Thom. The inscription was composed entirely in Sanskrit and mentions, among many other things, Queen Jayarajadevi's sponsorship of the Buddhist ordination *(prāvrājayat)* of a group of women (Coedès 1942, 2:171). K. 177, an inscription composed in Khmer during the late Angkor period, tells of a man named Śrīyasa who entered religion *(pvas)* and preached the *dhamma* in the capital city of Angkor. Later in the narrative, Śrīyasa undertook the *upasaṃpadā* ordination and became a *bhikkhu* (Coedès 1964, 38). The *pvas* ordination that Śrīyasa took prior to his *upasaṃpadā* ordination seems here to be equivalent to the Buddhist *pravrajyā* ordination.

The Sanskrit word *"pravrajyā"* and its Pāli equivalent, *"pabbajjā,"* mean "going forth." The *pabbajjā* ordination is characterized by the enunciation of the triple refuges (I take refuge in the Buddha, the *dharma,* the *sangha*) and is the formal statement of an individual's intention to leave household life in order to enter religious life. After undertaking the *pabbajjā,* a person who wishes to become a *bhikkhu* or *bhikkhunī* must next perform a ritual called the *upasaṃpadā* (Lamotte 1988, 166–167). The *upasaṃpadā* is founded on the *pabbajjā;* one cannot become a *bhikkhu* or *bhikkhunī* without first undertaking the *pabbajjā* (Bizot 1988, 13, 19). Although the *pabbajjā* forms the first part of the *upasaṃpadā,* it is technically separate from it. It is not a ritual that is exclusive to the ordination of the *bhikkhu* (or *bhikkhunī*) and can stand alone.

There is apparently no linguistic connection between the Sanskrit word *"pravrajyā,"* its Pāli equivalent, *"pabbajjā,"* and the Mon-Khmer word *"pos/pvas."*[10] *Pos/pvas* may be pre-Buddhist and first occurs in the inscriptions in a Śaivite context. However, by the Angkor period, the words *"pravrajyā"* and *"pvas"* seem to have become cognate. By the Middle period of Khmer history (fifteenth through eighteenth centuries), the word was used to refer to the Buddhist ordination of both men and women. A typical inscription from 1488 C.E. commemorates the meritorious deeds of a pious couple, Abhayarāj and Dhamm: they built a monastery, commissioned and consecrated statues of the Buddha, built a *cetiya,* planted a *bodhi* tree, had sacred texts copied, buried *sīmā* stones, and were themselves ordained *(papūs ātmā).* They also offered servants to be ordained *(bvumpus)* and attached to their monastery in the service of the Buddha images there. One of these servants received the *upasampat* (*upasampadā* ordination) as well as *pvas* (Pou 1971, 112–113). A similar inscription composed in 1669 C.E. describes the career of a government official, Vaṅsāaggarāj. Together with his wife and family, Vaṅsāaggarāj accomplished many meritorious acts, which he dedicated to his deceased parents during a ceremony in Braḥ Bān' (a gallery in the temple Angkor Wat). He also sponsored the ordination of his aunt Kaññakesar, his wife Srīratnakesar, his sister-in-law Kim, and his two nieces as *nāṅ jī (puoss jā nāṅ jīy)* (Pou 1974, 320, 324; Chandler 1971, 151–159).

It is difficult to be certain from these inscriptions exactly what *puos* entailed during the Middle period (Pou 1972, 120–121). But it is possible to establish certain facts. First, women as well as men were able to *puos*. Second, this ordination conferred some sort of religious status on its recipient. Third, the sponsorship of someone's *puos*—male or female—was considered a meritorious deed, something to be commemorated with stone inscriptions. Fourth, these ceremonies had some kind of official religious status. They took place in public, in important religious sites like Angkor Wat, and were attended by religious officiants as well as family members and loyal retainers. But today there has been a change, and the official status of ordained female ascetics has become ambiguous. As one monk, educated at the Pāli University in Phnom Penh, explained,

> I often hear the people at my temple say nuns "*puos*" or "*puos* as *yiey-chi*." Personally, I don't normally use the word "*puos*" for nuns. . . . I don't like this word because some people use the words for the monks with the nuns too. And some *yiey-chi* don't know their roles. They might think that they and the monks are the same. It's completely wrong! It is not a big deal to use that word "*puos*" to refer to the nuns. But it is better to add "as" after "*puos*."[11]

Two senior *ṭūn jī* associated with the Association of Nuns and Laywomen of Cambodia (ANLWC) meditation center at Wat Koḥ in Oudong explained to me that although people commonly say "*puos*," the correct term to use for *ṭūn jī* is "*thvāy khluon*" (*thvāy*, "to give, to offer"; and *khluon*, "oneself").[12] The ceremony of *thvāy khluon* consists of a personal commitment to undertake the five or eight precepts. *Thvāy khluon* does not need to take place at a wat; it can take place at home. There is no need to have a monk or *ācāry* to perform the ceremony, and there are no set numbers of participants. Other *ṭūn jī, upāsikā,* or family members can come as guests, but they do not play any part in the ceremony. When I asked them to describe the ceremony, they told me that first the woman shaves her head, puts on white robes, and finally recites her vows before a Buddha image.[13] The *thvāy khluon* vow is renewed every *thṅai sīl* (holy days that are observed once a fortnight).

The formula for *thvāy khluon* can be found in a paperback manual called the *Gihipatibat* (Rituals for the householder) (Churm 1996, 22–30). The *Gihipatibat* makes a very clear distinction between the rituals performed by laypeople and those used by *sāmaṇera* and *bhikkhu,* and the word "*puos*" does not appear in the book. The formula for *puos* can be found in the manual called *Sāmaṇeravinay* (Rules for novices) on pages 11–19 in a chapter titled "*Pabbajjā.*" The existence of printed manuals containing official versions of religious rituals is a relatively recent development in Cambodia. The *Gihipatibat* and *Sāmaṇeravinay* are part of a series of religious manuals compiled and translated by Pāli linguists under the direction of Chuon Nath (then a professor at the Pāli University in Phnom Penh) and published by the Buddhist Institute in the 1920s (see chap. 3). The purpose of these manuals was to reform and redefine the principles of Khmer Buddhism (Bizot 1976, 20). They have been reprinted many times, are part of the Buddhist curriculum taught today to young monks, and are readily available in bookshops.

Over the past decades, the Ministry of Cults and Religion has been charged with regulating and controlling Cambodia's exuberant if eclectic form of Theravāda Buddhism (see chap. 8). To this end, attempts have been made to clearly differentiate ascetics such as the *ṭūn jī* and *tāpas'* from the ordained *sangha* and to confine them to the sphere of the householder. One strategy has been the promotion of the *thvāy khluon* ceremony as an officially sanctioned alternative to *puos* for non-*bhikkhu* ascetics.[14] The irony, of course, is that *puos* first appeared in pre-Angkor-period inscriptions describing the ordination of female temple attendants and only much later became identified with the Buddhist *pabbajjā* ordination.

The fact that Cambodia's female ascetics are today denied access to their ancient ordination tradition has clearly had a negative effect on the status of the *ṭūn jī.* They have been further challenged by international organizations eager to promote the reintroduction of the *bhikkhunī* ordination into Theravāda Buddhism. Today it is estimated that there are at least three thousand *ṭūn jī* in Cambodia (Löschmann 1995, 5). Most of these are older women who in the traditional manner have left the householder life to pursue their personal spiritual goals. There are moves afoot to change this situation: several local and foreign nongovernmental organizations are attempting to reform, organize, and train these women. A pamphlet from the ANLWC tells us, "The enormous potential of this marginalized group as important partners in the national reconciliation and social development process of their country had not been recognized." In 1995 and 1997, international conferences attended by *bhikkhunī* and Buddhist laywomen from around the world were held in Cambodia. At these conferences, the participants voted to empower *ṭūn jī* and *upāsikā* and involve them in the reconciliation and development of Cambodia; to encourage these women to take on leadership roles in society; to change gender perceptions and achieve religious and social equality for women; to train them in social work practices, including counseling victims of domestic violence and trauma; and to encourage national and international networking.[15]

This agenda clearly reflects contemporary Western (and Christian) ideas about the appropriate behavior for female ascetics. However, the primary goal of a Buddhist ascetic—male or female—is personal salvation: the search for *braḥ nibbāna*. Encouraging *ṭūn jī* to get involved in secular society will only hinder their meditation and *dhamma* studies while further diminishing their status as religious ascetics in Cambodia.

Living religions are in a constant state of flux. The religious status of Theravāda Buddhist women is a concern for many people today, and there have been several attempts to reinstitute the order of *bhikkhunī* in Śri Lanka and Thailand. While such movements have had less impact on Cambodia's somewhat conservative society, they have nevertheless captured the imagination of some Cambodian *ṭūn jī* who are discouraged by their low status, poverty, and marginalization in the present religious system. As *ṭūn jī* Jhuan Sūmuan of Wat Khemavan, Kompong Cham, said, "In my era we did not have *bhikkhunī* but I hope that the era of my grandchildren will have *bhikkhunī*."[16] While the reintroduction of the *bhikkhunī sangha* into Theravāda Buddhism will doubtless provide opportunities for some Buddhist women, the loss of Cambodia's ancient tradition of female asceticism may further marginalize poor or rural women like Mau Phon or Sū' Muay, unable to meet the financial and educational requirements for full *bhikkhunī* ordination or unwilling to accept the institutional domination of the male *sangha*.

Notes

Thanks to Robert Didham, Paul Harrison, John Marston, Serge Thion, and Michael Vickery for their help with the many stages this chapter has gone through. Thanks also to Uon Ngai, Him Tāt, and Sek Sisokhom.

1. Skilling (1995, 55) writes that there is "no incontrovertible evidence that the *bhikkhunī* ordination was ever established in mainland or insular South-East Asia during any period." For a different opinion see Goonatilake 1996, 6.

2. The *Vinaya* requires novices *(sāmaṇera, sāmaṇerī)* to formally vow to keep the ten precepts. *Bhikkhu* must vow to keep 227 precepts and *bhikkhunī* 311 precepts. Buddhist laypeople often chose to follow the five, eight, or ten precepts as a form of religious devotion on holy days or in times of illness or special need.

3. This information comes from a report by Rīne Pān, "My View of the Future of the *ṭūn jī;* Why They Seek Ordination *(puos)*" (Löschmann 1995, 7–39). This report and the other quotations from the conference proceedings cited below are my translations.

4. For characterizations of this sort, see "Nuns seen as ideal teachers of society," *Phnom Penh Post,* May 19–June 1, 1995, 17.

5. The information about Wat Mangalavan comes from interviews in April 1994,

February 1996, August 1996, November 1997, and July 2000 with Uon Ngai (the son-in-law of Iuṅ Hoṅgsat), Ven. Pāl' Hān, *ācāry* Duan Jhun, *ṭūn jī* Him Tāt and Mau Phan, and Sek Sisokhom.

6. "Aids sufferers seek Buddhist comfort," *Phnom Penh Post,* January 26–February 8, 1996, 8.

7. Ven. Pal' Hān's reputation came under attack during the bitter 1998 national election campaign, and Wat Mangalavan has suffered as a result. During a brief visit in 2000, I found the abbot overseas, few lay devotees in evidence, and the *ṭūn jī* population much reduced.

8. Wat Saṃbau Mās is the headquarters of the Dhammayātrā movement described by Poethig in chapter 9.

9. J. Marston, personal communication, July 2002: a few men with shaved heads and dressed in white robes called *tā* (grandfather) *jī* can be found in Khmer wats.

10. M. Vickery, personal communications during 2000.

11. Lok S. S., personal communication, October 1998. The monk, a resident at a wat in the United States, was responding via e-mail to a question from Marston.

12. Field notes, Wat Koḥ, Oudong, July 2000.

13. It is interesting that the informants used the term "*puos*" here, apparently contradicting their earlier assertion that *ṭūn jī* do not *puos.*

14. There is no reference to a ritual called *thvāy khluon* in Coedès' *Inscriptions du Cambodge,* Jenner's *Lexicon of Undated Inscriptions,* Pou's old Khmer dictionary or in the Cambodian dictionary published by the Buddhist Institute. The term does appear in the title of a ritual for *upāsaka/upāsikā,* in Meas-Yang 1978, 36.

15. ANLWC Information Pamphlet, July 2000.

16. Caption, Löschmann 1995, photographic section.

–7–

A Medium Possession Practice and Its Relationship with Cambodian Buddhism

The *Grū Pāramī*

Didier Bertrand

The practices of possession are the living witness of a culture; they always inscribe themselves within social, economic, historical-political, and religious systems. I will attempt to describe here the relations between the type of medium called *grū pāramī* (pronounced "kru boramey") and Theravāda Buddhism in Cambodia.[1] Several studies analyzing Buddhism in Theravāda countries have shown the interconnection between Buddhism and supernatural practices. Taking as my point of departure the point of view of the mediums themselves, I attempt to understand the recent renewal of these practices within the context of contemporary Cambodia and how references to Buddhism support their activities and ethic.

Outside observers usually try to place different religious practices in separate categories, but mediums themselves tend to consider what is taking place not so much as a syncretism of two religions, but as a whole. As Tambiah (1976, 77) wrote, the researcher is investigating in a "single field characterized by hierarchy, opposition, complementarity, and linkage" among different levels. This applies to Cambodian religious practices, with individual variations representing only the emphasis put on one level or another.

The research presented here represents three years of participation in the life of Cambodian mediums and the different activities they perform: ceremonies to reinforce their powers *(abhiṣeka),* the construction of new altars, the celebration of anniversaries *(puṇy khup)* and holy days *(tṅai sīl),* healing, divination, and pilgrimages. I have interviewed nearly one hundred medium-healers, usually known as *grū cūl rūp* because of their practice of possession (*cūl rūp*, "enter the body"). And I have collected the names of more than three hundred spirits referred to as *pāramī*.

Research was conducted between November 1994 and December 1997. During those years, which followed United Nations-supported national elections, political life was very tense, with much anxiety due to the constant threat of fighting between the political factions, which culminated with a coup d'etat in July 1997.

Several key Khmer Rouge, after losing battles, joined the Royal Armed Forces but tended to follow the generals of one specific faction, bringing out more tensions. Some journalists were assassinated, and in some provinces the countryside was unsafe, due to what was called "Khmer Rouge banditry." There were permanent rumors that Cambodia was going to face a new civil war and a bleak future. Because of the free sale of weapons, violence was often used to solve conflicts at every level of social life. With the collapse of the socialist state infrastructure, many public services, including education and health, were unreliable and available only for fees, with the wealthiest preferring to rely on private services. Cambodian patron-clientism and support networks provided the main source of protection, while the judiciary and police hardly participated in supporting a state of law. So it was a period of turmoil while the country, step by step, with heavy international assistance and myriad uncoordinated nongovernmental organizations, was trying to recover from nearly thirty years of war, revolution, and international isolation.

Presentation of the *Pāramī*

Pāramī (Skt/Pāli, "perfection" or "completeness") is a Buddhist technical term referring to the ten perfections of the Buddha *(dasapāramī),* accomplishments or virtues that permitted the Buddha to reach *nibbāna.*[2] In a popular reappropriation of the word in Cambodia, *pāramī* are believed to constitute a benevolent form of power. Some mediums are attacked (but also chosen and possessed) by spirits called *pāramī* who are supposed to have these virtues. These *pāramī* take on the character of different mythico-historical personages and are usually clearly differentiated from the *khmoc* (spirits of those who died a sudden or violent death), or the other errant spirits who populate the Khmer universe known as *brāy*. Certain mediums believe that in some cases of malevolent possession, the *brāy* can be trained and pacified by a master medium so that it, too, will eventually come to be called a *pāramī*. As one medium explained,

> The *brāy* and *anak tā* speak as we do, they don't know the language of the monks, but they can help to tell the future. They don't see the patients and they don't help the humans, they can help to know but they need to be educated because they like to play and to listen to music and to harm others; they need to be taught.

In one wat, Ang (1980, 158) noted on the base of a Buddha statue an inscription referring to a "Brāy Braḥ Pāramī," a malevolent spirit who had been converted to Buddhism and now guarded the Buddha image, which demonstrates the fundamental ambivalence of these figures. Penny Van Esterik, working in Thailand, has documented similar malevolent guardian spirits called *phi* and benevolent angel-like deities called *devatā* (pronounced "tevoda") where they often serve to integrate deities from Hinduism into the order and hierarchy of the Thai Buddhist world (P. Van Esterik 1982a, 10, 13). In Cambodia, the spirits known as *devatā* and *pāramī* are opposed to the more malevolent *khmoc* and *brāy*. *Devatā* are so high ranking that they do not possess humans and manifest themselves only on the occasion of the New Year.[3] And as we will see, *pāramī* are closely associated with Buddhism.

It is often said that there are more than ten thousand *pāramī* in Cambodia. The most famous of these can be identified as well-known personages. During possession the communications of the *pāramī* are transmitted by the *snāṅ* (pronounced "snang," a Khmer word meaning "royal concubine," "servant," or "spirit medium"). The *snāṅ* dresses up in a distinctive manner and uses certain attributes (bow and arrow, flower, trident). The demeanor and the physical and verbal expression of the *snāṅ* inform us of the character and identity of the possessing spirit.

The lexical field and the terms used by mediums to relate their experiences often belong to the royal language, which is used to speak with kings and Buddhist monks, and is an indication of how language can assist the transformations of a human medium into a member of the spirit world. For example, the verb "*kruṅ*" is used to describe the moment when the *pāramī* enters into the *snāṅ* as if it has dressed itself in its power. "*Kruṅ*" also means "to govern, to administrate or maintain, protect a kingdom or its subjects," all of which are royal functions. The word "*saṇṭhit*" (to establish within) is a Buddhist technical term that means in this particular context "the instant during which possession takes place." One finds "*dhvoe samādhi samrāp' oy pāramī cūl mak saṇṭhit*, "to meditate so the power can enter." "*Yāṅ*" is the royal verb that means "to walk, to go" and is used to express the arrival of the *pāramī*.

The very identity of the *pāramī* can be understood by the social or therapeutic functions that it exercises through its *snāṅ* in which it manifests a physical form *(rūp)* through modification, for example when the *pāramī* of a princess enters into a *rūp* of a man. The medium has adopted a formula of cohabitation with his *pāramī* (singular or plural) that, although it is ritualized, cannot be formalized by a marriage because the human and spirit worlds cannot be mixed together.[4] While the possession is taking place, the human host is obliterated, and the medium becomes simultaneously the vehicle of the power and the power itself.

Pāramī Identity: An Expression of the Variety of Religious Life

The group of *pāramī* with religious associations represented 25 percent of the total subjects in our survey and consisted of a variety of personages, reflecting the range of social circumstances in Cambodia and the different local methods of reappropriation of certain deities. Certain *pāramī* (10 percent of the total) have taken on the identity of monks who belong to contemporary history. An example is the monk Chan Cheung, who meditated at Wat Phnom during the war of the Lon Nol regime.

The *nāga* king Mucalinda, who protected the meditating Buddha from the rain by encircling him with his coils and spreading out his seven heads to serve as an umbrella, manifests as the female Nāṅ Nāga (pronounced "neang neak") and, along with other denizens of the *nāga* realm, often possesses women. One can also find the names of Brahmanic divinities such as Umāvatī (Pārvatī), Braḥ Bhaghnes (Gaṇeśa), Champuḥ Gruḍ (Beak of Garuḍa, the vehicle of Viṣṇu), and Srī Khmau (the Black Lady), who evokes Kālī. Umāvatī (pronounced "oma vathei") is also understood as a sister of the mythological Somāvatī, who is supposed to be the founding ancestress of Cambodia.

Other personages are those who are mentioned in the Buddhist scriptures *(gambīr)* such as the Buddha's disciple, Braḥ Mokklean (Moggallāna), and the heroes of the *Jātaka*s (the stories of the former lives of the Buddha) like Braḥ Vesando (Vessantara) or Braḥ Mokklean (Moggallāna). However, their coming as *pāramī* is disputed by some mediums who are more closely aligned with Buddhism and who deny that these perfect beings can return to the earth. According to a *grū* living near a Phnom Penh market, "the disciples of the Buddha can have *snāṅ* but the personages of the earlier *Jātaka* before the Buddha do not have *snāṅ,* and if they come it is for no longer than an instant." The dispute about the coming of these personages is also based on the idea that the *rūp* are not pure enough to receive such holy dignitaries. It is commonly believed that such spirits cannot come down to the human world because they are in a higher sphere that has no connection with humans.

Also considered as a *pāramī* is the earth deity, *nāṅ gaṅhīṅ* Braḥ Dharaṇī (Lady Princess Venerable Earth), popularly known as Neang Kongheng, whose statue is present on almost all the mediums' altars. However, she is not supposed to take possession like the other *pāramī,* but instead provides suggestions or advice. And finally, very dominant are the personages seen as pursuing a spiritual path, such as the hermits Lok Tā Isī, Tāpas', or Anak Saccaṃ (the one who tells the truth).[5] These are generally men, but one can find some women who lead the life of a mystic, such as Nāṅ Peou from Phnom Kulen. The *pāramī* in this group are above all the propagators of the *dhamma.*

Some *pāramī* who are not religious figures also have strong links with Buddhism. Many *pāramī* generals *(me dăb)* accompanied by their soldiers organize rites of offerings and dances in the initial or final phase of certain ceremonies. The *pāramī* of the head of the army can fight with his troops for the defense of the *dhamma.* Again, the *pāramī* status of these persons is not universally agreed on, since during their human lifetimes they did not follow the five essential Buddhist precepts (not to kill, drink alcohol, lie, rob, or commit adultery).[6]

Royal servants *(mahātlik)* are called *parivār pāramī,* and they manifest themselves during festivals by dancing and throwing flowers at the statues of the Buddha. The *pāramī* kings who are figures from the *Jātaka* have strong links with Buddhism. The *pāramī* king, like the *cakkavattin* kings in Theravāda societies, is said to maintain peace, calm, tranquillity, and harmony and to protect the weak. He comes to correct the errors and imperfections of the humans who are his subjects. He is supposed to follow the *dhamma* and become a moral leader, working for the purification of Buddhism and the organization of the *sangha.*

The Indian or Sinhalese *pāramī* are supposed to speak Sanskrit or Pāli. Like the kings or queens of the *Jātaka* and the disciples of the Buddha, they are particularly venerated because they come from the land of the Buddha.

Descriptions of Some *Grū Pāramī*

Before getting into the general analysis of the *grū pāramī* I would like to introduce four *grū* in order to give some idea of their differences and similarities.

Lok Yāy Rim is a sixty-five-year-old female rice farmer living in Kompong Speu. I found her while looking around for *grū cūl* in the villages. When I arrived she was planting rice, so her daughter went to find her in the paddy field. For her, calling the spirits to respond to the requests of her visitors is not her main activity. After asking the reason for my visit, she changed from her work clothes to a white cotton shirt, scarf, and *kben.*[7] She instructed me to bring her the five traditional gifts, each in quantities of five: cigarettes, candles, incense sticks, betel leaves, and areca nuts. She sat with her eyes closed while reciting some Buddhist Pāli stanzas, trembled for a few seconds, and shrieked, and then I faced the *pāramī lok yāy.* She said she was living as a *ṭūn jī* in the forest on Phnom Saṃbau in Battambang Province[8] and asked what she could do for me. I explained that I was a researcher trying to get in touch with the *pāramī* in Cambodia. She then started to tell me about her human life and her present life as a spirit as well as what she could do to support the human lives of those who consulted her: perform some medical diagnoses and prescribe some medicine; help to deal with other spirits harassing the patients; and offer some divination skills. She chose Lok Yāy Rim as *rūp* because she was a very good person who respected the five precepts. When I finished my interview the *pāramī* left, and I could speak with Lok Yāy Rim again.

Lok Yāy Rim lives in a modest bamboo house with a roof of palm leaves and maintains a room with a Buddha altar in it. As I sat in front of it, she explained to me how she had become sick many years ago. She obtained powers of diagnosis after being caught by the spirit who appears as a *ṭūn jī*. Mediumship has not changed her life much; she receives a few clients a week without being allowed to charge any money. If she does receive any money she cannot keep it for herself and instead brings it to the temple, where she attends ceremonies every week. She also organizes a ritual ceremony, including inviting monks, that should take place every year, but she does not always have enough money for it. So it can be held only once every two to three years unless the *pāramī* reminds her by provoking sufferings. She is married with five children, so this *pāramī* is rather an extra duty for her; she would like to abandon it, but she can't because the *pāramī* needs her to help human beings. Lok Yāy Rim has no disciples, nor does she attend gatherings of mediums, as she is very busy rice farming, and she goes only to the temple festivals and rituals.

Mrs. T. is a medium in Phnom Penh near one of the main markets. Her small house is often full of visitors. She lives in a very small, windowless, ground-floor flat with her husband and two children. After the Pol Pot period, at the end of the 1970s, she started to get very high fevers that she was told were due to a *pāramī*. She spent several months having visions and learning through her dreams while sick before she started to receive patients who came for blessing, divination, or healing. She is a very strong woman and worships the earth deity Nāṅ Gaṅhīn, who never possesses her but protects her and makes suggestions to her. Several other *pāramī* possess her. For most of them she just wears a white shirt and *kben*, but has different colored scarves. The most famous *pāramī* is from Sri Lanka and speaks Pāli and once asked us to bring her a sari from Sri Lanka. She teaches students, patients who, once diagnosed as having a *pāramī*, must learn how to deal with it and control their possession. During this afternoon session, first she takes care of the patients, then puts on *biṇbādy* music on a cassette, and once all the students with a vocation to receive *pāramī* are possessed, her *pāramī* teaches them how to *poek bhlūv* (open the way) by dancing, movement, and speech. She lives very close to one wat near Phnom Penh where she holds an annual ceremony to raise money for the monks. She also organizes pilgrimages during which the pilgrims are supposed to make donations. She receives some fees for teaching and healing and declares she gives as much as possible to the temple, but she sometimes needs to keep some for her family, as her husband's government salary is too small. He is usually at her side every afternoon and helps her. She also makes and sells temple or altar decorations such as embroidered flags or *pāy sī* (offerings constructed from folded paper or plant material). Every year a big ceremony in her home brings together former students (disciples of a kind) and monks for prayers and dances. Mrs. T. always refers to *dhamma* as the source of her teaching and the rules of her behavior. She goes to the wat every week, and the Buddhist altar, in front of which everything happens, takes up a large area in her small house. Since she began her relation with *pāramī* she has followed the five precepts (fig. 7.1).

Lok Tā P lives in the *prāsād* he built next to his house about twenty kilometers from Phnom Penh. As a famous *ācary* he supported building most of the statues of Wat Srae Aṃbil, to which his first *pāramī* was attached. He built a red *prāsād* in Wat Slaket in Koki before building the last one as his own residence. His house, where he lives with his wife and children, is on the other side of the road. Lok Tā P leads a life very similar to that of monks, in some respects: he wears saffron-colored clothes, especially during the *vassā* period, and fasts on holy days. He even became a vegetarian for some time while trying to collect money for building. People come to visit him seeking health care or moral support and advice. In his answers Lok Tā P always refers to the Buddhist sūtras; he might give amulets *(yantra)* and organize ceremonies in the temple. His experience of possession is not very visible. Rather, it is a very discreet process that takes place during intense meditation, at which time he receives the information needed to help his clients. He does not visibly manifest multiple personalities at that time and no longer changes his clothes during possession, but he still keeps his *pāramī*'s clothes and hat on his altar. Lok Tā P teaches Pāli at the wat as well as to some new *snāṅ* in his own *prāsād*, where patients are allowed to stay for several days.

Fig. 7.1 Monk as *grū pāramī.* (D. Bertrand)

The last medium I will present is Grū L, who is without doubt one of the most famous in Cambodia and who lives about thirty kilometers from Phnom Penh on the Mekong (fig. 7.2). When his story started, he was married with five children and nearly went mad, running away with severe pains in his belly. Another *grū* told him that he had received a *pāramī* and should build an altar for him. Then in dreams he realized that he could heal people and started doing so after giving his wife to another man whose brother had come to live with Grū L.[9] With long hair, jewelry, and a hyperactive manner, Grū L provides shelter on the ground floor of his house not only for his current patients, but also for more than ten former patients who became his disciples and work in a kind of therapeutic community. His therapeutic actions are very diverse and depend on the *pāramī:* salvation, purification, reinforcement, trying to find solutions for malevolent spirits, or exorcism. Like all the other *grū pāramī,* Grū L pretends not to be aware of what takes place while he is possessed. He is also an *ācāry;* he receives a lot of patients every day for his four consultations, during which he is possessed by several different *pāramī.* More than thirty *pāramī* can possess him (although some come only rarely). This *grū* wears a lot of extravagant costumes for his *pāramī,* which include a princess and the *pāramī* he is most famous for, the leper king (see chaps. 4 and 5).[10] On the days of the full moon, monks celebrate their office at his house while on holy days he brings food to the temple. Monks also come to ask him and his

Fig. 7.2 Grū L. (D. Bertrand)

pāramī for financial or spiritual support or even healing. Full-moon nights attract crowds; while his private orchestra is playing, between five to ten *pāramī* might come to possess him until late into the night. The whole spectacle happens in front of a large altar with several Buddha statues, including a life-size one, as well as Brahmanic symbols of *yoni* and *linga.* Every night all of those living in the house join in prayer sessions. And people help support Grū L with his building projects in the temple compounds. He started recently to build his own *prāsād* on his land.[11] He makes constant references to Buddhism, both as he relates to and treats patients and in his own life, in which he follows the five precepts. At the beginning of *vassā* (the rainy season), he usually stays isolated without speaking for some days. Part of the money he receives is redistributed as donations, but another part helps to support the survival of his community.

It is difficult with these four brief portraits to give a detailed idea of the diversity of the *grū pāramī,* who can be simple farmers, with no special clothing apart from white pieces of cloth—usually referred as *grū cūl rūp*—or professional mediums with a large number of *pāramī* possessing them and who wear sumptuous costumes and prefer to be called *grū pāramī.* In rural areas the scenario is very limited, while in urban regions the number of *pāramī* is higher (twenty to thirty for one *grū* is not unusual): here *grū* teach disciples and command large audiences.

Grū Pāramī and Other Possession Cults

Two other kinds of mediums operating in Cambodia are the *rūp anak tā,* a type of medium receiving the local genies *(anak tā),* and the *rūp ārakkh,* who are possessed by spirits known as *ārakkh* (Pāli *rakkhasa,* "guardian," "demon").

However, at the present time the *anak tā* cults and rituals are apparently less practiced. Several villages have no more *rūp anak tā* or specific mediums for their *anak tā,* while the *grū cūl* now claim they can also be possessed by *anak tā.* One *grū pāramī* explained,

> The way of the *anak tā* and the way of the *pāramī* is the same; the best *anak tā* can pass an exam to become *pāramī.* Now very often they want to become *pāramī* because they cannot find a *rūp* in their village, and there is a need to help the whole country. If the *rūp* are dead of course they can enter other persons but it is difficult to find.
>
> The *pāramī* have a lot of knowledge, but the *anak tā* less; anyway they can change *(pdūr),* once they dedicate themselves to study and they are given their exam to become *pāramī.* Now the *pāramī* come with the *devatā* because the *anak tā* stopped protecting the Khmers. They are not as pure as *pāramī,* because they are generals and they killed. The real *pāramī* are sons of kings who come to help

> and never did bad action *(pāp)*; they never killed. Before the war there was a lot of *rūp* and *anak tā*, but now the *rūp* are dead and the *anak tā* left to enter the forest and they don't come back.

This understanding, that there are not enough valuable persons to be *rūp*, has been shared with us in several villages. A Buddhicization of *anak tā* (Forest 1992, 212) is taking place; to be *anak tā* becomes a kind of rebirth in a Buddhist mode. Many *anak tā* are dead people who were famous for their practice of the Buddhist virtues during their lives. The next step seems to be to become a *pāramī* and to be considered under the orders of the Buddha himself. Obeysekere (1970) mentions that in Sri Lanka there is a tendency toward a universalization of the pantheon while villages and regional deities are losing their authority and guardian deities are taking their power to a national rank.

There are likewise not as many *rūp ārakkh*, but in this case the patterns of possession fall along family lines. Even an *ārakkh* who never possesses somebody who is not a relative can be of some help to other people in bringing information concerning misfortune or sickness, as well as divination.

Both *rūp anak tā* (at the village level) and *rūp ārakkh* (at the family level) are supposed to organize an annual ceremony for the spirit called *līeṅ anak tā*. It seems that this tradition is not always followed unless special problems happen and are understood as a sign from the spirits.

Those two kinds of possession rituals are less connected with Buddhism than those of the *pāramī*. However, some *anak tā* are guardians of the wat.

Generalizations along lines of gender have to be made cautiously, but the *rūp arakkh* or *rūp anak tā* we met are mostly women, while many *anak tā* or *ārakkh* are male. For the *grū pāramī*, as many men as women are professionally involved in healing, but a larger number of their disciples or *snāṅ* who occasionally experience possession are women (about two-thirds).

Grū Pāramī Practices of Possession and Their Relationship to Buddhism in Cambodia

Compared to the mediums studied by the various scholars of Southeast Asia (Brac de la Perrière, Spiro, Selim, Tambiah, Doray, Kapferer), the behavior of Cambodian mediums is distinctive in that they have a close relationship with Buddhism. While Buddhist monks studied by Tambiah, Spiro, or Gombrich in Thailand, Burma, and Sri Lanka usually do not interfere much with mediums and do not let them use the temple premises, Cambodian mediums and their disciples regularly occupy the Buddhist ritual space. Monks address religious incantations to the spirits, and in doing so recognize their existence in most Buddhist countries, but in Cambodia the monks are invited and come to attend the medium's ceremonies and vice-versa. The interactions between the mediums and the *sangha,* and their references to Buddhism, are constant.

Grū Pāramī as Elected on the Basis of Buddhist Virtue and Guardians of the Moral Order

Adherence to virtue was originally one of the causes for the selection of the medium by the *pāramī.* As a *grū* explains: "The *grū pāramī* are those who can fully respect the rule of the Buddha; ordinary men who uphold the virtues." Penny Van Esterik (1982a, 8) wrote that in Thailand as well, the *devatā* can assist only those who practice Buddhism. A *pāramī* said to us, "I only help those who know the prayer of the Buddha; if anyone has need of me he must behave according to the *dhamma* (Braḥ Thor)." Mediums are supposed to respect the Buddhist virtues and to follow the precepts of the *dhamma* or risk losing their power—a power for which the Buddha will be the final guarantee. The *snāṅ* explain that they are persons of exemplary morality—that is to say, they respect the five precepts *(sīl).* The mediums are in a relation of dependence to the *pāramī*'s authority, since the *pāramī* is the one who knows and who says what to do. All mediums in Cambodia would say that they cannot engage in malefic activities such as casting spells, as they get their power when possessed by a spirit who does only good (although some recognize that they could get in touch with bad spirits as well).

This adherence to the *dhamma* is important in itself for healing. Certain mediums say that they are not able to treat patients who have committed very grave faults or who do not respect the ethical laws. "If an illness of the nerves/veins or the loss of morale is the result of evil actions, or from too many bad actions, I am not able to heal," a medium told me.

Another medium did not wish to treat sexual maladies because he attributed them to the retribution of *kamma* on licentious conduct. An old medium from the vicinity of Phnom Penh added, "Elderly persons who have taken the five or eight precepts are the most easy to heal, almost 100 percent."

Buddhist Rituals and Relations with Monks

The altars in front of which the rites take place consist in general of several statues or images of the Buddha or of Maitreya (the Buddha to come). Holy days are the object of special religious practices; some *grū* suspend their consultations and others go to the wat, where they invite the monks for a ceremony of prayer and make offerings of food to them. At the annual ceremony of renewal and reinforcement of power, monks play an essential role in the many rituals, which last for twenty-four hours and include teaching of *dhamma* and conducting the standard prayers.

The entry into the rainy season retreat for the monks, during which they are supposed to be concentrating on study and meditation, is for some mediums an opportunity to follow a vegetarian diet and observe a period of silent reclusion while refraining from going anywhere. In doing so they sometimes impose on themselves rules even stricter than those of the monks. They manifest their faith with a kind of asceticism from which they gain more respect.

Most of the rituals organized by mediums start with an expression of faith in the three jewels and reverence for the Buddha. The officiant administers the five precepts and invokes the Buddhist trinity as well. In therapeutic practices, the utilization of Pāli is regular and consists of magical verses derived from the Buddhist sūtras, of protective verses called *paritta,* and of recited prayers extracted from the *Kalyāṇamitta-sutta.* The word of the Buddha is used for protection against evil spells *(aṃboe).* Buddhist morality or psychology is employed in particular in order to give counsel to persons suffering from troubles that we would call depressive. This proximity to Buddhist texts stands in opposition to the magic judged as unwholesome; thus a *pāramī* called Braḥ Rāj Kūmār (the Child King) confided in us, "I prefer those who know religion and prayer but not the magical words [*mantrāgam,* pronounced "monakum"]. The sacred texts *(gāthā)* are better." As described in Sri Lanka (Ames 1966, 35), all kinds of rituals start with Buddhist stanzas. Chanting and veneration of the Buddha are performed in order to show that he is the superior one. The Buddha is a source of power transferred to his relics, the consecrated images or statues as well as the Buddhist holy texts, and the Pāli chants that are used in rituals, with some appropriated to deal with supernatural beings. This same sacred language is inscribed on the square pieces of cloth called *yantra* (pronounced "yuan") and the magical plaques distributed as amulets of protection *(ksae gāthā).* The liturgy chanted by the mediums resembles those used by the *sangha.* During these long litanies, the medium invokes the local genies *(anak tā),* the protectors of the earth *(lokapāla),* and the hermits *(isī)* who live on the sacred mountains. There is constant reference to the *dhamma* or to sacred texts, and the mediums say that they also, like the monks, are invested with the mission of propagating the *dhamma.* "I must pray and respect the three jewels," declares one medium. Another says, "The *pāramī* also has a mission to protect the books."

The *grū pāramī* regularly frequent the wat, especially on holy days or other festivities. Their participation in numerous ceremonies *(puṇy sīmā, puṇy phkā, puṇy kathin)* provides additional occasions to redistribute the money they have received as gifts. "I make offerings (*slā dok,* a type of offering constructed from betel leaves) to the monks on holy days or other festivals," explained one medium who did not undertake consultations on holy days. "I keep all the money to give to the pagoda," said an elderly *snāṅ* from Koki who lived in a miserable hut. Mediums receive offerings, as do the monks, but unlike the monks they can receive food anytime of the day, unless their *pāramī* specifies otherwise. They usually cannot keep offerings for themselves, fearing punishment by the *pāramī.* I have not seen signs of personal enrichment, even among the most reputed mediums in the region of Phnom Penh who have many clients.[12] Practicing the essential virtue of giving *(dān'),* the mediums say that they do not keep the money but redistribute it all to the monks and to maintain the wat.

The practice of gift giving is a major part of social identity in a society where individuals are more recognized for what they give than for what they have (Forest 1992, 221). To give is to show power; the higher the social status, the more one is supposed to give, and to give, for the medium, means to give to the monks. The mediums, whose fame is partly derived from what they give, enjoy privileged relations with the monks whom they financially support. They attend the ceremonies that they sponsor with all their disciples and might perform some possession as well. Some are also *ācāry* of the wat, and they organize festivals with the monks in order to construct *vihāra,* bridges, stairs of access, and towers in the wat. The *pāramī* are supposed to be supporting their *snāṅ* to raise funds and might appear at the inauguration or foundation ceremonies such as *puṇy sīmā* to consecrate a new *vihāra.*

Mediums are often asked for their assistance at inauguration ceremonies. The *pāramī* are invited not only for the financial blessings they may provide, but because they are expected to come to give protection to the new buildings. In June 1996, for the Chinese *vihāra* of Phnom Prasiddh near Phnom Penh, which shelters a statue of Nāṅ Gong Se Im (Kuanyin), a huge festival was organized. At this time a new Chinese *pāramī* possessed the medium, to the great pleasure of the audience.

The *pāramī* are often consulted about the arrangement of private altars and about *prāsād,* such as one built in the camp of demobilized, handicapped soldiers on Highway 1, where a medium was asked to come and call the *pāramī* to the place. The medium was closely associated with the building of the Buddhist shrine, its inauguration, and the annual ceremonies.

These events are also excuses for reunions of mediums, which can take place in the wat or in their homes. Buddhism plays a "networking" role here. For example, a well-known healer-monk in the Phnom Penh area who was supposed to be a very powerful *pāramī* organized an annual meeting of all the mediums around a *bodhi* tree in which his power resided. This meeting, which took place at least every three years, had increasing participation and brought together hundreds of *grū* and *snāṅ.*

Another monk, head of a temple, gathered hundreds of persons for the celebration of the opening of the *pāramī* way (the consecration of his relationship with a *pāramī*). It was a two-day festival, including all-night possession ceremonies held in his residence *(kuṭī),* in the main hall *(sālā),* and the *vihāra* of the temple.

There are close connections between Buddhism and *pāramī* at other levels as well. The vital energy of certain mediums (and of many Cambodians as well) can be fortified and enhanced by showers of water blessed by monks. One medium who is also a monk related that "it is only a monk who is very old and who knows much *dhamma* who can give me a shower of blessed water *(sroc dịk).*" But even a sick monk or a victim of bad luck may seek healing from a medium: "My *pāramī* is very strong; it can even heal those who are greater than me and those who wear the monastic robes," a young medium told us.

Others related that at certain times in their lives they have adopted the rules of monastic life, such as a woman in relation with a hermit *pāramī* (an *anak saccaṃ*) who said, "For six months I could only eat rice in the morning like the monks." During the initial phases of their experience as mediums, the rules about eating were often more strict than those of monks, even of monks during the *vassā.* A medium told us that for two years he ate only rice, salt, and fruit. Another explained, "Some years during the *vassā* I ate only in the morning like the monks, but this is according to the wishes of the *pāramī;* at other times I am a vegetarian." Most mediums follow dietary prohibitions (the most frequent and almost universal prohibition being beef). Some mediums restrict themselves on holy days to one meal of rice and sesame, unlike the monks, who, fed by the devotees, eat abundantly on these days. The *pāramī* who present themselves in dreams often wear monastic robes, and they are considered to be servants of the Buddha, but we have never found a medium who dresses exactly like a monk. However, some prefer to be shaved and to wear saffron-colored robes (a cape and long trousers) or even the robes of a monk, but white in color.

And most interesting of all, a marginal phenomenon that I have not yet found in the other Theravāda countries is the medium-monks who practice possession. The possession state that they undergo, for healing or divination, is a complete infraction of the *Vinaya,* the code of conduct that regulates the life of the monks. Of course, we have never seen those monks dancing in public, but they show obvious signs of trance, trembling while they sit listening to *bhleṅ bādy,* a form of traditional religious music. Trance is unacceptable for a monk, as it is proof of the absence of serenity and a lack of behavioral control. The monks who do practice possession disobey the most basic rules of monkhood, and one may ask beyond what point they should still be considered a monk. Certain mediums were ordained into the monastic life before they established their relationship with their *pāramī.* Then, if during the seances of possession the *pāramī* manifested themselves through expressive gesticulations and dance steps, they choose to defrock rather than break the monastic rules. A medium from Kratie spent six months as a monk in the wat at Phnom Kulen before also engaging in the way of the *snāṅ.* He became sick because he could not conduct the requisite ceremonies for his *pāramī* while wearing the robes of a monk. He left the *sangha* but has continued to lead the life of a religious ascetic, dressing in white robes.

The modification of the iconography and statues of a wat by mediums is a visible phenomenon. Mediums will often bring their personal touch, following the counsel of the *pāramī,* to the construction of new statues for the wat. An extraordinary example of this can be found at Wat Srī Ambil in the district of Kien Svay, Kandal Province, where there is a profusion of statues. The festival to bring statues of Neang Kongheng and a crocodile and tortoise to Phnom Sarang was organized in the *borei kīla* sport hall in Phnom Penh in May 1995 and attracted hundreds of persons (*grū, snāṅ,* and devotees). Some mediums borrow Buddhist symbols, which they use to construct new places for worship/cult in which statues of the Buddha hold the place of honor. A medium in Phnom Penh collected money to reconstruct on the tongue of land in front of the royal palace a great boat made of concrete encircled by eight *prāsād* in order to "save the religion and so Cambodia can live in peace, regain prosperity, and that the inhabitants can find serenity on the road to *nibbāna,*" as explained in an invitation letter to the inauguration ceremony in May 1996.

These derivations, which are at the periphery of Theravāda Buddhism, reveal a "certain eclecticism more than syncretism" (Forest 1992, 77), something that characterizes the religious practice of Cambodians today. An example of this ecumenicism took place during the five-day pilgrimage to Angkor organized by some

Fig. 7.3 *Snāṅ* dancing at Angkor (D. Bertrand)

mediums and their devotees in 1995 for Visākhā Pūjā Day with the patriarchs of the Dhammayut and Mahānikāya sects of Cambodian Buddhism. The *snāṅ* participated in all the prayers and offerings of food to the monks, but they added ceremonies on their own initiative, such as dancing in front of the statue of the Buddha and the dumbfounded patriarchs in order to honor the Buddha by throwing flowers on him. The *snāṅ* also danced at the beginning of the ceremony of prayers directed by the monks at the terrace of the leper king in order to obtain good fortune (fig. 7.3). In addition to the official Buddhist ceremonies that took place at night in the heart of the Bayon, the *snāṅ* made offerings to the territorial deity Kruṅ Bali, held seances around the symbolic attributes of the *linga* and the *yoni,* and collected funds to support the Dhammayātra.[13]

Such public displays of the good relationship between mediums and monks are, for the mediums, signs of their respectability and honesty. It seems to us that the mediums, with their acting and finery, are more vulnerable to criticism and suspicion than the healer monks. They must constantly prove that they are not enriching themselves personally and demonstrate their availability. The monks, on the other hand, secure in their robes, do not always respect the rules of the *Vinaya* and can be found going about during the rainy season retreat, enjoying television and music during leisure time, pursuing lucrative practices, or getting involved in politics. Today mediums are able to attract the respect of the public because they follow not only the *dhamma,* with its universal ideas and doctrines, but also the monastic rules for the monks, and they are deeply involved in merit making through donation and public displays of morality. Mediums are more or less royalists, as the king is a kind of *pāramī,* but they usually refrain from any political comments; some even forbid newspapers to be brought to their houses and never listen to the news.

Conclusion: The Role of Mediums and *Pāramī* in Contemporary Cambodia

I have shown how in Cambodia the practitioners of exorcism and possession recognize the power of spirits and use it in a very Buddhist setting. They always try to acquire the assistance of Buddhist spirits; in so doing they declare the primacy of Buddhism but also point out its insufficiencies. The way time and space are divided as well as the rituals performed in the festivals in which both monks and mediums participate deserves further study, but it is already clear that the boundaries between the two are not strictly delineated.

It is interesting—even amazing—to see to what degree rituals implemented by a *grū pāramī,* which should be separated from those implemented by monks, tend on the contrary to be close to them. But mediums are still peripheral in the sense that while monks and the wat are at the center of religious life in a village, most of the people who consult a medium come from outside the village. While this is due in part to the fame of individual *grū*, many people also welcome the opportunity to resolve personal problems away from their own villages in a place where they can have more anonymity.

If we recognize that spirits are an integral part of the Cambodian belief system, the recent history of Cambodia can explain the presence and the intersecting roles of the *pāramī* and the mediums. The multiplication of mediums elected by the *pāramī* is interpreted by some *grū* as the wish of the Buddha to aid mankind and also to pacify and educate all the souls of the dead killed under Pol Pot who continue to roam and disturb people. For the mediums, the *pāramī* have come to make order among the living and the dead and to repair a collective trauma. As a *grū* in Kien Svay told me,

> There were many deaths from Pol Pot and from the war, and if their families do not hold ceremonies for them, they return and visit the *snāṅ* because the *snāṅ* can have money to make a ceremony for them. Many of the *khmoc* and *brāy* come to trouble the people, and the Buddha has asked the *pāramī* to come down to protect the humans and combat the *brāy* or teach them.

Wijayaratna (1987) shows that in Sri Lanka most spirits can be converted to Buddhism, even the most demonic ones such as the *yakkha* (pronounced "yeak"). This conversion operates on an even larger scale in Cambodia, with malevolent spirits learning the *dhamma* alongside the mediums.

The ancestral heroes, whom we can find as *pāramī*, represent new kinds of iconic figures that are needed in the rebuilding of Cambodia. These heroes offer models that are needed in the political sphere, such as the supremely virtuous King Vessantara or Braḥ Sdec Gaṃlaṅ, the leprous king who took great care of the sick and the indigent.[14] These *pāramī* identities link political, social, and cosmological orders so that they can address the contemporary situation and expectations of Cambodian society.

It is difficult to say to what degree this is a renewal or a new phenomenon, as quantitative data concerning Cambodian society before 1970 are lacking. There were mediums before the Civil War, and some were famous, but according to most of our informants there were not so many, and they did not interact as much with monks and the wat. In particular it seems that the existence of monk-mediums is a new phenomenon.[15] The proliferation of spiritual building projects in existing temple compounds and on new sites is new as well.[16] The projects are usually considered the expression of the will of the *pāramī*. One can wonder how long the *pāramī* will be worshiped as savior and protector after their *rūp* dies.

The consequences of the war and genocide in terms of social destruction are still readily apparent. Old figures of traditional wisdom have disappeared or do not inspire the same confidence that they once did. At the same time, family relationships have become more constrained, with individuals displaying mistrust toward other family members. Some persons, their families decimated during the Pol Pot years, are isolated and impoverished, living out their lives in a permanent state of depression. They go to the wat and to the communities that encircle the most charismatic of the mediums to recreate social links. The medium listens and speaks; he is an ally. Consulted outside the village of residence, he can become the guide or the confidant; in responding to the worry of comprehension and the quest for meaning, he researches and proposes explanations for what has happened to their families, and he guarantees a superior protection. In contrast to the monks, who refer to *dukkha* (suffering) as an inherent and inexorable part of life that we must endure with patience and wisdom, the medium acts to restore order and meaning in society as a means to lighten suffering or to heal. He brings also an individualized response (in relation to, e.g., the spirits of the ancestors).

One function of the medium today is to channel the stress induced by change and the loss of bearings and to respond to the Cambodian population's need to understand. Linked to areas of strong internal migration, of problems of land and labor, and of poverty, the increase in the phenomenon of possession and divination corresponds to the management of uncertainty and vulnerability. Mediums alleviate the lack of boundaries by providing mediation in a society agitated by numerous conflicts, at the heart of which the *pāramī* intervene as judges in the present (without waiting for the *kammic* retribution of acts). The responses of the *pāramī* appear to be appropriate to the necessities of an individual's social and political life.

The *pāramī* are accessible figures that help people who are marginal, or in a state of crisis, to recuperate. The medium does not only appear in a therapeutic role, but he also diagnoses illness, aggression, and evil. The medium has a social role, and he also serves as an intermediary between the spirits and men, and between men in social tension. He does this through the force of autosuggestion divided up, a sort of conditioning maintained between the rituals and the cult that participated in the reorganization of the pathology and tensions existing between the individuals and, moreover, the social groups. The role of these practices is to reestablish order amid the loss and separation at different individual, familial, and social levels through access to information that permits the individual to find underlying meaning and to reorganize disorder for the self and others. The mediums participate in the maintenance of tradition at the same time that they accompany change. The *pāramī* demand goodness from their representatives and respect of the laws of the *dhamma;* they stand for strictness, purity of heart, and good relations, while the persons they aid and counsel are explicitly those with good morality.

Not all the *pāramī* have iconic representations, but the statue of the Buddha of which they are guardians is an emblematic representation of the power that they incarnate. The *pāramī* constitute a visible manifestation of the power of the Buddha through the intermediary of the *snāṅ*, and the pairing of Buddha/*pāramī* reveals a meeting and reappropriation that merits further historical investigation. While some mediums put emphasis on their close relation with Buddhism, others would like to be the first voice of a new era during which spirits will be omnipotent and the ultimate reference for humans.

These mediums, more and more numerous in the urban and peri-urban zones, reveal the creative vitality that animates Cambodian society, in terms of spirituality or mysticism, while it faces an increasing materialism.

The needs that people express to the mediums they consult—the desire for wealth and success in school exams, work, or social promotion, as well as help with sickness or misfortune—may seem contradictory to the Buddhist ideal of morality, asceticism, and inner spiritual development. But in Cambodia, where sacred words are used both to exorcise and to teach morality, the desire for material success and well-being is believed to be complementary to the Buddhist path. In the face of an exterior world that is chaotic and politically uncertain, Theravāda Buddhism, preaching impermanence and endurance of suffering, does not seem to provide much immediate help. Nor does animism, which plunges one into the heart of hostile forces that he/she must ceaselessly try to conciliate. On the other hand, the *pāramī* sent by the Buddha through the medium ensure well-being while promoting Buddhist morality, and valorize continuity, security, and stability while guiding change.

Notes

This research has been supported by the Fyssen Foundation, Paris. My warm thanks to Elizabeth Guthrie for helping with the translation from French.

1. *Grū*, Skt: master, teacher; *pāramī*, Skt: sacred Buddhist powers or perfections. We will translate *pāramī* here as "power," but there is some ambiguity about the term, its origins, and its use in Cambodia. The Buddhist term "*pāramī*" is pronounced in Khmer as "baramey." However, some *grū*, when talking about spirit possession, substitute "boramey," thus making a distinction between "baramey" and "boramey." They reserve the first term for the virtues of the Buddha and the second for spirit possession, arguing that human beings cannot have *pāramī*. Bizot (1994, 116) suggests that the word pronounced "boramey" is spelled *pāramī* and is used to express "the force, the power or the sacred energy which emanated from a cult-object in the greater sense, and notably the gods in the service of Buddhism." But according to de Bernon (personal communication) the word pronounced "boramey" is actually derived from Skt *pūraṇa* + *rasmī* and means the "day of the full moon." This word conveys positive notions of fullness, completion, abundance, accomplishment, and perfection as well as negative associations with supernatural activities that take place on full-moon nights. We can thus think that the semantic field of "boramey"

captures some of the representations advanced by Bizot, although its origin is different from the Buddhist technical term "*pāramī*."

2. Braḥ Pāramī, "venerable powerful one" or "venerable virtuous one," is also a form of address for the Buddha.

3. The difference between the *devatā* and the *pāramī* has not been analyzed in detail, and it seems difficult to reach any conclusion at the present time.

4. However, I once attended a wedding of two *pāramī* who were represented by their *snāṅ*.

5. See chap. 8 on the ascetic Tāpas'.

6. The presence or absence of alcoholic beverages is usually a signal as to whether a religious ceremony is predominantly Theravāda Buddhist in nature or not. Most of the medium ceremonies we attended had no alcohol, with the exception of general feasts, which are, we believe, more closely related to the rituals dedicated to the local terrestrial spirits called *anak tā*.

7. The *kben* is a traditional lower garment made from a length of cloth wrapped around the waist with the end drawn up between the legs, creating something not unlike pantaloons.

8. Phnom Saṃbau is a sacred site in Battambang associated with *ṭūn jī* meditation.

9. Ed. note: his decision to leave his wife echoes the *Vessantara Jātaka*.

10. Ed. note: Another *pāramī* is Yāy Dep. Statues of the leper king and Yāy Deb are conspicuous at his new *prāsād*. Unlike the Yāy Dep statues Hang describes in chap. 5, Grū L's have distinguishable feminine features.

11. Ed. note: The *prāsād* is one of several mentioned in chap. 8 that parallel the activity of Tāpas'. In fact, it is not far from Tāpas' *prāsād* and was doubtless built with consciousness of Tāpas' activity. Like several other movements surrounding *prāsād*, it has millennial implications. Some followers say he is the savior prophesied in the *Buddh Daṃnāy*, Braḥ Pād Dhammik.

12. The only mediums I met who had obviously accumulated wealth as a result of their practices were two monks who had cars and mobile phones and had traveled extensively in the Cambodian overseas community in Europe, America, and Australia.

13. See chap. 9.

14. For more information about the leper king, see chaps. 4 and 5.

15. During my research, I met five of these monk-mediums. Some religious leaders complained to me about this kind of mixing, which they reject.

16. For more on this subject, see chap. 8.

–8–

Clay into Stone

A Modern-Day Tāpas'

John Marston

State policies toward religion in Cambodia liberalized in 1989 when a new constitution was adopted. In hindsight, the 1989 Constitution fits into a broad pattern of political and social changes that, in the context of international peace negotiations, would go on to bring about the 1991 Paris Agreements, the 1993 U.N.-sponsored elections, and a shift from a socialist to a free-market economy. All had some bearing on the fact that this was also a time of the birth of religious projects in Cambodia. Small cults surrounding persons believed to possess spiritual power had always existed, even in the socialist 1980s, but flourished dramatically at this time.

One cult grew up in a rural area close to Phnom Penh around a man who claimed to have the power to turn clay into stone. This movement was widely known and discussed and attracted many followers in the years immediately after the U.N.-sponsored elections, perhaps climaxing at the beginning of March 1996 during the mass festivities celebrating the scheduled completion of a clay temple/shrine. By 1999 the man had few followers and his compound was closed to the public. Probably by then most well-informed Cambodians believed that the movement involved fraud. Since then the compound has reopened but seems to be hobbling along with only the support of a few followers.

From one perspective, it was just another saga of religious charlatanism of the kind that plagues every country. The movement, however, has fascinated me, as a non-Cambodian observer, for reasons I believe are not completely different from those that succeeded in attracting so many followers: that despite (or because) of its absurdity, it managed to constitute a particularly dense and suggestive locus of

Cambodian cultural symbols—symbols that could be seen playing themselves out in direct relation to the social dynamics of the time. Like many religious movements in Cambodia in the 1990s, it claimed to be a resurrection of the past and of something essential about Cambodian culture. It claimed as well to be the fulfillment of prophecy. At the same time, it was patently a new synthesis, and part of the excitement it generated derived from its attraction as a new synthesis. It was fueled by the freedoms of a new political and economic order while it stood both as a critique of this order and a form of symbolic agency in relation to it.

This chapter will try to show the movement both as an example of basic tensions that have figured historically in Cambodian religion and of the particular pattern of development of Cambodian religion in the 1990s—the power, in Cambodian terms, of specific religious iconography and of deep-seated ambiguities about what is and is not Buddhism; the way, at this particular time, religion could figure in the ways persons related their identity to national identity; the role of overseas Khmer, negotiating their own senses of identity, in the trajectory of a religious project; and the parallels with other religious projects from the same period.

Kien Svay District lies immediately east of Phnom Penh on Highway 1, the road running parallel to the Mekong, which leads to the Nek Loeng ferry crossing and from there to Vietnam. This district has always been famous as a lush fruit- and vegetable-farming region. In recent years, with the introduction of a free-market economy, the privatization of land, and the new flow of wealth into a sector of the Phnom Penh economy, Kien Svay has been a site of particularly widespread land speculation, not only because of the fertility of the land, but because it is seen as a pleasant site for country homes accessible to the city and because people know that the city itself may soon extend into the district.

Phnom Penh people think of Kien Svay as a destination for day excursions, both to restaurants, nightclubs, and boat rental sites along the Mekong River and to the many famous Buddhist temples lining the national road, which in the wake of the Pol Pot period have gradually been restored and returned to active use. About twelve kilometers from Phnom Penh is the road to Wat Candaraṅsī, a modest temple lying to the south of the national road across a wide canal, in Prey Thom Village, Kbal Koh commune. Down the road from the wat is the compound of a religious figure generally referred to as Tāpas'.

The name Tāpas' (pronounced "tapoh") is derived from the Sanskrit/Pāli word for a religious ascetic: *tāpasa* (a hermit, one who practices austerities). *Tāpasa* are an icon of Cambodian folk literature and theater, and statues and paintings representing long-haired and bearded hermits garbed in tiger skins are common at Buddhist temples and religious shrines.

Tāpas' given name was Ras' Lī. He appeared, when his movement came to prominence, to be in his mid-thirties. His compound lies on his parents' land in the village where he grew up. Villagers say he became a monk at Wat Candaraṅsī in the late 1980s but left the monkhood after a few months, at which time he disappeared from the village. A year later he reappeared in the village and worked for a time on the family farm, only to disappear once again. Tāpas' claimed to have studied meditation at this time somewhere on the Thai-Burmese border (Angkor Thom 1996). When he reappeared in 1994, it was in the role of a religious ascetic hermit. His hair, which had been allowed to grow freely, was matted on top of his head in an arching mound, peaking in a rounded ridge. He returned to live at Wat Candaraṅsī but was asked to leave when he refused to cut his hair in the traditional manner of a Theravāda monk. It was at this time, in early 1994, not long after the U.N.-sponsored elections in Cambodia, that he set up his compound on his parents' land and began to attract a wide following based on his reputation of being able to turn clay and other substances into stone.

When I met Tāpas' in 1995, he was wearing robes that from a distance appeared to be the traditional robes of a Theravāda monk, folded in *graṅ* style with one shoulder bare. On closer inspection the robes were seen to be made from orange cloth on which were printed swirls of specks in a darker orange color. He referred to the robes as "leopard-skin pattern," in keeping with the traditional icon of the hermit wearing animal skins, and in some of the photographs of Tāpas' in circulation, he is shown more clearly wearing robes made from leopard-skin-patterned cloth (fig. 8.1). I was later told by provincial Ministry of Religion officials that when Tāpas' left the wat he kept using the traditional saffron-colored monks' robes for a time, but was told by them not to. He then wore white robes for a while, and finally began wearing the leopard-skin pattern.

Tāpas' high-pitched voice and ebullient manner approach the Western stereotype of a gay man, leading the observer to speculate that gender ambiguity may relate to the construction of liminality that created his charisma. Watching different videotapes of him in circulation in the Seattle Cambodian community, I was struck by how different his persona could appear at different times. Sometimes in videotaped conversations, Tāpas' seems childlike and passive, and it was hard to conceive of him as the leader of any kind of charismatic cult. At other times while preaching, his persona became focused and intense. On one tape, when Tāpas' was reading off a list of names of Cambodians who had sent contributions from the United States, he displayed difficulty reading the longer names and eventually turned the list over to a key follower, suggesting that there may be a limit to his degree of literacy. In 1999, when the mystique of Tāpas' had largely disappeared, villagers in the vicinity recalled that as a child Tāpas' had always been a terrible student. Nevertheless, the videotapes show that at times he is capable of considerable verbal artistry.

I first heard of Tāpas' in late 1994 when a videotape of him was played at a Buddhist ceremony held at a Cambodian home in Seattle, Washington. The video showed the groundwork being laid for a building called a museum or *sāramandīr* (pronounced "saraqmonti"). It also showed groups of people laying on the ground hundreds of clay blocks, disks of hardened sugar, mango seeds, and other objects, including wood and clay figures of iconic Khmer images such as *apsarā,* Braḥ Go-Braḥ Kaev, and Nāṅ Cek-Nāṅ Cam. These objects were then covered with dirt. My Cambodian friends told me that Tāpas' claimed that in three years the sugar would be transformed into gold and other objects would be transformed into bronze. These would then be displayed in the museum and would bring worldwide attention to Cambodia.

I visited Tāpas' compound in September 1995. Speaking to me and other people assembled, he explained that through meditation he had gained access to a kind of "mine" *(r'ae)* that gave him the power to turn substances into stones and

Fig. 8.1 Tāpas', 1995 (photo for sale at site)

metals. His knowledge of these mines, he said, did not come from any teacher, but from the practice of forest meditation. He described two broad categories into which seven specific kinds of mines were organized. In the highest category were three mines: laterite, marble, and granite. These three mines gave him access to a process whereby objects could be transformed materially after being buried for a period of months or years. In the remaining category there were four kinds of mines, named using Khmer folk terms for stone *(thma ān, thma gruos, āc(m) phkāy, thma gruos boḥ vīen, thma saṃlīeṅ kāṃbit).* When he created the stone blocks out of which the museum was being built, he drew on these four mines. The process of turning substances into stone, he said, was not one of magic *(mantāgam)* but of science.

Henri Mouhot, the nineteenth-century French naturalist and explorer whose posthumous writings first informed popular European consciousness of the existence of Angkor, wrote about a folk belief that the monuments were made of clay and then transformed into stone. This involved the holes in the blocks of stone.

> According to Cambodian legend, these are prints of the fingers of a giant, who, after kneading an enormous quantity of clay, had cut it into blocks and carved it, turning it into hard and, at the same time, light stone by pouring over it some marvelous liquid. (Mouhot 1989 [1864], 299)

One of the startling things about the cult surrounding Tāpas' is that it demonstrates the degree to which aspects of this folk belief are still current in Cambodia. The idea of a monk having the power to turn clay into stone is not new. There are many references in the history of mainland Southeast Asia to spiritual leaders skilled in alchemy and to times of social catastrophe in which pebbles would be turned into gold and silver, and gold and silver would become pebbles, lead, or iron (Ishii 1975; Keyes 1977b, 296–297, Mendelson 1975, 144–145; Spiro 1967, 231; Tambiah 1984, 312–313). However, Tāpas' cult is built on the premise that he draws on the same processes once used to create the temples of Angkor and suggests that, by creating glories like those of Angkor, he can usher in an era of new Cambodian greatness.

Tāpas' compound is on a dirt road that runs along a canal to the east of Wat Candaraṅsī. In the center of the compound behind a metal fence, the grillwork of which is decorated with *dhamma* wheel configurations, is the rather surreal temple/shrine with five turrets, constructed from sun-dried clay. This building, whose foundations I saw being lain in the video in Seattle in 1994, is the chief public focus of the movement (fig. 8.2).

Both the shrine and the compound have changed notably over the course of my periodic visits since 1995. In 1995 the shrine was still referred to as a *sāramandīr* (museum), emphasizing the idea that it would eventually house the objects to turn to precious metals. By 1998, it was more common to call it a *prāsād* (Skt, *prāsāda*). The word "*prāsād*" (temple) is most commonly used in Cambodia today to refer to the temple-monuments of the Angkor period or to religious structures that in some way make reference to antiquity.

In 1995 visitors could sit and talk to Tāpas' in a large porched-in area of a wooden building behind the *sāramandīr*. Farther back in the compound was a mound where truckloads of donated clay soil were deposited. Near it was a covered work area where followers of Tāpas' broke the clay into fine pieces to be worked by artisans. Across from this, on the west side of the compound, was a long dormitory where visitors stayed, both volunteers working on the *sāramandīr* and the sick who came for healing. At the far end of the compound were three long, low, barnlike buildings made of bamboo and thatch where the finely ground pieces of clay were taken to be molded into building materials or decorations and set out to dry—the claim being that Tāpas' powers would enable the blocks of clay to harden faster and be more truly transformed into stone than would occur by natural processes alone.

On the road in front of the compound there are usually three or four stalls where women sell sundries to the neighborhood as well as, especially in 1995, items that visitors are likely to want to bring to the *prāsād:* incense and candles,

Fig. 8.2 Tāpas' *sāramandīr-prāsād,* Kien Svay (J. Marston)

fruit and sugar. They also sell items visitors commonly wanted blessed by Tāpas': canisters of tiger balm and bottled water—the latter, having been blessed, to be sprinkled on a car for protection against road accidents.

Viewed for the first time in 1998, across the compound behind another grill-work gate was a long, gardened walkway leading to an impressive white villa. One of the ladies selling sundries readily volunteered the information (with only a touch of irony) that the new villa also belonged to the ascetic Tāpas'.

The *sāramandīr/prāsād* has changed several times during the process of construction between 1995 and 1998. The building has a simple rectangular shape with three arched doorways facing the front and a single arched doorway on each side. It is made entirely out of sun-dried clay blocks whose hardness, it is claimed, has been induced by Tāpas' powers. No metal frame or cement was used. In September 1995, the building had been built only up to the level of the archways above the doors and was still surrounded by wooden scaffolding. At this time the walls were decorated with a rough imitation of floral designs on Angkor temples, and on either side of the front doorway was a plaintively crude molded image of an *apsarā,* the female divinities that decorate many of the temples at Angkor. Even in 1995, the rough-hewn building, worlds apart from the artistry of Angkor Wat, nevertheless arrested the visitor with its weirdly ambitious, very-much handmade artifice (fig. 8.3).

I was able to follow work on the site over the next two years by watching the videos in circulation in the Seattle Cambodian community.[1] At the end of February and beginning of March 1996, at the time the *prāsād* was scheduled for completion, even though the work was behind schedule and the five towers had not yet been placed on the roof, a three-day festival was held that attracted thousands of visitors—probably the high point of the popularity of the movement. It ended up being some time later before the builders were able to successfully put the turrets on the *prāsād.* By June 1996 the turrets had been placed on the roof, but this caused the unreinforced sides of the building to curve precipitously.[2] By 1998, when I was allowed to freely enter the shrine, these structural problems had apparently been ironed out.

The building covered fourteen square meters and was twelve meters high.[3] The *apsarā* on the outside of the building had been replaced by new bas-reliefs of the Buddha in seated meditation above each of the three doorways and on the sides of the temple; in general there was greater emphasis on specifically Buddhist imagery than before.

As you enter each of the three doorways, on both sides of each of the three foyers are bas-reliefs of what at first seems to also be a seated Buddha. Under each of the six bas-reliefs is an inscription saying that the temple was built by Tāpas' (or Ras' Lī) and was dedicated to Dhamma and Civilization, A.D. 1994, 2537 B.E. To me, the face of the Buddha figure looked like that of Tāpas' himself, but the thirty-year-old man who originally guided us into the building said that it was the face of the Buddha. Later, the principal public spokesman for Tāpas', known as Tā Siem Reap, appeared and assured us that the bas-relief was of Tāpas' and not of the Buddha.

In general, the bas-reliefs that we saw in 1998 were of a much higher artistic standard than those I had seen in 1995; the spokesman Tā Siem Reap reported that a Cambodian returning from California who had had formal artistic training had created them. More primitive, and more consistent with the style I had seen in 1995, were the five turrets now on top of the building, each of the four faces looking out in different directions, like those of the Bayon (although compared to Bayon, a much flatter, expressionless, and makeshift face on a simple, onion-like, bulb-shaped head), which nevertheless created a dramatic if surreal presence.

In 1995, when Tāpas' was meeting the public, typical visitors would park their motorbikes or cars near the road and then go to the vendors to purchase incense and other items, also getting the use of a tray for presenting them to Tāpas'. In addition to items purchased from vendors, visitors would bring other items to place on the tray and be blessed, such as lotion, perfume, or lipstick, as well as amulets. At the back of the porched area where Tāpas' met visitors was a traditional stepped altar on which were several Buddha images made in the compound as well as the usual artificial flowers, candles, and multitiered *pāy sī* offerings. Photographs

Fig. 8.3 Detail of clay molding of *sāramandīr-prāsād* (E. Guthrie)

were for sale of Tāpas' standing next to the stepped altar: either a regular three-by-five-inch photo or a smaller size, which, it was pointed out, was convenient to carry in a shirt pocket as a talisman. Pāli letters were written on the back in marker—not actual Pāli words, but a series of sounds representing a mantra to be chanted. Once purchased, the photographs were also added to the tray.

After talking to visitors and answering their questions, Tāpas', much like many other Cambodian monks reputed to have the capacity to convey spiritual or healing power, would bless the objects on the tray, chanting and blowing onto the photographs and into each canister of tiger balm or bottle of perfume or lotion.

My inquiries in the neighboring village did not detect any hostility at this time. The abbot of the nearby wat recounted asking Tāpas' to leave when he refused to cut his hair. I was surprised, though, at the degree to which he and other villagers I met at the wat seemed to genuinely hold Tāpas' and his powers in awe. The abbot now described a dream that had foretold a monk attracting many followers. Villagers told me Tāpas' would disappear suddenly for days, with no one having seen him come or leave. His shoes were found left behind. Later, when Cambodians began speaking dismissively of Tāpas', they said he claimed to have transported himself to the Himalayas.

Tāpas' and Nationalism

Like many other religious movements that have appeared in the postcolonial world, the cult surrounding Tāpas' is interesting for the degree to which national identity colors the construction of religion. A Cambodian preoccupation with defining and asserting national identity grows naturally out of its recent history and the processes by which, since independence, it has negotiated its relation to world politics and economy. No doubt it is fair to say (like Edwards 1996 and Keyes 1994) that the ways in which Cambodian national identity has been constructed relate to the discourse of French colonialism and that the use of Angkor as a national symbol is part of this colonial construction. Be that as it may, there is at the present time no more recurrent symbol of national greatness for Cambodians than Angkor Wat, the Angkor period, and associated iconography. The use of Angkorean icons in Cambodian religious architecture is not new. But Tāpas' project is distinctive in the degree to which a conscious attempt to symbolically *recreate* a vision of Angkor becomes the thrust of a religious movement, and in the degree it stresses Khmer autonomy on the project.

Tāpas' stressed that the *sāramandīr* was the "handiwork of the nation" *(snāṭai rapas' jāti)*. In his conversation with me, he said that Cambodia had received much help from many countries, but his project was one that gave to Cambodians themselves the task of rebuilding the country's greatness. In the same vein, in a videotaped conversation with Cambodian-American visitors, he stressed that the building was being made "without help from foreigners." The workers on the temple, he said, were "all purely Khmers like us" *(dāṃṅ as' soddhtae khmaer yoeṅ),* people, he said, who did not have a lot of training or education, but who had ideals. Unquestionably, the *sāramandīr*'s essential Khmerness was seen as basic to its power and its virtue. On another tape he disparaged aid from foreign countries more generally, saying that "as long as they like what we are doing they will help us, but they stop helping if they don't like what we are doing."

In the discourse surrounding Tāpas', his power is, moreover, of a kind to be guarded from other nationalities. A disciple of Tāpas' told us that Tāpas' might someday pass on his secrets, but only to fellow Khmer. Tāpas' himself, in his conversation with me and a Cambodian friend, compared his situation to that of North Korea, recently in the news, saying that he could understand why North Korea did not want outsiders examining their nuclear power facilities. However absurd this may seem to an outsider, it is a revealing analogy that showed the scale at which Tāpas' conceived his own power and pointed to the degree that the attraction of Tāpas' and his project was related to their capacity to stand as a complex symbol of subaltern agency in relation to preponderant outside powers. We should keep in mind that Tāpas' came on the scene after an extended period of domination of Cambodia by Soviet-bloc countries, followed by a year-long U.N. mission entailing the presence of some twenty thousand foreign troops and civilians. Tāpas' started building his *sāramandīr* soon after an elected constitutional assembly had written a constitution setting up a new government, at a time of debate and rhetoric about the country's new direction. Cambodians were painfully aware how easily the country could be dominated and hyperconscious of the idea of its sovereignty.

The movement's appeal had a millennial aspect. On videotapes and, in particular, on an audiotape of one of Tāpas' sermons that circulated in the Seattle Cambodian community, Tāpas' makes reference to the *Buddh Daṃnāy* (Buddhist prophecies), the Khmer prophetic text in various written and oral versions described in chapter 2, which is believed to have predicted the Pol Pot period (see also Smith 1989; Chaumeau 1996; de Bernon 1998). On the tape Tāpas' talks about three crises, or "rising of the water," the first of which was the Pol Pot period, and the bloodshed that will accompany coming crises. He describes a period of reversal in which the grandchild will teach the grandparent and the child carry the parent like a baby in its arms. He also predicts a period of peace but says it can come only following a renewal of culture like that of his project.

The Iconography of Brahmanism and Theravāda Buddhism

Tāpas' and the images associated with his movement at once exemplify Cambodia's traditional Buddhist iconography and illustrate that iconography's ambiguities—those it has always implicitly had and those peculiar to its contemporary situation.

In the printed invitation to the 1996 dedication festival, Tāpas' name was given as "Maṇī Tāpas' Īsī." *Maṇī* signifies "jewel" (a word with Buddhist overtones), *tāpasa,* as we have seen earlier, means "religious ascetic," and *Īsī* is derived from the Pāli *isi* (and Skt *ṛṣi*): "hermit, religious ascetic, sage." Cambodia's most ancient inscriptions make references to such religious ascetics, and artists carved their bearded, topknotted forms into the walls of Angkorean temples. Religious ascetics also figure in the *Jātaka* stories, especially that of *Vessāntara,* and are often depicted in the painted murals of Cambodian wats.

The idea of "*tāpas'*" is closely related to the forest-monks tradition and the fascination this has held in Theravāda Buddhist countries, something especially well documented for Thailand (see Tambiah 1984; Taylor 1993; Kamala 1997). However, while a fully ordained Buddhist monk who practices religious austerities, known as *lok dhutaṅg* (Pāli, *dhuta + anga*), may share some of the characteristics of a "*tāpas',*" the iconography of the "*tāpas'*" (and Tāpas') is quite separate. The hermit is always depicted as an old, bearded man with a topknot, dressed in white cloth or animal skins, walking with a cane through the forest, a sage with access to supernatural powers. Such figures appear in Khmer primers, illustrating the Khmer letter "Ī." During the 1980s, they were sometimes pilloried in comedy routines on Cambodian television, perhaps a socialist critique of religion; they also appear in movies about the supernatural. Statues of the hermit clad in tiger skin often appear near shrines on Cambodian hills considered spiritually powerful. These are more crudely constructed than, for example, the statues of a Buddha that can be found in a wat and always seemed to me slightly comic. Nevertheless, they are also objects of devotion, receiving offerings and prayers.

As an icon, then, *tāpas'* can be associated with actual ascetics who have practiced religious austerities in Cambodia over the years, but he represents something more: a spiritual entity that can communicate with or enter a human being, much like the *pāramī* that enter mediums described by Bertrand in chapter 7. As such, Tāpas' is an icon that, although not exactly "Buddhist," has existed in conjunction with Cambodian Buddhism for a long time.

One pre-1975 precedent is described by Bareau (1969, 23), who wrote about a Tāpas'-like figure at Phnom Kulen in Siem Reap Province. The ascetic, dressed in white robes with his hair in a chignon, claimed to be a direct descendent of bearded Brahmanical ascetics depicted in Angkorean bas-reliefs. In 1995 conversations, Tāpas' similarly identified his practice as "Brahmanist" rather than Buddhist. He said he recognized that the aim of Buddhism was the pursuit of *nibbāna,* not earthly goals; as such, what he was doing was not Buddhism. Perhaps at some later stage or future life he would progress to the level of Buddhism, he said, but for now felt called to pursue the work he was doing.

These statements may reflect his discussions with Ministry of Religion officials and other skeptical visitors, an attempt to define himself in relation to official categories. In carving out a Brahmanist niche for himself, the way Tāpas' exploited and expanded discursive categories represented shifts in the ways Brahmanism figures in Cambodian national consciousness.

Brahmanist practices have, of course, always been deeply intertwined with the everyday Cambodian practice of Buddhism, and Tāpas' statement serves less to place him in opposition to mainstream Cambodian Buddhism than to justify his position on its periphery. Traditional Cambodian Buddhist phraseology and ritual practice very much find a place in the practice of Tāpas' cult, to the extent that Tāpas' refers to his disciples as *buddhaparisăt* ("Buddhist disciples," a term commonly used to refer to the members of the lay congregation of a Buddhist wat in Cambodia). In 1995, his workshop produced Buddha images, which were given to visitors and displayed prominently on the altar where Tāpas' receives visitors.

Cambodian Buddhist monks at this time did not hesitate to visit the complex, and he was widely discussed among the monkhood. The 1996 dedication ceremony included Buddhist monks, who chanted, gave sermons, and were presented with food.[4]

The iconography associated with Tāpas' movement became more Buddhist over time. In videos of the 1996 dedication ceremony, one is struck by the hundreds of paper and cardboard Buddha images adorning the site. The most prominent bas-reliefs and images on the final version of the *prāsād* are of the Buddha. Nāṅ Gaṅhīṅ Braḥ Dharaṇī, situated conspicuously on the walls of the building, is also closely associated with Buddhist iconography. The four-faced turrets on the top of the *prāsād* that evoke the four-faced images of the Bayon and Ta Prohm, built by Buddhist King Jayavarman VII, are widely recognized by Cambodians as the most "Buddhist" of the Angkorean images in Cambodian folk iconography.[5]

Tāpas' specific association with the figure of the Buddha is ambiguous. Tā Siem Reap responded with a resounding "no" when asked whether Tāpas' could be considered an *anak mān puṇy* (person with merit), referring to powerful figures who have led Buddhist millennial movements; he gave the same response when asked whether Tāpas' was a Maitreya figure. Nevertheless, some ambiguity exists in both cases. As described above, the walls of the entryways of the finished *prāsād* have bas-reliefs of what at first sight seem to be images of the Buddha, but whose face is similar to that of Tāpas'. The point to be made is that, whether or not it is intended, some iconographical ambiguity exists that associates Tāpas' with the Buddha, just as, even when he was not wearing monks' robes, there was some iconography that associated him with monks. One of two photographs of Tāpas' being sold at the shrine in 1998 showed him with hair coming to a point in a cone, in a style reminiscent of Maitreya's *jaṭā* (see chap. 1). Similarly, the four-faced towers of the completed *prāsād,* while replicating the images of the Bayon, have conical peaks similar to Tāpas' hairstyle but unlike the hair on the Bayon heads.

I do not intend to suggest that Tāpas' is not primarily identified as a Brahmanical ascetic, or that his shrine is not primarily conceived of as neo-Angkorean; I mean to emphasize the multivocality of Tāpas' and the images associated with him. The very ambiguity of the symbolic associations of Tāpas' may have had something to do with his followers' attraction to him. This ambiguity extends to the movement's ability to symbolize complex ideas about nation.

Followers in Cambodia and the United States

The question of who Tāpas' followers were is difficult to answer definitively, although there is much anecdotal evidence. Tāpas' original devotees were the people in the farm communities surrounding the site of the compound. It is clear that eventually he generated followers and curiosity seekers from all parts of Cambodia. Most observers say that the core followers and volunteer laborers came from poor, rural backgrounds. Nevertheless, my own visits to the compound and the conversations I have had with many Cambodians lead me to believe that there were also significant urban and middle-class visitors who made financial contributions and took seriously his advice and predictions.

My own understanding of Tāpas' is heavily filtered by the particular ways he presented himself to Cambodian Americans. Despite his emphasis on the notion of Khmer autonomy in his project, Tāpas' unquestionably received substantial support from overseas Khmer. A six-hour video begins with Tāpas' reading a long list of names of Cambodian Americans who had sent donations totaling over four thousand U.S. dollars. In 1998 Tā Siem Reap acknowledged that although Cambodians inside the country represented by far the greatest numbers of supporters of Tāpas', the financial support from overseas Khmer had been greater.[6] Overseas Khmer were very much in evidence as visitors to his compound. His case was between 1994 and 1996 widely known and discussed by Cambodians in the United States and probably other countries of resettlement. It is interesting that the spread of interest in Tāpas' in the United States was largely effected by the exchange of video and audio tapes and by the casual playing of the tapes at parties and religious celebrations held in Cambodian homes, pointing to the degree to which this kind of exchange contributes among overseas Khmer to a sense of community and of connection to Cambodia.

The Decline of Tāpas'

The question of whether Tāpas' movement was a deliberate scam is a relevant one, although not one that this chapter can answer. I myself have tended to believe that Tāpas', if not all those managing his movement, really believed in his own powers, although this is also contradicted by some details: the most convincing evidence of fraud, to me, was a marble vase that he claimed had been transformed from wood. The most convincing evidence that the movement was not a mere scam is the very absurdity of it. Who would have believed that such an idea would attract followers? Given the total departure from Khmer building styles, who would have predicted that someone would come up with a scheme for building a *prāsād* out of clay, or that it would be able to achieve a semblance of structural soundness? How could such a complex concatenation of symbols be generated merely out of the desire to dupe? The answer may lie in the ways Tāpas' acted in relation to persons managing his movement. There may also be some shift over time in the motivations of Tāpas' himself and his core followers.

Ministry of Religion officials for Kandal Province, interviewed during 1998, displayed an obvious skepticism about Tāpas' project. As stated to me, their philosophy of religion, apparently reflecting socialist 1980s ideologies, was to educate the people not to be superstitious and to encourage religion consistent with science and modernity. They showed me photographs from a similar religious movement in S'ang District also involving a charismatic figure raising money among local and overseas Cambodians to build a series of *prāsād,* which seemed to fulfill prophecy. They had shut down this movement for misconduct and fraud, including the sexual license of the leader and a cave full of weapons, as well as improper solicitation of contributions. They implied that this might someday be necessary with Tāpas'; they were still waiting for clear evidence of malfeasance. (I suspected that they wanted to be absolutely sure that Tāpas' did not really have the power to turn clay into stone.)

The abbot of Wat Mahā Mantrī, Saṃtec Oum Sum, told me in 1998 that when he visited the site of the compound, they would not let him enter the *prāsād,* presumably for fear it might collapse on one of the highest-ranking Cambodian monks. He commented that in the old days (i.e., the 1980s) they would have just thrown Tāpas' in jail, but now you had to take into consideration things like "rights."

The turning point for the movement seems to have been late 1996, three years after the burial of the objects, when Tāpas' was unwilling to dig them up to see if they had turned to precious metals. At this time, according to an article in the newspaper *Seṭṭhakicc niṅ Jīvit* (1999), tens of thousands of people came from different provinces of Cambodia, camping out in the village and the grounds of the wat near Tāpas' compound for more than two weeks, hoping to see the objects dug up and the supernatural powers of Tāpas' revealed. However, Tāpas' was simply absent. According to one woman interviewed in the article, some children died of diarrhea as a result of the crowded conditions among those who gathered at this time. Since that time, according to the article, Tāpas' has not been readily available to the public. The stated date for the unearthing of the buried objects continues to be projected further in the future. According to villagers interviewed in 1999, Tāpas' said he was waiting for the moment to be signaled by the appearance of a *devatā.*

This was roughly the time when videos of Tāpas' compound stopped circulating in the Seattle Cambodian community, although I was never given a specific explanation. There was another reason for the loss of interest in Tāpas': the fact that the building project was completed and there was no longer the excitement of seeing the building progressing.

When I visited the compound in July 1998, I had heard rumors of disillusionment with Tāpas' and half expected that the *prāsād* would no longer be standing. It was, and seemed in good condition, but Tāpas' was not present. I was told he had gone into forest meditation shortly after a ribbon-cutting ceremony the previous February. (Actually, according to a lady tending one of the stalls on the road, he was in the small house at the back of the compound.) There was much less activity than there had been in 1995. The man who showed us into the *prāsād* said the number of builders had shrunk from 1,000 to 150, but it was hard to believe that even this number of people was present. Despite this, the project seemed far from dead, the compound was in orderly condition, and there were occasional weekend visitors other than myself videotaped by Tā Siem Reap.

In pictures of Tāpas' for sale in 1998, and in pictures accompanying the 1999 newspaper article, he had gained considerable weight and was now quite chubby (figure 8.4).

The 1999 newspaper article claimed that, according to villagers, the *prāsād* showed signs of damage after rains. Somewhat contradictorily, villagers interviewed at that time speculated that the clay used to build the *prāsād* was mixed with cement or iron filings to make it hard. They jokingly made a word play with the name "Tāpas'" and "Tā Pok," or "Granddad Cheat." In the course of the conversation it came out that in 1997, at the time that Tāpas' was making a trip to the United States, my hostess had loaned him ten thousand U.S. dollars but had never gotten it back.

When I visited the compound in 1999, the gate was closed and no one would open it for us. I asked if I could speak to Tā Siem Reap, and he came out to talk to us through the gate. He said the grounds had been closed to the public for two months because "security" was afraid that people would come and commit acts of vandalism or theft against the property. I asked him whether "security" meant the police or the Ministry of Religion. (It may have meant the security apparatus of the movement itself.) He said that the *prāsād* had nothing to do with the Ministry of Religion, which was responsible only for wats. With a typical knack for associating any vulnerability of the movement to the vulnerability of the nation, he said that the compound was the "property of the nation" *(kammasiddhi jāti)* and had to be protected. He said that anything that was dedicated in a ribbon-cutting ceremony was "property of the nation" and needed to be protected. He said that the people we saw inside the compound were the project's core workers. (A young man from the area who accompanied me later said that these were believers who "swallowed it whole" *(jīeo s'up)*. The article in *Seṭṭhakicc niṅ Jīvit*, which came out after this visit, stated that the Ministry of Religion was closing the compound to the public.

When Tāpas' compound was closed in 1999 I assumed that it was the end of the movement; on subsequent visits to Cambodia I found it open again but with many fewer visitors and much less fanfare. A new building was begun, this one not of clay turned to stone. While the building with turrets was now called a *prāsād*, this would be the *sāramandīr* to house the buried objects once transformed. Spokespersons for the movement now more modestly claimed that they would turn into stone instead of precious metals.

In August 2002, making what I felt was my obligatory visit to the site while in Cambodia, without expecting any new revelations, children on the grounds told my research assistant that Tāpas' was present and pointed to him as he walked by the construction site in the distance. We followed and asked to talk. Amazingly, he had shaved his head and was now dressed as a Buddhist monk. He said he had done this in 1999; people still called him Tāpas' even though he no longer assumed that role. The shaved hair was placed at a shrine when it was cut off.

Fig. 8.4 Tāpas', 1998 (photo for sale at site)

The hair had given him the power *(pāramī)* to build the *prāsād,* he said, but he acknowledged that his powers had now diminished. He now had no intention of doing forest meditation and was, as it were, lying fallow, trying to calm his emotions *(sṅap' āramm(ṇ)).* His organization was much weaker than before. People left, he said, to go on with their lives.

He said that, having been ordained at Wat Candaraṅsī several years earlier, he had always considered himself a monk and had not felt the need to go through another ordination when he shaved his head. However, his status as a monk was clearly in some sense ambiguous. He was sometimes invited to Phnom Penh to chant or sprinkle water in private ceremonies, but would never go with monks from other wats, only with an older layman or *acāry.* Forest monks *(lok dhutaṅg)* would be welcome at his compound, but it was not a place where regular monks could come to stay, like a wat.

He seemed rather sheepish about his past claims to fame, as though it was something he would rather not talk about. At the same time, while he probably would have preferred avoiding us, he was open and amiable, and there was no clear indication that he was hiding anything—leaving a favorable impression.

The abbot of Wat Candaraṅsī had died a year previously and the old *vihāra* had been razed. Under Tāpas' supervision and apparently with his financial help, a new *vihāra* was being built.

I was in general amazed at the degree to which Tāpas' had managed to land on his feet, extricating himself from the more extravagant claims of the movement in ways that maintained face for his core followers and allowed him to blend into the woodwork of more traditional Buddhism. His decision to direct his talent for building to a traditional wat was a perfect form of reconciliation—an appropriate gesture of penance in the eyes of those who did not believe in him and a further investment of his spiritual power for those who did.

Analysis

The movement surrounding Tāpas' stands, first of all, as an example of Cambodian cultural iconography in actual practice, both the iconography of the hermit and the iconography of Angkor. In ways that parallel the *pāramī* described by Bertrand in chapter 7 or the way Cambodian classical dancers perform rituals to invoke the spirit of the role they are dancing (Chan 1987, 14–16), we see the degree to which such an icon is not merely an abstract idea on which to meditate, but an active source of power that can enhance that of the person who interacts with it. In the case of the hermit icon it represents power integrated with a kind of personhood with which someone can communicate or with which there can be a fluid exchange of identity. Icons can inhabit or be inhabited. It is logical to assume that this kind of relation to an icon has a long history in Southeast Asia, given the historical existence of mediums and given a conception of power as something inhabiting images of the Buddha and other objects such as amulets (Tambiah 1984). Nevertheless, we should not assume that these practices are timelessly traditional or rule out the possibility that spiritual practice in relation to icons may have crystallized in new ways or taken on a particular intensity in postsocialist Cambodia.

The fact that alongside Buddhism there exist practices that do not seem to be specifically Buddhist is a characteristic of Theravāda Buddhism from its earliest times. Different authors have stressed to different degrees the extent to which these non-Buddhist elements could represent a cultural divide or a single integrated system (Tambiah 1970; Kirsch 1977; Ang 1988). Tāpas' movement perhaps tells us something about the nature of this divide in the degree to which the ambiguities—whether the movement is or is not Buddhism, or whether, more generally, is the movement orthodox—create the possibility for it to represent simultaneously deference toward religion and national culture and ideas of subalternity and opposition.

But if the movement surrounding Tāpas' in some ways exploited traditional ambiguities between Buddhist and non-Buddhist elements in Cambodian religion, it is not at all clear that what was called Brahmanist in the movement has a clear link to what was called Brahmanist in pre-1975 Cambodia.

The impact of Tāpas' and the movement surrounding him clearly related to the capacity of the icon and the movement, in the very ambiguities they configured, to combine a variety of symbolic meanings, some of them contradictory; its iconography was, that is, multivocal. Ambiguities surrounding religious practice in Cambodia were heightened by the fact that, throughout the socialist years, there were state-imposed restrictions. The fact that religious practice then had to be reinvented in relation to new social circumstances meant that what should or should not be practiced was open to conscious decision in a way that released new possibilities. By the nature of memory, there was ambiguity about what pre-1975 religious practice really was. These ambiguities were even more heightened in the attempts of overseas Khmer to reconstruct religious authenticity. Tāpas' movement flourished, then, in its capacity to evoke powerful meanings in relation to the very ambiguities surrounding him. It is likely that the symbolic density of the iconography surrounding Tāpas' was actually heightened among overseas Khmer by the very technical imperfections of video and audio tapes by which it was known and the vagueness of oral reports by visitors.

That the multivocality of the religious iconography extends to representation of the nation is new to Cambodia; this is part of what puts the movement in the category of the modern. It is beyond the scope of this chapter to examine in detail the history of postcolonial Cambodia in relation to Chatterjee's idea of how, in postcolonial Asia and Africa, the idea of nation counters Western ideas of science, technology, and statecraft with an insistence on an "'inner' domain bearing the 'essential' marks of cultural identity" (1993, 6; see also 1986, 50–52). (This is discussed in chap. 2.) Tāpas' movement does not represent the dignity of mainstream nationalist thought in Cambodia; it finally exalts the instrumentality of a righteous "Brahmanism" over what it acknowledges as the greater purity of Buddhism. But, along Chatterjee's lines, the nationalism it constructs is one that claims to tap the essence of Khmer identity; this nationalism is constructed as subaltern in relation to the international order and as giving agency in relation to that international order.

The movement surrounding Tāpas' illustrates a practice of individuals exercising symbolic agency to build the nation, thus relating individual identity to national identity. The obvious irony, that an important motor of this national process was the transnational contributions of overseas Khmer, does not really contradict this. It is perhaps overseas Khmer who are most conscious of Cambodia's subaltern position in the community of nations and most in need of enacting their own national identity. Ledgerwood (1998) has emphasized that nation building can include the contributions of diaspora Khmer.

It is difficult, if not impossible, to evaluate the range of new religious phenomena in Cambodia in the 1990s. The *grū khmaer,* the mediums, and the monks gifted in blessings with water had always existed in one form or another, but now seemed to flourish or take on greater public visibility because of the relaxation of state controls.

In trying to compare the different religious projects of the time, we find ourselves lumping together projects of very different stripes and, seemingly, different degrees of legitimacy, but most, in one way or another, shared traits with Tāpas' movement, and all shared the same general momentum of the time. Few would put the Dhammayātrā (described by Poethig in chap. 9) in the same category as Tāpas' movement, but both represented religious innovation at a time when religious conventions were very much in flux. Like Tāpas' cult, the Dhammayātrā was conceived in terms of the Cambodian nation and in some ways tries to create a new definition of the nation. Like Tāpas' cult, it attempted to provide to Cambodians agency in relation to their national future in a situation where there seemed to be little other possibility of providing real agency.

For me the most interesting religious movements in comparison with Tāpas' are those that also involve a building project and, as with Tāpas', the belief, with reference to prophecies in the *Buddh Daṃnāy,* that once this building is finally completed it will signal the beginning of an era of peace and prosperity for Cambodia. I know of five such projects in Cambodia besides that of Tāpas' and would not be surprised if there were more.

One was the project in S'ang District, mentioned above, which was closed down by the Kandal provincial Ministry of Religion. Following references in some versions of the *Buddh Daṃnāy,* it involved the construction of three *prāsād:* one silver, one gold, and one diamond.

Near Wat Bhnaṃ Rāp, at Phnom Prasiddh, also in Kandal Province, is another massive building project, which also involved creating a silver, gold, and diamond *prāsād.* This was followed by the construction of an elaborate three-towered structure in Angkor style. Since 1999, near the same location, a new wat has been established with an elaborate esplanade in imitation of the ones at the four entrances to Angkor Thom, with lines of *devā* and *asura* pulling a giant *nāga.* A huge new ritual center is also being built on the site. Although most Cambodians view the site as a simple tourist destination, the movement has millennial overtones for a core of followers.

The building project that received the most international press was a small wat built on an island in the Mekong River directly in front of the palace—again with the specific belief that the construction could bring peace to the country (Chea 1999; Johnson 1999). In addition to references in the *Buddh Daṃnāy* to silver and gold *prāsād,* the prophecies make reference to the temple being constructed at the meeting of four rivers, which the island precisely does. The wat was consequently flooded during the annual rise in the river's water levels. Then, because government officials found that the newly formed island was causing significant damage to delicate water flows that affect fishing, the entire project had to be dismantled and the island dredged.

Lok Tā Lṅaṅ' Āyu Vaeṅ (Uneducated Granddad with Long Life) has a compound in Kandal Province near the border with Takeo Province. His persona emphasizes the role of the humble peasant man. He has also built a series of *prāsād,* following the instructions given to him in a vision by the god Indra. These *prāsād* are intended to house the *anak mān puṇy* who will welcome in an era in which Cambodia will become an international power and Khmer will be an international language.

One of the *grū pāramī* mentioned in chapter 7 has built an elaborate cruciform neo-Angkorean *prāsād* not far down the national road from Tāpas' compound.[7] Some followers claim he is the righteous ruler prophesied in the *Buddh Daṃnāy.*

These five projects are among countless less dramatic building projects that took place in the 1990s as momentum gained to rebuild the country in the wake of the devastations of Pol Pot. Such projects flourished because of the lifting of government controls on religion and because of new infusions of wealth as the country opened up to a free-market economy. They also flourished because of the contributions of overseas Khmer, many who focused on rebuilding wats in their home villages.

The five projects described above involved significant contributions by overseas Khmer, as well as local contributors. While individual contributors may play key roles on a given project, there is invariably an appeal to general contributors, as well as, of course, the assumption that contributions constitute a particularly strong form of merit. What is not always acknowledged is that such fund-raising represents a key way in which personal networks and ideas of hierarchy within these networks are enacted—to the extent that it is not an exaggeration to say that the building project exists to empower the fund-raising networks as much as the fund-raising networks exist to empower the building project. This is important in Cambodia itself; it is especially true among overseas Cambodians, where it is one of relatively few ways that a sense of community is enacted.

The movement surrounding Tāpas', and other movements that appeared at the same time, must be analyzed in terms of the momentum they were able to achieve. Ultimately they grew as projects because the very processes of growth generated more followers. This momentum relates to several factors. First, as I have said, was the economic momentum. The fact that in the 1990s there was more money to devote to religious projects (especially money coming from overseas) meant that such movements could achieve dramatic material momentum.

Political changes meant that, after the socialist 1980s, brand-new nongovernmental organizations, including religious bodies, were created, and there was much excitement about the possibility of new forms of social organization. It also meant that the state was not entirely clear about what its role should be in relation to the new nongovernmental bodies—an ambiguity underlined by the fact that traditional government bodies shared power with the U.N. Transitional Authority in Cambodia in 1992 and 1993. As cited above, a monk ranking high in the Ministry of Religion said that in the old days they would have just thrown Tāpas' in jail, but now they had to take into consideration issues of rights. Without underplaying the new concern for rights, it is fair to say that he was in part acknowledging that there was a confusion about what the role of government should and could be under the new order—a confusion that, for good or for bad, allowed eccentric religious movements like that of Tāpas' to gain momentum.

The momentum of Tāpas' movement spread by word-of-mouth discussion, the circulation of photographs and amulets, and, at least to a small degree, coverage in newspapers and on television. Among Cambodians overseas word-of-mouth discussion of Tāpas' was supplemented by the circulation of audio and video cassettes (by "small media," to use the formulation of Sreberny-Mohammadi and Mohammadi 1994), underlining the importance of the circulation of such "small media" in overseas Khmers' sense of community.

It should be obvious from the overall content of this chapter that, in conjunction with economic and political momentum and the momentum created by media, I see religious projects such as Tāpas' as gaining momentum by the very power of their ideas to capture the imagination of the population. The disproportionate social momentum that revived religious practices could take on after the long silence of the socialist periods may derive in part from the fact that they represented what Scott (1990) has called "hidden transcripts," long quietly discussed in private and mulled over in thought, as a hidden, subaltern truth, which only at length is allowed public voice, sometimes much transformed from the religious practice it "remembers." Combined with this, I would argue, is a process of working out, in practice, the logical possibilities of a given set of ideas in relation to a changing social framework: it is a process of exploring, in new social circumstances, the degree to which a set of ideas really does provide agency—ideas of nation and democracy and a new Cambodian sovereignty, as well as the ideas implicit in religious categorization and iconography.

Can the movement surrounding Tāpas' be described as millennial? In the fullest sense of the word, probably not. Despite the massive number of people who visited Tāpas', made small financial contributions, and to some degree believed in him, there were relatively few who were the immediate disciples of Tāpas', and their activities seem to be limited to building construction. Despite the prophecies that the movement could bring about a new order in Cambodia, there seemed to never have been any danger of the movement bubbling over into political activity.

Nevertheless, like the other building projects I have described, the movement was millennial to the extent that it predicted the miraculous coming of a reign of peace and prosperity. Whether or not we can categorize the movement surrounding Tāpas' as millennial, it does shed some light on religious-oriented social momentum in Cambodian and Southeast Asia more generally.

Tāpas' movement fits Keyes' criteria that "millennial movements are caused primarily by a crisis centering around political power" (Keyes 1977b, 284), both in the sense that the political confusion of the early 1990s was a reason that Cambodians sought the psychic framework of religious systems, and in the sense that a lack of political controls helped create the conditions for the movement to gain momentum.

At the same time, the millennialism of Tāpas' movement was a very modern phenomenon to the degree that the chosen people who would reap the benefits of the movement were conceived in terms of the nation—a Cambodian nation descended from Angkor. It was a very modern phenomenon, as well, in the degree to which the movement drew strength and momentum from the fact of the Cambodian diaspora, and the degree to which the movement existed in relation to global inequalities. These inequalities in turn served to feed the movement economically, creating astounding economic momentum in Cambodian terms at the same time that a heightened, very modern sense of global inequality was part of what the movement appealed to as it represented, symbolically, the subaltern nature of Cambodian nationality.

With reference to the large question of how millennial movements can fit into the belief system of Theravāda Buddhist societies (see discussion in Kitsiri 1970, Keyes 1977b), Tāpas' movement suggests several possibilities: the degree to which iconic elements peripheral to Buddhism can come to take on central roles; the degree to which traditional ideas of the millennial savior, as a Maitreya or an *anak mān puṇy*, can be called on even when they do not play an explicit role in the ambiguity of symbolic systems; the degree to which the association of Buddhism with the nation lends itself to the dream of national salvation; the degree to which one conventional way of building merit, by building buildings, can extend itself to the idea that building a building can create the conditions of a new order.

Notes

My thanks to Hong Siphanna, who first brought me to see Tāpas' and who was a source of help and insight in my initial explorations. Ven. Sath Sakkarak, Leng Lim, and Yin Luoth have also helped clarify questions of Cambodian customs. This chapter grew out of three conference presentations, and I am grateful for the discussant comments by Charles Keyes, John Pemberton, and Maury Eisenbruch. I would also like to thank Elizabeth Guthrie for photographs from Tāpas' compound and ongoing comments and discussion.

1. Many Cambodian Americans who visited Cambodia during this period included Tāpas' compound on their itinerary. They videotaped the construction and then circulated the videotapes among other Cambodians upon their return to the United States.

2. Hong, personal communication, 1996.

3. These dimensions were given in a printed invitation for the 1996 dedication ceremony.

4. Hong, personal communication, 1996. At this ceremony, Tāpas' was seated lower than the monks, an indication of his lower religious status.

5. Cambodians have told me in conversation that the four faces represent the four ideal traits of *mettā* (loving kindness), *karuṇā* (compassion), *upekkhā* (equanimity), and *paññā* (wisdom).

6. Tā Siem Reap himself had lived in the United States for a period of time. He returned to Cambodia to do forest meditation before linking with Tāpas'. Networks of support for Tāpas' seem to have been especially strong in places where Tā Siem Reap had lived.

7. This is the *grū pāramī* Bertrand calls Grū L. Construction of the *prāsād* was only beginning when Bertrand wrote his chapter.

PART IV

The Transnationalism of Cambodian Religion

In a sense Cambodian religion has been transnational at least as long as the concept of "nation" could be applied to Cambodia. As chapters 2 (Hansen) and 3 (Edwards) have shown, French colonial authorities were responding to a tendency of Cambodian monks to see Thailand as a center of Buddhist learning when they worked to establish a more Cambodia-centered system of education and administration for the monkhood. The French colonial interaction with Buddhism that they describe was of course itself a transnational process even as it served to define nationalism. At least since the French colonial period there have been ethnic Khmer monks from southern Vietnam (Khmer Krom) coming for residency and education in Cambodian wats. When Buddhism was reestablished in Cambodia in the early years of the Peoples' Republic of Kampuchea, senior Khmer Krom monks were brought to Cambodia to reestablish the ordination lineage. According to at least one former Khmer Krom monk, authorities also resettled a number of more junior Khmer Krom monks in Cambodia in the early 1980s to foster the rebirth of a particular kind of Theravāda Buddhism. More have come individually and for more personal reasons of religious and ethnic identity. Cambodian monks still find ways of going, by formal and informal means, to Thai wats for education.

But contemporary transnationalism goes beyond this. It is a truism that the global phenomenon of transnationalism is in recent times intensifying, to the extent that it is sometimes described as ushering in a new cultural era. In Cambodian terms, this is most dramatically illustrated by the Khmer diaspora that occurred in the wake of the Pol Pot period, and with the rapid opening of the country to Western markets and the international nongovernmental organization (NGO) community that has taken place since 1989, especially since the 1993 U.N.-sponsored elections.

The flow of refugees from Cambodia into Thailand began during the 1975–1979 Pol Pot period but achieved its greatest momentum in the early years of the Peoples' Republic of Kampuchea, after Vietnamese troops defeated the Khmer Rouge. Enormous border settlements of Cambodian refugees formed, larger than any Cambodian city besides Phnom Penh, to be supervised by U.N. agencies. They included what the U.N. called holding centers, like Khao I Dang, which were technically inside Thai territory, and camps straddling the border, which the U.N. regarded as in Cambodian territory and which were more closely linked to resistance movements. As Poethig brings out in chapter 9, camp authorities supported the creation of Buddhist temples and the promotion of Buddhist education. The temples serve the straightforward goal of meeting the religious needs of the camp population. They also became a way of symbolically preserving aspects of Cambodian culture that were perceived as threatened and, in border camps, implicitly made the political statement that the areas controlled by the resistance more truly represented the continuation of Khmer culture than did the territory controlled by Phnom Penh.

Many of the relief organizations working in the camps were Christian and a small but a significant proportion of the Cambodians in the camps also converted to Christianity.

As Yamada describes in chapter 10, hundreds of thousands of Cambodian refugees were eventually resettled in industrialized countries, primarily the United States, France, Australia, and New Zealand, where they established Cambodian Buddhist temples. In these new temples there was often confusion and dispute over what was essential to Cambodian Buddhism and what could be changed or left behind. One of the biggest problems these communities faced was a lack of monks.

Many Cambodian immigrants have converted to Christianity, most often, according to Smith-Hefner, to conservative Protestant religions. While some Cambodian Christians cut all ties with Buddhism, many new converts have maintained close connections to the Cambodian Buddhist wat and continued to participate in traditional Buddhist ceremonies despite attending Christian churches.

Throughout most of the 1980s, there was almost no formal means of communication between Cambodia and either the refugee camps or the refugee communities overseas. This would change dramatically with the peace negotiations in the late 1980s, which led to the 1991 Paris Agreements.

The period leading up to and immediately following the 1993 U.N.-sponsored elections represents a watershed in the opening of Cambodia to transnational processes—in particular insofar as transnationalism is associated with the West. The U.N.-sponsored elections made possible a diplomatic opening of the country, which in turn meant there could be aid from countries that had blockaded Cambodia during the 1980s. There was a general opening of the country to international organizations and NGOs, some of whom had previously restricted their activities to the border camps because the "government" situated there was recognized by the U.N. and many Western-bloc countries. The Dhammayātra march from the border to Phnom Penh that Poethig describes represented in part the expanded focus of border-based NGOs.

At the same time, there was a dramatic opening of the possibility of communication between Cambodians in the country and those overseas. With peace negotiations, overseas Cambodians began hesitantly to make visits to the country, and the number of visitors gained more and more momentum at the time of the U.N. elections. Visitors invariably played the role of courier, bringing the money that other Cambodians were sending to their relatives—for general support, but often also, significantly, to sponsor ritual activities, including ceremonies to those who died during the Pol Pot regime. Overseas Cambodians, eager to make merit for dead relatives and themselves, have donated enormous sums of money to refurbish and rebuild their village wats (usually damaged or destroyed during the war or the Pol Pot period), as well as more eccentric religious building projects of the sort described in chapter 8.

The first two monks to travel officially to the United States (in 1990) were the Mahānikāy patriarch, Ven. Tep Vong, and a similarly high-ranking figure, Ven. Oum Sum,[1] under the auspices of the U.S.-Indochina Reconciliation Project. Their visit, though politically controversial among the leaders of the Cambodian community, was welcomed enthusiastically by rank-and-file Cambodians in the cities they visited. In 1992 it became possible for monks from Cambodia to be sponsored by wats in the United States and to become residents there. This would sometimes create complex situations merely in terms of immigration regulations, but it very much served the needs of the Cambodian wats, which could rarely recruit young men as monks from the refugee community. This also served to underscore connections to Cambodia, since the monks had solid links to specific wats in the home country and were often committed to raising funds for these wats. Similar processes occurred in other countries of resettlement.

The new opening also meant that monks and *ṭūn jī* affiliated with overseas communities could travel to Cambodia and visit wats there and that monks and other religious leaders in Cambodia could make visits overseas to broaden their followings and raise funds—including the medium monks described by Bertrand in chapter 7 and the "forest ascetic" described by Marston in chapter 8.

While Christian missionaries to Cambodia before 1975 had never gained a significant foothold among the ethnic Khmer population, the return of refugees from the border in 1992 meant that for the first time there was a small community of confirmed Cambodian Christians. The opening to the West also created new opportunities for Western missionary groups, who frequently brought with them Christian pastors from the overseas Cambodian communities. There is some evidence of continuing conversions of Cambodians to Christianity, as well as some tension between Christians and Buddhists in rural areas.

Transnationalism figures in very different ways in the two chapters of this section. Poethig's chapter discusses the transnational aspects of the Dhammayātra peace marches, which began in Cambodia in 1992. Poethig discusses the origins of the marches among monks and relief workers based in camps on the Thai border, as well as the background of the monk that has been its most charismatic leader, Ven. Mahā Ghosananda. She discusses the place of the movement in relation to the larger global movement of Engaged Buddhism. The Dhammayātrā has been transnational in the way it has linked international movements to the local situation of Cambodia, in its links to the NGO movement, and in the way it has brought together Cambodians returning from refugee camps and Cambodians long resident in the country, with the support of Cambodians and non-Cambodians overseas. The Dhammayātrā stands out from the other Cambodian religious practices discussed in this book in its clear stance of social activism—but like the other chapters on contemporary religious practice, Poethig's describes a phenomenon very much linked to social developments taking place in Cambodia at a particular time.

Chapter 10, by Teri Yamada, is a detailed ethnographic description of a ceremony that took place in the Cambodian community in Long Beach, California, the largest Cambodian community in the United States. Yamada describes how the ceremony draws on and extends myth and ritual as it was practiced in Cambodia, in this case a ceremony associated with a well-known legend about a Khmer ruler who commits suicide in order to raise an army of ghosts to fight Siamese invaders. As Yamada shows, the ceremony is very much a Khmer ceremony, and as such illuminates other religious practice found in Cambodia proper. (The dramatic use of mediums in the ceremony extends our understanding of Bertrand's description of mediums in chap. 7, for example.) At the same time, Yamada shows the ceremony as directly linked to the social organization of the Long Beach Khmer community and its particular concerns as a community.

Both chapters, I believe, illustrate the complexity of the relation between transnational processes, nation, and national identity, whereby nation and national identity are sometimes defined or underlined by transnationalism, at the same time that they are challenged by it.

Note

1. They would each later be given the title Saṃtec.

–9–

Locating the Transnational in Cambodia's Dhammayātrā

KATHRYN POETHIG

In the high heat of April 1992, a dusty band of Cambodian refugees and orange-swathed monks walked across the Thai border back into Cambodia after nearly twenty years of exile. Mahā Ghosananda, the elderly monk who led that first Dhammayātrā,[1] had conceived of the walk as a mindful means to initiate a peaceful exchange between former refugees returning and those left behind. They did not know then that the decision to repatriate on foot would blossom into an internationally acclaimed movement.

The massive multilateral buildup toward Cambodia's transition to democracy after the signing of the Paris Agreement in 1991 brought U.N. agencies, election monitors, and a wide range of international development organizations intent on establishing a "civil society" in Cambodia. In the next two years, with this international encouragement, a host of local nongovernmental organizations (NGOs) sprung up to address the unmet needs of Cambodian citizens. Unlike any of these first Cambodian NGOs, the Dhammayātrā and its organizing body, the Coalition for Peace and Reconciliation (CPR), focused on the intractable conflict in Cambodia through religious philosophy and practice. It offered a vivid sign of a socially engaged Buddhism: a Buddhist practice of nonviolence that had been forged through contemporary circuits of transnational exchange.

The Dhammayātrā quickly established itself as an annual peace walk. For eight years, a stunning visual assembly of monks in saffron robes and laypeople dressed in white traversed Cambodia's embattled terrain. Thousands of Cambodians lined the roads as the monks passed, ready for the *dịk mant* (lustral water blessed by Pāli prayers) and incense plunged into the water to "extinguish the fire of war." Each evening, the walkers assembled in the local wat for rest and *dhamma* talks by Mahā Ghosananda who reflected on the Dhammayātrā's purpose: "Peace is growing in Cambodia, slowly, step by step. . . . Each step is a meditation. Each step is a prayer." (Ghosananda 1991, 65)

Socially engaged Buddhism is a concept that has gained great currency in both Asia and North America in the last two decades. The Dhammayātrā thrived because of a transnational network forged by its expatriate founders and the prominence of its leader, sometimes called the "Gandhi of Cambodia," Saṃtec Braḥ Mahā Ghosananda. I will show how the Dhammayātrā balanced local legitimacy and strategic transnationalism in its philosophy and practice.

Engaged, Transnational Buddhism

"Socially engaged Buddhism" is a moniker created by the South Vietnamese monk Thich Nhat Hanh in the 1960s to refer to Buddhist social action. Thich Nhat Hanh became well known for his neutrality during the Vietnam War, which earned him a nomination for the Nobel Peace Prize by Martin Luther King, Jr.—and premature exile to France when he was cautioned against returning to Vietnam.

From the beginning, engaged Buddhism was a transnational movement. The term "transnational" gives stress to the phenomenon of a world no longer merely divided into nation-states but also critically defined by cross-boundaried forma-

Fig. 9.1 Dhammayātrā 1993 (P. Gyallay-Pap)

tions—Appadurai (1990) calls them "scapes"—that may usurp the state's claims to sovereignty. It has often been noted that religion is one of the oldest transnational institutions—transcending the political boundaries that carve up our world.

Queen and King refer to engaged Buddhism in Asia as "voluntary groups and non-governmental organizations committed to realizing a just and peaceful society by Buddhist means" (Queen 1996, 20). Leaders of these movements, such as Thich Nath Hanh, Sulak Sivaraksa, and the Dalai Lama, share Mahā Ghosananda's emphasis on both mundane goals (peace in Cambodia) and supramundane goals of Buddhism *(nibbāna)* in their work for peace. Queen and King argue that these liberation movements mark a sea change in Buddhism across Asia in the last two decades (Queen, Prebisch, and Keown 2001). This sea change is part of the trend toward an increasingly global civil society in which political moralities (such as nonviolent approaches to civil conflict) are transmitted by transnational religious movements (Casanova 1994; Keck and Sikkink 1998; Rudolph and Piscatori 1997).

A vigorous cross-Pacific exchange of Buddhist activists since the late-1970s *ṭūn jī* movements attests to Buddhism's new transnationalism. Sulak Sivaraksa, an outspoken Thai lawyer, has employed the term "engaged Buddhism" in his Buddhist critique of development strategies in Thailand (Sivaraksa 1988, 1993; Swearer 1996). In the 1980s, American Buddhists were also seeking justification for social activism in their religious practice (Eppsteiner 1988; Jones 1992; Kraft 1992; Macy 1983). The U.S.-based Buddhist Peace Fellowship and other social action groups emerged (Queen 2000). By 1989, the International Network of Engaged Buddhists (INEB) was established at an international Buddhist conference to serve this growing network of engaged Buddhists. By the late 1990s, INEB's membership spanned thirty countries. Saṃtec Braḥ Mahā Ghosananda and the Dhammayātrā, having emerged only since 1992, have appeared only recently in the scholarship on engaged Buddhism (Skidmore 1997; Appleby 2000, 123–140; Moser-Puangsuwan 2000).

The Trajectory of Cambodian Buddhism

During the past twenty-five years of civil war and revolution, Cambodian Buddhism has been both the hammer and anvil of various political agendas. This chapter is primarily concerned with the late 1980s and the 1990s, a period when international negotiations led to a plan for elections under U.N. supervision, entailing the reintegration into the country thousands of refugees who had been living in refugee camps on the country's borders. (The mission ultimately failed in its goal of integrating the Khmer Rouge into the plan.)

The story begins in the refugee camps, with Mahā Ghosananda and NGO relief workers. Expatriate relief workers at Site II were greatly divided over the implications of aiding resistance forces fighting against Cambodia's existing regime. Bob Maat, a Jesuit brother who had been working in the camps since 1980, attended the ASEAN-sponsored Jakarta peace talks that had convened the four Cambodian factions.[2] There he met Mahā Ghosananda and an entourage of monks who presented themselves as an "army of peace." Maat recalls that Mahā Ghosananda thanked him for his efforts in the camp and then added, "Why do you help only one faction?"[3] Thus challenged, the Jesuit brother founded the CPR along with Ven. Yos Hut Khemacaro, another prominent Cambodian monk who had been out of the country during the Khmer Rouge regime. After living in France and Australia, Ven. Yos Hut returned to Site II to assist U.N. human rights training. Elizabeth Bernstein, originally an English teacher in the camp, soon joined them as a major organizer.

They secured neutral space for expatriate staff to reflect on the political situation, organizing speakers, videos, and a monthly discussion so that when advocacy was required, there was a network in place. The primary strength of CPR was its vision of a reconciled Cambodia brought together through information exchange between the border camps and Cambodia and training in nonviolence.

The Paris Agreement signed in 1991 called for the closure of Thai camps and repatriation of their three hundred thousand occupants. In order to prepare the *sangha* and Buddhist laypeople for reunification, CPR contacted INEB in Bangkok to develop a series of workshops on nonviolence. They were joined by Yeshua Moser, an American working in Bangkok with INEB, and an NGO called Nonviolence International. Those sympathetic with CPR's mission sought ways to symbolize and support a reunified Cambodia. Moser recalls that one night, Maat mused, "I was thinking about doing a peace walk in Cambodia."[4] In the following days, they discussed the idea with increasing seriousness. Mahā Ghosananda, already celebrated as a peace advocate, was attending an INEB conference in Thailand. Bernstein and Moser invited him to participate. In order to initiate dialogue between high-ranking monks in the border camps and Cambodia, CPR and INEB sponsored a workshop in Thailand (Coalition for Peace and Reconciliation in Cambodia and the World 1992). One of the objectives was garnering support for the peace walk. The Phnom Penh-based Mahānikāy *sangharāj*, Ven. Tep Vong, supported the idea at the workshop but retracted his position when he returned to Phnom Penh. Other monks invited to walk also declined. It thus fell to Mahā Ghosananda to assume leadership. He insisted that walkers carry a picture of the former Mahānikāy patriarch Chuon Nath, his mentor and a revered figure. He referred to the walk as the Dhammayātrā, intended to bring peace to Cambodia "step-by-step."[5]

Only with difficulty would Thai, Cambodian, or U.N. officials grant permission for the refugees to cross the border. But finally, on April 12, 1992, over a hundred refugees and international walkers, including monks from Sri Lanka, Thailand, and Japan, crossed into Cambodia. Daily, walkers were reunited with long-lost family members. The walkers arrived in Phnom Penh on May 13, Visākhā Pūjā, the holiday celebrating the life of the Buddha. Crowds gathered on the roadside to watch or join in, and by the time they reached the royal palace, their numbers had swelled to over a thousand (Bernstein and Moser 1993).

Mahā Ghosananda: Exile and Return

Mahā Ghosananda's return to Cambodia inspired a rumor that he was the fulfillment of an old prophecy that after the brutal reign of the *damiḷ* (dark ones or infidels; pronounced "thmil") a "holy man from the west" who was a light-skinned Khmer would appear, and the prince would come back to save his people.[6] Mahā Ghosananda's exile in the West had been a long one. Born the only son of poor farmers in Takeo Province, his gifts and attraction to the monkhood were recognized early. He studied at Buddhist universities in Phnom Penh and Battambang, progressing rapidly to the higher echelons of the Mahānikāy under the tutelage of its Supreme Patriarch, Chuon Nath. In 1951, at the age of twenty-seven, he left for doctoral work at Nalandā University in India. For the next forty years, he would spend little time in his homeland. In India Mahā Ghosananda received his title.[7] There he also met Nichidatsu Fujii, a Japanese Buddhist whose long friendship with Mahātma Gandhi had inspired him to found the Nipponzan Myohoji, an order dedicated to world peace. At the Fujii ashram in Rajgir, Mahā Ghosananda learned the Gandhian philosophy and practice of Satyagraha that would later inform his work in Cambodia. After fifteen years in India, he visited other wats throughout Asia, returning to Cambodia briefly before leaving for Thailand in 1965 to study in the forest monastery of the meditation master Ajahn *(ācāry)* Dhammadaro. He was there when the Khmer Rouge occupied Phnom Penh.

When waves of starving refugees flooded the border in 1978, Mahā Ghosananda joined an international delegation to Sakeo, a camp occupied by Khmer Rouge and their hostages fleeing Vietnamese troops. He used donations given to him for an airline ticket to France to print forty thousand leaflets of the *metta sutta,* the Buddha's discourse on loving-kindness. These he handed silently from his cloth bag as he walked through the camp. The sight of an orange-robed Cambodian monk in the camp proved so cathartic that many refugees fell prostrate at his feet and wept uncontrollably (Mahoney and Edmonds 1992).

Throughout 1979, Mahā Ghosananda established wats at the refugee camps that lined the Thai-Cambodian border and ordained monks against the orders of the Thai military. Reportedly fluent in ten languages and accomplished in interfaith interchange, he quickly formed alliances with various faith-based organizations.

His work along the border, however, lasted a little over a year. When the Khmer Rouge resistance movement forced conscription of refugees, Ghosananda and Protestant activist Rev. Peter Pond circulated a letter assuring that repatriation was not mandatory and outlining opportunities for resettlement. Ghosananda offered his wat as a sanctuary for those fleeing conscription. Thousands took refuge there, relinquishing their weapons at the door (Mahoney n.d.). Thai military officials who had quietly backed the forced conscription were furious. Rev. Pond and his son were arrested, but the Queen Mother, a devout Buddhist, intervened on behalf of the monk (Cooper 1981). Rev. Pond reports that Ghosananda visited him in prison and, with characteristic wit, whispered "body of Christ" as he pushed a sandwich and a soft drink between the bars. Banned from the refugee camps, Mahā Ghosananda accepted a U.N. appointment to represent Cambodians in exile at the Economic and Social Council in 1980. Later that year, he resettled in Providence, Rhode Island, where he set up one of the first Cambodian wats in the United States.[8]

Over the next decade, Mahā Ghosananda established more than forty wats around the globe. The exiled *sangha* in France elected him a Sangharāja (Supreme Patriarch) of the Mahānikāy order in 1988.[9] This pointed to a basic division in lines of authority, since the socialist government in Phnom Penh had already made Tep Vong the chief of the Cambodian *sangha;* when Sihanouk returned, Tep Vong would be given the title of Sangharāja. Mahā Ghosananda promised to resign when the overseas *sangha* and Cambodian *sangha* were reunited, and did so in 1992. At that time, King Sihanouk bestowed on Mahā Ghosananda the honorary title of Saṃtec Braḥ.[10]

As one of the few multilingual Cambodian monks able to communicate with the American public, Mahā Ghosananda was quickly recruited as the Cambodian face of interfaith peace activism. At Rev. Pond's urging, the two cofounded the Inter-Religious Mission for Peace in Cambodia and the World. This led to several meetings with Pope John Paul II and other engaged Buddhist leaders. American engaged Buddhists also drew him into their ambit. His supporters collected his *dhamma* talks into a small book, *Step by Step,* to introduce him to the American public (Mahoney and Edmonds 1992).

Out of the Temple, into the World: Ghosananda's Philosophy

As a Cambodian refugee engrossed with his country's "tragedy of history," Mahā Ghosananda drew the connection between individual and social suffering that is the strongest feature of an engaged Buddhist philosophy (Ghosananda 1991, 66). Noting that Cambodians are not alone in their anguish—Buddhists in India, Burma, and Sri Lanka also know political strife—he argues that all this suffering is "but a mirror of the suffering of the world." The means by which the *sangha* addresses this suffering is also engaged. Mahā Ghosananda often notes that the Buddha conducted "conflict mediation" when he walked onto the battlefield between the Śakyas and Koliyas. This Buddha act, argues Ghosananda, should inspire Buddhists to "leave our temples and enter the temples of human experience that are filled with suffering" (Ghosananda 1991, 63). He notes that Buddha, Christ, and Gandhi offer examples of this. Like them, the monks must "go to the people. They sustain us and feed us and give us refuge, if they suffer we suffer" (Burslem 1993).

What is sometimes called "loving-kindness" (Pāli, *mettā*) is a complex Buddhist concept suggesting ideas such as love, compassion, friendliness, sympathy, and well-wishing. It is Ghosananda's antidote to the rage and despair of the victims of war. Ghosananda likens loving-kindness to water.

> Just like water, it can stay everywhere—in a glass, in the mouth, in the belly. When water boils, it becomes very hot; but if we leave water for some time it naturally becomes cool again. Sometimes we are angry, but if we have loving kindness we can cool down easily. (Ghosananda 1989)

This loving-kindness is cultivated through meditation. For Mahā Ghosananda, the essence of Buddhist *dhamma* is the practice of peacemaking. It requires skillful means, the ability to listen with compassion to the perspective of the one who has done you and others harm, and being mindful and selfless in negotiating a peaceful resolution to conflict. During the Jakarta peace talks in 1988 he called his contingency of monks a "fifth army of peace." This army of the Buddha, armored with mindfulness, he said, would "shoot the people with bullets of loving-kindness" to disarm the four Cambodian factions. His monks opened daily sessions with prayer and meditation, offered a formal ceremony for peace and unity, and circulated a statement of peace.

As a Buddhist monk highly trained in techniques of meditation, Mahā Ghosananda has promoted walking meditation as a skillful means toward mindfulness. The Dhammayātrā as a walking meditation helps its participants understand that both personal and national peacemaking is incremental ("step-by-step") and requires mindfulness, compassion, and nonattachment.

Training the People to Walk

While the Dhammayātrā began as a celebration of the refugees' return to Cambodia, its practice and underlying philosophy captured the country's imagination and inspired a second walk. In order to encourage participation in the U.N.-monitored elections in 1993, another walk was organized, starting at Angkor Wat in Siem Reap Province and ending in Phnom Penh 350 kilometers away. At that time much of the province of Siem Reap was still controlled by Khmer Rouge forces, but the region was important for the march because of its deep associations with Cambodian nationalism. The resolve of the Dhammayātrā leaders was tested at Wat Damnak in Siem Reap Town two days before the march began. During meditation, Mahā Ghosananda recalls that they "could hear fighting going on outside and bullets were fired through the temple walls. Three of our people were wounded, one was shot in the shoulder."[11] A grenade flew through the window and landed in front of the statue of the Buddha. Everyone but the meditating monk fell to the floor. When it did not explode, Mahā Ghosananda exclaimed, "The Buddha saved us!"[12]

The walkers gained the respect of the U.N. Transitional Authority in Cambodia as they moved through Khmer Rouge territory at the height of pre-election tensions, assaulted by the constant sounds of rockets, mortars, and AK-47 rifle shots. U.N. helicopters and ground troops monitored the walk with grave concern. By the time the marchers reached Phnom Penh, an estimated three thousand people joined the procession through the streets and circled the Independence Monument.

As a further demonstration of Buddhist concern for democratic practices, Mahā Ghosananda organized monks and nuns to meditate for a "just constitution" during the Constitutional Assembly following the election. The venerated monk's leadership was acknowledged when a coalition of Cambodian NGOs formed the umbrella organization Ponloeu Khmer and elected him as honorary chairman. His wat, Saṃbau Mās, hosted the new Dhammayātrā Center, which shared offices with the Coalition for Peace and Reconciliation in Cambodia and the World and Ponloeu Khmer.

The schema of the Dhammayātrā was established by the second walk. Between 1993–1999, when the "big walks" sponsored by the Dhammayātrā Center in Phnom Penh were replaced by more localized walks, certain features of the walks were replicated. By far the greatest percentage of walkers (and the most disciplined) have been the *ṭūn jī*, Cambodia's female Buddhist "nuns." All participants were required to attend nonviolence workshops before the May event. Each walk lasted about two weeks, covering between twenty and twenty-three kilometers a day. To avoid the heat, walkers started between four and five o'clock in the morning. Along the route, *bodhi* trees were planted. Villagers usually lined the road before their arrival, awaiting a blessing. Meals and lodging were arranged beforehand by designated wats along the route. Villagers provided much of the food, although the World Food Program provided several tons of rice, canned fish, and oil. King Sihanouk and international NGOs donated part of the financial support for the walk and prewalk training; additional donations were collected along the route.[13] Mahā Ghosananda or a senior monk usually offered *dhamma* talks several times each day.

The third Dhammayātrā in 1994 tested the nonviolence preparedness of its walkers. It was routed from Battambang to Pailin through the war zone in western Cambodia, intending to "spread our message of compassion, loving kindness and respect for human rights to all Cambodians who are victims of war" (Mang 1994). Dhammayātrā's organizers had secured permission from Khieu Samphan, a top-ranking Khmer Rouge official, to pass through their territory, but renewed combat had shifted the front lines. Several days into the walk, Dhammayātrā walkers grew increasingly anxious as they passed deserted villages and heard distant rocket fire. Warned of intense fighting ahead, Dhammayātrā organizers decided to retreat to Wat Andaek in Bịṅ Aṃbil, joining thousands of fleeing families. That night, a "quieter" route was chosen, but it proved no less dangerous. As they tracked single file through the landmined forest, government soldiers joined the walk to protect them, and Khmer Rouge soldiers opened fire. In the mayhem, a monk and nun were killed, several walkers were wounded, and nine walkers (six were foreigners) were taken hostage. After an hour of walking, the hostage party met the Khmer Rouge commander. He motioned for them to sit under a tree and issued an appeal "that you remind all foreigners working in Cambodia that all Cambodians, including those of the Democratic Kampuchea, want peace as well" (Mang 1994). During the following hour of conversation, he apologized for killing the monk and asked about Mahā Ghosananda and the Dhammayātrā. Then he designated a soldier to take them back. Bernstein remarks,

> The point of the walk was to meet Khmer Rouge. We had said we would walk until our enemies become our friends, and yet we had been fleeing them from the beginning. At that point we had nowhere to flee to. We were there in front of them. It was the only occasion we had to meet them, and in some ways it was very positive. It opened the door. (Moon 1995)

With the walk in disarray, the organizing committee wrestled with the decision to disband. The walk resumed, rerouted to Siem Reap.

The crisis of the third Dhammayātrā wrought significant changes in its organizational framework. Moser-Puangsuwan (2000) identifies three changes. First, a more disciplined formation program for nonviolent behavior was instituted. Nonviolence workshops multiplied at each subsequent walk. Dhammayātrā organizers set up trainer-training workshops and designed a new curriculum for prewalk workshops. Between 1994–1997, George Lakey ran trainers' workshops for the Dhammayātrā (Coalition for Peace and Reconciliation 1994). These two workshops became the primary sources for nonviolent training for the Dhammayātrā. The training included stories of individual peacemaking, introduction to the theory of Buddhism and nonviolence, ways to handle fear, role-playing of situations the participants might encounter, and a practice walk around town. Walkers were required to sign a pledge stating

> I will maintain a discipline of nonviolence at all times while on the Dhammayātrā. I will sustain a practice of meditation daily while on the walk. I make a commitment of service to others while on the Dhammayātrā, and knowingly sacrifice

> my usual comforts for the duration of the walk. I acknowledge that my participation in this event carries potential risks to my personal well being.[14]

Potential walkers also agreed to attend prewalk training, not ride vehicles, and avoid drugs, alcohol, and weapons.[15] Monks or nuns were required to present a letter of approval from their abbot. Participants who violated the rules of the walk were given three chances before they were expelled. Dhammayātrā organizers also demanded that government soldiers refrain from accompanying them along the route, as this had obviously incited Khmer Rouge reprisal. While weapons were always forbidden, Dhammayātrā leaders now required civilian clothing. In order to discourage political figures from co-opting the walk, they were required to find a place with laypersons behind the monks.

Second, groups were organized into twenty (and later ten) walkers, with a group leader responsible for distributing supplies, food and water, medical attention, and information. Subcommittees of volunteers also were organized for specific tasks such as transporting food and supplies, receiving donations, and distributing leaflets. Third, the organizing committee was recomposed to constitute a membership representative of the walkers—monks, nuns, and laypeople living in Cambodia.[16] Its gender ratio was unusual for Cambodian organizations, and in fact the most prominent figure in the walk and training was Kim Leng, a laywoman. It became more formalized, and decision making occurred by consensus.

In 1995, Dhammayātrā IV greeted the Interfaith Pilgrimage for Peace at the Thai-Cambodian border and accompanied the pilgrimage to the Vietnamese border at Svay Rieng. The yearlong pilgrimage was organized by the Nipponzan Myohoji to commemorate the fiftieth anniversary of the bombing of Hiroshima and started at Auschwitz. Some of the Dhammayātrā organizers went with the pilgrimage to Japan. During that walk Dhammayātrā participants solicited twenty thousand signatures for the International Campaign to Ban Landmines. The following year, Dhammayātrā V traveled southwest from Phnom Penh, illuminating the connection between the Civil War, illegal logging, and deforestation for the first time. Two thousand trees were planted along the route.

In 1997, Dhammayātrā VI retraced the route of the tragic third walk. It traveled from Battambang to Pailin, ending in Banteay Meanchey. After Ieng Sary, third in command to Pol Pot, defected with his battalion a year earlier, Pailin, a former Khmer Rouge stronghold, was slated for "reintegration." Unfamiliar with the Dhammayātrā, Khmer Rouge families watched the procession curiously and sometimes with a welling up of emotion. In a moving reunion, the Khmer Rouge officer who had released the Dhammayātrā hostages in 1994 met with the organizers.[17] This time the walkers reached Pailin without incident and were welcomed by Ieng Sary before going on to their final destination. In addition to now common educational components of landmines and deforestation, there was attention to domestic violence for the first time.

While Dhammayātrā VI drew attention to the end of the war in the western provinces recently under fierce Khmer Rouge control, violence erupted elsewhere in Cambodia. As pre-election tensions rose, grenades were tossed into an opposition campaign rally in Phnom Penh, killing sixteen. Then, on July 2–7 a brief but violent coup upset the fragile balance between the FUNCINPEC and the Cambodian People's Party in the government.[18] A new group was formed to address the violence. Metta Thor, a Forum for Peace through Love and Compassion, was organized by a small group of women from various NGOs, with a Cambodian American as its spokeswoman. At their request, Mahā Ghosananda led a march in Phnom Penh sponsored by this group.

Built around the goal of reconciling Cambodia's warring factions and upset by factionalism of its own, the force and scope of the Dhammayātrā waned in the following years. A second round of national elections was scheduled for 1998. Concerned about the existing level of political violence, an ad hoc collective of NGOs organized the Campaign to Reduce Violence for Peace (CRVP) and held pre-election peace walks in sixteen provinces. That year, the Dhammayātrā Center organized the pre-election walk in Phnom Penh (Dhammayātrā VIII) and also Dhammayātrā VII through Rattanakiri, a much-neglected province in the northeast and site of great deforestation. Focusing on the environment, a tree was ordained during the walk. "When we ordained a tree, it became a monk," explained Mahā Ghosananda, "and we told the people. When you kill the tree, then you kill the monk."[19] Only two hundred completed this walk.

In 1999, Dhammayātrā IX recruited only two hundred participants and did not reach its intended goal. Intending to traverse former Khmer Rouge territory from Siem Reap to Prāsād Preah Vihear, it got stuck in the mud, making it as far as Anlong Veng. By 2000, Mahā Ghosananda, ill and in his late seventies, no longer attended the walks. This time, new walks, organized by a former member of the Dhammayātrā organizing committee who lives in Sisophon at the Cambodian border, took place in western Cambodia. They went shorter distances, were led by different monks, and encouraged local participation. The CPR-Dhammayātrā Center in Battambang run by Bob Maat has offered support. While the Dhammayātrā Center became dormant in 2000, it scheduled a small walk to Preah Vihear in 2001. This time they made it.

Local Meanings: Dhammayātrā as Engaged Cambodian

Appadurai (1990) argues that dominant cultural forms localize differently; there is a dialectical relationship between an action and its response. The integration of engaged Buddhism into Cambodia's religious and political landscape occurred along four vectors—its look, its message, its relevance to a young, undisciplined *sangha,* and its adaptability to a maturing civil society. I will take each in turn.

The philosophy and practice of engaged Buddhism could take root in Cambodia only if it *looked* Khmer. The visible presence of Saṃtec Braḥ Mahā Ghosananda, his patronage by King Sihanouk, the Dhammayātrā Center's presence at Wat Saṃbau Mās, and the Dhammayātrā's embrace of the *sangha* through walk participation, philosophy, and hospitality along the route established the Dhammayātrā's Cambodian identity. The foreign organizers and overseas Cambodians who first organized the walks have gone on to other pursuits, leaving Cambodians in charge. By 1995, Cambodians were both the primary architects and recipients of the message of the walk. Cambodian organizers have argued that the foreign presence at its inception and behind its funding has been incidental to its continued success, but foreign supporters had the language to communicate with donors, accounting skills, and familiarity with governance structures. The absence of these weakened the Dhammayātrā Center's ability to maintain itself in the last few years (Sasse 1999).

The Dhammayātrā's local success has also been attributed to its social relevance in responding to some of Cambodia's most pressing issues: repatriation, peaceful elections, the Khmer Rouge/government conflict, landmines ban, and illegal logging. For those who participated in the walks and for those along the routes, its message of nonviolence was unequivocal. Skidmore (1997) suggested that the first Dhammayātrā walks were more immediate in their connection to the populace's needs. It could also be argued that the Dhammayātrā's practice of walking continued to address some of the most troubling aspects of Cambodian history—displacement, flight, and mined land.

Third, the Dhammayātrā's stress on self-disciplined nonviolence and meditation has been critical for the formation of a postsocialist generation of young monks. It was perceived as a reconstruction of the pre-revolution Khmer moral order. Ven. Nhem Kim Teng, senior monk of the Dhammayātrā, has suggested that "in essence, Mahā Ghosananda is trying to bring back the things we have lost. Khmers used to be gentle, honest and forgiving. We would help each other in times of difficulty, speak respectfully of all those things we have lost because of the war and violence and destruction" (Coalition for Peace and Reconciliation 1995). Guthrie, in chapter 6, has illustrated the connection between the *ṭūn jī* and the Dhammayātrā movement. In addition to training monks, the Dhammayātrā Center contributed to the empowerment of the *ṭūn jī*. The Dhammayātrā Center/CPR helped to plan the first national seminar in 1995 for *ṭūn jī*, which included training in *dhamma*, meditation, and engaged Buddhism. Ghosananda's presence at this conference lent them additional legitimacy. Finally, the Dhammayātrā Center and CPR strengthened Cambodia's civil society in many ways. They encouraged initiatives rising from monks and *ṭūn jī* who participated in the walks, such as Ven. Kim Teng's Sante Sena community forestry project in Svay Rieng. It was most evident through the educational component of the walks, which set up workshops to educate villagers about landmines, domestic violence, and deforestation. By far the most significant contribution has been training a generation of peace activists. By the late 1980s, the Dhammayātrā's Buddhist philosophy of nonviolence, its workshops, and its practice of walking had been replicated by other peace-based local and international NGOs in Cambodia.

This mantle of Cambodian leadership and Buddhist peacemaking, however, has cloaked more complicated transnational arrangements. Indeed, Mahā Ghosananda's global connections have significantly contributed to the transnational features of the Dhammayātrā just as Maat and Bernstein's CPR connections gave it the NGO support it needed. Certainly its origin story begins with foreigners and refugee monks crossing borders. Its constituency, though predominantly Cambodian, regularly includes expatriate staff from NGOs and the peripatetic Japanese monks of the Nipponzan Myohoji.

It is this strategic transnationalism that has given the Dhammayātrā its shape, support, and visibility in its first decade. By strategic I mean that the Dhammayātrā's expatriate organizers and Mahā Ghosananda chose to situate the Dhammayātrā in a global network. This transnational vision influenced the ways in which local organizing took on the broader focus of international issues that also impacted Cambodia, such as the international campaign to ban landmines and the campaign against nuclear testing in the Pacific in 1998. It also integrated the Dhammayātrā's philosophy with other agents of peacemaking—Gandhi, Martin Luther King, Jr., Quakers teaching Buddhism, American nonviolence trainers, Japanese peace monks, Thai engaged Buddhists, and the global interfaith peace network that Mahā Ghosananda has known since the early 1980s, when he was a refugee. As the "Buddha of the Battlefields," Saṃtec Braḥ Mahā Ghosananda's message of peacemaking as *dhamma* is shared with his contemporaries, Thich Nhat Hanh and the Dalai Lama. There is thus nothing particularly Khmer about the Buddhist philosophy and practice promoted by the walk.

A similar statement might be made about Mahā Ghosananda's complex relationship to his former homeland. Hailed as the "Gandhi of Cambodia" in international circles, he is the most celebrated figure of Cambodia's postwar peacemaking efforts. In addition to five Nobel Peace Prize nominations, he has been the recipient of many peace awards around the world, including Norway's Rafto Foundation Prize for Human Rights (1992), a peacemaking award from Sri Lanka's Sarvodaya (1997), and the coveted Niwano Peace Prize from Japan (1998). But unlike Gandhi, who returned to his homeland to build a movement, Mahā Ghosananda has rarely stayed in Cambodia for any length of time except during the Dhammayātrās. This follows a pattern set early in life. His itinerary for the last decade shows a constant series of appearances at conferences or peace gatherings.[20] According to some reports, Mahā Ghosananda is a U.S. citizen, and while this is not unusual in Cambodia (the Cambodian political party FUNCINPEC is dominated by dual citizens), it presses the question of citizenship and place in former refugees' avowal of national identity. Mahā Ghosananda's choice to signify as singularly Cambodian is balanced with a complex, cosmopolitan embrace.

There has been a strong incentive in the international community to depict the Dhammayātrā as a fully realized, indigenous Buddhist-based peace movement in Cambodia. This is evident in the global media, feature articles, and a growing number of video documentaries. This has also been the agenda of most international NGOs and donors aligned with the Dhammayātrā Center, though they have been more realistic about its realization and conflicting visions of the walk (Sasse 1999). Unfortunately, the expense of prewalk trainings and the size and duration of the walks has required substantial assistance. The symbiotic relationship between the Cambodian staff of the Dhammayātrā Center and expatriate donors who also consider themselves allies has been at times confused and conflicting. This is a common feature of North-South NGO partnerships, but it challenges the notion that "local" movements, especially in the South, can be unhampered by "global" interests.

Moser-Puangsuwan (2000) argues that the Dhammayātrā's philosophy and practice are not culturally specific but transferable to other forms of conflict. He posits that its Buddhist philosophy of compassion is a unique contribution to the peace movement (Moser-Puangsuwan 2000, 266). One example of this is an eponymous Thai version of the walk that focuses on the environment (Santikare 1999).

Conclusion

The Dhammayātrā as an example of the transnational networks and philosophy of engaged Buddhism attests to a fluid mixture of political forms and philosophies in an era of global cultural melange. Mahā Ghosananda's peacemaking efforts both in the diaspora and back in Cambodia can be seen as paradigmatic of this new Buddhism. Can engaged Buddhism be seen in terms of Appadurai's model "dominant cultural forms" that "locals" then integrate? Given its multiple influences and sources, engaged Buddhism cannot be represented as homogenizing or hegemonic. As for its local integration, while neither its message nor its practice is derived from any Khmer model, the Dhammayātrā's legitimacy is a result of its success "on the ground." In the decade of diaspora return and national reconstruction in Cambodia, the Dhammayātrā and its philosophy of nonviolence have been a particularly powerful message for poor Cambodians tired of war.

I have pressed the transnational features of the Dhammayātrā and Mahā Ghosananda to counter a tendency for both local and transnational allies to simplify the representation of the Dhammayātrā and Mahā Ghosananda in order to maintain their Cambodian authenticity. The notion that transnational alliances can dilute the efficacy of a Buddhist peace walk is a curious concern given the transnational nature of religious institutions. In an era of permeable borders, Cambodia's *sangha* has garnered much transnational support—wat reconstruction paid by overseas Cambodians, texts from Japan, funding through German donors, and training for monks in Thailand and Sri Lanka.

As a multisourced entity of engaged Buddhism, the Dhammayātrā in Cambodia has left a considerable legacy for peace activists in this country and elsewhere. Although the walks have not wrought significant changes on the political front, the replication of nonviolence and conflict mediation techniques among a larger group of players signifies an effective transfer into public discourse. While fighting between the Khmer Rouge and Cambodian armed forces has ended, other conflicts continue to require vigilant efforts on the part of a more empowered Buddhist community. It remains to be seen how a decade of engaged Buddhist peace walks has contributed to a practice and philosophy of nonviolence in Cambodia's civil society, and what peace walks elsewhere in the future might be inspired by the Dhammayātrā.

Notes

I wish to thank Phil Edmonds, Bob Maat, Victoria Rue, and John Marston for their help.

1. *Dhammayātrā* (pronounced "dhammayietra") is a Pāli-language compound. "*Dhamma*" is a Buddhist technical term that may be translated as "doctrine," "righteousness," or "law," and "*yātrā*" means "walk," "to go." In its Khmer context here, *Dhammayātrā* can be translated as "journey" or "walk for righteousness."

2. ASEAN (Association of South-East Asian Nations) is a political organization representing nations in Southeast Asia, which at that time included Indonesia, Malaysia, Thailand, Singapore, the Philippines, and Brunei. The four Cambodian factions were Democratic Kampuchea (the Khmer Rouge), two noncommunist resistance groups (the royalist FUNCINPEC and the Republican Khmer People's National Liberation Front (KPNLF), and the Phnom Penh-based government (People's Republic of Kampuchea [PRK], later called the State of Cambodia [SOC]).

3. B. Maat, personal communication, November 13, 1994.

4. Moser-Puangsuwan, personal communication, August 2001.

5. Moser-Puangsuwan offers a detailed account of the first and second walks in "The Buddha in the Battlefield."

6. Ibid. Ed. note: this seems to be a reference to the Buddhamnāy.

7. The movement translates the name Mahā Ghosananda as "Great Joyful Proclaimer." It could be translated more simply as "The Great Talker."

8. Mahā Ghosananda has kept Providence as his residence despite his hectic international schedule.

9. "Cambodian Buddhists Elect Patriarch," *Providence Journal-Bulletin*, July 30, 1988.

10. While there have been recent changes, at the time the research for this chapter was being conducted there were five monks with the title of Saṃtec, an Old Khmer word mean-

ing "powerful person," one given to officials of high rank. They include the *sanghrāj* of the Mahānikāy at Wat Unnalom and the Dhammayut at Wat Botum Vadey, a second abbot at Wat Botum Vadey, the abbot of Wat Mahā Mantri, and Mahā Ghosananda at Wat Saṃbau Mās, who is called "member-at-large."

11. "Mahā Ghosananda, a True Peacemaker," *Bangkok Post,* May 30, 1993.

12. B. Maat, personal communication, November 13, 1994.

13. The most consistent support has come from the Peace Partnership between the American Friends Service Committee (AFSC) and Mennonite Central Committee (MCC), both Christian churches with a theology of pacifism. Other NGOs include Church World Service, Oxfam, Great Britain, Catholic Relief Services, CIDSE (Cooperation Internationale pour le Developpement et la Solidarite), and STAR Kampuchea.

14. "Dhammayatra VIII—Pre-Election Peace Walk," 1998 press release.

15. This was particularly a problem with the younger monks, who abused the respect of the community by soliciting money for their own personal use and requesting rides when they grew tired of walking. See Sasse 1999.

16. From 1993–1995, the most active members of this committee were Ven. Nhem Kim Leng and Ven. Yos Hut. Lay leaders included Kim Teng and her husband Ong Vuthy, the driver for Mahā Ghosananda on his first visits to Cambodia in 1991 and 1992. Lay activists included Chea Mouy Kry (founder of Youth Resources Development Project), Thida Khus (founder of SILAKA and Metta Thor), and Mu Sochua (founder of the first women's NGO, Khemara, and now minister of women's affairs).

17. For an extended interview, see the video of the walk, "Army of Peace—Quest for a Non-violent Cambodia."

18. "More than 1,000 Meditate, March for Peace in Phnom Penh," *The Cambodia Daily,* August 4, 1997.

19. "A Monk tells of Lifelong Commitment to Peace through Compassion," *World Buddhism Supplement, The Cambodia Daily,* May 1998.

20. See Niwano Peace Prize web site: www.interfaith-center.org/oxford/press/niwano98.htm.

–10–

The Spirit Cult of Khleang Moeung in Long Beach, California

Teri Shaffer Yamada

Don't reject the crooked road and don't take the straight one; instead, take the road traveled by the ancestors.

—Quoted in translation in Karen Fisher-Nguyen, "Khmer Proverbs: Images and Rules"

Cambodians share a hauntingly tragic past (Chandler 1991; Martin 1994). The Khmer Rouge era of traumatic social reengineering (1975–1979) decimated traditional Cambodian religion, a rich fusion of folk beliefs, Brahmanism, and Buddhism[1] that formed the basis of a Cambodian sense of order.[2] During this four-year period, Buddhist monks, who also served as respected teachers in temple schools and as advisers in community and domestic issues, were defrocked or killed. Temples—the center of social gatherings, education, and religious life—were dismantled or used for animal and human shelters, warehouses, and prisons. Buddhist scriptures were burned for fuel, and Buddhist statues were destroyed or dumped into lakes and rivers (Higbee 1992; Ngor 1987).

Religion was a prime target of the Khmer Rouge as they deconstructed Cambodian culture and society through a system of ideology, violence, and intimidation known as the "Organization" *(aṅkā)* (Chandler 1991; Kiernan 1996; Marston 1997; Martin 1994). When Vietnamese troops invaded in 1979, many Cambodians fled to the Thai border. Over the next ten to fifteen years, 150,000 Cambodians emigrated to the United States (Haines 1985; Hein 1995). Cambodian religion, specifically Buddhism, with its temple structure and ritual cycles, subsequently became an organizing principle for the reconstruction of Cambodian identity in the diaspora (Mortland 1994; Smith-Hefner 1999). Coleman notes that in 1970 there were only two hundred Cambodians and three Cambodian Buddhist temples in the United States. By the year 2000 there were approximately 260,000 Cambodians and at least eighty Khmer Buddhist temples or sites of worship in the United States (Lerch 2000). In California's Long Beach Cambodian community there are presently five Buddhist temples serving an estimated population of forty thousand Khmer.

Although temples have been built, "the Khmer way of the ancestors" has been difficult to reconstruct in America's high-tech urban setting for the peasant rice farmers who comprise the majority of the Cambodian community dispersed in racially mixed central Long Beach.[3] The syncretic nature of Khmer religion encompasses various beliefs in both malevolent spirits *(brāy)* and benevolent spirits, including various guardian spirits *(anak tā)*[4] typically associated with a given locale in Cambodia, sometimes in the persona of legendary heroes or ancestors. These spirits appear to have made the move to Long Beach, along with a number of healers *(grū)*.[5] Some of these *grū* practice the art of love potions, others provide advice through communication with various spirits, including predictions about the future. The older generation may seek advice from both Buddhist monks and the traditional healers.

The community has also experienced political and class factionalism, which

Fig. 10.1 Flag-raising ceremony, UCC parking lot, Long Beach (T. Yamada)

has constrained the development of a politically viable Cambodian presence in Long Beach.[6] It was partially in response to this factionalism and the divisiveness within the United Cambodian Community (UCC), one of the two major mutual-aid associations serving Cambodians in Long Beach, that Sakphan Keam decided to organize and sponsor a traditional religious ritual to honor and communicate with the ancestors as a symbolic act of community healing.[7]

On Sunday, March 3, 1996, the first public spirit-flag-raising ritual in the thirty-year history of the Long Beach Cambodian community was held due to Sakphan Keam's efforts (fig. 10.1). This ritual, in honor of the ancestor spirit Lok Tā Ukñā Khleang Moeung,[8] his wife Lok Yāy Jaṃdāv Kan Kaev, and various other spirits, took place at the UCC Plaza located on Anaheim Street in the center of Little Phnom Penh.[9] This was the first public recognition of the ancestor cult of Khleang Moeung, which has been reestablished in Long Beach.[10]

The Spirit-Flag-Raising Ceremony

According to Sakphan Keam, the sponsor of the ritual, although privately held ceremonies for Khleang Moeung involving traditional healers *(grū khmaer)* and spirit mediums have been held in the Long Beach Cambodian community for many years, this was the first successful public spirit-flag-raising ceremony.[11] Unable to find a text describing the ritual, Keam asked a respected local *grū khmaer* to construct the altar and organize the ritual, including its time sequence.[12] Another highly respected traditional healer from La Puente,[13] medium Heng Kim, was consulted about the auspicious date to hold this event and asked to serve as official medium for the ceremony.[14]

The event itself was a great success in terms of both attendance and enthusiasm. Several hundred Cambodians from Long Beach, Los Angeles, and outlying areas, and a small number of non-Cambodians, participated in the ceremony.

The altar area was assembled gradually from 6:30 A.M. on the day of the event. A canopy was erected over the altar constructed toward the left side of the empty UCC parking lot. Grass mats were spread on the ground beneath the main altar and the area in front of it. A strip of white cloth, approximately eighteen inches wide, was placed on the grass mats leading to the altar. On either side of the white cloth were arranged one pair of flower vases and four pairs of silver bowls with fruit. A large, covered silver container was placed between these two rows of paired fruit bowls near the edge of the grass mat where worshipers would come to bow, pray, and offer incense.

The strip of cloth, now unfolded to a width of several feet, led up to the altar table, where it was laid across the table surface. A banana trunk[15] covered with fifty-seven stacks of five pointed-leaf clusters in a circumference pattern of five was erected in the center of this table.[16] One candle, surrounded by nine yellow flowers and five palm fruits, was placed on the top of this trunk, and four hollow green coconuts *(slā thor)*, with five green betel leaves and three sticks of incense placed in the center of each, were placed at its base.[17] As more people arrived, vases of flowers and flower arrangements were randomly placed on both the main altar and the grass mats below it.

The musicians belonging to a traditional Khmer *biṇbādy* percussion ensemble arrived around 7:30 A.M., took about thirty minutes to set up their instruments, and then began playing for the arriving spectators. According to the formal invitation,

> The program will begin with sunrise prayers and will include the music of the Pinpeat Orchestra and a meeting of the spirits. Several monks and other spiritual guides will offer prayers and food offerings and will perform an ancient flag raising.
>
> The flags represent the Spirit of Lokta Ukgna Klang Moeung [*sic*] a legendary Cambodian Army Commander who lived in the XV Century, and his wife, Lok Yeay Chumteav Kan Keav. The rulers are memorialized for sacrificing their lives to defend Cambodia against enemies.
>
> The flags that will be used at the ceremony were made under special instruction by the spirit of Lokta Ukgna through a spirit practitioner from the city of Pauthiksat [Pursat], in the Kingdom of Cambodia. Spirit practitioners are called Rup or Kru, meaning Master. The flags are 15 feet long and three feet wide and are made of a peach colored cloth in the shape of a giant lizard.[18] The creature carries a pair of bronze bells in its mouth, and is decorated with sequins and colorful orange tassels.
>
> The mythological creature has roots in both the Buddhist and Hindu religions. The sacred flags are thought to bring unity, trust and prosperity to all people.[19]

The opening ceremony actually began around 9:00 A.M., after the raising of both the American and Cambodian flags and introductions by UCC officials, as well as by Keam and Sandy Blankenship, a Cambodian American involved in Long Beach City politics.[20] The audience then waited for the arrival of the La Puente *grū khmaer* group, who appeared nearly two hours later in a white van.

White cloth was spread on the ground as a pathway for the chief female medium Heng Kim, who channels the spirit of a distant ancestor of King Sihanouk (fig. 10.2). She arrived dressed in orange silk monk's robes, accompanied by Sary Khiev, a female medium referred to as her spirit wife.[21] Another female medium, Yang Neang,[22] there since early morning, rose in dance to greet them. Carefully attended by her son, she would later dance in trance, wielding a sword as Khleang Moeung.

As the *biṇbādy* ensemble played the same song seven times, the entourage of the La Puente and Santa Ana medium groups, dressed gaily in bright, traditional Cambodian dress, danced in trance, some of them repeatedly falling unconscious to the ground. During this time the spirit flag was blessed and raised. After the raising of the spirit flag, Heng Kim, embodying Sihanouk's ancestor, gave a speech in which s/he stated that the ancestor spirits wanted peace within Cambodia and the Long Beach Cambodian community. She continued to declare that there should be no more fighting and no more bloodshed in Cambodia. Urging all Cambodians to reunite, she proclaimed that, as prophesied, Cambodia would have a restorative king called Braḥ Pād Dhammik.[23]

After the speech, white cloth was spread for Heng Kim to walk upon and rose petals were scattered in her path as she and the entourage proceeded inside the UCC building. The entire group, including the musicians, reassembled in the large second-floor meeting room, where another, more informal altar was set up in front of her, while Cambodian food was served to all the participants in the rooms below.

As the musicians played and women danced, Heng Kim and Sary Khiev sprayed the heads of participants with perfume. One after another, people would approach Heng Kim to ask a series of questions about their personal lives and future prospects. This activity lasted well into the evening.

Fig. 10.2 Medium Heng Kim, flag-raising ceremony (T. Yamada)

The Legend of Khleang Moeung

Over a year after the event, while interviewing Keam about his role as sponsor, he revealed to me that a Cambodian text detailing the ritual for Khleang Moeung had been unexpectedly found. According to Keam this text was discovered, somewhat miraculously, on the desk of his mother-in-law, who apparently had it in her personal library.[24] According to the text, the ceremony to honor Khleang Moeung and all others who have sacrificed their lives for Cambodia since 1516 C.E. takes place once a year on a Saturday during the sixth month of the lunar year[25] at Khleang Moeung's sacred compound *(āsram)* in the Bakan District of Pursat.

Most Cambodians know the story of Khleang Moeung, a high official of the capital city of Lovek during 1502, when Cambodia was under the domination of Siam. At this time, the Cambodian king Braḥ Chan Rājā arranged for his bodyguards to kill the son of the Siamese king, sent by his father to oversee Cambodian territory. When the king of Siam heard of his son's death, he assembled an army to destroy Braḥ Chan Rājā and his family. When the Siamese army arrived at the city of Lovek, they surrounded it, then seized and executed the king along with his family, sacked the treasury, and enslaved the city's inhabitants.

Among those who escaped were General Khleang Moeung, his wife and their four children, and a consort of the king now pregnant with his son, Chey Aschar. She was subsequently captured and concealed the identity of her son. With his royal identity unknown, Chey Aschar was able to learn methods of tending elephants during his youth and ultimately became the head of the Siamese king's army of elephants. Ready to reclaim his rightful kingdom, clever Chey Aschar devised a plan to trick the Siamese king into giving him the king's royal sword to help in pursuit of capturing a wild, great white elephant that actually did not exist.

Having successfully fled with the king's elephants and royal sword, Chey Aschar made known his true identity. With only a few Khmer soldiers to accomplish his plan, he summoned his loyal retainers and asked them for a strategy that would succeed anyway. General Khleang Moeung was the only one to respond. He proposed to sacrifice his life in order to raise an army of ghosts to attack the Siamese troops. He made a large pit lined at the bottom with sharp blades that would impale him when he jumped inside.[26] Before his sacrifice, he ordered all the soldiers to come and listen to his last exhortation. Khleang Moeung told them that when he died, he would summon an army of ghosts. Seven days after his death, the soldiers would hear a loud noise like thunder; this would indicate that they would be victorious in battle. He requested that they fight with all their heart and strength to protect Khmer territory. After saying this he then leapt into the pit, followed by his wife (and in some versions of the story, his two sons).

Seven days later the tremendous sound of thunder was heard just as Khleang Moeung had foretold. By this time the Siamese army had arrived in Battambang and met the troops of Chey Aschar. The ghost army then manifested its power, tormenting the Siamese soldiers. They became dizzy or experienced violent stomach cramps and fell to the earth, where the Khmer soldiers massacred them in great numbers, thus routing the Siamese army, who returned to Siam in defeat. Chey Aschar was enthroned as rightful king. Out of respect and appreciation, the new king organized a solemn ceremony to be carried out each year in memory of *anak tā* Khleang Moeung, now a "national" hero and the ancestor-spirit who protects Cambodia.

This legend of Khleang Moeung has inspired Cambodian freedom fighters from its inception. In the twentieth century the legend was also utilized by the French due to the Vichy regime's emphasis on the construction of a Cambodian national identity linked to an idealization of the Angkorean era and the promotion of wartime heroes like Khleang Moeung (Edwards 1999). A 1943 article in the newspaper *Kampuchea* likened the spirit of self-sacrifice demonstrated by Khleang Moeung and his wife to Joan of Arc's "valiant conduct and patriotic fervor" (Edwards 1999).

After the demise of the colonial era, Khleang Moeung appeared in a nationalist song, "The Advice of Khleang Moeung," recorded in Kien Svay Village during the civil disruption of the Lon Nol era (1970–1975).

> The advice of the story of Khleang Moeung's love
> for the nation is to sacrifice oneself
> and to die with good reputation,
> full of glory, well-known everywhere,
> with your name engraved on scrolls of gold,
> to appease and care for the nation.[27]

Toan Chay, one of the first figures to organize armed resistance to the Khmer Rouge, also chose Khleang Moeung as the symbol of his movement.[28]

The protective power of ancestor Khleang Moeung is illustrated in Daran Kravanh's memoir, *Music through the Dark: A Tale of Survival in Cambodia*, written in collaboration with Bree Lafreniere. In his account of survival during the Khmer Rouge period, Kravanh, also a native of Pursat, relates an incident where he evoked the power of Khleang Moeung and other spirits to save him from certain death. He attributes his miraculous escape to their power (Lafreniere and Kravanh 2000, 48–49).

The range of activities regarding Khleang Moeung extends from private initiation, political identification, and deployment as a symbol of resistance to a new form of public ritual intended "to protect and bring peace" to both the Long Beach Cambodian community and Cambodia. Initially without a ritual text, Keam relied upon the advice of respected mediums in the community to devise an appropriate altar setting and ritual context. According to Moore and Myerhoff, "even in the case of a newly invented ritual (or ritual performed only once), the ritual is constructed in such a way that its internal repetitions of form and content make it tradition-like" because "it is supposed to carry the same unreflective conviction as any traditional repetitive ritual" (Tambiah 1985, 132). At the March 3, 1996, ceremony, the altar construction and use of monks, mediums, and music made the event "similar enough" to other events remembered by the older generation of Cambodians to seem authentic. Keam declared he had not seen anything like this since his childhood.

Social and Personal Context

The creative force behind the public Khleang Moeung spirit-flag-raising ceremony was Keam. Tambiah's comment regarding the linkage of rituals "to status claims and interests of the participants" is directly confirmed by the fact that without Sakphan Keam, its sponsor, the event would not have occurred. He financed the event, succeeding in obtaining support from UCC, and organized the ceremony and the medium participants.

Keam is a Cambodian intellectual originally from Pursat. A long-term resident of the Long Beach Cambodian community who belongs to the relatively small sector of upper-middle-class Cambodian professionals, he currently works as a translator for the Long Beach Municipal Court. For some time, Keam has expressed concern about the reconstruction of traditional Khmer culture for the refugee community. This concern has been publicly expressed in his role as a cultural activist to promote the traditional Khmer boat racing festival in Long Beach, the yearly Cambodian New Year festival, and now this public spirit-flag-raising ritual.

But more than cultural activism, the public spirit-flag-raising ritual was intimately interwoven with Keam's public aspirations, politics, and personal spiritual life. This event gave him the opportunity to reconstruct a "traditional" public ritual. Since he traveled to Cambodia to obtain the spirit flags, he fulfilled his desire to facilitate linkages between the Long Beach refugee community and the homeland. He also hoped to use this ceremony as a means to bridge the gap between UCC and different social segments of the Long Beach refugee community and to mend factionalism with UCC itself.[29] The two social service agencies in the community, UCC and the Cambodian Association of America (CAA), both run by Cambodians, are organized as institutions in ways consistent with the principles of the American social service sector. CAA is the oldest mutual-aid society for Cambodians in the United States. UCC split from it due to political differences, and these political differences have only recently been healed to the extent that both organizations can work together on various projects. Both agencies are run and staffed by educated Cambodians, typically from wealthy, urban backgrounds.

Ironically, many features of Cambodia's traditional hierarchical society have been unintentionally reconstructed, and these "upper-class" social workers control the services and benefits supplied to their "clients"—who in Cambodia were uneducated, rice-farming peasants. As a result, social service agencies have not been very effective in providing meaningful services to this large sector of the Long Beach Khmer population.

Due to the reemergence of traditional class conflicts within the refugee Cambodian community, social service agencies have had difficulties reaching many members of the Long Beach Cambodian community.[30] By symbolically holding an event at the UCC Plaza that would appeal to what he described as the "spiritual" aesthetics of the "lower classes," Keam hoped to link these elite and non-elite groups as he affirmed his own rural roots.

According to one of the information sheets in Khmer available at the event and Keam's personal explanation to me, the ritual began with a command by Moeung to hold a spirit-flag-raising ceremony in Long Beach that would promote peace. This injunction for a ceremony occurred when Keam went to Cambodia in January 1996, the first visit since his father's death, to see his mother, also a *grū khmaer* in Pursat. Two spirit flags were to be created and raised according to Khleang Moeung's instructions as given through a medium in Pursat. He asked his mother to make the flags according to the medium's directions. They were to be kept with the medium near Khleang Moeung's grave.

Keam traveled again to Cambodia to pick up a second flag and bring it to Long Beach for the flag-raising ceremony there. After the Long Beach event on March 3, he returned to Cambodia in April for seven days and seven nights, during which time he visited Angkor Wat, where, he states, he had a unique religious experience. The returned flag was then raised on a full-moon day in May in honor of Khleang Moeung and Keam's deceased father.

This description reveals a complex interweaving of levels of intent and geographical spaces. It clearly illustrates Tambiah's observations (1970, 125) that rituals, "however prescribed they may be, are always linked to status claims and interests of the participants." Keam, acting in accordance with the instructions of Khleang Moeung through a Pursat medium in Cambodia, could work toward linkage of the fractured Cambodian community in Long Beach while pursuing his own spiritual life. This impetus, manifested as an urgent call for ritual when a community is in crisis, has been studied by Victor Turner (1969) in an African context. The shock of a coup in Cambodia during the summer of 1997 caused Keam to reevaluate his hopes for peace there. A Long Beach *grū khmaer* with whom Keam frequently consults has advised him against going to Cambodia for several years. Since the coup he has retreated from overt promotion of Cambodian cultural activities. According to him there has been a proliferation of Khleang Moeung spirit medium groups since the March 3, 1996, event. In 1997 a request was made by one such group to have the yearly ceremony held at the Willow Street Temple. The abbot, Ven. Kong Chhean,[31] apparently refused due to the fact that such a ritual was too "Brahmanical."

The popularity of this "one-time event" reflects how difficult it is to hold public rituals outside the Buddhist temple, especially when those rituals have been traditionally associated with a geographical site in Cambodia, such as Khleang Moeung's sacred site. There is nothing sacred about the UCC parking lot (Rappaport 1999).

The Significance of Public Ritual for the Long Beach Cambodian Community

Researchers who study the Cambodian diaspora have long recognized the importance of ritual in the reconstruction of traditional culture (Mortland 1994; Higbee 1992; Kalab 1994; Smith-Hefner 1999). The building of a Buddhist temple and the presence of monks serve to signify a degree of cultural reconstruction for most diasporic Cambodians. Public cultural events that incorporate traditional ritual, such as the New Year's festival, serve as important culturally unifying symbolic systems within the fragmented diasporic Cambodian Long Beach community, where there is a small but significant pattern of conversion to Christianity.[32]

In 1998 the Cambodian New Year's festival, the major yearly event that brings the entire community together, was not held in El Dorado Park for the first time in a decade because the city of Long Beach and its police department refused to subsidize the anti-gang security services the city authorities felt were needed for the three-day event.[33] In 2000 the city incurred debts for the event due to security costs, and city officials refused to sanction the 2001 festival until just four weeks before its proposed date. The 2001 New Year's festival in El Dorado Park was ultimately canceled against strong protest.

As the Cambodian community reveals its fragmentation, reflecting in part politics in Cambodia, public events like the New Year's festival, serving to unify the community across political and class lines, become harder to organize as more and more of the community's leaders leave to run for political office or for business opportunities in Phnom Penh. The community may be left with only cultural rituals that take place within the confines of the major Khmer Buddhist temples in the area, also sites of political contestation.[34]

The March 3 Khleang Moeung spirit-flag-raising ceremony appears retrospectively to be a unique event in the community's history. That such religious rituals serve to foster a cooperative sense of cultural cohesion is apparent from the 1998–2001 struggle to find a Long Beach location for the New Year's festival. Such events take place in outdoor public arenas where a larger Cambodian population representing diverse economic sectors and generations is able to commingle.

Even if many American-educated, elite Cambodians no longer profess belief in spirit mediums as healers, they may participate as observers or as organizers of such communal events and thus remain indirectly linked to indigenous Khmer traditions. For those who value Khmer culture, public rituals are an important symbol of cultural identity and continuity in a postmodern, multiethnic urban American environment.

Notes

This chapter would have been impossible without the generosity of Sakphan Keam, who spent many hours with me discussing the March 3, 1996, ceremony and his own personal belief system. Vuth Reth also provided invaluable assistance regarding the analysis of the Cambodian texts.

1. Cambodian Buddhism is fused with folk beliefs. It includes elements from Brahmanism, Śaivism, animism, ancestor spirits, and other supernatural entities, as well as various forms of Buddhism. On this topic see Ebihara 1966 and Canniff 1999.

2. For a description of the Khmer sense of order, refer to Chandler 1982 and Thompson 1996.

3. Kalab (Ebihara, Mortland, and Ledgerwood 1994) describes similar difficulties for Cambodians in Paris. Cambodians in smaller urban areas (Fresno, Stockton, and San Jose, California) seem to fare better in gaining cooperation from city officials and police regarding public ceremonies.

4. *Anak tā,* pronounced "neak ta," is often translated into English as "local genies" based upon the French translation, *génies territoriaux;* Porée-Maspero 1955, 375–377. They are guardian deities or spirits, most frequently associated with specific geographical locations. Leclère (1916, 559) glosses the term *"anak tā"* as *ancêtres devenus génies* and *"āraks"* as *génies locaux.* For further information on *anak tā,* see Ang 1986, Forest 1992, Porée-Maspéro 1962–1969, and Touch 2001.

5. This relationship is further explored by Bertrand in chap. 7 and Forest 1992.

6. Other Cambodian communities in the United States seem to have less conflict than the Long Beach Cambodian community. This is partly due to the larger population in Long Beach. The Cambodian community has historically experienced conflict with the city government, police, and public school district. This is the only Cambodian community with two competing mutual-aid associations run by Cambodians. Smith-Hefner's (1999) treatment of the Boston Khmer community should be cautiously applied to other Cambodian communities in the United States. For a study of conflict in other Cambodian mutual-aid associations, see Niedzwiecki 1998.

7. Community ritual activity parallel to this has been seen in Lao refugee camps; see Conquergood 1988.

8. *Glāṃṅ* (Khmer, "keeper of the treasury, storehouse"); *mīoeṅ* (Thai, "municipality, region, or country"), thus: "keeper of the local treasury," "a high official." Lok Tā Ukñā and Lok Yāy Jaṃdāv are honorific titles indicating seniority, gender, and rank.

9. An information sheet in Khmer for the event stated that many spirits in addition to Khleang Moeung might arrive for the ceremony.

10. For the story of Khleang Moeung, see Forest 1992, 242–247; and Khin Sok 1988, 121–128.

11. According to Keam, the Santa Ana medium group tried to have a public flag-raising ceremony for Khleang Moeung several years ago, but it was unsuccessful.

12. This is a male *grū*. He is associated with the Braḥ Go-Braḥ Kaev cult.

13. The major mediums and their cohorts are known by geographical location. There are groups in La Puente, El Monte, Pamona, and Santa Ana, and several in Long Beach.

14. No distinction is made in the program or by Keam between male and female *grū*. Two of the female participants, including Heng Kim, were *cūl rūp arākkh,* mediums who become possessed by spirits. On this type of medium, usually a woman, see Lavelle et al. 1996, 60; on traditional healers in Cambodia, see Eisenbruch 1992 and Ebihara 1968. For a general discussion of the significance of spirit possession, see Crapanzano and Garrison 1977.

15. This resembles, perhaps unconsciously, a Śiva *linga.* In Pursat, a large termite hill is used to symbolize Khleang Moeung.

16. The symbolism of the number five is explained by Porée-Maspéro 1958, 22.

17. Similar ceremonial offerings have been described by Porée-Maspéro 1958, 7–10; 1962, 49–50.

18. "Giant lizard" means *nāga* or crocodile in this context. The history of crocodile banners and associated legends are explained by Porée-Maspero 1962, 103–117.

19. This text comes from an information sheet titled "Ancient Flag Raising Ceremony" handed out in both Khmer and English on the day of the ceremony. The program schedule was listed as follows: 6:30 A.M. Reception; 7:00 A.M. Opening ceremony; 7:15 A.M. Pinpeat Orchestra, individual prayers with candles, the raising of the flags; 8:00 A.M. Meeting of the spirits through the *Grū Khmaer* with accompaniment by the orchestra. Light food will be provided by the Arts of Apsara Gallery located in the UCC Plaza; 10:00 A.M. Seven Buddhist monks will pray and make a food offering; 11:00 A.M. Cambodian Cultural Shows.

20. Sandy Blankenship is now known as San Arun and is living in Cambodia.

21. Sary Khiev passed away the following year. According to Sakphan Keam, personal communication, October 6, 2002, Heng Kim returned to Cambodia and is currently living in a temple outside of Phnom Penh, where she is not allowed to wear monk's robes.

22. Aged seventy-two in 1998.

23. Sakphan Keam, personal communication, October 6, 2002, explained that since Cambodia is now a republic with a marginalized monarch, this prophesied king will come to restore the monarchy. Because of his integrity and compassion, the living and social conditions of all the people in Cambodia will be restored. The prophecy described comes from the *Buddh Daṃnāy,* described by Hansen in chap. 2 and referred to by Marston in chap. 8.

24. The story of Khleang Moeung appears in the multivolume *Prajuṃ rīoeṅ breṅ khmaer* (Collection of old Khmer stories), republished many times by the Buddhist Institute. This is in fact one of the most commonly found Khmer-language texts, both in Cambodia and overseas.

25. According to Forest 1992, 238, this special day is always on a Saturday in the month called Pisaaq, when the moon is either waxing or waning.

26. The legend has a number of versions; this version comes from a translation by Khing Hoc in Forest 1992. Different versions can be found in Khin Sok 1988 and Andelle 1940, 5–7.

27. Verse three of the translation, "Advice of Khleang Moeung," is a song on a CD titled *Goodbye Sweetheart I'm Going to War,* remastered by Chlangden Productions, Signal Hill, California, reissue no. 191; translation from Khmer by Guthrie.

28. K. Robinson, Reuters, "Toan Chay, Moderate Who May Become New Cambodian PM," July 15, 1997.

29. Over 80 percent of the Long Beach Cambodian community belongs to the functionally illiterate rice-farming class. The Cambodian community, along with the Hmong, has the largest long-term welfare rate (70 percent) and the lowest success rate as measured by high school and college graduates.

30. For a general understanding of "class" issues within Cambodian culture, see Marston 1997.

31. He refers to himself as "Rev. Kong Chhean."

32. There are currently over five Christian churches attended by Cambodians, including Catholic, Methodist, Quaker, and Seventh-Day Adventist denominations. The number of Khmer Christians appears to be much higher among third-generation Khmer Americans, many of whom are rapidly losing their heritage and language skills.

33. The event was moved to the Santa Fe Dam Park area, miles away from the community. It had to be held there again in 2001 when negotiations to move it back to El Dorado Park in Long Beach broke down between the community organizers and Long Beach City officials aligned with the Long Beach police department. It was finally reestablished in 2002, but now two separate New Year's festivals are being organized by competing community factions.

34. The importance of "reparative" public rituals in Cambodia is reflected by the Dhammayātrā Movement; see chap. 9.

References

AEFEO:	Archives École Française d'Extrême-Orient, Paris
BEFEO:	*Bulletin de l'École Française d'Extrême-Orient,* Paris et Hanoi
BN:	Rare Book Collection, Bibliothèque Nationale, Paris
Cedoreck:	Centre de Documentation et de Recherche sur la Civilisation Khmère
EFEO:	École Française d'Extrême-Orient, Paris et Hanoi
GL:	*Gatilok*
IC:	*Inscriptions du Cambodge,* by George Coedès (each inscription is identified by the letter "K" followed by an inventory number)
IMA:	*Inscriptions Modernes d'Angkor Vat*
JAS:	*Journal of Asian Studies*
JSS:	*Journal of the Siam Society*
NAC:	National Archives of Cambodia, Phnom Penh

Adas, Michael. 1979. *Prophets of Rebellion.* Chapel Hill: University of North Carolina Press.

Ames, Michael M. 1966. "Ritual Prestations and the Structure of the Singhalese Pantheon." In *Anthropological Studies of Theravāda Buddhism,* June Nash, ed. New Haven, Conn.: Yale University Press, 27–50.

An, Leang Hap. 1970. *Buddhism in Cambodia.* Tome 8, Série de Culture et Civilisation Khmères. Phnom Penh: Institut Bouddhique.

Andaya, Barbara. 2002. "Localizing the Universal: Women, Motherhood and the Appeal of Early Theravāda Buddhism." *Journal of Southeast Asian Studies* 33.1:1–30.

Andelle, Pierre. 1940. "Folklore et légendes du Cambodge: Le génie Khléang-Moeung." *Indochine Hebdomaire Illustreé* 1.11 (November 21):5–7.

Anderson, Benedict. 1991. *Imagined Communities: Reflections on the Origin and Spread of Nationalism.* London: Verso.

Ang Chouléan. 1986. *Les êtres surnaturels dans la religion populaire khmère.* Paris: Cedoreck.

———. 1988. "The Place of Animism within Popular Buddhism in Cambodia: The Example of the Monastery." *Asian Folklore Studies* 47:35–41.

———. 1990. "La communauté rurale khmère du point de vue du sacré." *Journal Asiatique* 278.1–2:135–154.

Angkor Thom. 1996. "Tāpas' Ros Lī Min Maen Jā Acchariya Baggal De!" January 30–31.

Appadurai, Arjun. 1990. "Disjuncture and Difference in Global Cultural Economy. *Public Culture* 2.2:1–24.

Appleby, Scott. 2000. *The Ambivalence of the Sacred: Religion, Violence and Reconciliation.* Lanham, Md.: Rowman and Littlefield.

Au Chhieng. 1968. "À propos de la statue dite du 'roi lépreux' (Études de Philologie khmère V)." *JA* 256.2:185–202.

Aymonier, Étienne. 1900–1904. *Le Cambodge.* 3 vols. Paris: E. Leroux.

Bareau, André. 1960. "La construction et le culte des *stūpa* d'après les *Vinayapiṭaka.*" *BEFEO* 50.2:229–274.

———. 1969. "Quelques érmitages et centres de méditation bouddhiques au Cambodge." *BEFEO* 56:2–30.

———. 1974. "Sur l'origine des piliers dits d'Asoka, des stupa et des arbres sacrés du Bouddhisme primitif." *Indologica Taurensia* 2:9–36.

Barth, Auguste. 1882. "Bulletin critique des religions de l'Inde." *Revue de l'Histoire des Religions* 5:227–252.

———. 1903. "Les doublets de la stèle de Say Fong." *BEFEO* 3:460–466.

Barth, Auguste, and A. Bergaigne. 1893. *Inscriptions sanscrites du Campa et du Cambodge.* Paris: Imprimerie national.

Basch, Linda, Nina Glick Schiller, and Cristina Szanton Blanc. 1994. *Nations Unbound: Transnational Projects, Postcolonial Predicaments, and Deterritorialized States.* Amsterdam: Gordon and Breach Publishers.

Bechert, Heinz. 1978. "On the Popular Religion of the Sinhalese." In *Buddhism in Ceylon and Studies on Religious Syncretism in Buddhist Countries,* Heinz Bechert, ed. Gottingen: Vandenhoek and Ruprecht, 217–233.

Becker, Elizabeth. 1985. *When the War Was Over: The Voices of Cambodia's Revolution and Its People.* New York: Simon and Schuster.

Benoist, Jean. 1982. "Possession, guérison, médiations." *L'ethnographie* 78 87/88.2–3:227–239.

Benveniste, Émile. 1969. *Le vocabulaire des institutions indo-européenees. 1. Economie, parenté, société.* Paris: Les Éditions de Minuit, Paris.

Bernstein, Elizabeth, and Yeshua Moser. 1993. "Washing Away the Blood." Dhammayietra Center.

Bhabha, Homi. 1994. *The Location of Culture.* London: Routledge.

Bhattacharya, Gouriswar. 1980. "The Stupa as Maitreya's Emblem." In *The Stupa: Its Religious, Historical and Architectural Significance,* A. L. Dallopiccola, ed. Weisbaden: Steiner.

Bhattacharya, Kamaleswar. 1997. "The Religions of Ancient Cambodia." In *Sculpture of Angkor and Ancient Cambodia: Millennium of Glory,* H. I. Jessup and T. Zephir, eds. New York: Thames and Hudson, 34–52.

Birnbaum, Raoul. 1979. *The Healing Buddha.* Boulder, Colo.: Shambala.

Bizot, François. 1976. *Le figuier à cinq branches: Recherche sur le bouddhisme khmer.* Paris: EFEO.

———. 1988. *Les traditions de la pabbajjā en Asie du Sud-Est.* Göttingen: Vandenhoeck and Ruprecht.

———. 1992. *Le Chemin de Langka*. Paris: EFEO.
———. 1993. *Le Bouddhisme des Thaïs*. Bangkok: Éditions des Cahiers de France.
———. 1994. "La consécration des statues et le culte des morts." In *Recherches nouvelles sur le Cambodge*, François Bizot, ed. Paris: EFEO, 101–112.
Bloch, M. 1983. *Les rois thaumaturges*. Paris: Gallimard (Corrected version of 1924 ed. by the Publications de la Faculté des Lettres de Strasbourg and a 1961 ed. by the Librairie Armand Colin).
Bloss, Lowell W. 1987 "The Female Renunciants of Sri Lanka: The Dasasilmattawa." *Journal of the International Association of Buddhist Studies* 10.1:21–31.
Bode, Mabel. 1893. "Women Leaders of the Buddhist Reformation." *Journal of the Royal Asiatic Society of Great Britain & Ireland*, 517–566, 763–798.
Bond, George. 1988. *The Buddhist Revival in Sri Lanka*. Durham: University of South Carolina Press.
Bosch, F.D.K. 1932. "Notes archéologiques." *BEFEO* 31.3–4:485–497.
Bouchy, Anne. 1992. *Les oracles de Shirataka*. Arles: Éditions Philippe Piquier.
Bowie, Katherine A. 1996. "Slavery in Nineteenth-Century Northern Thailand: Archival Anecdotes and Village Voices." In *State Power and Culture in Thailand*, E. Paul Durrenberger, ed. New Haven, Conn.: Yale Southeast Asia Studies Monograph no. 44, 114–126.
Brac de la Perrière, Bénédicte. 1989. *Les rituels de possession en Birmanie, du culte d'état aux cérémonies privées*. Paris: ERC.
Brocheux, P. 1995. *The Mekong Delta: Ecology, Economy and Revolution 1860–1960*. Madison: University of Wisconsin-Madison, Center of Southeast Asian Studies Monograph no. 12.
Brötel, Dieter. 1986. "Imperialist Domination in Vietnam and Cambodia: A Long-Term View." In *Imperalism and After: Continuities and Discontinuities*, Wolfgang J. Mommsen and Jurgen Osterhammel, eds. London: Allen and Unwin.
Bulletin mensuel de documentation (compiled by the Private Secretariat of His Majesty the King of Cambodia). 1998 (June 24–July 9).
Bunnag, Jane. 1973. *Buddhist Monk, Buddhist Layman*. Cambridge: Cambridge University Press.
Burslem, C. 1993. "Mahā Ghosananda's Peace Revolution," *Phnom Penh Post*, July 16–29.
Cabezón, José Ignacio. 1996. "Buddhist Principles in the Tibetan Liberation Movement." In *Engaged Buddhists: Buddhist Liberation Movements in Southeast Asia*, Christopher Queen and Sallie King, eds. Albany: State University of New York Press.
Canniff, Julie G. 1999. "Traveling the Middle Path: The Cultural Epistemology of Success, a Case Study of Three Cambodian Families." Ph.D. dissertation, Harvard University.
Casanova, Jose. 1994. *Public Religions in the Modern World*. Chicago: University of Chicago Press.
Chakrabarty, Dipesh. 2000. *Provincializing Europe: Postcolonial Thought and Historical Difference*. Princeton, N.J.: Princeton University Press.
Chan Moly Sam. 1987. *Khmer Court Dance: A Comprehensive Study of Movements, Gestures, and Postures as Applied Techniques*. Newington, Conn.: Khmer Studies Institute.
Chandler, David. 1971. "An Eighteenth Century Inscription from Angkor Wat." *JSS* 59.2: 151–159.

———. 1974. "Royally Sponsored Human Sacrifices in Nineteenth Century Cambodia: The Cult of *Nak Tā* Me Sa (Mahisāsuramardini) at Ba Phnom." *JSS* 62.2:207–222.
———. 1976. "Maps for the Ancestors: Sacralized Topograpy and Echoes of Angkor in Two Cambodian Texts." *JSS* 64.2:170–187.
———. 1982. "Songs at the Edge of the Forest: Perceptions of Order in Three Cambodian Texts." In *Moral Order and the Question of Change: Essays on Southeast Asian Thought,* David K. Wyatt and Alexander Woodsides, eds. New Haven, Conn.: Yale University Southeast Asia Studies Monograph Series no. 24, 53–77.
———. 1983. "Going through the Motions: Ritual Aspects of the Reign of King Ang Duang of Cambodia (1848–1860)." In *Centers, Symbols and Hierarchies: Essays on the Classical States of Southeast Asia,* Lorraine Gesick, ed. New Haven, Conn.: Yale University Press, 106–124.
———. 1991. *The Tragedy of Cambodian History: Politics, War, and Revolution since 1945.* New Haven, Conn.: Yale University Press.
———. 1992. *A History of Cambodia.* Boulder, Colo.: Westview Press.
———. 1996a. *A History of Cambodia.* 2d. ed., updated. Boulder, Colo.: Westview Press.
———. 1996b. *Facing the Cambodian Past: Selected Essays 1971–1994.* Chiangmai: Silkworm Books.
Chatterjee, Partha. 1986. *Nationalist Thought and the Colonial World: A Derivative Discourse?* London: Zed Books for The United Nations University.
———. 1993. *The Nation and Its Fragments: Colonial and Postcolonial Histories.* Princeton, N.J.: Princeton University Press.
Chau Seng. 1961. *L'organisation buddhique au Cambodge.* Phnom Penh: Université Buddhique Preah Sihanouk Raj.
Chaumeau, Christine. 1996. "The Future Is Written: As Fast as Cooking a Shrimp." *Phnom Penh Post,* May 3–16, 1.
Chea Sotheacheath. 1999. "Rising Rivers Threaten Island *Wat.*" *Phnom Penh Post,* August 6–19, 1, 16.
Chhun Ratanak. 1999. "Prāsāt Dī Min Klāy Jā Mās." *Settakicch niṅ Jīvit,* August 30, 10.
Chou Ta-Kuan. 1993. *The Customs of Cambodia,* J. Gilman d'Arcy Paul, trans. Bangkok: The Siam Society.
Churm Duc, ed. 1996 (reprint). *The Longer Kihipadibat: An Anthology of 35 Ceremonies.* Phnom Penh: Triratana Bookshop.
Chutiwongs, Nandana, and Denise Patry Leidy. 1994. *Buddha of the Future: An Early Maitreya from Thailand.* New York: Asia Society Galleries.
Clifford, James. 1994. "Diasporas." *Cultural Anthropology* 9:302–338.
Coalition for Peace and Reconciliation. 1994. *Year-End Activities Report from the Coalition for Peace and Reconciliation and the Dhammayatra Center.* Phonm Penh, December 30.
———. 1995. *Report of the Dhammayietra 4/Interfaith Pilgrimage for Peace and Life 1995.* Phnom Penh, Funder's Report, July.
Coalition for Peace and Reconciliation and International Network of Engaged Buddhists. 1993. *Meditation for a Peaceful Future in Cambodia: Buddhism for Reconciliation and Reconstruction in Cambodia, November 15, 1992–February 7, 1993.* Funder's Report.

Coalition for Peace and Reconciliation and Thai Inter-Religious Commission for Development and International Network of Engaged Buddhists. 1992. *Buddhist and Conflict Resolution: A Training Seminar for Cambodians, December 14, 1991–January 6, 1992.* Funder's Report.

Coalition for Peace and Reconciliation in Cambodia and the World, Thai Inter-Religious Commission for Development and International Network of Engaged Buddhists. 1992. *Buddhism and Conflict Resolution: A Training Seminar for Cambodians, December 14, 1991–January 6, 1992.* Thailand. Funder's Report.

Coedès, George. 1913. "Études Cambodgiennes, part 7." *BEFEO* 13.2:16–17.

———. 1924. *The Vajirañāṇa Library.* Bangkok: Bangkok Times Press.

———. 1929. "Études cambodgiennes, 19. La date du Bayon." *BEFEO* 28.1–2:81–112.

———. 1930. "Études cambodgiennes, 24: Nouvelles données chronologiques et généalogiques sur la dynastie de Mahīdharapura." *BEFEO* 29:297–330.

———. 1937. *Inscriptions du Cambdoge.* Vol. 1. Hanoi: École Française d'Extrême-Orient.

———. 1938. "Dictionnaire Cambodgien." *BEFEO* 38:314–321.

———. 1941. "Études Cambodgiennes 33: La destination funéraire des grands monuments Khmers." *BEFEO* 40.2:315–343.

———. 1942. *Inscriptions du Cambdoge.* Vol. 2. Hanoi: École Française d'Extrême-Orient.

———. 1943. *Pour mieux comprendre Angkor.* Hanoi: Imprimerie d'Extrême-Orient.

———. 1951. *Inscriptions du Cambdoge.* Vol. 3. Paris: É. de Boccard.

———. 1952. *Inscriptions du Cambdoge.* Vol. 4. Paris: É. de Boccard.

———. 1954. *Inscriptions du Cambdoge.* Vol. 6. Paris: École Française d'Extrême-Orient.

———. 1957. "The *Traibhūmikathā,* Buddhist Cosmology and Treaty on Ethics." *East and West* 7.4:349–352.

———. 1960. Le portrait dans l'art Khmer. *Arts Asiatiques* 7.3:179–198.

———. 1963. *Angkor.* Hong Kong: Oxford University Press.

———. 1964. *Inscriptions du Cambdoge.* Vol. 7. Paris: École Française d'Extrême-Orient.

———. 1966. *Inscriptions du Cambdoge.* Vol. 8. Paris: École Française d'Extrême-Orient.

———. 1968. *The Indianized States of Southeast Asia,* Walter Villa, ed., Susan Brown Cowing, trans. Honolulu: East-West Center Press.

———. 1989. *Les états indouisés d'Indochine et d'Indonésie.* Paris: De Boccard.

Cohn, Bernard. 1996. *Colonialism and Its Forms of Knowledge: The British in India.* Princeton, N.J.: Princeton University Press.

Coleman, Cynthia M. 1987. "Cambodians in the United States." In *The Cambodian Agony,* D. A. Ablin and M. Hood, eds. Armonk, N.Y.: M. E. Sharpe, 354–374.

Collard, Paul. 1925. *Cambodge et Cambodgiens.* Paris: Société d'Éditions.

Collection of Old Khmer Stories (Prajuṃ Rïoeṅ Pren Khmaer). BE 2515, vol. 2. Phnom Penh: Institute Bouddhique.

Collins, Steven. 1998. *Nirvana and Other Buddhist Felicities.* Cambridge: Cambridge University Press.

Commission des Moeurs et Coutumes (CMC) (re-edited by E. Porée-Maspero et al). 1985. *Cérémonies des douze mois.* Paris: Cedoreck. (1st ed.: Buddhist Institute, Phnom Penh.)

Condominas, Georges. 1985. "Quelques aspects du chamanisme et des cultes de possession en Asie du Sud Est et dans le monde insulindien." In *L'autre et l'ailleurs, Hommages à Roger Bastide Georges.* Paris: Berger Levrault, 215–232.

Conquergood, Dwight. 1988. "Health Theatre in a Hmong Refugee Camp: Performance, Communication, and Culture." *The Drama Review* 32.3:174–206.

Cook, Nerida. 1982. "The Position of Nuns in Thai Buddhism: The Parameters of Religious Recognition." M.A. thesis, Prehistory and Anthropology, Australian National University.

Cooper, Andrew. 1981. "The Activity of Friendship," *Ten Directions.* Los Angeles: Zen Center.

Crapanzano, Vincent, and Vivian Garrison, eds. 1977. *Case Studies in Spirit Possession.* New York: John Wiley & Sons.

Cruz, Gaspar da. 1953. [1569]. "Treatise in Which the Things of China are Related at Great Length, with Their Particularities, as Likewise of the Kingdom of Ormuz." In *South China in the Sixteenth Century,* C. R. Boxer, ed. London: Hakluyt Society, 59–79.

de Bernon, Olivier. 1994. "Le *Buddh Daṃnāy:* Note sur un Texte Apocalyptique Khmer." *BEFEO* 81:83–85.

———. 1996. "*Chi (jī)* un mot d'origine khmère en usage dans la langue thïe." *JSS* 84.1:87–91.

———. 1997. "À propos du retour des bakous dans le palais royal de Phnom Penh." In *Renouveaux Religieux en Asie,* Catherine Clémentin-Ojha, ed. Paris: *BEFEO,* 33–58.

———. 1998. "La Prédiction du Bouddha." *Aséanie* 1:43–66.

de Casparis, J. G., and I. W. Mabbett. 1992. "Religion and Popular Beliefs of Southeast Asia before c. 1500." In *The Cambridge History of Southeast Asia, Vol. 1,* N. Tarling, ed. Cambridge, New York, and Oakleigh, Victoria: Cambridge University Press, 281–339.

de Coral Rémusat, G. 1940. *L'art khmer, Les grandes étapes de son évolution (Études d'Art et d'Ethnologie Asiatique 1).* Paris: Éditions d'Art et d'Histoire.

de la Brosse, P. 1907. "Dans les provinces Cambodgiennes retrocedées." *Revue Indochinoise,* 2d semester, 1151–1240.

de Pourtalés, Guy. 1931. *Nous a qui rien n'appartiennent.* Paris: Flammarion.

de Villemereuil, M.A.B. 1883. *Explorations et Missions de Doudart de Lagrée.* Paris: Imprimerie et Librairie de Madame Veuve Bouchard-Huzard.

Derrida, Jacques. 1995. *Mal d'Archive.* Paris: Galilée.

———. 1996. "Foi et savoir. Les deux sources de la 'religion' aux limites de la simple raison." In *La religion: Seminaire de Capri,* sous la direction de Jacques Derrida et Gianni Vattimo. Paris: Éditions du Seuil.

Devereux, Georges. 1972. *Ethnopsychanalyse complémentariste.* Paris: Flammarion.

Dhammarama, P. S. 1962. *Initiation Practique au Buddhisme.* Phnom Penh: Imprimerie du Ministere de l'Information.

Doré, Amphay. 1979. "Profils médiumniques lao." *Cahiers de l'Asie du Sud Est.,* no. 5, 7–25.

Duara, Prasenjit. 1995. *Rescuing History from the Nation: Questioning Narratives of Modern China.* Chicago: Chicago University Press.

Ebihara, May. 1966. "Interrelations between Buddhism and Social Systems in Cambodian Peasant Culture." In *Conference on Theravada Buddhism,* Manning Nash, ed. New Haven, Conn.: Yale University Press, 175–196.

———. 1968. "Svay, a Khmer Village in Cambodia." Ph.D. dissertation, Columbia University. Ann Arbor, Mich.: University Microfilms.

———. 1990. "Revolution and Reformulation in Kampuchean Village Culture." In *The Cambodian Agony,* David A. Ablin and Marlowe Hood, eds. Armonk, New York: M. E. Sharpe.

Ebihara, May, Carol Mortland, and Judy Ledgerwood, eds. 1994. *Cambodian Culture since 1975: Homeland and Exile.* Ithaca, N.Y.: Cornell University Press.

Edwards, Michael, and David Hulme. 1997. *Magic Bullet?* West Hartford, Conn.: Kumarian Press.

Edwards, Penny. 1996. "Imagining the Other in Cambodian Nationalist Discourse before and during the UNTAC Period." In *Propaganda, Politics, and Violence in Cambodia: Democratic Transition under United Nations Peace-Keeping,* S. Heder and J. Ledgerwood, eds. Armonk, N.Y.: M. E. Sharpe, 50–72.

———. 1999. "Cambodge: The Cultivation of a Nation, 1860–1940." Ph.D. dissertation, Monash University.

———. 2001. "Propagander: Marianne, Joan of Arc and the Export of French Gender Ideology to Cambodia." In *Promoting the Colonial Idea: Propaganda and Visions of Empire in France,* T. Chafer and A. Sackur, eds. London: Macmillan.

———. forthcoming. *Cambodge, the Cultivation of a Nation 1860–1945.* Honolulu: University of Hawai'i Press.

Eisenbruch, Maurice. 1992. "The Ritual Space of Patients and Traditional Healers in Cambodia." *BEFEO* 79.2:283–316.

Eppsteiner, Fred, ed. 1988. *The Path of Compassion: Writings on Socially Engaged Buddhism.* Berkeley, Calif.: Parallax Press.

Les Étudiants de la Faculté d'Archeologie de Phnom Penh. 1969. "Le Monasterie Bouddhique de Tep Pranam." *BEFEO* 56:29–62.

Evers, H. David. 1972. *Monks, Priests and Peasants.* Leiden: Brill.

Feer, M. 1884. *"Pañcagatidīpana." Journal of the Pali Text Society,* 152–161.

Ferguson, John P., and Sharladchai Ramitanondh. 1976. "Monks and Hierarchy in Northern Thailand." *JASS* 64:104–149.

Filliozat, Jean. 1969a. "Suzanne Karpelès." *BEFEO* 56:1–3.

———. 1969b. "Une inscription cambodgienne en pali et en khmer de 1566 (K 82 Vatt Nagar)." *Académie des Inscriptions et Belles Lettres. Comptes rendus des séances de l'année 1969, janvier-mars.* Paris, 93–106.

Finot, Louis. 1903. "Notes d'épigraphie. L'inscription sanskrite de Say-Fong." *BEFEO* 3:18–33 (with note by P. Pelliot, Le Bhaisajyaguru, 33–37).

———. 1927. "Mahā Vimaladhamma." *BEFEO* 27.

Finot, Louis, and V. Goloubew. 1931. "Chronique: Rapport de mission à Ceylan." *BEFEO* 30.3–4:627–643.

Fisher-Nguyen, Karen. 1994. "Khmer Proverbs: Images and Rules." In *Cambodian Culture since 1975: Homeland and Exile,* 91–104.

Flauguerges, E. 1914. "La mort du chef suprême des bonzes." *Revue Indochinoise* 2 (Février):175–182.

Florida, Nancy. 1995. *Writing the Past, Inscribing the Future: History as Prophecy in Colonial Java.* Durham, N.C., and London: Duke University Press.

Foucault, Michel. 1976. "Droit de mort et pouvoir sur la vie." In *Histoire de la sexualité I: La volonté de savoir.* Paris: Gallimard.

Forest, Alain. 1980. *Le Cambodge et la colonization Française: histoire d'une colonization sans heurts (1897–1920).* Paris: L'Harmattan.

———. 1992. *Le culte des génies protecteurs au Cambodge: Analyse et traduction d'un corpus de textes sur les "neak ta."* Paris: L'Harmattan.

———. 1995. "Cambodge: Pouvoir de roi et puissance de génie." In *Cultes populaires et sociétés asiatiques,* A. Forest et al., eds. Paris: L'Harmattan, 185–222.

Frazer, J. G. 1911–1915. *The Golden Bough: A Study in Magic and Religion.* 3d ed. (12 vols.) London: Macmillan.

Frédéric, Louis. 1992. *Les dieux du Bouddhisme. Guide Iconographique.* Paris: Flammarion.

French, Lindsay. 1994. "Enduring Holocaust, Surviving History: Displaced Cambodians on the Thai-Cambodian border, 1989–1991." Ph.D. dissertation, Harvard University.

Freud, Sigmund. 1918. *Totem and Taboo,* A. A. Brill, trans. New York: Random House.

Ganguly, Debjani. 2001. "Hierarchy and Its Discontents: Caste, Postcoloniality and the New Humanities." Ph.D. dissertation, Australian National University.

Gastaldy, P. 1931. *La Cochinchine.* Saigon: Société des Études Indochinoises.

Geertz, Clifford. 1973. *The Interpretation of Cultures.* New York: Basic Books.

Gellner, David N. 1992. *Monk, Householder, and Tantric Priest.* Cambridge: Cambridge University Press.

Gervais-Courtellemont, Vandelet, et al. n.d., ca. 1902. *Empire Colonial de la France: Indochine.* Paris: Librairie Coloniale.

Ghosh, M. 1968. *A History of Cambodia from the Earliest Times to the End of the French Protectorate.* Calcutta: Oriental Book Agency.

Giteau, Madeleine. 1967. "Note sur les frontons du sanctuaire central de Vatt Nagar." *Arts Asiatiques* 5.16:125–140.

———. 1975. *Iconographie du Cambodge post-Angkorien.* Paris: EFEO.

Goloubew, Victor. 1925. "Mèlange sur le Cambodge ancien, II. Une idole khmère de Lokeṛvara au Musée de Colombo." *BEFEO* 24.3–4:510–512.

———. 1935. "Nécrologie: In memoriam." *BEFEO* 35.

———. 1936. "Sylvain Lévi et l'Indochine." *BEFEO* 35.2:551–574.

Gombrich, Richard. 1984. "Temporary Ordination in Sri Lanka." *The Journal of the International Association of Buddhist Studies* 7.2:41–65.

———. 1988. *Theravada Buddhism: A Social History from Ancient Benares to Modern Colombo.* London and New York: Routledge.

Gombrich, Richard, and Gananath Obeyesekere. 1988. *Buddhism Transformed.* Princeton, N.J.: Princeton University Press.

Goonatilake, Hema. 1996. "The Role of Ancient Cambodian Women in the Promotion of Buddhism." Unpublished paper read at the International Conference on Khmer Studies, August 26–30, University of Phnom Penh, Cambodia.

Goscha, Christopher. 1995. *Vietnam or Indochina? Contesting Concepts of Space in Vietnamese Nationalism 1887–1954.* Copenhagen: Nordic Institute of Asian Studies NIAS Report Series no. 28.

Griswold, Alexander B. 1961. *King Mongkut of Siam.* New York: The Asia Society.

Groslier, Bernard Philippe. 1969. "La terrasse du roi lépreux." *Nokor Khmer* 1:19–32.

———. 1973. *Inscriptions du Bayon. Mémoires Archéologiques.* Paris: EFEO.

———. 1985–1986. "L'image d'Angkor dans la conscience khmère. For a geographic history of Cambodia." *Seksa Khmer* 8–9:31–78.

Guelden, Marlane. 1995. *Thailand into the Spirit World.* Bangkok: Asia Books.

Guesdon, Joseph. 1930. *Dictionnaire Cambodgien-Français.* Vols. 1–2. Paris: Librairie Plon.

Gupta, Akhil, and James Ferguson. 1992. "Beyond 'Culture': Space, Identity, and the Politics of Difference." *Cultural Anthropology* 7:6–23.

Gutschow, Neils. 1997. *The Nepalese Caitya: 1500 Years of Buddhist Votive Architecture in the Kathmandu Valley.* Stuttgart: Axel Menges.

Ha, Marie-Paule. 1999. "Engendering French Colonial History: The Case of Indochina." *Historical Reflections/Reflexions Historiques* 25.1:95–125.

Haines, David W., ed. 1985. *Refugees in the United States: A Reference Handbook.* Westport, Conn.: Greenwood Press.

Hall, Kenneth R. 1985. *Maritime Trade and State Development in Early Southeast Asia.* Honolulu: University of Hawai'i Press.

Hallisey, Charles. 1995. "Roads Taken and Not Taken in the Study of Theravada Buddhism." In *Curators of the Buddha: The Study of Buddhism under Colonialism,* Donald S. Lopez, Jr., ed. Chicago: The University of Chicago Press.

Hallisey, Charles, and Anne Hansen. 1996. "Narrative, Sub-ethics and the Moral Life: Some Evidence from Theravada Buddhism." *Journal of Religious Studies* 24.2: 305–328.

Hansen, Anne R. 1999. "Ways of the World: Moral Discernment and Narrative Ethics in a Cambodian Buddhist Text." Ph.D. dissertation, Harvard University.

Harper, Edward B., ed. 1964. *Religion in South Asia.* Seattle: University of Washington Press.

Harris, Ian. 2000. "Buddhism in Extremis." In *Buddhism and Politics in Twentieth-Century Asia,* Ian Harris, ed. London: Cassell.

Harrison, Paul. 1992. "Is the Dharma-*kāya* the Real 'Phantom Body' of the Buddha?" *Journal of the International Association of Buddhist Studies* 15.1:44–94.

Hein, Jeremy. 1995. *From Vietnam, Laos, and Cambodia: A Refugee Experience in the United States.* New York: Twayne Publishers.

Heine-Geldern, Robert. 1956. *Conceptions of State and Kingship in Southeast Asia.* Southeast Asia Program Data Paper no. 18. Ithaca, N.Y.: Cornell University Press.

Heinze, Ruth-Inge. 1988. *Trance and Healing in South East Asia Today.* Bangkok: White Lotus.

Herbert, Patricia M. 1982. *The Hsaya San Rebellion (1930–1932) Reappraised.* Clayton, Victoria: Monash University Centre of Southeast Asian Studies.

Higbee, Elizabeth Guthrie. 1992. "Khmer Buddhism in New Zealand." M.A. thesis, University of Otago.

Hinton, Alexander Laban. 1998. "Why Did You Kill? The Cambodian Genocide and the Dark Side of Face and Honor." *JAS* 57.1:93–122.

Hitchcock, John, and Rex Jones. 1994. *Spirit Possession in the Nepal Himalayas.* New Delhi: Vikas.

Hong Siphanna. 1996. Letter, July 12.

Horner, I. B. 1930. *Women under Primitive Buddhism.* London: George Routledge and Sons, Ltd.

Hours, Bernard. 1981. "Pouvoir et territoire bouddhiste." *L'homme* 21.3:95–113.

Hours, Bernard, and Monique Sélim. 1997. *Anthropologie politique du Laos contemporain.* Paris: L'Harmattan.

Ind, Ukña Suttantaprījā. 1971 [1921?]. *Gatilok.* Vols. 1–10. Phnom Penh: Buddhist Institute.

Institut Bouddhique. 1963. *Centres d'études bouddhiques au Cambodge/Centers of Buddhist Studies in Cambodia.* Phnom Penh: Institut Bouddhique.

———. 1963 [1938]. Reprinted 1989. *Vacanukram Khmaer [Dictionnaire Cambodgien].* Phnom Penh: Institut Bouddhique.

———. 1970. *Biography of Samdech Preah Sanghareach Chuon Nath.* Serie de Culture et Civilisation Khmeres, vol. 7. Phnom Phenh: Institut Bouddhique.

Irvine, Walter. 1984. "Decline of Spirit Cults and Growth of Urban Spirit Mediumship: The Persistence of Spirit Beliefs, the Position of Women and Modernization." *Mankind* 14.4:315–324.

Ishii, Yoneo. 1975. "A Note on Buddhist Millenarian Revolts in Northeast Siam." *Journal of Southeast Asian Studies* 6.2: 121–126.

———. 1986. *Sangha, State and Society.* Peter Hawkes, trans. Honolulu: University of Hawai'i Press.

Iukanthor, Areno. 1931. *Au seuil du narthex Khmère: Boniments sur les conflits de deux points cardinaux.* Paris: Éditions d'Asie.

———. 1935. *Destin de l'empire.* Paris: Pierre Bossuet.

Ivarsson, Sören. 1995. "The Study of Traiphum Phra Ruang: Some Considerations." In *Thai Literary Traditions,* Manas Chitakasem, ed. Bangkok: Institute of Thai Studies, Chulalongorn University Press, 56–86.

Jackson, Peter. 1989. *Thai Buddhism.* Singapore: Institute of Southeast Asian Studies.

Jacob, Judith. 1986. "The Deliberate Use of Foreign Vocabulary by the Khmer: Changing Fashions, Methods and Sources." In *Context, Meaning and Power,* M. Hobart and R. Taylor, eds. Ithaca, N.Y.: Cornell University Southeast Asia Program.

———. 1996. *The Traditional Literature of Cambodia.* Oxford: Oxford University Press.

Jaini, Padmanabh S. 2001. "Stages in the Bodhisattva Career of the Tathagatha Maitreya." In *Collected Papers on Buddhist Studies.* Delhi: Motilal Banarsidass Publishers.

Janneau, G. 1914. "Le Cambodge d'Autrefois." *Revue Indochinoise* 31.6(Juin):617–632.

Jenner, P. 1982. *A Chrestomathy of Pre-Angkorian Khmer, Lexicon of Undated Inscriptions.* Southeast Asia Paper no. 20, pt. 4. Honolulu: University of Hawai'i, Center for Southeast Asian Studies.

Jessup, H. I., and T. Zephir, eds. 1997. *Angkor et dix siècles d'art khmer.* Paris: Réunion des musées nationaux.

Johnson, Kay. 1999. "Warning over Plan to Dredge Holy Islet." *South China Morning Post,* September 30.

Jones, Ken. 1992. *The Social Face of Buddhism: An Approach to Political and Social Activism.* London and Boston: Wisdom.

Jory, Patrick. 2002. "Thai and Western Buddhist Scholarship in the Age of Colonialism: King Chulalongkorn Redefines the Jatakas." *JAS* 61.3:891–918.

Juergensmeyer, Mark. 1993. *The New Cold War? Religious Nationalism Confronts the Secular State.* Berkeley: University of California Press.

Kabilsingh, Chatsumarn. 1988. *Thai Women in Buddhism.* Berkeley: Parallax Press.

———. 1994. "The Problem of Ordination: Women in Buddhism." In *Buddhist Behavioral Codes and the Modern World,* Charles Wei-hsun Fu and Sandra Wawrytko, eds. Westport, Conn.: Greenwood Press.

Kalab, Milada. 1968. "Study of a Cambodian Village." *Geographical Journal* 13.4:521–537.

———. 1994. "Cambodian Buddhist Minorities in Paris: Continuing Tradition and Changing Patterns." In *Cambodian Culture since 1975: Homeland and Exile,* 57–71.

Kamala, Tiyavanich. 1997. *Forest Recollections: Wandering Monks in Twentieth-Century Thailand.* Honolulu: University of Hawai'i Press.

Kantorowicz, E. 1997 [1957]. *The King's Two Bodies.* Princeton, N.J.: Princeton University Press.

Kapferer, Bernard. 1995. *A Celebration of Demons.* Oxford: Bergs Publishers.

Kariyawasam, A.G.S. 1995. *Buddhist Ceremonies and Rituals of Sri Lanka.* Kandy, Sri Lanka: The Wheel Publications, Buddhist Publication Society.

Karma Lekshe Tsomo, ed. 1988. *Sakyadhita Daughters of the Buddha.* Ithaca, N.Y.: Snow Lion Publications.

Kawanami, Hiroko. 1990. "The Religious Standing of Burmese Buddhist Nuns *(thila-shin):* The Ten Precepts and Religious Respect Words." *The Journal of the International Association of Buddhist Studies* 12.1:17–39.

Keck, Margaret, and Kathryn Sikkink. 1998. *Activists beyond Borders.* Ithaca, N.Y.: Cornell University Press.

Kern, Hendrik. 1879. "Opschriften op oude bouwwerken in Kambodja." *Bijdragen tot de Taal-, Land-en Volkenkunde,* 268–272.

Keyes, Charles F. 1977a. *The Golden Peninsula: Culture and Adaptation in Mainland Southeast Asia.* New York: Macmillan.

———. 1977b. "Millennialism, Theravada Buddhism, and Thai Society." *JAS* 36.2:283–302.

———. 1984. "Mother or Mistress but Never a Monk: Buddhist Notions of Female Gender." *American Ethnologist* 11.2:223–241.

———. 1994. "Communist Revolution and the Buddhist Past in Cambodia." In *Asian Visions of Authority: Religion and the Modern States of East and Southeast Asia,* C. F. Keyes, L. Kendall, and H. Hardacre, eds. Honolulu: University of Hawai'i Press, 43–73.

Khaing, Mi Mi. 1984. *The World of Burmese Women.* London: Zed Books.

Khin Sok. 1988. *Chroniques royales du Cambodge: De Bañā Yāt à la prise de Laṅvaek.* Paris: EFEO.

———. 1991. *Le Cambodge entre le Siam et le Viêtnam (de 1775 à 1860).* Paris: EFEO.

Khin Thitsa. 1980. *Providence and Prostitution: Image and Reality for Women and Reality in Buddhist Thailand.* London: Change International Reports (Women and Society).

———. 1983. "Nuns, Mediums and Prostitutes in Chiangmai: A Study of Some Marginal Categories of Women." In *Women and Developments in Southeast Asia,* I.C.W. Watson, ed. Centre of South-East Asian Studies Occasional Paper no. 1. Canterbury: University of Kent, 4–45.

Khing Hoc Dy. 1993. *Écrivains et expressions littéraires du Cambodia au XXème siècle.* Paris: L'Harmattan.

Khmer Buddhist Research Center. 1986. *Buddhism and the Future of Cambodia.* Rithisen, Thailand: Khmer Buddhist Research Center.

Kiernan, Ben. 1985. *How Pol Pot Came to Power.* London: Verso.

———. 1996. *The Pol Pot Regime: Race, Power, and Genocide in Cambodia under the Khmer Rouge, 1975–79.* New Haven, Conn.: Yale University Press.

Kihipadibat. 1997 reprint. Oum Sour and Chuon Nath, eds. Phnom Penh: Institut Bouddhique.

King, Winston. 1964. *In the Hope of Nibbana.* LaSalle, Ill.: Open Court.

Kingshill, Konrad. 1976 [1960]. *Ku Daeng—The Red Tomb: A Village Study in Northern Thailand.* Rev. 3d ed. Bangkok: Suriyaban Publishers.

Kirsch, A. Thomas. 1977. "Complexity in the Thai Religious System: An Interpretation." *JAS* 36.2:241–266.

———. 1985. "Text and Context: Buddhist Sex Roles/Culture of Gender Revisited." *American Ethnologist* 12:302–320.

Kitsiri Malalgoda. 1970. "Millennialism in Relation to Buddhism." *Comparative Studies in Society and History* 12.4:424–441.

Klubokowski, A. 1909. *Discours prononcé par M. A. Klobukowski Gouverneur Général de l'Indochine à l'ouverture de la session ordinaire du Conseil Supérieure le 27 novembre 1909.* Saigon: Imprimerie Commerciale Marcellin Rey.

Kornfield, Jack. 1998. "Is Buddhism Changing in North America?" In *Buddhist America: Centers, Retreats, Practices,* Don Morreale, ed. Santa Fe, N.M.: John Muir.

Kraft, Kenneth. 1992. *Inner Peace, World Peace: Essays on Buddhism and Nonviolence.* Albany: State University of New York Press.

Krassem, Mahā Bidūr, ed. 1985. *Silācārịk Nagar Vatt* [Inscriptions modernes d'Angkor]. Re-edited with a new preface by Saveros Pou. Paris: Cedoreck.

Lafreniere, Bree, and Daran Kravanh. 2000. *Music through the Dark: A Tale of Survival in Cambodia.* Honolulu: University of Hawai'i Press.

Lam Sopheak and So Chheng. 1997. "Bicāranā loe rīoeṅ bren tael nidān ambī prāsād" [Analysis of legends told about temples]. Senior thesis, Department of Archaeology, Royal University of Fine Arts, Phnom Penh.

Lamotte, Etienne. 1988. *History of Indian Buddhism,* S. Webb-Boin, trans. Louvain-La-Neuve: Institut Orientaliste.

Lando, Richard. 1972. "The Spirits Aren't So Powerful Anymore: Spirit Belief and Irrigation Organization in North Thailand." *JSS* 60.2:121–148.

Lavelle, James, et al. 1996. *Harvard Guide to Khmer Mental Health.* Cambridge, Mass.: Harvard University, Harvard Program in Refugee Trauma.

Law, Bimala Churn. 1981. *Women in Buddhist Literature.* Varanasi, India: Indological Book House.

le Grauclaude, Henri. 1935. *Le Réveil du Peuple Khmer: Notes en marge d'un voyage au Cambodge de M. Robin, Gouverneur Général de l'Indochine.* Hanoi: Éditions de la Presse Populaire de L'Empire Annam.

Leclère, Adhémard. 1899. *Le Buddhisme au Cambodge.* Paris: Ernest Leroux.

———. 1900. "Mémoire sur les fêtes Funéraires et les Incinérations Qui ont eu lieu à Phnôm-Penh (Cambodge) du 27 Avril au 25 Mai 1899." *Journal Asiatique* 9.15: 368–376.

———. 1904. "Le *Phok Tuk Prah Vipheak Sachar.*" *Revue Indochinoise* 30 (November): 735–741.

———. 1906a. *Cambodge: La crémation et les rites funéraires.* Hanoi: F. H. Schneider.
———. 1906b. *Livres sacrés.* Paris: E. Leroux.
———. 1914. *Histoire du Cambodge.* Paris: Librairie Paul Geuthner.
———. 1916. *Cambodge. Fêtes civiles et religieuses.* Paris: Imprimerie nationale.
———. 1975 [1899]. *Le Buddhisme au Cambodge.* New York: AMS Press.
Ledgerwood, Judy L. 1990. "Changing Khmer Conceptions of Gender: Woman, Stories, and the Social Order." Ph.D. dissertation, Cornell University.
———. 1995. "Khmer Kinship: The Matriliny/Matriarchy Myth." *Journal of Anthropological Research* 51:247–261.
———. 1998. "Does Cambodia Exist? Nationalism and Diasporic Constructions of a Homeland." In *Diasporic Identity,* C. Mortland, ed. Arlington, Va.: American Anthropological Association, 92–112.
Leiris, Michel. 1993. *La possession et ses aspects théàtraux chez les éthiopiens de Gondar.* Paris: Plon.
Lerch, Philippe. 2000. *Cambodia in the United States.* Paris: La Chaîne de l'Espoir.
Lester, Robert. 1973. *Theravada Buddhism in Southeast Asia.* Ann Arbor: University of Michigan Press.
Lévi, Sylvain. 1931. *Indochine.* Paris: Sociétés d'éditions geographiques, maritimes et coloniale.
———. 1932. "Maitreya le consolateur." In *Mélanges Raymonde Linossier,* 2. Paris: Ernest Leroux.
Lévy, P. 1981–1984. "Le leng trot ou danses rituelles et rustiques du nouvel an khmer." *Seksa Khmer* 3–4:59–85; 5:61–102; 6:109–133; 7:187–213.
Lewitz, Saveros. 1969. "Note sur la translittération du Cambodgien." *BEFEO* 55:163–169.
———. 1970. "Inscriptions modernes d'Angkor 2 et 3." *BEFEO* 57:99–126.
———. 1971. "Inscriptions modernes d'Angkor 4, 5, 6 et 7." *BEFEO* 58:105–123.
Ling, Trevor O. 1962. *Buddhism and the Mythology of Evil.* London: Allen and Unwin.
———. 1993. *Buddhist Trends in South East Asia.* Singapore: ISEAS.
Lingat, Robert. 1938. "Vinaya et Droit Laique." *BEFEO* 37.2:415–477.
Lopez, Donald S., Jr. 1995. *Curators of the Buddha: The Study of Buddhism under Colonialism.* Chicago: University of Chicago Press.
Lowenthal, David. 1985. *The Past Is a Foreign Country.* Cambridge: Cambridge University Press.
Löschmann, Heike, ed. 1995. *Proceedings of the First Conference on the Role of Khmer Buddhist Don Chee and Lay Women in the Reconciliation of Cambodia.* Prek Ho, Kandal Province: Center for Culture and Vipassana, May 1–4.
Ly Daravuth and Ingrid Muan. 2001. *Preah Ko Preah Keo: A Cambodian Legend.* Phnom Penh: Reyum.
Macy, Joanna. 1983. *Dharma and Development.* West Hartford, Conn.: Kumarian Press.
Maen Chon, ed. 1989 (reprint). *Pabbajjā Khantaka and Samaṇeravinay.* Phnom Penh: n.p.
Mahā Ghosananda. 1989. "Loving-kindness." Unpublished manuscript presented at the Sonoma Mountain Zen Center, Santa Rosa, California, October.
———. 1991. *Step by Step.* Berkeley: Parallax Press.
Mahoney, Jane. n.d. "Step by Step: The Journey for Cambodian Peace and the Work of Venerable Samdech Preah Mahā Ghosananda." Unpublished manuscript.

Mahoney, Jane Sharada, and Philip Edmonds. 1992. Editor's Introduction. In *Step by Step.*
Mak Phoeun. 1984. *Chroniques royals du Cambodge (des origins legendaries jusqu'à Paramaraja 1er).* Paris: EFEO.
Makhali Phâl. 1937. *Chant de Paix.* Phnom Penh: Bibliothèque Royale du Cambodge.
Malalasekera, G. P. 1974 [1938]. *Dictionary of Pali Proper Names.* London: Pali Text Society.
Mang Channo. 1994. "Pailin March Presses Ahead," *Phnom Penh Post,* April 22–May 5.
Mannikka, Eleanor. 1996. *Angkor Wat, Time, Space, and Kingship.* Honolulu: University of Hawai'i Press.
Marchal, Henri. 1954. "Note sur la forme du stupa au Cambodge." *BEFEO* 44.2:581–590.
Marchal, Henri, and G. Trouvé. 1935. "Chronique: Cambodge." *BEFEO* 34.2:762–772.
———. 1936. "Chronique: Cambodge." *BEFEO* 35.2:473–493.
Marcucci, John. 1994. "Sharing the Pain: Critical Values and Behaviors in Khmer Culture." In *Cambodian Culture since 1975: Homeland and Exile,* 129–140.
Marquet, J. 1931. *La France mondiale au XXé siècle, Indochine.* Paris: Delalain.
Marston, John. 1994. "Metaphors of the Khmer Rouge." In *Cambodian Culture since 1975: Homeland and Exile,* 105–118.
———. 1997. "Cambodia 1991–94: Hierarchy, Neutrality and Etiquettes of Discourse." Ph.D. dissertation, University of Washington.
Martel, Gabrielle. 1975. *Lovea, village des environs d'Angkor: aspects démographiques, économiques et sociologiques du monde rural cambodgien dans la province de Siem Réap.* Paris: EFEO.
Martin, Marie Alexandrine. 1994. *Cambodia: A Shattered Society,* Mark W. McLeod, trans. Berkeley: University of California Press.
Martini, Ginette, ed. and trans. 1969. *"Pañcabuddhabyākaraṇa."* *BEFEO* 55:125–144.
Mas. 1908? *Rīoengpandanm Tā Mas* [The recommendations of Tā Mas], microfilm, BN, Paris.
Maspéro, George. 1929. *L'Indochine: Un Empire Colonial Française.* Vols. 1–2. Paris: Les Éditions G. Van Oest.
McGill, Forrest. 1997. "Painting the 'Great Life.'" In *Sacred Biography in the Buddhist Traditions of South and Southeast Asia,* Juliane Schober, ed. Honolulu: University of Hawai'i Press.
Meas-Yang. 1978. *Le Bouddhisme au Cambodge.* Than-Long, Vietnam: Études Orientales.
Mendelson, E. Michael. 1975. *Sangha and State in Burma: A Study of Monastic Sectarianism and Leadership,* J. P. Ferguson, ed. Ithaca, N.Y.: Cornell University Press.
Meyer, Charles. 1971. *Derrière le sourire khmer.* Paris: Plon.
Migot, André. 1960. *Les Khmers, des origines d'Angkor au Cambodia d'aujourd'hui.* Paris: Le Livre Contemporaine.
Monod, G. H. 1907. "L'orthographie dite 'Quoc-Ngu' appliquée au Cambodgien." *Revue Indochinoise,* 2d semester.
Moon, S. "Portraits from Cambodia." *Turning Wheel* (summer 1995).
Morizon, René. 1930. *Monographie du Cambodge.* Hanoi: Imprimerie d'Extrême Orient.
Mortland, Carol. 1994. "Khmer Buddhists in the United States: Ultimate Questions." In *Cambodian Culture since 1975: Homeland and Exile,* 72–90.
Moser-Puangsuwan, Yeshua. n.d. "One Million Kilometers for Peace. Five Years of Peace Walks in Cambodia." (www.igc.org/nonviolence/niseasia/dymwalk.dyl.html).

———. 2000. "The Buddha in the Battlefield: Maha Ghosananda Bhikku and the Dhammayietra Army of Peace." In *Non-Violence in the Third Millennium,* Simon Harak, ed. Macon, Ga.: Mercer University Press.

Mouhot, Henri. 1989 [1864]. *Travels in Siam, Cambodia, and Laos, 1858–1860.* New York: Oxford University Press.

Moura, Jean. 1883. *Le Royaume du Cambodge.* Vols. 1–2. Paris: Ernest Leroux.

Mowry, Robert D. 1985. "An Image of Maitreya and Other Pre-Angkor Prakhonchai Bronzes." *Orientations* 16.12 (December).

Mul, Bunchan. 1982 [1971]. "The Umbrella War," Chantou Boua and Ben Kiernan, trans. In *Peasants and Politics in Kampuchea, 1942–1981,* B. Kiernan and C. Boua, eds. London: Zed Press, 115–126.

Murcott, Susan. 1991. *The First Buddhist Women.* Berkeley: Parallax Press.

Mus, Paul. 1928. "Le Bouddha paré. Son origine indienne. Cakayamuni dans le Mahayanisme moyen." *BEFEO* 28.1 and 28.2: 7–134; 153–278.

———. 1936. "Le symbolisme à Angkor-Thom: Le grand miracle du Bayon." *Comptes rendus de l'Académie des Inscriptions et Belles Lettres.*

———. 1975. *India Seen from the East: Indian and Indigenous Cults in Champa,* I. W. Mabbett, trans.; I. W. Chandler and D. P. Chandler, eds. Monash Papers on Southeast Asia no. 3. Melbourne: Centre of Southeast Asian Studies.

Nagaravatta. 1938. December 17:1–3.

Nash, Manning, et al. 1966. *Anthropological Studies in Theravada Buddhism.* Cultural Report Series no. 13. New Haven, Conn.: Yale University Press, South East Asia Studies.

Nattier, Jan. 1988. "The Meanings of the Maitreya Myth." In *Maitreya, the Future Buddha,* Alan Sponberg and Helen Hardacre, eds. Cambridge: Cambridge University Press, 23–47.

Neher-Bernheim, Renée. 2002. *Histoire juive de la Revolution a l'État d'Israël.* Paris: Éditions du Seuil.

Népote, Jacques, and Khing Hoc Dy. 1981. "Literature and Society in Modern Cambodia." In *Essays on Literature and Society in Southeast Asia,* Tham Seong Chee, ed. Singapore: Singapore University Press.

Niedzwiecki, William R. 1998. "The World Turned Upside-Down: Khmer-American Status, Identity, and Cultural Conflicts in Institutional Contexts." Ph.D. dissertation, Boston University.

Ngor, Haing. 1987. *Haing Ngor: A Cambodian Odyssey.* New York: Macmillan.

Nolot, Edith. 1991. *Règles de Discipline des Nonnes Boudhhistes Le Bhikṣuṇīvinaya de l'École Mahāsāṃghika Lokottaravadin.* Paris: Diffusion de Boccard.

Obeysekere, Gananath. 1970. "The Idiom of Demonic Possession: A Case Study." *Social Sciences and Medicine* 4:97–111.

Osborne, Milton. 1969. *The French Presence in Cochinchina and Cambodia, Rule and Response (1859–1905).* Ithaca, N.Y.: Cornell University Press.

Phang Kat. 2493 BE [1950]. *Śri Hitopadeś.* Phnom Penh: Pannagār Ghin-Chai.

———. 1963. *Centres d'Études Bouddhiques au Cambodge.* Phnom Penh: Institut Bouddhique, 105–116.

Parmentier, Henri. 1917. "Vat Nokor." *BEFEO* 16.4.

Pavie, Auguste. 1898. *Mission Pavie Indo-chine: 1879–1895, vol. 1, Recherches sur la Littérature du Cambodge, du Laos et du Siam.* Paris: Ernest Leroux.

———. 1995 [1921]. *Au pays des millions d'éléphants et du parasol blanc (à la conquête des coeurs).* Rennes: Terre de Brume Éditions.

Pelliot, Paul, trans. 1997 [1951]. *Mémoires sur les coutumes du Cambodge de Tcheou Ta-Kouan.* Paris: Librairie d'Amérique et d'Orient, Adrien Maisonneuve.

Phal, Makhali. n.d., ca. 1932. *Chant de Paix: Poème au peuple khmèr pour saluer l'édition cambodgienne du Vinaya Pitaka. La premiere corbeille du canon Bouddhique.* Phnom Penh: Institut Bouddhique.

Phnom Penh Post. 1995. "Nuns Seen as Ideal Teachers of Society." May 19–June 1, 17.

Poethig, Kathryn. 2001. "Visa Troubles: Cambodian American Christians and their Defense of Multiple Citizenship." In *Religions/Globalizations: Theories and Cases,* D. N. Hopkins, D. Batstone, and E. Mendieta, eds. Durham, N.C.: Duke University Press, 187–202.

Pollock, Sheldon. 1996. "The Sanskrit Cosmopolis, 300–1300: Transculturation, Vernacularization and the Question of Ideology." In *The Ideology and Status of Sanskrit,* Jan E. M. Houben, ed. Leiden: Brill.

———. 1998. "The Cosmopolitan Vernacular." *JAS* 57.1:6–37.

Ponchaud, François. 1989. "Social Change in the Vortex of Revolution." In *Cambodia 1975–1978: Rendezvous with Death,* Karl D. Jackson, ed. Princeton, N.J.: Princeton University Press.

———. 1990. *The Cathedral of the Rice Paddy: 450 Years of History of the Church in Cambodia.* Paris: Le Sarment; Fayard.

Porée-Maspero, Éveline. 1947–1950. "Notes sur les particularités du culte chez les Cambodgiens." *BEFEO* 44.

———. 1955. "Les néak ta." *France-Asie* 12:114–115, 375–377.

———. 1958. *Cérémonies privées des Cambogiens.* Phnom Penh: Commission de Moeurs et Coutumes du Cambodge, Institut Bouddhique.

———. 1962–1969. *Études sur les rites agraires des cambodgiens.* 3 vols. Paris-La Haye: Mouton.

———. 1975. "Rites de possession au Cambodge." *Objets et monde* 15:39–46.

Porée, Guy, and Éveline Porée-Maspero. 1938. *Moeurs et Coutumes des Khmèrs.* Paris: Payot.

Pou, Saveros Lewitz. 1969. "Note sur la transliteration du Cambodgien." *BEFEO* 55:163–169.

Pou, Saveros. 1971. "Inscriptions modernes d'Angkor 4, 5, 6 et 7." *BEFEO* 58:105–123.

———. 1972. "Inscriptions modernes d'Angkor 1, 8 et 9." *BEFEO* 59:101–121.

———. 1974. "Inscriptions modernes d'Angkor 35, 37 et 39." *BEFEO* 61:301–337.

——— (trans. with commentary). 1977a. *Rāmakerti (XVIè–XVIIè siècles).* Paris: EFEO.

———. 1977b. *Études sur le Rāmakerti (XVIè–XVIIè siècles).* Paris: EFEO.

———. 1979. *Rāmakerti (XVIè–XVIIè siècles). Texte khmer publié.* Paris: EFEO.

———. 1982. *Rāmakerti II (Deuxième version du Ramayana khmer), Texte khmer, traduction et annotations.* Paris: EFEO.

———. 1989. *Nouvelle Inscriptions du Cambodge 1.* Paris: Cedoreck.

———. 1992. *Dictionnaire Vieux Khmer-Français-Anglais/An Old Khmer-French-English Dictionary.* Paris: Cedoreck.

Prebisch, Charles, and Kenneth Tanaka. 1999. *Faces of Buddhism in America.* Berkeley: University of California Press.

Pym, Christopher. 1959. *The Road to Angkor.* London: R. Hale.

Queen, Christopher. 1996. Introduction. In *Engaged Buddhists: Buddhist Liberation Movements in Southeast Asia,* Christopher Queen and Sallie King, eds. Albany: State University of New York Press.

———, ed. 2000. *Engaged Buddhism in the West.* Somerville, Mass.: Wisdom.

Queen, Christopher, and Sallie King, eds. 1996. *Engaged Buddhists: Buddhist Liberation Movements in Southeast Asia.* Albany: State University of New York Press.

Queen, Christopher, Charles S. Prebish, and Damien Keown, eds. 2003. *Action Dharma: New Studies in Engaged Buddhism.* London: Curzon.

Raffin, Anne. 2002. "The Integration of Difference in French Indochina During World War II: Organizations and Ideology concerning Youth." *Theory and Society* 31.3:365–390.

Rappaport, Al, ed. 1997. *Buddhism in America: Proceedings from the First Buddhism in America Conference.* Boston, Mass.: Charles Tuttle.

Rappaport, Roy A. 1999. *Ritual and Religion in the Making of Humanity.* Cambridge: Cambridge University Press.

Reddi, V. M. 1970. *A History of the Cambodian Independence Movement: 1863–1955.* Tirupati, India: Sri Venkateswara University.

Reynell, Josephine. 1989. *Political Pawns, Refugees on the Thai-Kampuchean Border.* Oxford: Refugee Studies Programme.

Reynolds, Craig J. 1972. "The Buddhist Monkhood in Nineteenth-Century Thailand." Ph.D. dissertation, Cornell University.

Reynolds, Frank E. 1976a. "Buddhist Cosmography in Thai History, with Special Reference to Nineteenth-Century Culture Change." *JAS* 35.2:203–220.

———. 1976b. "The Many Lives of the Buddha: A Study of Sacred Biography and Theravāda Tradition." In *The Biographical Process: Studies in the History and Psychology of Religion,* Frank E. Reynolds and Donald Capps, eds. The Hague: Mouton, 37–61.

———. 1978. "The Holy Emerald Jewel: Some Aspects of Buddhist Symbolism and Political Legitimation in Thailand and Laos." In *Religion and Legitimation of Power in Thailand, Laos, and Burma,* Bardwell Smith, ed. Chambersburg, Pa.: Anima Books, 175–193.

Reynolds, Frank E., and Regina T. Clifford. 1987. "Theravada." In *The Encyclopedia of Religion.* Vol. 14, M. Eliade, ed. New York: Collier-Macmillan Publishers, 469–479.

Reynolds, Frank E., and Mani B. Reynolds, trans. 1982. *The Three Worlds According to King Ruang.* Berkeley: Asian Humanities Press, Motilal Banarsidass.

Rhys Davids, C.A.F., and K. R. Norman, eds. 1989. *Poems of Early Buddhist Nuns.* Oxford: The Pali Text Society.

Robertson, Roland, and William Garrett, eds. 1991. *Religion and Global Order.* New York: Paragon.

Rouse, Roger. 1995. "Questions of Identity: Personhood and Collectivity in Transnational Migration to the United States." *Critique of Anthropology* 15.4:351–380.

Rudolph, Suzanne Hoeber, and James Piscatori, eds. 1997. *Transnational Religion and Fading States.* Boulder, Colo.: Westview.

Ryuken, Duncan W., and Christopher Queen, eds. 1999. *American Buddhism, Methods and Findings in Recent Scholarship.* Surrey, U.K.: Curzon Press.

Sadler, A. W. 1970. "Pagoda and Monastery: Reflections of the Social Morphology of Burmese Buddhism." *Journal of Asian and African Studies* 5.4:282–293.

Said, Edward. 1978. *Orientalism.* New York: Random House.

Sam, Yang. 1987. *Khmer Buddhism and Politics from 1954 to 1984.* Newington, Conn.: Khmer Studies Institute.

Santikare Bikkhu. "Not the Duty *(kicca)* of Monks." *Turning Wheel* (fall 1999):35–36.

Sao Htun Hmat Win. 1986. *The Initiation of Novicehood and the Ordination of Monkhood in the Burmese Buddhist Culture.* Rangoon: Department of Religious Affairs.

Sarkisyanz, Emanuel. 1965. *Buddhist Backgrounds of the Burmese Revolution.* The Hague: Martinus Nijhoff.

Sasse, R. 1999. "A Long March to Peace. Evaluation of the Dhammayatra Center for Peace and Nonviolence (1993–1999)." Phnom Penh, February/March.

Schober, Juliane. 1995. "The Theravada Buddhist Engagement with Modernity in Southeast Asia: Whither the Social paradigm of the Galactic Polity?" *JAS* 26.2:307–325.

Schopen, Gregory. 1978. "The *Baiṣajyaguru Sūtra* and the Buddhism of Gilgit." Ph.D. dissertation, Australian National University.

———. 1989. "The Stupa Cult and the Extant Pāli Vinaya." *Journal of the Pāli Text Society* 13:83–100.

———. 1991. "Archaeology and Protestant Suppositions in the Study of Buddhism." *History of Religions* 31.1:1–23.

Scott, James. 1990. *Domination and the Arts of Resistance: Hidden Transcripts.* New Haven, Conn.: Yale University Press.

Selim, Monique. 1996a. *Génies blessures et peurs dans le Laos contemporain.* Unpublished manuscript, 18 pages.

———. 1996b. "Les génies thérapeutes au service du marché." *Mondes en développement* 24.93:71–89.

Shils, Edwards. 1966. "The Intellectuals in the Political Development of the New States." *World Politics* 12:329–368.

Shlaim, Avi. 2000. *The Iron Wall: Israel and the Arab World.* London: Penguin.

Sivaraksa, Sulak. 1988. *A Socially Engaged Buddhism.* Bangkok: Thai Inter-Religious Commission for Development.

———. 1993. *Seeds of Peace: A Buddhist Vision of Renewing Society.* Berkeley: Parallax.

Skidmore, Monique. 1997. "In the Shade of the Bodhi Tree: Dhammayietra and the Reawakening of Community in Cambodia." *Crossroads* 10.1:1–32.

Skilling, Peter. 1995. "Female Renunciants *(nang chi)* in Siam According to Early Travellers' Accounts." *JASS* 83.1 and 2:55–61.

———. 2001. "Nuns, Laywomen, Donors, Goddesses: Female Roles in Early Indian Buddhism." *Journal of the International Association of Buddhist Studies* 24.2:241–274.

Slamet-Velsink, Ina E. 1995. *Emerging Hierarchies: Processes of Stratification and Early State Formation in the Indonesian Archipelago: Prehistory and the Ethnographic Present.* Leiden: KITLV Press.

Smith, Frank. 1989. *Interpretive Accounts of the Khmer Rouge Years: Personal Experience in*

Cambodian Peasant World View. Occasional Paper no. 18. Madison, Wis.: Center for Southeast Asian Studies.

Smith-Hefner, Nancy Joan. 1999. *Khmer-American: Identity and Moral Education in a Diasporic Community.* Berkeley: University of California Press.

Snellgrove, David L., ed. 1978. *The Image of the Buddha.* Paris: UNESCO.

Snodgrass, Adrian. 1985. *The Symbolism of the Stupa.* Ithaca, N.Y.: Cornell University, Southeast Asia Program.

Spiro, Melford E. 1967. *Burmese Supernaturalism.* Expanded ed. Philadelphia: Institute for the Study of Human Issues.

———. 1982. *Buddhism and Society, a Great Tradition and Its Vicissitudes.* 2d expanded ed. Berkeley: University of California Press.

Sponberg, Alan, and Helen Hardacre, eds. 1988. *Maitreya, the Future Buddha.* Cambridge: Cambridge University Press.

Sreberny-Mohammadi, Annabelle, and Ali Mahammadi. 1994. *Small Media, Big Revolution: Communication, Culture, and the Iranian Revolution.* Minneapolis: University of Minnesota Press.

Strong, John S. 1992. *The Legend and Cult of Upagupta: Sanskrit Buddhism in North India and Southeast Asia.* Princeton, N.J.: Princeton University Press.

Suksamran, Sombon. 1993. "Buddhism, Political Authority and Legitimacy in Thailand and Cambodia." In *Buddhist Trends in Southeast Asia,* Trevor Ling, ed. Singapore: Institute of Southeast Asian Studies.

Swearer, Donald K. 1976. "The Role of the Layman Éxtraordinaire in Northern Thai Buddhism." *JSS* 64:151–168.

———. 1995. *The Buddhist World in Southeast Asia.* Albany: State University of New York Press.

———. 1996. "Sulak Sivaraksa' s Buddhist Vision for Renewing Society." In *Engaged Buddhists: Buddhist Liberation Movements in Southeast Asia,* 195–235.

Tai, Hue Tam Ho. 1983. *Millenarianism and Peasant Politics in Vietnam.* Cambridge, Mass.: Harvard University Press.

Tambiah, Stanley J. 1970. *Buddhism and the Spirit Cults in Northeast Thailand.* Cambridge: Cambridge University Press.

———. 1976. *World Conqueror and World Renouncer.* Cambridge: Cambridge University Press.

———. 1984. *The Buddhist Saints of the Forest and the Cult of Amulets.* Cambridge: Cambridge University Press.

———. 1985. *Culture, Thought and Action: An Anthropological Perspective.* Cambridge, Mass.: Harvard University Press.

Tat, Huoth [Tāt, Huot]. 1993. *Kalyāṇamitta rabas' khñuṃ.* Phnom Penh: Buddhist Institute.

———. n.d. *L'enseignement du Bouddhisme des origines a nos jours,* no. 1. Phnom Penh: Université Bouddhique Preah Sihanouk Raj.

Tauch Chhuong. 1994. *Battambang during the Time of the Lord Governor,* Hin Sithan, Carol Mortland, and Judy Ledgerwood, trans. Phnom Penh: Cedoreck.

Taylor, J. L. 1993. *Forest Monks and the Nation-State.* Singapore: Institute of Southeast Asian Studies.

Teston, E., and M. Percheron. 1931. *L'Indochine Moderne: Encyclopédie Administrative Touristique, Artistique et Économique.* Paris: Librairie de France.

Thanet Aphornsuvan. 1998. "Slavery and Modernity: Freedom in the Making of Modern Siam." In *Asian Freedoms: The Idea of Freedom in East and Southeast Asia,* David Kelly and Anthony Reid, eds. Cambridge: Cambridge University Press, 161–186.

Thich Nhat Hanh. 1967. *Vietnam: Lotus in a Sea of Fire.* New York: Hill and Wang.

———. 1997. *Interbeing: Fourteen Guidelines for Engaged Buddhism.* Berkeley: Parallax.

Thierry, Jean. 1955. *L'Évolution de la Condition de la Femme en Droit Privé Cambodgien.* Phnom Penh: Institut National d'Études Juridiques Politiques et Économiques.

Thompson, Ashley. 1993. "Le Hau Pralin, étude du texte et du rite." *Mémoire pour la maitrise d'études indiennes.* University of Paris 3.

———. 1996. *The Calling of Souls: A Study of the Khmer Ritual* Hau Braliṅ. Working Paper no. 98. Clayton, Victoria, Australia: Monash University, Monash Asia Institute.

———. 1998. "The Ancestral Cult in Transition: Reflections on Spatial Organization of Cambodia's early Theravada Complex." In *Southeast Asian Archaeology 1996. Proceedings of the 6th International Conference of the European Association of Southeast Asian Archaeologists, Leiden, 2–6 September 1996,* Marijke J. Klokke and Thomas de Brujin, eds. Hull: University of Hull, Centre for Southeast Asian Studies.

———. 1999. "Mémoires du Cambodge." Ph.D. dissertation, Université de Paris 8.

———. 2000. "Introductory Remarks Between the Lines: Writing Histories of Middle Cambodia." In *Other Pasts: Women, Gender and History in Early Modern Southeast Asia,* Barbara Andaya, ed. Honolulu: University of Hawai'i Press.

———. forthcoming. "Lost and Found: The Stupa, the Four-Faced Buddha, and the Seat of Royal Power in Middle Cambodia." In *Southeast Asian Archaeology 1998. Proceedings of the 7th International Conference of the European Association of Southeast Asian Archaeologists, Berlin, September 1998.*

Thongchai Winichakul. 1994. *Siam Mapped.* Honolulu: University of Hawai'i Press.

Touch Phara. 2001. "The Neak Ta in Khmer Society." *Aksarsastra-Manossastra* 2:43–47.

Trainor, Kevin. 1997. *Relics, Ritual and Representation in Buddhism: Rematerializing the Sri Lankan Tradition.* Cambridge: Cambridge University Press.

Turner, Victor. 1969. *The Ritual Process: Structure and Anti-Structure.* Ithaca, N.Y.: Cornell University Press.

Um, Khatarya. 1996. "Transnationalism and Reconstruction." Paper presented at the conference Cambodia: Power, Myth and Memory. Monash University in Clayton, Victoria, Australia, December 11–13.

Vāṃṅ Juon. 1929, 1934. *Braḥ rāj baṅsāvatār kruṅ kambujādhipateyy* (August royal chronicle of the sovereign country of Kampuchea). Phnom Penh.

Van Esterik, John L. 1977. "Cultural Interpretation of Canonical Paradox: Lay Meditation in a Central Thai Village." Ph.D. dissertation, University of Illinois at Urbana-Champaign.

Van Esterik, Penny. 1982a. "Interpreting a Cosmology, Guardian Spirits in Thai Buddhism. *Anthropos* 77.6:2–15.

———, ed. 1982b. *Women of Southeast Asia.* Occasional Paper no. 9. DeKalb, Ill.: Northern Illinois University, Center for Southeast Asian Studies.

Vickery, Michael. 1998. *Society, Economics and Politics in Pre-Angkor Cambodia—The 7th–8th centuries.* Tokyo: The Toyo Bunko.
Villemereuil, M.A.B de. 1883. *Explorations et Missions de Doudart de Lagrée.* Paris: Imprimerie et Librairie de Madame Veuve Bouchard-Huzard.
Walters, Johnathan S. 1994. "A Voice from the Silence: The Buddha's Mother's Story." *History of Religions* 33.4:358–379.
Wei-hsun Fu, Charles, and Sandra Wawrytko, eds. 1994. *Buddhist Behavioral Codes and the Modern World.* London: Greenwood Press.
Welaratna, Usha, ed. 1993. *Beyond the Killing Fields: Voices of Nine Cambodian Survivors in America.* Stanford, Calif.: Stanford University Press.
Wijayaratna, Mohan. 1987. *Le culte des dieux chez les bouddhistes singhalais, la religion populaire de Ceylan face au bouddhisme theravada.* Paris: Cerf.
———. 1990. *Buddhist Monastic Life.* Cambridge: Cambridge University Press.
Wijeyewardene, Gehan, and E. C. Chapman, eds. 1993. *Patterns and Illusions in Thai History and Thought.* Canberra: Australian National University.
Williams, P. 1989. *Mahayana Buddhism: The Doctrinal Foundations.* London: Routledge.
Willis, Janice. 1985. "Nuns and Benefactresses: The Role of Women in the Development of Buddhism." In *Women, Religion and Social Change,* Yvonne Hadda and Ellison B. Findly, eds. Albany, N.Y.: State University of New York Press, 59–85.
———, ed. 1989. *Feminine Ground: Essays on Women and Tibet.* Ithaca, N.Y.: Snow Lion Publications.
Wolters, Oliver W. 1979. "Khmer 'Hinduism' in the Seventh Century." In *Early Southeast Asia in Archaeology, History and Historical Geography,* R. B. Smith and W. Watson, eds. Oxford. University of Oxford Press, 438–442.
———. 1999. *History, Culture, and Region in Southeast Asian Perspectives.* Rev. ed. Singapore: Institute of Southeast Asian Studies.
Woodward, Hiram W. 1981. "Tantric Buddhism at Angkor Thom." *Ars Orientalis* 12:57–67.
Wyatt, David K. 1969. *The Politics of Reform in Thailand: Education in the Reign of King Chulalongkorn.* New Haven, Conn.: Yale University Press.
Wyatt, David K., and Alexander Woodside, eds. 1982. *Moral Order and the Question of Change: Essays on Southeast Asian Thought.* New Haven, Conn.: Yale University Southeast Asian Studies Monograph Series no. 24.
Yamada, Teri Shaffer. 1996. "Nostalgia and Collective Memory: The Formation and History of Cambodian Culture in Long Beach, California (1958–1996)." Paper presented at the conference Cambodia: Power, Myth, and Memory. Monash University in Clayton, Victoria, Australia, December 11–13.

Contributors

Didier Bertrand, Ph.D. in cultural psychology, is currently working on a psychosocial study of child victims of unexploded ordnance accidents in Laos for Handicap International Belgium. His research has focused on mental health and mental health care in societies where psychiatry is not yet developed (Vietnam, Cambodia, Laos). This has brought him into contact with local therapists, especially the traditional therapy of possession cults. He has also conducted research with Southeast Asian refugees in France and the United Kingdom. He recently completed a mental-health situation analysis for the World Health Organization in Laos.

Penny Edwards is a Research Fellow at the Centre for Cross-Cultural Research, Australian National University. Her main interests are ethnicity, gender, heritage, and identity in Cambodia and Burma, and she has also edited two volumes on the Chinese diaspora in Southeast Asia and Australia. Her book manuscript, *Cambodge: The Cultivation of a Nation, 1860–1945,* is forthcoming.

Elizabeth Guthrie completed a Ph.D. at the University of Canterbury, Christchurch, New Zealand. Her Ph.D. research topic was the iconography and text of the Buddhist earth deity, Nāṅ Gaṅhīn Braḥ Dharaṇī, a beautiful female deity who wrings water from her hair at the time of the Buddha's enlightenment. Although this episode is absent from the Pāli canon, images of the hair-wringing earth deity are found throughout Theravāda Buddhist mainland Southeast Asia, in Cambodia, Thailand, Laos, Burma, and Sipsong Panna (PRC). To date, her publications have been concerned with the presence and absence of the earth deity episode in the Buddha's biographical tradition; tracing the earth deity motif in the Buddhist kingdoms of Arakan, Pagan, and Angkor; and the contemporary cult of the earth deity in Cambodia and Thailand. She lives in Dunedin, New Zealand, with her husband and three children.

Hang Chan Sophea studied archaeology at the Royal University of Fine Arts in Phnom Penh from 1991–1995. She worked for UNESCO in Cambodia from 1996 to 1999. Since 1999 she has been a researcher with the Apsara authority in Siem Reap, Cambodia.

Anne Hansen teaches Buddhist history and comparative religions at the University of Wisconsin, Milwaukee, in the Department of History and Program in the Comparative Study of Religion. Her research interests focus on the history of the Theravāda tradition in Southeast Asia, and particularly on the development of vernacular Buddhist ethical literature. She is currently completing her manuscript, *Cambodian Buddhism, 1860–1930: Local Values and Modern Identity in Colonial Cambodia.*

John Marston's interest in Cambodia grew out of his experience of teaching English in refugee camps in Thailand and the Philippines. After doing research with Cambodians in the United States, he decided to pursue graduate work in anthropology. While completing fieldwork in Cambodia at the time of the 1993 elections, he worked for the United Nations for one year. Since completing a Ph.D. at the University of Washington, he has taught at the Center for Asian and African Studies of El Colegio de México in Mexico City. His articles have appeared in several edited volumes and in *Southeast Asian Journal of Social Science, Estudios de Asia y África,* and *Crossroads: An Interdisciplinary Journal of Southeast Asian Studies.*

Kathryn Poethig has a B.A. from the University of Chicago, an M.Div. from Union Theological Seminary (New York) in feminist theology and ecumenics, and a Ph.D. in religion and society from the Graduate Theological Union (Berkeley). She has worked for fifteen years in refugee programs in the United States and Southeast Asia, and her dissertation, "Ambivalent Moralities: Cambodian Americans as Dual Citizens in Phnom Penh," applied postmodern and transnational theory to the moral discourses of Cambodian Americans returning to work in post-socialist Cambodia. Her current research is concerned with the globalization of such moral discourses (transnational feminisms, human rights, liberation theologies); most recently, research has focused on a Filipino feminist theology of just peace as a response to the U.S. war on terrorism. She teaches global studies at California State University, Monterey Bay.

Ashley Thompson is an assistant professor in South and Southeast Asian studies at the University of California, Berkeley. A specialist in Khmer studies with experience in comparative regional work concerning mainland Southeast Asia, her research interests involve questions of memory and cultural transition, cult and ritual practices, sexual difference, and the history of Theravāda Buddhism. Her publications to date have focused largely on the construction of historiographical discourses in and on the post-Angkorean period (thirteenth to eighteenth centuries). She is presently working on a book titled *Engendering History, Cambodia and the Arts of Remembrance*, which treats questions of ancient as well as contemporary history from a textual point of view.

Teri Shaffer Yamada received an M.A. in Southeast Asian languages and literatures in 1975 and a Ph.D. in Buddhist studies from the University of California, Berkeley, in 1985. Currently she is an associate professor in the Department of Comparative World Literature and Classics at California State University, Long Beach. In 2002 the University of Michigan Press published the anthology *Virtual Lotus: Modern Fiction of Southeast Asia*, which she organized and edited. She has written numerous articles on modern Cambodian literature and the diaspora. Currently she is the senior adviser of the Nou Hach Literary Project for the promotion of modern Cambodian literature, based in Phnom Penh.

Index

128, 136, 152; worship of, 32, 58, 125); multiple appearances of, 29, 94, 96, 111; power of, 161, 168; ten perfections of (see also *pāramī*), 43, 151, 168
Buddh Daṃnāy, 48–49, 169n. 11, 188, 211, 224n. 23; referred to by Tāpas', 179, 189
Buddhism (*see also* Mahāyāna Buddhism; Theravāda Buddhism) 16, 23, 40–41, 73, 99, 199; ambiguities implicit in, 171, 179; and Brahmanism, 5, 84, 179–181, 187–188, 223n. 1; cosmology, 41–43, 49, 52–54, 82; Engaged Buddhism, 196, 197–199, 207–208, 210; European scholarship, 54, 67, 69; and French, 52, 70, 76, 79, 82; and kingship, 91, 104–105; as national religion, 64, 74–75, 79, 81–82, 192; and nonviolence, 197, 199–200, 204–205, 208–209; reform movements, 42, 53–54, 57, 74, 78–79, 82–83, 147 (their Siamese roots, 53, 64, 67); scriptures, 10, 72–73; social role, 69–70, 129, 165; texts, 10–11, 43, 45, 54, 67–68, 73, 81, 161, 213; in Thailand, 49, 130; in U.S., 199
bulls: as image of Prajāpati, 96, 105
Burma: Cambodia compared to, 48, 77, 159, 202; monks from, 9; scribes from, 68–69; texts from, 74

cakkavattin (cakravartin) (*see also* kingship): 15–19, 17, 32, 35, 43, 45, 47, 154
Cambodian People's Party, 89, 122–123, 207
ceremonies. *See* holidays, rituals
Champa, 17, 29, 97
Chan Rājā, King, 218
Chatterjee, Partha, 51, 187–188
chediy. See stupa
Le chemin de Langka (Bizot), 142
Christianity, 5, 148, 225n. 32; before 1975; Catholicism, 135; compared to Buddhism, 52, 203; conversion to, 194–196, 222; Protestantism, 194, 201; in refugee camps, 194
chronicles, 2, 27–28, 40, 42, 91; and kingship, 18, 26, 52
Chuon Nath, 12, 53, 64–65, 70–75, 77, 84n. 21, 147, 200–201; and national identity, 73–74, 80–82
civil society (*see also* non-governmental organizations): 197, 199, 207
Coalition for Peace and Reconciliation, 197, 200, 204, 207, 209
Cœdès, George, 2, 54, 69, 76, 80, 102; Jewish background of, 74, 79
colonialism (*see also* French colonialism): 2, 41–42, 51, 66, 69, 83; essentialism of, 67, 91, 99
constitution: of 1989, 170; of 1993, 99–100, 179, 204
coup d'etat of July 1997, 124, 151, 207, 221
culture, 3, 50, 77–79, 94, 107, 150, 171; Cambodian national, 2, 41, 70, 80–82, 171, 187; as concept, 57, 99; as framing identity, 60, 223; preservation of, 73, 80, 194, 220, 222

Dalai Lama, 199, 209
democracy, 109, 191
Democratic Kampuchea period, 138, 142, 166, 179, 194, 201; aftermath of, 127, 155, 166–167, 189, 193; destruction of statuary, 116, 120, 213; opposition to religion, 60, 130, 137, 195, 213
dhamma (dharma), 19, 56, 60, 107, 125, 153, 211n. 1; decline and regeneration of, 16, 42, 47–49; *dharma*-body of Buddha, 94, 111n. 6; instruction in, 16, 140, 142, 148, 160, 166, 208; and peacemaking, 203, 209; as preached, 16, 145, 160, 198, 202; protection of, 154; upheld by individuals, 141–142, 160; upheld by kings, 45–46, 107, 154; upheld by mediums, 153–156, 160–161, 165, 167
Dhammakāy movement, 12, 64, 66, 75, 76–81
Dhammarāja (Dharmarāja). *See* kingship
Dhammayātrā, 165, 188, 206, 211n. 1, 225n. 34; Cambodian focus of, 198, 207–209; Dhammayātrā Center, 204, 207–208, 210; and Khmer Rouge, 203–208; and NGOs, 195, 197; non-violence training, 200, 204–205, 208; participation of *ṭūn jī,* 141, 204, 206, 208; and transnationalism, 196–197, 209–211
Dhammayut Order: antipathy to new Buddhist institutions, 77–79, 82; in Cambodia, 50, 53, 61–62n. 14, 67–68, 72, 130; and French, 53, 54, 69; patriarch of, 165, 212n. 10; relation to Mahānikāy, 64, 68, 77–78; textual bias of, 50, 68; Thai orientation, 70, 78; in Thailand, 49, 50, 59, 67, 130
dhammik. See Braḥ Pād Dhammik
diaspora, Cambodian (*see also* refugees), 3–4, 169n. 12, 183, 193–195, 200, 222; community among, 189–190, 196,

213–214, 222; contributions to Tāpas', 172, 182, 190, 192; identity and, 42, 187–188, 223
Dien, Saṃtec Saṅgharāj, 53, 71–72
divination (*see also* prophecy): 150, 154, 155, 163, 167
dukkha. See suffering

École Française d'Extrême Orient, 2, 54, 64, 69–74, 76
École Supérior de Pāli, 55, 64, 70, 72–77, 80–81, 147
education, 42, 52–53, 76; in 1990s, 151; French in Cambodia, 66, 78; reforms in, 41, 66, 69, 71; in refugee camps, 194; temple schools, 68–69, 71–72, 74–76, 78, 83
elections, 109, 116, 208; of 1993, 33, 121–123, 141, 172, 194, 203 (and socio-political change, 151, 170, 179, 194, 199); of 1998, 110, 116, 149n. 7, 207

Finot, Louis, 69, 71, 73, 76, 101, 111n. 4
folklore, 52, 55, 57, 60
Foucault, Michel, 91, 102–104
France, 198; fall to Germany, 79; folk stories from, 55
Frazer, J. G., 92, 99, 111n. 4
French: study by monks, 65, 70, 73; use in Cambodia, 69, 77
French colonialism, 11, 12, 49, 63, 79, 219; arrival of, 10, 11, 46; colonial perception of Cambodians, 51–52, 60; discourse of, 83, 178; opposition to, 48, 63, 80; reforms of, 3, 47, 50–52, 63; scholars during, 12, 54, 65, 68, 76, 78, 82; transnationalism of, 193
Freud, Sigmund, 91–93, 108
FUNCINPEC, 33, 89, 121–122, 207, 209, 211n. 2

Gatilok, 55, 57, 60
gender: ambiguity (of statues, 89, 116–117; of Tāpas', 172); and Buddhism, 133, 144; equality, 147; of mediums, 159; Vichy perspective on, 80
Gandhi, Mahātma, 198, 201, 203, 209
Gihipatibat, 147
Golden Bough, The (Frazer), 92, 99
grū (see also *grū pārāmi;* healing): 57, 122–124, 168n. 1, 214; *grū khmaer,* 89, 129, 188, 215–216, 221, 224
grū pārāmī (*see also* mediums; *pārāmī*): 61n. 6, 87, 89, 129–131, 150; compared to monks, 156, 161, 163, 165; dancing by, 154–155, 163–165, 216; interaction with monks, 158, 162, 165–166; money and, 155, 158, 161–162, 165; observance of *vassā,* 156, 158, 161; and *prāsāt,* 156, 158, 189, 192

Harben, William, 87–89
healing (*see also* Jayavarman VII): 57–58, 97–98, 108, 175; health care, 93–94, 110, 151; Khmer conceptions of, 88–89, 91; by mediums, 150, 154–155, 157–158, 160, 163; and wholeness, 93, 110
Hem Chieu, Achar, 63–64, 80, 83
Heng Kim, 215–217, 224
hierarchy, 41, 43–45, 49–50
Hinduism. *See* Brahamanism
history, 42, 73, 75; Cambodian tradition of, 13, 52, 107; linear view of, 4, 13–14, 66; of religion, 13, 73
holidays (*see also* rituals): 128; Auṃ Dik, 121, 220; Bhjuṃ Piṇḍ, 116, 125n. 5, 128–129; Kathin, 129, 161; New Year, 109, 116, 118, 125n. 5, 152 (in Long Beach, Calif., 220, 222, 225n. 33; as wat celebration, 128–129, 136); Visākhā Pūjā, 165, 201
holy days, 115, 118, 135, 146, 148n. 2; observed by *grū pāramī,* 150, 156–158, 160, 163
Hospital Edicts, 94–95, 98, 102, 104, 111nn. 4, 6
hospitals, 94–96, 98, 103
human rights, 42, 61, 183, 189–190, 200, 204
Hun Sen, 110–111, 137
Huot Tat, 12, 53, 64–65, 70–75, 77, 80–82, 84n. 21

iconography (*see also* Braḥ Go and Braḥ Kaev; leper king; Maitreya; Nāṅ Cek-Nāṅ Cam): 3, 4, 22, 32–33, 89, 186–187; of Angkor, 4, 178, 181; *apsarā,* 173, 176; ascetic figures, 9, 31, 89, 131, 186 (*isī,* 153, 161, 180; *tāpas,* 144, 153, 171, 180; *anak saccaṃ,* 153, 163); of Bayon, 29–30; heroic figures, 166, 214; Middle period modifications, 19, 39n. 41; multivocality of, 32, 34, 187; power of, 3, 171, 186
identity, 42–43, 47, 53, 60, 171; Buddhist, 57, 60; as Cambodian or Khmer, 1, 40, 41, 51, 55, 59–60, 74, 81, 89, 188, 193, 208; of community, 43, 52, 56; cultural, 187–188, 223; of diaspora Cambodian, 4, 40, 171,

188, 213–214; national, 41, 69, 89, 171, 178, 196, 209–210, 219; of *pāramī,* 152; religion-shaped, 55–56, 60, 130, 193
Ieng Sary, 100–101, 206
Ind, Ukña Suttantaprījā, 12, 55–60, 62n. 18, 64, 82
India, 11, 55, 74, 201–202; colonialism in, 51, 67; influence on Cambodia, 2, 7, 8, 10, 113
Indra, 30, 189
Inscriptions du Cambodge (Cœdès), 2
Institute Bouddhique (Buddhist Institute), 2, 40, 75–81, 147
international assistance, 151, 178–179, 195
International Network of Engaged Buddhists, 199–200

Japan, 79, 200, 206, 209, 211
Jātakas, 43, 54, 134, 153–154; critique of, 50, 71, 81; *Vessantara-jātaka,* 43, 166, 169n. 9, 180
Jayavarman VII, 29, 31, 97, 100–101; Buddhism of, 9, 17, 29, 93, 104, 107, 181; buildings constructed under, 19, 21, 28, 102, 108, 181; and healing, 88, 93–98, 104, 107; and leper king legend, 88, 101–102, 104, 112n. 16, 115; and pardon, 100–101; reign of, 30, 95, 112
Jews (*see also* Karpelès, Suzanne): Vichy policy on, 64, 79–80

Kambujā Suriyā, 57, 62n. 18, 75
kamma (karma), 17, 42, 46, 56, 112n. 7, 160, 167; inconsistency with pardon, 99–101; as ordering existence, 49, 51
Kampuchea Krom, 75–76, 78, 193
Kantorowisz, E., 91–92
Karpelès, Suzanne, 12, 54, 69, 78, 80, 84n. 21; and Institute Bouddhique, 76, 81; Jewish background of, 64, 74, 77, 79–80; and Royal Library, 74–75, 77, 81
Keam, Sakphan, 215, 218–219, 220, 223
Khieu Samphan, 204, 205
Khleang Moeung, 11, 196, 216, 218–219, 223n. 8, 224; spirit of, 216, 221
Khmer, 73–74, 76–78, 128, 189; linguistic study of, 52, 55; as national language, 41, 66, 74, 80, 82; printing of, 63, 68, 75, 77; Romanization of, 80, 83; school texts, 76; studied by French, 65, 67; vernacular medium for Buddhist teaching, 65–66, 70, 71, 75, 78, 81
Khmer Krom. *See* Kampuchea Krom
Khmer Republic, 87–88, 120, 153, 219
Khmer Rouge (*see also* Democratic Kampuchea): 100, 151, 199, 201, 203–205, 211n. 2
kingship, 3, 33–34, 46–47, 113, 165; cosmology surrounding, 30, 44, 47, 97, 125; and democracy, 109–110; and divinity, 8, 31, 113–114; embodiment of Buddha, 94, 99–100, 109, 111; embodiment of dharma or Dhammarāja, 47, 92, 107–108; embodiment of kingdom, 88, 92, 97, 105–106, 109, 111; and healing, 88, 93–94, 97, 103–104, 110; and monkhood, 52, 154; multiple bodies of, 89, 91–92, 94, 96, 105, 107, 109, 111n. 6; and pardon, 88, 98–101, 108; and power, 102–104; regicide, 105, 108–110, 112n. 21; reinstatement of, 10, 18, 130, 224; as social center, 8, 44–46; as substitute body, 89, 91, 98–99, 107–108, 110; succession among, 8, 31, 34, 92, 95
Kitchanukit, 50, 53
Kravanh, Daran, 219
Kulen mountains, 102, 115, 118, 153, 163, 180

Lafraniere, Bree, 219
Laos, 9, 11, 76, 79, 130, 134
law, 7, 42, 68, 98, 151; and *dhamma,* 107; influence of Western, 99
lay Buddhists, 59, 128, 137, 143–144, 148n. 2, 181, 200; rituals of, 147; women, 133–134, 142, 147, 206
Leclère, Adhemard, 2, 43, 53, 67–69, 143
Leper King, 87–88, 101–102, 112n. 16, 105; in bas reliefs, 102–104, 108; confusion with Yama, 106–107, 115; at National Museum, 89, 114–116, 125nn. 3,4; as *pāramī,* 116, 124, 157, 166; at Phnom Penh riverfront, 120–122; statuary of, 88–89, 104, 106–107, 169n. 10; Terrace of the (Angkor Thom), 115, 124–125, 165; at Wat Unnalom, 122–123
leprosy, 101–102, 104–105
libraries, 67, 73–75, 83; monastic, 9, 137; Royal Library, 74–78, 81
literacy, 8, 10, 68, 128, 140, 172, 225n. 29
literature: Cambodian tradition of, 40, 52, 55, 67, 73, 75; poetry, 43, 45, 55, 75, 94–96, 100
Livres Sacrés (Leclère), 68
Lon Nol, 88, 110
Lon Nol period. *See* Khmer Republic

Long Beach, 196, 214–215, 220–222
Lovek, 13, 18, 23–25, 108

Maat, Bob, 200, 207, 209
Mahā Ghosananda, Samṭec, 141, 196–197, 200, 208–210, 211n. 7, 212n. 10; in refugee camps, 199–202; teachings of, 198, 202–204
Mahānikāy Order: administration of, 69, 71, 120n. 1, 201; in Cambodia, 53, 55, 64, 70–71, 81, 83n. 1; and Dhammayut, 50, 78–79, 130; doctrines of, 94; opposition to reforms, 66, 68, 72–73, 82; patriarch of, 72, 79, 165, 195, 200–202, 212n. 10; in Thailand, 55
Mahāyāna Buddhism, 9, 15, 19, 28–29, 36n. 4, 47, 93–94; replaced by Theravāda, 17, 93
Maitreya, 13, 36nn. 1, 5, 7, 181; cult of, 3, 11, 15, 17, 22; images, 27–28, 31–33, 160; in Middle period, 21–22; prophecies of, 15–16, 47–48; rebirth in time of, 23, 24; in Theravāda Buddhism, 15, 191; and Viṣnu, 32–33
maṇḍala. *See* political organization
meditation, 16, 48, 128, 138, 152, 161, 186; cultivation of *metta*, 203; in forests, 180, 192, 201; and Mahā Ghosananda, 198, 203–205, 208; of Tāpas', 172–173, 184; by *ṭūn jī* and other women, 130–131, 135–136, 140–143, 169n. 8, 208; Western influence on, 142
mediums (see also *grū pāramī*): 150, 186–188, 196, 215, 219–220; and Buddhism, 131, 150, 159–165, 168; before Civil War period, 129, 166; *cūl rūp*, 129, 151, 158–159, 216; gatherings by, 155, 162, 221; gender of, 153, 159, 224; healing by, 154, 160, 223; psychological therapy provided by, 152, 157, 161, 167; role of *snāṅ*, 152; *rūp anak tā*, 129, 158–159; *rūp ārakkh*, 129, 158–159, 224
Memoirs on the Customs of Cambodia (Zhou), 101
merit-making, 68, 146, 192; as determining rebirth, 16–17, 42; of donations, 128, 161–162, 165, 172, 189–190, 195; by Khmer people, 79, 96; by kings, 45; transfer of merit, 24–25, 43; by women, 133, 134
metta, 192, 201, 203, 210
Middle period, 10, 11, 33–34, 99; and Maitreya, 13, 18, 32; statuary, 32; transition from Angkor period, 14, 17, 29, 31
military, 46, 48, 151, 154, 206; in French period, 66, 76–80; personnel making religious petition, 118, 162
millenarianism, 4, 11, 169n. 11, 179, 181, 189–192; in 19th century, 12, 46–49, 52
Ministry of Religion, 130, 147, 172, 180–181, 183–184, 188, 190
modernity, 7, 41, 80–81, 88, 183; and French colonialism, 11, 12, 52, 83; and nation, 3, 66, 80, 187
Mongkut, King (of Thailand), 49–50, 54–55
Monivong, King Sisowath (r. 1927–1941), 72, 76, 78–79
monkhood (*see also* ordination): 4, 6, 52–53, 76, 80, 133, 200; *bikkhu* vs. novice, 128, 148; Cambodians in Thailand, 52–55, 68, 70, 74, 130, 193, 201, 211; in countries of resettlement, 194–195, 202, 222; during Democratic Kampuchea period, 137, 213; disciplinary practices, 128, 130, 131n. 2, 165, 169n. 12, 207, 212n. 15; education among, 43, 53; forest monks, 180, 186; and French, 48, 63–65, 76, 80; and literacy, 10, 52–53, 128; in medium rituals, 155, 159–160, 162; numbers of, 10, 130; offerings to, 133, 162, 165, 181; participation in ceremonies, 116, 128, 146–147, 165; preaching, 70–71, 75, 77–78, 80, 181; reforms among, 41–42, 50, 64, 72, 78–79, 82; spirit possession among, 163, 166, 169n. 15, 195; as teachers, 69, 78, 213; Thai influence on Cambodian, 50, 76, 79–80; in Thailand, 130, 131n. 2, 180
Mus, Paul, 7, 31
museums, 66, 69, 83; *sāramandir* of Tāpas', 172–175, 178, 185
music, 158; *biṇ bādy*, 116, 155, 163, 216–217; listened to by monks, 163, 165; religious, 136; and spirits, 151
Music Through the Dark: A Tale of Survival in Cambodia (Lafraniere and Kravanh), 219

Nagaravatta, 57, 78–80
nāgas, 22, 102, 153, 189, 224n. 18
Nāṅ Cek-Nāṅ Cam, 118, 125–126n. 8, 173
Nāṅ Gaṅhīn Braḥ Dharanī, 153, 164, 181
nation (*see also* identity): 64, 141, 182, 187–188; concept of, 1, 3–4, 56–57, 66, 75, 80–82, 191, 196; nation-state, 11, 41–42, 60, 88, 198
National Museum (Phnom Penh), 26; *pāramī*

of, 115; statues in 32–33, 89, 114–116, 125nn. 3, 4, 5
nationalism, 99, 178–179, 188, 203; in colonial period, 40, 51, 57, 60, 66, 74–75, 78–80, 82, 193
newspapers. *See* print media
Nhem Kim Teng, Ven., 208, 212n. 16
nibbāna (nirvana), 16, 24, 68, 133, 151, 164; as goal, 137, 143, 148, 180, 199
Nipponzan Myohoji, 201, 206, 209
non-governmental organizations (NGOs), 151, 190, 193–197; and Dhammayātrā, 199, 204, 207, 209–210, 212n. 13
Norodom, King (r. 1860–1904), 46–47, 52, 61n. 12, 62n. 14, 68–69, 120
nuns. *See bikkhunī; ṭūn jī*

ordination (*see also* monkhood): 43, 134, 138, 201; early traditions, 10, 131, 144–147; female, 131, 144–145, 148n. 1; *pabbajjā,* 145, 147; puos, 134, 144–147, 148n. 3, 149n. 13; *upasaṃpadā,* 135, 145
Oudong, 120, 143, 146
Oum Sum, Saṃtec, 138, 183, 195

Pach Choeun, 78
Pāl' Han, Ven., 136, 138–140, 149n. 7
Pāli (*see also* École Supérior de Pàli): 54–55, 128, 178; canon, 67, 144; instruction in, 2, 52–54, 60, 70, 73, 156; manuscripts in, 68, 74; preaching in, 71, 81; printed texts in, 43, 70, 77; in rituals, 139, 154, 161, 197; spoken by *pāramī,* 154, 155; translation from, 55, 71, 77, 147
Pān, Saṃtec Sugaidhādhipahī, 53, 72
Paramarāja I, 18, 26
pāramī (see also *grū pāramī;* mediums): 4, 151, 166, 186; as perfection of Buddha, 151, 168n. 1; as "power," 151–152, 167–168, 168n. 1, 186; as type of spirit, 87, 115, 151–152, 158–159, 165, 180 (marriage between two, 152, 169n. 4, 216; range of different, 4, 89, 131, 153–154, 159; of Yāy Deb, 116, 118, 120, 169n. 10)
Paris Agreement (of 1991), 99, 170, 194
pāy sī, 120, 155, 177
People's Republic of Kampuchea, 130, 138, 170, 193–194, 211
Phnom Prasiddh, 162, 189
Phnom Saṃbau, 154, 169n. 8
pilgrimages (*see also* Dhammayātrā): 135, 142, 150, 155, 164–165
Pol Pot period. *See* Democratic Kampuchea period
political organization, 42, 45–46, 114; after Democratic Kampuchea, 167; *maṇḍala*/galactic polity, 3, 8, 12, 28, 44; transformation by French, 41, 46, 49, 50; after UNTAC, 171, 190
Pollock, Sheldon, 41, 99
Porée-Maspéro, Eveline, 127
possession. *See* mediums
Prajāpati, 95–96, 105
prāsād. See temple structures
precepts, 128, 134–135, 141–143, 148n. 2; kept by mediums, 154, 156, 158, 160
print media, 66, 68, 70, 78–83, 147; books, 50, 55, 70, 72–73, 82; and Dhammakāy, 12, 64, 73, 75, 81–82; newspapers, 82, 110, 165, 190
prophecy (see also *Buddhamnāy*): 12, 42, 47–48, 171, 183

Rāma, 18, 33, 39, 101
Ras' Lī. *See* Tāpas'
rebellions. *See* social unrest
refugees (*see also* diaspora): camps, 3, 5, 194, 196, 199, 213; repatriation of, 197, 199–201, 203, 208, 213, 220
resistance movements, 194, 199–200
rituals (*see also* holidays; Khleang Moeung; ordination): 2, 42, 109, 128, 130, 147, 220, 222; *bhịk-dịk saṃpath,* 45, blessing, 136, 138–139, 155, 176–177, 204; funerary, 43, 92, 195; of mediums, 150, 155–156, 159–161, 165; *puṇy phkā,* 161; *puṇy sīma,* 161–162; and reforms, 54, 147; spirit-flag raising, 215–217, 220–222; Trot ceremony, 109, 112n. 21; water sprinkling, 139–140, 162, 163, 186, 188, 197
Royal University of Fine Arts, 116, 120, 143

Saen Chrik, 119–120, 125n. 3
Sāmanera Vinaya, 147
sangha. See monkhood
Sanskrit, 36n. 1, 41, 55, 65, 70, 73, 154
science, 49–51, 73, 81–82, 174, 183, 187
Siam. *See* Thailand
Siem Reap, 44, 54, 70, 78, 116, 203
Sihanouk, King Norodom (r. 1941–1955, 1993–present), 33–34, 88, 109–111, 202, 216–217; abdication in 1955, 109–110; and democracy, 109–110; deposed in 1970, 137; and Dhammayātra, 204, 208;

and pardon, 100–101; return to throne, 110, 121; ritual activity of, 113, 116, 118, 121–122
Sisovong Vong, King, 76
Sisowath, King (r. 1904–1927), 43, 69, 72, 74
Siva, 7–9, 36n. 5, 39n. 39, 59, 145, 223n. 1, 224n. 15
Sivutha Rebellion, 63–64, 68
slavery, 8–9, 41, 46, 50–51, 61n. 12
social unrest: millenarial, 46, 48, 52; nineteenth century, 44, 47, 63–64, 71; tax related, 46–48; urban, 64–65, 80
Son Ngoc Thanh, 78
spirits (see also *pāramī;* Khleang Moeung): 58, 124, 167–168; *anak tā,* 129, 151, 158, 161, 169n. 6, 214, 223n. 4 (annual ceremonies for, 159, 219; Buddhicization of, 152, 159, 166; shrines to, 7, 33, 89; at wats, 129, 159); animism, 5, 54, 60, 113, 168, 223n. 1; *ārrakkh,* 158; and belief system, 66, 166, 186; *brāy,* 151–152, 166, 214; *devatā,* 89, 152, 158, 160, 169n. 3, 183; ghosts, 196, 218; *kmoc,* 151–152, 166; *phi,* 152; transformation into *pāramī,* 151–152, 158; *yakkha,* 166
Sri Lanka, 9–11, 39n. 41, 148, 155, 200; Cambodia compared to, 77, 159, 161, 166, 202
Sruk Khmaer, 75, 77
statuary (*see also* Buddha; leper king; Yāy Dep): 32, 108, 125, 161, 180; of Bhaiṣajyaguru, 95, 98; during Democratic Kampuchea period, 116, 119–120, 213; dual pattern among, 89, 116–120, 124; of four faces, 29–31, 102; as substitute body, 108; in wats, 162–164; worship of, 89, 113, 115–116
Sṭec Gaṃlaṅ'. *See* leper king
Step by Step (Mahā Ghosananda), 202
stūp, 22, 23, 25, 28
stūpa, 13, 16, 92, 120; as funerary monument, 26, 36n. 2; in headdress of Maitreya, 15, 16, 33–34, 37n. 8; and Maitreya, 15, 22, 34–35; representing absence, 22, 34–35; surrounded by four Buddhas, 13, 21, 23, 25, 29, 31n. 17, 38n. 21; as temple architecture, 19, 128, 138, 145; as wombs, 14, 22, 36n. 3
suffering, 167–168, 202–203; kingship and the peoples', 95, 97–98, 102, 104, 108
Sulak Sivaraksa, 199
synchretism, 4, 5, 8, 150, 164–165, 187, 214
Tā Siem Reap, 177, 181–182, 184, 192
Tambiah, Stanley, 150, 159, 220–221
Tāpas', 89, 130–131, 169n. 11, 170, 195; and Brahmanism, 179–182; and Buddha, 176–177, 181; as Buddhist monk, 171–172, 185–186; building project of, 172–176, 181, 183–185; followers of, 178–179, 182, 184, 186, 191; meditation practices of, 172–173, 184, 186; nationalism of, 178–179, 184
television (*see also* video): 165, 180, 190
temple structures (*see also* stūpa), 10, 36n. 4, 44–45; *kuṭi,* 128, 138, 162; murals in, 35, 55, 138, 180; *prāsād,* 156, 162, 175 (ancient Khmer, 15, 24, 36n. 4, 38, 113, 125; associated with religious movements, 158, 164, 169n. 11, 183, 185–190; becoming *cetiya,* 15, 19, 21); *sāla chān',* 128, 138, 162; *vihāra,* 19, 21, 24, 27–28, 35, 36n. 4, 128, 137–138, 162, 186
Tep Vong, Saṃṭec, 186, 195, 200, 202
Thailand (Siam), 11, 57, 68–69, 74, 199–200; Cambodia compared to, 48, 77, 130, 159; conquests of Cambodia, 10–11, 25, 44, 108; female ascetics in, 134–135, 148; influence of, 50, 52, 53, 64; invasion by, 196, 218–219; modernization in, 46, 52; and refugees, 194, 201–202
Theravāda Buddhism, 13, 15, 30, 47, 79, 191; coming of, 9–10, 17, 19, 22, 40, 93; as global, 42; and Khmer identity, 40, 60–61; with "non-Buddhist" practice, 4–5, 150, 180, 187; orthodoxy, 41, 187; peripheral phenomena of, 134, 164–165, 181; women's role in, 133–135, 142, 148
Thich Nhat Hanh, 198–199, 209
Thong, 71, 73
Three Jewels / Three Refuges, 59, 145, 161
time, 42; as concept, 67, 81; timelessness, 21, 22, 37n. 8, 127
Tipiṭaka, 54, 77–78
titles, 19, 45, 61n. 2, 196n. 1, 201–202, 211–212n. 10, 223n. 8
Totem and Taboo (Freud), 92
Trai Bhūm, 43–44, 50
Tralaeng Kaeng, 13, 23, 28, 38n. 21
transnationalism, 4, 42, 131, 193, 196, 198–199, 209–211
ṭūn jī, 128–131, 133, 148, 154–155, 169n. 8, 195; activism of, 147–148, 199; and ancient ordination traditions, 134, 147; defined, 134–135; in Dhammayātrā, 141, 204, 208; mendicancy of, 135, 138, 142;